Stories of the Prophet

Biography of the Prophet

Peace and Blessings be Upon Him

Imam Ibn Kathir

Dr. al-Mubarakpuri

Dr. al-Qarni

Islamic Books
www.al-Qarni.com

Copyright ©
TX0009117719.TX0009056026.TX0009012705

All rights reserved. King Fahd Complex for the Printing of the Holy Qur'an and the Prophet's Sunnah, peace and blessings be upon him. No part of this book may be reproduced or transmitted in any form or by any means, electronic or mechanical, including photocopying, recording, or by any information storage and retrieval system, without written permission from the Publisher.

Imam Ibn Kathir wrote the original versions of this book, then Dr. Mubarakpuri and Dr. al-Qarni summarized it further and added their invaluable comments.

Biography of the Prophet

Beyond a shadow of doubt, the biography of Prophet Muhammad (Peace be upon him) manifestedly represents an exhaustive embodiment of the sublime Divine Message that he communicated in order to deliver the human race from the swamp of darkness and polytheism to the paradise of light and monotheism. An image, authentic as well as comprehensive, of this Message is therefore only attainable through careful study and profound analysis of both backgrounds and issues of such a biography. In view of this, a whole chapter is here introduced about the nature and development of Arab tribes prior to Islam as well as the circumstantial environment that enwrapped the Prophet's mission.

LOCATION OF THE ARABS:

Linguistically, the word "Arab" means deserts and waste barren land well-nigh waterless and treeless. Ever since the dawn of history, the Arabian Peninsula and its people have been called as such.

The Arabian Peninsula is enclosed in the west by the Red Sea and Sinai, in the east by the Arabian Gulf, in the south by the Arabian Sea, which is an extension of the Indian Ocean, and in the north by old Syria and part of Iraq. The area is estimated between a million and a million and a quarter square miles.

Thanks to its geographical position, the peninsula has always maintained great importance.. Considering its internal setting, it is mostly deserts and sandy places, which has rendered it inaccessible to foreigners and invaders, and allowed its people complete liberty and independence through the ages, despite the presence of two neighbouring great empires.

Its external setting, on the other hand, caused it to be the centre of the old world and provided it with sea and land links with most nations at the time. Thanks to this strategic position the Arabian Peninsula had become the centre for trade, culture, religion and art.

ARAB TRIBES:

Arab kinfolks have been divided according to lineage into three groups:
Perishing Arabs: The ancient Arabs, of whose history little is known, and of whom were 'Ad, Thamûd, Tasam, Jadis, Emlaq, and others.
Pure Arabs: Who originated from the progeny of Ya'rub bin Yashjub bin Qahtan. They were also called Qahtanian Arabs.
Arabized Arabs: Who originated from the progeny of Ishmael. They were also called 'Adnanian Arabs.

The pure Arabs – the people of Qahtan – originally lived in Yemen and comprised many tribes, two of which were very famous:

1. Himyar: The most famous of whose septs were Zaid Al-Jamhur, Quda'a and Sakasic.
2. Kahlan: The most famous of whose septs were Hamdan, Anmar, Tai', Mudhhij, Kinda, Lakhm, Judham, Azd, Aws, Khazraj and the descendants of Jafna — the kings of old Syria.

Kahlan septs emigrated from Yemen to dwell in the different parts of the Arabian Peninsula prior to the Great Flood (Sail Al-'Arim of Ma'rib Dam), due to the failure of trade under the Roman pressure and domain on both sea and land trade routes following Roman occupation of Egypt and Syria.

Naturally enough, the competition between Kahlan and Himyar led to the evacuation of the first and the settlement of the second in Yemen.

THE EMIGRATING SEPTS OF KAHLAN CAN BE INTO FOUR GROUPS:

1. **Azd**: Who, under the leadership of 'Imran bin 'Amr Muzaiqbâ', wandered in Yemen, sent pioneers and finally headed northwards. Details of their emigration can be summed up as follows:
2. Tha'labah bin 'Amr left his tribe Al-Azd for Hijaz and dwelt between Tha'labiyah and Dhi Qar. When he gained strength, he headed for Madinah where he stayed. Of his seed are Aws and Khazraj, sons of Haritha bin Tha'labah.

   Haritha bin 'Amr, known as Khuza'a, wandered with his folks in Hijaz until they came to Mar Az-Zahran. Later, they conquered the Haram, and settled in Makkah after having driven away its people, the tribe of Jurhum.

   'Imran bin 'Amr and his folks went to 'Oman where they established the tribe of Azd whose children inhabited Tihama and were known as Azd-of-Shanu'a.

   Jafna bin 'Amr and his family, headed for Syria where he settled and initiated the kingdom of Ghassan who was so named after a spring of water, in Hijaz, where they stopped on their way to Syria.
2. **Lakhm and Judham**: Of whom was Nasr bin Rabi'a, father of Manadhira, Kings of Heerah.
3. **Banu Tai'**: Who also emigrated northwards to settle by the so-called Aja and Salma Mountains which were consequently named as Tai' Mountains.
4. **Kinda**: Who dwelt in Bahrain but were expelled to Hadramout and Najd where they instituted a powerful government but not for long, for the whole tribe soon faded away.

- Another tribe of Himyar, known as Quda'a, also left Yemen and dwelt in Samawa semi-desert on the borders of Iraq.

The Arabized Arabs go back in ancestry to their great grandfather Abraham (Peace be upon him) from a town called "Ar" near Kufa on the west bank of the Euphrates in Iraq. Excavations brought to light great details of the town, Abraham's family, and the prevalent religions and social circumstances.

It is known that Abrahaml (Peace be upon him) eft Ar for Harran and then for Palestine, which he made headquarters for his Message. He wandered all over the area. When he went to Egypt, the Pharaoh tried to do evil to his wife Sarah, but Allâh saved her and the Pharaoh's wicked scheme recoiled on him. He thus came to realize her strong attachment to Allâh, and, in acknowledgment of her grace, the Pharaoh rendered his daughter Hagar at Sarah's service, but Sarah gave Hagar to Abraham as a wife.

Abraham returned to Palestine where Hagar gave birth to Ishmael. Sarah became so jealous of Hagar that she forced Abraham to send Hagar and her baby away to a plantless valley on a small hill in Hijaz, by the Sacred House, exposed to the wearing of floods coming right and left. He chose for them a place under a lofty tree above Zamzam near the upper side of the Mosque in Makkah where neither people nor water was available, and went back to Palestine leaving with his wife and baby a leather case with some dates and a pot of water. Not before long, they ran out of both food and water, but thanks to Allâh's favour water gushed forth to sustain them for sometime. The whole story of Zamzam spring is already known to everybody.

Another Yemeni tribe – Jurhum the Second – came and lived in Makkah upon Hagar's permission, after being said to have lived in the valleys around Makkah. It is mentioned in the Sahih Al-Bukhari that this tribe came to Makkah before Ishmael was a young man while they had passed through that valley long before this event.

Abraham used to go to Makkah every now and then to see his wife and son. The number of these journeys is still unknown, but authentic historical resources spoke of four ones.

Allâh, the Sublime, stated in the Noble Qur'ân that He had Abraham see, in his dream, that he slaughtered his son Ishmael, and therefore Abraham stood up to fulfill His Order:

- "Then, when they had both submitted themselves (to the Will of Allâh), and he had laid him prostrate on his forehead (or on the side of his forehead for slaughtering); and We called out to him: "O Abraham! You have fulfilled the dream (vision)!" Verily! Thus do we reward the Muhsinûn (good-doers, who perform good deeds totally for Allâh's sake only, without any show off or to gain praise or fame, etc. and do them in accordance to Allâh's Orders). Verily, that indeed was a manifest trial — and We ransomed him with a great sacrifice (i.e. a ram)" [37:103-107]

It is mentioned in the Genesis that Ishmael was thirteen years older than his brother Ishaq. The sequence of the story of the sacrifice of Ishmael shows that it really happened before Ishaq's birth, and that Allâh's Promise to give Abraham another son, Ishaq, came after narration of the whole story.

This story spoke of one journey – at least – before Ishmael became a young man. Al-Bukhari, on the authority of Ibn 'Abbas, reported the other three journeys; a summary of which goes as follows:

When Ishmael became a young man, he learned Arabic at the hand of the tribe of Jurhum, who loved him with great admiration and gave him one of their women as a wife, soon after his mother died. Having wanted to see his wife and son again, Abraham came to Makkah, Ishmael's marriage, but he didn't find him at home. He asked Ishmael's wife about her husband and how they were doing. She complained of poverty, so he asked her to tell Ishmael to change his doorstep. Ishmael understood the message, divorced his wife and got married to the daughter of Mudad bin 'Amr, chief of the tribe of Jurhum.

Once more, Abraham came to see his son, but again didn't find him at home. He asked his new wife the same previous question, to which she thanked Allâh. Abraham asked her to tell Ishmael to keep his doorstep (i.e. to keep her as wife) and went back to Palestine.

A third time, Abraham came to Makkah to find Ishmael sharpening an arrow under a lofty tree near Zamzam. The meeting, after a very long journey of separation, was very touching for a father so affectionate and a so dutiful and righteous son. This time, father and son built Al-Ka'bah and raised its pillars, and Abraham, in compliance with Allâh's Commandment, called unto people to make pilgrimage to it.

By the grace of Allâh, Ishmael had twelve sons from the daughter of Mudad, whose names were Nabet, Qidar, Edbael, Mebsham, Mishma', Duma, Micha, Hudud, Yetma, Yetour, Nafis and Qidman, and who ultimately formed twelve tribes inhabiting Makkah and trading between Yemen, geographical Syria and Egypt. Later on, these tribes spread all over, and even outside, the peninsula. All their tidings went into oblivion except for the descendants of Nabet and Qidar.

The Nabeteans – sons of Nabet – established a flourishing civilization in the north of Hijaz, they instituted a powerful government which spread out its domain over all neighbouring tribes, and made Petra their capital. Nobody dared challenge their authority until the Romans came and managed to eliminate their kingdom. After extensive research and painstaking investigation, Mr. Sulaiman An-Nadwi came to the conclusion that the Ghassanide kings, along with the Aws and Khazraj were not likely to be Qahtanians but rather Nabeteans.

Descendants of Qidar, the son of Ishmael, lived long in Makkah increasing in number, of them issued 'Adnan and son Ma'ad, to whom 'Adnanian Arabs traced back their ancestry. 'Adnan is the twenty-first grandfather in the series of the Prophetic ancestry. It was said that whenever Prophet Muhammad صلى الله عليه وسلم spoke of his ancestry he would stop at 'Adnan and say: "Genealogists tell lies" and did not go farther than him. A group of scholars, however, favoured the probability of going beyond 'Adnan attaching no significance to the aforementioned Prophetic Hadith. They went on to say that there were exactly forty fathers between 'Adnan and Abraham (Peace be upon them).

Nizar, Ma'ad's only son, had four sons who branched out into four great tribes; Eyad, Anmar, Rabi'a and Mudar. These last two sub-branched into several septs. Rabi'a fathered Asad, 'Anazah, 'Abdul Qais, and Wa'il's two sons (Bakr and Taghlib), Hanifa and many others.

Mudar tribes branched out into two great divisions: Qais 'Ailan bin Mudar and septs of Elias bin Mudar. Of Qais 'Ailan were the Banu Saleem, Banu Hawazin, and Banu Ghatafan of whom descended 'Abs, Zubyan, Ashja' and Ghani bin A'sur. Of Elias bin Mudar were Tamim bin Murra, Hudhail bin Mudrika, Banu Asad bin Khuzaimah and septs of Kinana bin Khuzaimah, of whom came Quraish, the descendants of Fahr bin Malik bin An-Nadr bin Kinana.

Quraish branched out into various tribes, the most famous of whom were Jumah, Sahm, 'Adi, Makhzum, Tayim, Zahra and the three septs of Qusai bin Kilab: 'Abdud-Dar bin Qusai, Asad bin 'Abdul 'Uzza bin Qusai and 'Abd Manaf bin Qusai.

'Abd Manaf branched out into four tribes: 'Abd Shams, Nawfal, Muttalib and Hashim. It is, however, from the family of Hashim that Allâh selected Prophet Muhammad bin 'Abdullah bin 'Abdul-Muttalib bin Hashim (Peace be upon him).

Prophet Muhammad (Peace be upon him) said:

- "Allâh selected Ishmael from the sons of Abraham, Kinana from the sons of Ishmael, Quraish from the sons of Kinana, Hashim from the sons of Quraish and He selected me from the sons of Hashim."

Al-'Abbas bin 'Abdul-Muttalib quoted the Messenger of Allâh (Peace be upon him) as saying:

- "Allâh created mankind and chose me from the best whereof, He chose the tribes and selected me from the best whereof; and He chose families and selected me from the best whereof. I am the very best in person and family."

Having increased in number, children of 'Adnan, in pursuit of pastures and water, spread out over various parts of Arabia.
The tribe of 'Abdul Qais, together with some septs of Bakr bin Wa'il and Tamim, emigrated to Bahrain where they dwelt.

Banu Hanifa bin Sa'b bin Ali bin Bakr went to settle in Hijr, the capital of Yamama. All the tribes of Bakr bin Wa'il lived in an area of land which included Yamama, Bahrain, Saif Kazima, the sea shore, the outer borders of Iraq, Ablah and Hait.

Most of the tribe of Taghlib lived in the Euphrates area while some of them lived with Bakr.
Banu Tamim lived in Basra semi-desert.
Banu Saleem lived in the vicinity of Madinah on the land stretching from Wadi Al-Qura to Khaibar onwards to the eastern mountains to Harrah.
Thaqif dwelt in Ta'if and Hawazin east of Makkah near Autas on the road from Makkah to Basra.
Banu Asad lived on the land east of Taimâ' and west of Kufa, while family of Tai' lived between Banu Asad and Taimâ'. They were five-day-walk far from Kufa.

Zubyan inhabited the plot of and between Taimâ' and Hawran.

Some septs of Kinana lived in Tihama, while septs of Quraish dwelt in Makkah and its suburbs. Quraish remained completely disunited until Qusai bin Kilab managed to rally their ranks on honourable terms attaching major prominence to their status and importance.

RULERSHIP AND PRINCESHIP AMONG THE ARABS

When talking about the Arabs before Islam, we deem it necessary to draw a mini-picture of the history of rulership, princeship, sectarianism and the religious dominations of the Arabs, so as to facilitate the understanding of emergent circumstances when Islam appeared.

When the sun of Islam rose, rulers of Arabia were of two kinds: crowned kings, who were in fact not independent; and heads of tribes and clans, who enjoyed the same authorities and privileges possessed by crowned kings and were mostly independent, though some of whom could have shown some kind of submission to a crowned king. The crowned kings were only those of Yemen, Heerah and Ghassan. All other rulers of Arabia were non-crowned.

RULERSHIP IN YEMEN:

The folks of Sheba were one of the oldest nations of the pure Arabs, who lived in Yemen. Excavations at "Or" brought to light their existence twenty five centuries B.C. Their civilization flourished, and their domain spread eleven centuries B.C.

It is possible to divide their ages according to the following estimation:

1. The centuries before 650 B.C., during which their kings were called "Makrib Sheba". Their capital was "Sarwah", also known as "Khriba", whose ruins lie in a spot, a day's walk from the western side of "Ma'rib". During this period, they started building the "Dam of Ma'rib" which had great importance in the history of Yemen. Sheba was also said to have had so great a domain that they had colonies inside and outside Arabia.
2. From 650 B.C. until 115 B.C. During this era, they gave up the name "Makrib" and assumed the designation of "Kings of Sheba". They also made Ma'rib their capital instead of Sarwah. The ruins of Ma'rib lie at a distance of sixty miles east of San'a.
3. From 115 B.C. until 300 A.D. During this period, the tribe of Himyar conquered the kingdom of Sheba and took Redan for capital instead of Ma'rib. Later on, Redan was called "Zifar". Its ruins still lie on Mudawwar Mountain near the town of "Yarim". During this period, they began to decline and fall. Their trade failed to a very great extent, firstly, because of the Nabetean domain over the north of Hijaz; secondly, because of the Roman superiority over the naval trade routes after the Roman conquest of Egypt, Syria and the north of Hijaz; and thirdly, because of the inter-tribal warfare. Thanks to the three above-mentioned factors, families of Qahtan were disunited and scattered out.
4. From 300 A.D. until Islam dawned on Yemen. This period witnessed a lot of disorder and turmoil. The great many and civil wars rendered the people of Yemen liable to foreign subjection and hence loss of independence. During this era, the Romans conquered 'Adn and even helped the Abyssinians (Ethiopians) to occupy Yemen for the first time in 340 A.D., making use of the constant intra-tribal conflict of Hamdan and Himyar. The Abyssinian (Ethiopian) occupation of Yemen lasted until 378 A.D., whereafter Yemen regained its independence. Later on, cracks began to show in Ma'rib Dam which led to the Great Flood (450 or 451 A.D.) mentioned in the Noble Qur'ân. This was a great event which caused the fall of the entire Yemeni civilization and the dispersal of the nations living therein.

In 523, Dhu Nawas, a Jew, despatched a great campaign against the Christians of Najran in order to force them to convert into Judaism. Having refused to do so, they were thrown alive into a big ditch where a great fire had been set. The Qur'ân referred to this event:

- "Cursed were the people of the ditch." [85:4]

This aroused great wrath among the Christians, and especially the Roman emperors, who not only instigated the Abyssinians (Ethiopians) against Arabs but also assembled a large fleet which helped the Abyssinian (Ethiopian) army, of seventy thousand warriors, to effect a second conquest of Yemen in

525 A.D., under the leadership of Eriat, who was granted rulership over Yemen, a position he held until he was assassinated by one of his army leaders, Abraha, who, after reconciliation with the king of Abyssinia, took rulership over Yemen and, later on, deployed his soldiers to demolish Al-Ka'bah, and , hence, he and his soldiers came to be known as the "Men of the Elephant".

After the "Elephant" incident, the people of Yemen, under the leadership of Ma'dikarib bin Saif Dhu Yazin Al-Himyari, and through Persian assistance, revolted against the Abyssinian (Ethiopian) invaders, restored independence and appointed Ma'dikarib as their king. However, Ma'dikarib was assassinated by an Abyssinian (Ethiopian) he used to have him around for service and protection. The family of Dhu Yazin was thus deprived of royalty forever. Kisra, the Persian king, appointed a Persian ruler over San'a and thus made Yemen a Persian colony. Persian rulers maintained rulership of Yemen until Badhan, the last of them, embraced Islam in 638 A.D., thus terminating the Persian domain over Yemen.

RULERSHIP IN HEERAH:

Ever since Korosh the Great (557-529 B.C.) united the Persians, they ruled Iraq and its neighbourhood. Nobody could shake off their authority until Alexander the Great vanquished their king Dara I and thus subdued the Persians in 326 B.C. Persian lands were thenceforth divided and ruled by kings known as "the Kings of Sects", an era which lasted until 230 A.D. Meanwhile, the Qahtanians occupied some Iraqi territories, and were later followed by some 'Adnanians who managed to share some parts of Mesopotamia with them.

The Persians, under the leadership of Ardashir, who had established the Sasanian state in 226 A.D, regained enough unity and power to subdue the Arabs living in the vicinity of their kingdom, and force Quda'a to leave for Syria , leaving the people of Heerah and Anbar under the Persian domain.

During the time of Ardashir, Juzaima Alwaddah exercised rulership over Heerah, Rabi'a and Mudar, and Mesopotamia. Ardashir had reckoned that it was impossible for him to rule the Arabs directly and prevent them from attacking his borders unless he appointed as king one of them who enjoyed support and power of his tribe. He had also seen that he could make use of them against the Byzantine kings who always used to harass him. At the same time, the Arabs of Iraq could face the Arabs of Syria who were in the hold of Byzantine kings. However, he deemed it fit to keep a Persian battalion under command of the king of Heerah to be used against those Arabs who might rebel against him.

After the death of Juzaima around 268 A.D., 'Amr bin 'Adi bin Nasr Al-Lakhmi was appointed as king by the Persian King Sabour bin Ardashir. 'Amr was the first of the Lakhmi kings who ruled Heerah until the Persians appointed Qabaz bin Fairuz in whose reign appeared someone called Mazdak, who called for dissoluteness in social life. Qabaz, and many of his subjects, embraced Mazdak's religion and even called upon the king of Heerah, Al-Munzir bin Ma' As-Sama', to follow after. When the latter, because of his pride and self-respect, rejected their orders, Qabaz discharged him and nominated Harith bin 'Amr bin Hajar Al-Kindi, who had accepted the Mazdaki doctrine.

No sooner did Kisra Anu Shairwan succeed Qabaz than he, due to hatred of Mazdak's philosophy, killed Mazdak and many of his followers, restored Munzir to the throne of Heerah and gave orders to summon under arrest Harith who sought refuge with Al-Kalb tribe where he spent the rest of his life.

Sons of Al-Munzir bin Ma' As-Sama' maintained kingship a long time until An-Nu'man bin Al-Munzir took over. Because of a calumny borne by Zaid bin 'Adi Al-'Abbadi, the Persian king got angry with An-Nu'man and summoned him to his palace. An-Nu'man went secretly to Hani bin Mas'ud, chief of Shaiban tribe, and left his wealth and family under the latter's protection, and then presented himself before the Persian king, who immediately threw him into prison where he perished. Kisra, then, appointed Eyas bin Qubaisa At-Ta'i as king of Heerah. Eyas was ordered to tell Hani bin Mas'ud to deliver An-Nu'man's charge up to Kisra. No sooner than had the Persian king received the fanatically motivated rejection on the part of the Arab chief, he declared war against the tribe of Shaiban and mobilized his troops and warriors under the leadership of King Eyas to a place called Dhee Qar which witnessed a most furious battle wherein the Persians were severely routed by the Arabs for the first time in history. That was very soon after the birth of Prophet Muhammad ﷺ eight months after Eyas bin Qubaisah's rise to power over Heerah.

After Eyas, a Persian ruler was appointed over Heerah, but in 632 A.D. the authority there returned to the family of Lukhm when Al-Munzir Al-Ma'rur took over. Hardly had the latter's reign lasted for eight months when Khalid bin Al-Waleed fell upon him with Muslim soldiers.

RULERSHIP IN GEOGRAPHICAL SYRIA:

In the process of the tribal emigrations, some septs of Quda'a reached the borders of Syria where they settled down. They belonged to the family of Sulaih bin Halwan, of whose offspring were the sons of Duj'am bin Sulaih known as Ad-Duja'ima. Such septs of Quda'a were used by the Byzantines in the defence of the Byzantine borders against both Arab Bedouin raiders and the Persians, and enjoyed autonomy for a considerable phase of time which is said to have lasted for the whole second century A.D. One of their most famous kings was Zyiad bin Al-Habula. Their authority however came to an end upon defeat by the Ghassanides who were consequently granted the proxy rulership over the Arabs of Syria and had Dumat Al-Jandal as their headquarters, which lasted until the battle of Yarmuk in the year 13 A.H. Their last king Jabala bin Al-Aihum embraced Islam during the reign of the Chief of Believers, 'Umar bin Al-Khattab (May Allah be pleased with him).

RULERSHIP IN HIJAZ:

Ishmael (Peace be upon him) administered authority over Makkah as well as custodianship of the Holy Sanctuary throughout his lifetime. Upon his death, at the age of 137, two of his sons, Nabet and Qidar, succeeded him. Later on, their maternal grandfather, Mudad bin 'Amr Al-Jurhumi took over, thus transferring rulership over Makkah to the tribe of Jurhum, preserving a venerable position, though very little authority for Ishmael's sons due to their father's exploits in building the Holy Sanctuary, a position they held until the decline of the tribe of Jurhum shortly before the rise of Bukhtanassar.

The political role of the 'Adnanides had begun to gain firmer grounds in Makkah, which could be clearly attested by the fact that upon Bukhtanassar's first invasion of the Arabs in 'Dhati 'Irq', the leader of the Arabs was not from Jurhum.

Upon Bukhtanassar's second invasion in 587 B.C., however, the 'Adnanides were frightened out to Yemen, while Burmia An-Nabi fled to Syria with Ma'ad, but when Bukhtanassar's pressure lessened, Ma'ad returned to Makkah to find none of the tribe of Jurhum except Jursham bin Jalhamah, whose daughter, Mu'ana, was given to Ma'ad as wife who, later, had a son by him named Nizar.

On account of difficult living conditions and destitution prevalent in Makkah, the tribe of Jurhum began to ill-treat visitors of the Holy Sanctuary and extort its funds, which aroused resentment and hatred of the 'Adnanides (sons of Bakr bin 'Abd Munaf bin Kinana) who, with the help of the tribe of Khuza'a that had come to settle in a neighbouring area called Marr Az-Zahran, invaded Jurhum and frightened them out of Makkah leaving rulership to Quda'a in the middle of the second century A.D.

Upon leaving Makkah, Jurhum filled up the well of Zamzam, levelled its place and buried a great many things in it. 'Amr bin Al-Harith bin Mudad Al-Jurhumi was reported by Ibn Ishaq, the well-known historian, to have buried the two gold deer together with the Black Stone as well as a lot of jewelry and swords in Zamzam, prior to their sorrowful escape to Yemen.

Ishmael's epoch is estimated to have lasted for twenty centuries B.C., which means that Jurhum stayed in Makkah for twenty-one centuries and held rulership there for about twenty centuries.

Upon defeat of Jurhum, the tribe of Khuza'a monopolized rulership over Makkah. Mudar tribes, however, enjoyed three privileges:

- **The First:** Leading pilgrims from 'Arafat to Muzdalifah and then from Mina to the 'Aqabah Stoning Pillar. This was the authority of the family of Al-Ghawth bin Murra, one of the septs of Elias bin Mudar, who were called 'Sofa'. This privilege meant that the pilgrims were not allowed to throw stones at Al-'Aqabah until one of the 'Sofa' men did that. When they had finished stoning and wanted to leave the valley of Mina, 'Sofa' men stood on the two sides of Al-'Aqabah and nobody would pass that position until the men of 'Sofa' passed and cleared the way for the pilgrims. When Sofa perished, the family of Sa'd bin Zaid Manat from Tamim tribe took over.

  The Second: Al-Ifadah (leaving for Mina after Muzdalifah) on sacrifice morning, and this was the responsibility of the family of Adwan.

  The Third: Deferment of the sacred months, and this was the responsibility of the family of Tamim bin 'Adi from Bani Kinana.

Khuza'a's reign in Makkah lasted for three hundred years, during which, the 'Adnanides spread all over Najd and the sides of Bahrain and Iraq, while small septs of Quraish remained on the sides of Makkah; they were Haloul, Harum and some families of Kinana. They enjoyed no privileges in Makkah or in the Sacred House until the appearance of Qusai bin Kilab, whose father is said to have died when he was still a baby, and whose mother was subsequently married to Rabi'a bin Haram, from the tribe of Bani 'Udhra. Rabi'a took his wife and her baby to his homeland on the borders of Syria. When Qusai became a young man, he returned to Makkah, which was ruled by Halil bin Habsha from Khuza'a, who gave Qusai his daughter, Hobba, as wife. After Halil's death, a war between Khuza'a and Quraish broke out and resulted in Qusai's taking hold of Makkah and the Sacred House.

THE REASONS OF THIS WAR HAVE BEEN ILLUSTRATED IN THREE VERSIONS:

- **The First:** Having noticed the spread of his offspring, increase of his property and exalt of his honour after Halil's death, Qusai found himself more entitled to shoulder responsibility of rulership over Makkah and custodianship of the Sacred House than the tribes of Khuza'a and Bani Bakr. He also advocated that Quraish were the chiefs of Ishmael's descendants. Therefore he consulted some men from Quraish and Kinana concerning his desire to evacuate Khuza'a and Bani Bakr from Makkah. They took a liking to his opinion and supported him.

  The Second: Khuza'a claimed that Halil requested Qusai to hold custodianship of Al-Ka'bah and rulership over Makkah after his death.

  The Third: Halil gave the right of Al-Ka'bah service to his daughter Hobba and appointed Abu Ghabshan Al-Khuza'i to function as her agent whereof. Upon Halil's death, Qusai bought this right for a leather bag of wine, which aroused dissatisfaction among the men of Khuza'a and they tried to keep the custodianship of the Sacred House away from Qusai. The latter, however, with the help of Quraish and Kinana, managed to take over and even to expel Khuza'a completely from Makkah.

  Whatever the truth might have been, the whole affair resulted in the deprivation of Sofa of their privileges, previously mentioned, evacuation of Khuza'a and Bakr from Makkah and transfer of rulership over Makkah and custodianship of the Holy Sanctuary to Qusai, after fierce wars between Qusai and Khuza'a inflicting heavy casualties on both sides, reconciliation and then arbitration of Ya'mur bin 'Awf, from the tribe of Bakr, whose judgement entailed eligibility of Qusai's rulership over Makkah and custodianship of the Sacred House, Qusai's irresponsibility for Khuza'a's blood shed, and imposition of blood money on Khuza'a. Qusai's reign over Makkah and the Sacred House began in 440 A.D. and allowed him, and Quraish afterwards, absolute rulership over Makkah and undisputed custodianship of the Sacred House to which Arabs from all over Arabia came to pay homage.

Qusai brought his kinspeople to Makkah and allocated it to them, allowing Quraish some dwellings there. An-Nus'a, the families of Safwan, Adwan, Murra bin 'Awf preserved the same rights they used to enjoy before his arrival.

A significant achievement credited to Qusai was the establishment of An-Nadwa House (an assembly house) on the northern side of Al-Ka'bah Mosque, to serve as a meeting place for Quraish. This very house had benefited Quraish a lot because it secured unity of opinions amongst them and cordial solution to their problem.

QUSAI HOWEVER ENJOYED THE FOLLONG PRIVILEGED OF LEADERSHIP AND HONOUR:

1. Presiding over An-Nadwa House meetings where consultations relating to serious issues were conducted, and marriage contracts were announced.
2. The Standard: He monopolized in his hand issues relevant to war launching.
3. Doorkeeping of Al-Ka'bah: He was the only one eligible to open its gate, and was responsible for its service and protection.
4. Providing water for the Pilgrims: This means that he used to fill basins sweetened by dates and raisins for the pilgrims to drink.
5. Feeding Pilgrims: This means making food for pilgrims who could not afford it. Qusai even imposed on Quraish annual land tax, paid at the season of pilgrimage, for food.

It is noteworthy however that Qusai singled out 'Abd Manaf, a son of his, for honour and prestige though he was not his elder son ('Abd Ad-Dar was), and entrusted him with such responsibilities as chairing of An-Nadwa House, the standard, the doorkeeping of Al-Ka'bah, providing water and food for pilgrims. Due to the fact that Qusai's deeds were regarded as unquestionable and his orders inviolable, his death gave no rise to conflicts among his sons, but it later did among his grand children, for no sooner than 'Abd Munaf had died, his sons began to have rows with their cousins —sons of 'Abd Ad-Dar, which would have given rise to dissension and fighting among the whole tribe of Quraish, had it not been for a peace treaty whereby posts were reallocated so as to preserve feeding and providing water for pilgrims for the sons of 'Abd Munaf; while An-Nadwa House, the flag and the doorkeeping of Al-Ka'bah were maintained for the sons of 'Abd Ad-Dar. The sons of 'Abd Munaf, however, cast the lot for their charge, and consequently left the charge of food and water giving to Hashim bin 'Abd Munaf, upon whose death, the charge was taken over by a brother of his called Al-Muttalib bin 'Abd Manaf and afterwards by 'Abd Al-Muttalib bin Hashim, the Prophet's grandfather, whose sons assumed this position until the rise of Islam, during which 'Abbas bin 'Abdul-Muttalib was in charge.

Many other posts were distriamong people of Quraish for establishing the pillars of a new democratic petite state with government offices and councils similar to those of today. Enlisted as follows are some of these posts.

1. Casting the lots for the idols was allocated to Bani Jumah.
2. Noting of offers and sacrifices, settlement of disputes and relevant issues were to lie in the hands of Bani Sahm.
3. Consultation was to go to Bani Asad.
4. Organization of blood-money and fines was with Bani Tayim.
5. Bearing the national banner was with Bani Omaiyah.
6. The military institute, footmen and cavalry would be Bani Makhzum's responsibility.
7. Bani 'Adi would function as foreign mediators.

RULERSHIP IN PAN-ARABIA:

We have previously mentioned the Qahtanide and 'Adnanide emigrations, and division of Arabia between these two tribes. Those tribes dwelling near Heerah were subordinate to the Arabian king of Heerah, while those dwelling in the Syrian semi-desert were under domain of the Arabian Ghassanide king, a sort of dependency that was in reality formal rather than actual. However, those living in the hinder deserts enjoyed full autonomy.

These tribes in fact had heads chosen by the whole tribe which was a demi-government based on tribal solidarity and collective interests in defence of land and property.

Heads of tribes enjoyed dictatorial privileges similar to those of kings, and were rendered full obedience and subordination in both war and peace. Rivalry among cousins for rulership, however, often drove them to outdo one another in entertaining guests, affecting generosity, wisdom and chivalry for the sole purpose of outranking their rivals, and gaining fame among people especially poets who were the official spokesmen at the time.

Heads of tribes and masters had special claims to spoils of war such as the quarter of the spoils, whatever he chose for himself, or found on his way back or even the remaining indivisible spoils.

THE POLITICAL SITUATION:

The three Arab regions adjacent to foreigners suffered great weakness and inferiority. The people there were either masters or slaves, rulers or subordinates. Masters, especially the foreigners, had claim to every advantage; slaves had nothing but responsibilities to shoulder. In other words, arbitrary autocratic rulership brought about encroachment on the rights of subordinates, ignorance, oppression, iniquity, injustice and hardship, and turning them into people groping in darkness and ignorance, viz., fertile land which rendered its fruits to the rulers and men of power to extravagantly dissipate on their pleasures and enjoyments, whims and desires, tyranny and aggression. The tribes living near these regions were fluctuating between Syria and Iraq, whereas those living inside Arabia were disunited and governed by tribal conflicts and racial and religious disputes.

They had neither a king to sustain their independence nor a supporter to seek advice from, or depend upon, in hardships.

The rulers of Hijaz, however, were greatly esteemed and respected by the Arabs, and were considered as rulers and servants of the religious centre. Rulership of Hijaz was, in fact, a mixture of secular and official precedence as well as religious leadership. They ruled among the Arabs in the name of religious leadership and always monopolized the custodianship of the Holy Sanctuary and its neighbourhood. They looked after the interests of Al-Ka'bah visitors and were in charge of putting Abraham's code into effect. They even had such offices and departments like those of the parliaments of today. However, they were too weak to carry the heavy burden, as this evidently came to light during the Abyssinian (Ethiopian) invasion.

RELIGIONS OF THE ARABS

Most of the Arabs had complied with the call of Ishmael (Peace be upon him) , and professed the religion of his father Abraham (Peace be upon him) They had worshipped Allâh, professed His Oneness and followed His religion a long time until they forgot part of what they had been reminded of. However, they still maintained such fundamental beliefs such as monotheism as well as various other aspects of Abraham's religion, until the time when a chief of Khuza'a, namely 'Amr bin Luhai, who was renowned for righteousness, charity, reverence and care for religion, and was granted unreserved love and obedience by his tribesmen, came back from a trip to Syria where he saw people worship idols, a phenomenon he approved of and believed it to be righteous since Syria was the locus of Messengers and Scriptures, he brought with him an idol (Hubal) which he placed in the middle of Al-Ka'bah and summoned people to worship it. Readily enough, paganism spread all over Makkah and, thence, to Hijaz, people of Makkah being custodians of not only the Sacred House but the whole Haram as well. A great many idols, bearing different names, were introduced into the area.

An idol called 'Manat', for instance, was worshipped in a place known as Al-Mushallal near Qadid on the Red Sea. Another, 'Al-Lat' in Ta'if, a third, 'Al-'Uzza' in the valley of Nakhlah, and so on and so forth.

Polytheism prevailed and the number of idols increased everywhere in Hijaz. It was even mentioned that 'Amr bin Luhai, with the help of a jinn companion who told him that the idols of Noah's folk – Wadd, Suwa', Yaguth, Ya'uk and Nasr – were buried in Jeddah, dug them out and took them to Tihama. Upon pilgrimage time, the idols were distributed among the tribes to take back home. Every tribe, and house, had their own idols, and the Sacred House was also overcrowded with them. On the Prophet's conquest of Makkah, 360 idols were found around Al-Ka'bah. He broke them down and had them removed and burned up.

Polytheism and worship of idols became the most prominent feature of the religion of pre-Islam Arabs despite alleged profession of Abraham's religion.

Traditions and ceremonies of the worship of their idols had been mostly created by 'Amr bin Luhai, and were deemed as good innovations rather than deviations from Abraham's religion. Some features of their worship of idols were:

- Self-devotion to the idols, seeking refuge with them, acclamation of their names, calling for their help in hardship, and supplication to them for fulfillment of wishes, hopefully that the idols (i.e., heathen gods) would mediate with Allâh for the fulfillment of people's wishes.
- Performing pilgrimage to the idols, circumrotation round them, self-abasement and even prostrating themselves before them.
- Seeking favour of idols through various kinds of sacrifices and immolations, which is mentioned in the Qur'ânic verses:
- "And that which is sacrificed (slaughtered) on An-Nusub (stone-altars)" [5:3]

Allâh also says:

- "Eat not (O believers) of that (meat) on which Allâh's Name has not been pronounced (at the time of the slaughtering of the animal)." [6:121]

- Consecration of certain portions of food, drink, cattle, and crops to idols. Surprisingly enough, portions were also consecrated to Allâh Himself, but people often found reasons to transfer parts of Allâh's portion to idols, but never did the opposite. To this effect, the Qur'ânic verses go:

- "And they assign to Allâh a share of the tilth and cattle which He has created, and they say: 'This is for Allâh according to their pretending, and this is for our (Allâh's so-called) partners.' But the share of their (Allâh's so-called) 'partners', reaches not Allâh, while the share of Allâh reaches their (Allâh's so-called) 'partners'. Evil is the way they judge." [6:136]

- Currying favours with these idols through votive offerings of crops and cattle, to which effect, the Qur'ân goes:

- "And according to their pretending, they say that such and such cattle and crops are forbidden, and none should eat of them except those whom we allow. And (they say) there are cattle forbidden to be used for burden or any other work, and cattle on which (at slaughtering) the Name of Allâh is not pronounced; lying against Him (Allâh)." [6:138]

- Dedication of certain animals (such as Bahira, Sa'iba, Wasila and Hami) to idols, which meant sparing such animals from useful work for the sake of these heathen gods. Bahira, as reported by the well-known historian, Ibn Ish, was daughter of Sa'iba which was a female camel that gave birth to ten successive female animals, but no male ones, was set free and forbidden to yoke, burden or being sheared off its wool, or milked (but for guests to drink from); and so was done to all her female offspring which were given the name 'Bahira', after having their ears slit. The Wasila was a female sheep which had ten successive female daughters in five pregnancies. Any new births from this Wasila were assigned only for male people. The Hami was a male camel which produced ten progressive females, and was thus similarly forbidden. In mention of this, the Qur'ânic verses go:

- "Allâh has not instituted things like Bahira (a she-camel whose milk was spared for the idols and nobody was allowed to milk it) or a Sa'iba (a she camel let loose for free pasture for their false gods, e.g. idols, etc., and nothing was allowed to be carried on it), or a Wasila (a she-camel set free for idols because it has given birth to a she-camel at its first delivery and then again gives birth to a she-camel at its second delivery) or a Hâm (a stallion-camel freed from work for their idols, after it had finished a number of copulations assigned for it, all these animals were liberated in honour of idols as practised by pagan Arabs in the pre-Islamic period). But those who disbelieve, invent lies against Allâh, and most of them have no understanding." [5:103]

Allâh also says:

- "And they say: What is in the bellies of such and such cattle (milk or foetus) is for our males alone, and forbidden to our females (girls and women), but if it is born dead, then all have shares therein." [6:139]

It has been authentically reported that such superstitions were first invented by 'Amr bin Luhai.

The Arabs believed that such idols, or heathen gods, would bring them nearer to Allâh, lead them to Him, and mediate with Him for their sake, to which effect, the Qur'ân goes:

- "We worship them only that they may bring us near to Allâh." [39:3], and

    "And they worship besides Allâh things that hurt them not, nor profit them, and they say: These are our intercessors with Allâh." [10:18]

Another divinatory tradition among the Arabs was casting of Azlam (i.e. featherless arrows which were of three kinds: one showing 'yes', another 'no' and a third was blank) which they used to do in case of serious matters like travel, marriage and the like. If the lot showed 'yes', they would do, if 'no', they would delay for the next year. Other kinds of Azlam were cast for water, blood-money or showed 'from you', 'not from you', or 'Mulsaq' (consociated). In cases of doubt in filiation they would resort to the idol of Hubal, with a hundred-camel gift, for the arrow caster. Only the arrows would then decide the sort of relationship.If the arrow showed (from you), then it was decided that the child belonged to the tribe; if it showed (from others), he would then be regarded as an ally, but if (consociated) appeared, the person would retain his position but with no lineage or alliance contract.

This was very much like gambling and arrow-shafting whereby they used to divide the meat of the camels they slaughtered according to this tradition.

Moreover, they used to have a deep conviction in the tidings of soothsayers, diviners and astrologers. A soothsayer used to traffic in the business of foretelling future events and claim knowledge of private secrets and having jinn subordinates who would communicate the news to him. Some soothsayers claimed that they could uncover the unknown by means of a granted power, while other diviners boasted they could divulge the secrets through a cause-and-effect-inductive process that would lead to detecting a stolen commodity, location of a theft, a stray animal, and the like. The astrologer belonged to a third category who used to observe the stars and calculate their movements and orbits whereby he would foretell the future. Lending credence to this news constituted a clue to their conviction that attached special significance to the movements of particular stars with regard to rainfall.

The belief in signs as betokening future events, was, of course common among the Arabians. Some days and months and particular animals were regarded as ominous. They also believed that the soul of a murdered person would fly in the wilderness and would never rest at rest until revenge was taken. Superstition was rampant. Should a deer or bird, when released, turn right then what they embarked on would be regarded auspicious, otherwise they would get pessimistic and withhold from pursuing it.

People of pre-Islamic period, whilst believing in superstition, they still retained some of the Abrahamic traditions such as devotion to the Holy Sanctuary, circumambulation, observance of pilgrimage, the vigil on 'Arafah and offering sacrifices, all of these were observed fully despite some innovations that adulterated these holy rituals. Quraish, for example, out of arrogance, feeling of superiority to other tribes and pride in their custodianship of the Sacred House, would refrain from going to 'Arafah with the crowd, instead they would stop short at Muzdalifah. The Noble Qur'ân rebuked and told them:

- "Then depart from the place whence all the people depart." [2:199]

Another heresy, deeply established in their social tradition, dictated that they would not eat dried yoghurt or cooked fat, nor would they enter a tent made of camel hair or seek shade unless in a house of adobe bricks, so long as they were committed to the intention of pilgrimage. They also, out of a deeply-rooted misconception, denied pilgrims, other than Makkans, access to the food they had brought when they wanted to make pilgrimage or lesser pilgrimage.

They ordered pilgrims coming from outside Makkah to circumambulate Al-Ka'bah in Quraish uniform clothes, but if they could not afford them, men were to do so in a state of nudity, and women with only some piece of cloth to hide their groins. Allâh says in this concern:

- "O Children of Adam! Take your adornment (by wearing your clean clothes), while praying [and going round (the Tawaf of) the Ka'bah". [7:31]

If men or women were generous enough to go round Al-Ka'bah in their clothes, they had to discard them after circumambulation for good.

When the Makkans were in a pilgrimage consecration state, they would not enter their houses through the doors but through holes they used to dig in the back walls. They used to regard such behaviour as deeds of piety and god-fearing. This practice was prohibited by the Qur'ân:

- "It is not Al-Birr (piety, righteousness, etc.) that you enter the houses from the back but Al-Birr (is the quality of the one) who fears Allâh. So enter houses through their proper doors, and fear Allâh that you may be successful." [2:189]

Such was the religious life in Arabia, polytheism, idolatry, and superstition.

Judaism, Christianity, Magianism and Sabianism, however, could find their ways easily into Arabia.

The migration of the Jews from Palestine to Arabia passed through two phases: first, as a result of the pressure to which they were exposed, the destruction of the their temple, and taking most of them as captives to Babylon, at the hand of the King Bukhtanassar. In the year B.C. 587 some Jews left Palestine for Hijaz and settled in the northern areas whereof. The second phase started with the Roman occupation of Palestine under the leadership of Roman Buts in 70 A.D. This resulted in a tidal wave of Jewish migration into Hijaz, and Yathrib, Khaibar and Taima', in particular. Here, they made proselytes of several tribes, built forts and castles, and lived in villages. Judaism managed to play an important role in the pre-Islam political life. When Islam dawned on that land, there had already been several famous Jewish tribes — Khabeer, Al-Mustaliq, An-Nadeer, Quraizah and Qainuqa'. In some versions, the Jewish tribes counted as many as twenty.

Judaism was introduced into Yemen by someone called As'ad Abi Karb. He had gone to fight in Yathrib and there he embraced Judaism and then went back taking with him two rabbis from Bani Quraizah to instruct thpeople of Yemen in this new religion. Judaism found a fertile soil there to propagate and gain adherents. After his death, his son Yusuf Dhu Nawas rose to power, attacked the Christian community in Najran and ordered them to embrace Judaism. When they refused, he ordered that a pit of fire be dug and all the Christians indiscriminately be dropped to burn therein. Estimates say that between 20-40 thousand Christians were killed in that human massacre. The Qur'ân related part of that story in Al-Buruj (zodiacal signs) Chapter.

Christianity had first made its appearance in Arabia following the entry of the Abyssinian (Ethiopian) and Roman colonists into that country. The Abyssinian (Ethiopian) colonization forces in league with Christian missions entered Yemen as a retaliatory reaction for the iniquities of Dhu Nawas, and started vehemently to propagate their faith ardently. They even built a church and called it Yemeni Al-Ka'bah with the aim of directing the Arab pilgrimage caravans towards Yemen, and then made an attempt to demolish the Sacred House in Makkah. Allâh, the Almighty, however did punish them and made an example of them – here and hereafter.

A Christian missionary called Fimion, and known for his ascetic behaviour and working miracles, had likewise infiltrated into Najran. There he called people to Christianity, and by virtue of his honesty and truthful devotion, he managed to persuade them to respond positively to his invitation and embrace Christianity.

The principal tribes that embraced Christianity were Ghassan, Taghlib, Tai' and some Himyarite kings as well as other tribes living on the borders of the Roman Empire.

Magianism was also popular among the Arabs living in the neighbourhood of Persia, Iraq, Bahrain, Al-Ahsâ' and some areas on the Arabian Gulf coast. Some Yemenis are also reported to have professed Magianism during the Persian occupation.

As for Sabianism, excavations in Iraq revealed that it had been popular amongst Kaldanian folks, the Syrians and Yemenis. With the advent of Judaism and Christianity, however, Sabianism began to give way to the new religions, although it retained some followers mixed or adjacent to the Magians in Iraq and the Arabian Gulf.

THE RELIGIOUS SITUATION:

Such was the religious life of the Arabians before the advent of Islam. The role that the religions prevalent played was so marginal, in fact it was next to nothing. The polytheists, who faked Abrahamism, were so far detached from its precepts, and totally oblivious of its immanent good manners. They plunged into disobedience and ungodliness, and developed certain peculiar religious superstitions that managed to leave a serious impact on the religious and socio-political life in the whole of Arabia.

Judaism turned into abominable hypocrisy in league with hegemony. Rabbis turned into lords to the exclusion of the Lord. They got involved in the practice of dictatorial subjection of people and calling their subordinates to account for the least word or idea. Their sole target turned into acquisition of wealth and power even if it were at the risk of losing their religion, or the emergence of atheism and disbelief.

Christianity likewise opened its doors wide to polytheism, and got too difficult to comprehend as a heavenly religion. As a religious practice, it developed a sort of peculiar medley of man and God. It exercised no bearing whatsoever on the souls of the Arabs who professed it simply because it was alien to their style of life and did not have the least relationship with their practical life.

People of other religions were similar to the polytheists with respect to their inclinations, dogmas, customs and traditions

ASPECT OF PRE-ISLAMIC ARABIAN SOCIETY

After the research we have made into the religious and political life of Arabia, it is appropriate to speak briefly about the social, economic and ethical conditions prevalent therein.

SOCIAL LIFE OF THE ARABS:

The Arabian Society presented a social medley, with different and heterogeneous social strata. The status of the woman among the nobility recorded an advanced degree of esteem. The woman enjoyed a considerable portion of free will, and her decision would most often be enforced. She was so highly cherished that blood would be easily shed in defence of her honour. In fact, she was the most decisive key to bloody fight or friendly peace. These privileges notwithstanding, the family system in Arabia was wholly patriarchal. The marriage contract rested completely in the hands of the woman's legal guardian whose words with regard to her marital status could never be questioned.

On the other hand, there were other social strata where prostitution and indecency were rampant and in full operation. Abu Da'ûd, on the authority of 'Aishah(May Allah be pleased with her) reported four kinds of marriage in pre-Islamic Arabia: The first was similar to present-day marriage procedures, in which case a man gives his daughter in marriage to another man after a dowry has been agreed on. In the second, the husband would send his wife – after the menstruation period – to cohabit with another man in order to conceive. After conception her husband would, if he desired, have a sexual intercourse with her. A third kind was that a group of less than ten men would have sexual intercourse with a woman. If she conceived and gave birth to a child, she would send for these men, and nobody could abstain. They would come together to her house. She would say: 'You know what you have done. I have given birth to a child and it is your child' (pointing to one of them). The man meant would have to accept. The fourth kind was that a lot of men would have sexual intercourse with a certain woman (a whore). She would not prevent anybody. Such women used to put a certain flag at their gates to invite in anyone who liked. If this whore got pregnant and gave birth to a child, she would collect those men, and a seeress would tell whose child it was. The appointed father would take the child and declare him/her his own. When Prophet Muhammad (Peace be upon him) declared Islam in Arabia, he cancelled all these forms of sexual contacts except that of present Islamic marriage

Women always accompanied men in their wars. The winners would freely have sexual intercourse with such women, but disgrace would follow the children conceived in this way all their lives.

Pre-Islam Arabs had no limited number of wives. They could marry two sisters at the same time, or even the wives of their fathers if divorced or widowed. Divorce was to a very great extent in the power of the husband.

The obscenity of adultery prevailed almost among all social classes except few men and women whose self-dignity prevented them from committing such an act. Free women were in much better conditions than the female slaves who constituted the greatest calamity. It seemed that the greatest majority of pre-Islam Arabs did not feel ashamed of committing this obscenity. Abu Da'ûd reported: A man stood up in front of Prophet Muhammad (Peace be upon him) and said: "O Prophet of Allâh! that boy is my son. I had sexual intercourse with his mother in the pre-Islamic period." The Prophet (Peace be upon him) said:

- "No claim in Islam for pre-Islamic affairs. The child is to be attributed to the one on whose bed it was born, and stoning is the lot of a fornicator."

With respect to the pre-Islam Arab's relation with his offspring, we see that life in Arabia was paradoxical and presented a gloomy picture. Whilst some Arabs held children dear to their hearts and cherished them greatly, others buried their female children alive because an illusory fear of poverty and shame weighed heavily on them. The practice of infanticide cannot, however, be seen as irrevocably rampant because of their dire need for children to guard themselves against their enemies.

Another aspect of the Arabs' life which deserves mention is the bedouin's deep-seated emotional attachment to his clan. Family, or perhaps tribal-pride, was one of the strongest passions with him. The doctrine of unity of blood as the principle that bound the Arabs into a social unity was formed andsupported by tribal-pride. Their undisputed motto was: "انصر أخاك ظالما أو مظلوما — Support your brother whether he is an oppressor or oppressed" in its literal meaning; they disregarded the Islamic amendment which states that supporting an oppressor brother implies deterring him from transgression.

Avarice for leadership, and keen sense of emulation often resulted in bitter tribal warfare despite descendency from one common ancestor. In this regard, the continued bloody conflicts of Aws and Khazraj, 'Abs and Dhubyan, Bakr and Taghlib, etc. are striking examples.

Inter-tribal relationships were fragile and weak due to continual inter-tribal wars of attrition. Deep devotion to religious superstitions and some customs held in veneration, however, used to curb their impetuous tendency to quench their thirst for blood. In other cases, there were the motives of, and respect for, alliance, loyalty and dependency which could successfully bring about a spirit of rapport, and abort groundless bases of dispute. A time-honoured custom of suspending hostilities during the prohibited months (Muharram, Rajab, Dhul-Qa'dah, and Dhul-Hijjah) functioned favourably and provided an opportunity for them to earn their living and coexist in peace.

We may sum up the social situation in Arabia by saying that the Arabs of the pre-Islamic period were groping about in the dark and ignorance, entangled in a mesh of superstitions paralyzing their mind and driving them to lead an animal-like life. The woman was a marketable commodity and regarded as a piece of inanimate property. Inter-tribal relationships were fragile. Avarice for wealth and involvement in futile wars were the main objectives that governed their chiefs' self-centred policies.

THE ECONOMIC SITUATION:

The economic situation ran in line with the social atmosphere. The Arabian ways of living would illustrate this phenomenon quite clearly. Trade was the most common means of providing their needs of life. The trade journeys could not be fulfilled unless security of caravan routes and inter-tribal peaceful co-existence were provided – two imperative exigencies unfortunately lacking in Arabia except during the prohibited months within which the Arabs held their assemblies of 'Ukaz, Dhil-Majaz, Mijannah and others.

Industry was alien to the Arabian psychology. Most of available industries of knitting and tannage in Arabia were done by people coming from Yemen, Heerah and the borders of Syria. Inside Arabia there was some sort of farming and stock-breeding. Almost all the Arabian women worked in yarn spinning but even this practice was continually threatened by wars. On the whole, poverty, hunger and insufficient clothing were the prevailing features in Arabia, economically.

ETHICS:

We cannot deny that the pre-Islam Arabs had such a large bulk of evils. Admittedly, vices and evils, utterly rejected by reason, were rampant amongst the pre-Islam Arabs, but this could never screen off the surprise-provoking existence of highly praiseworthy virtues, of which we could adduce the following:

1. Hospitality: They used to emulate one another at hospitality and take utmost pride in it. Almost half of their poetry heritage was dedicated to the merits and nobility attached to entertaining one's guest. They were generous and hospitable on the point of fault. They would sacrifice their private sustenance to a cold or hungry guest. They would not hesitate to incur heavy blood-money and relevant burdens just to stop blood-shed, and consequently merit praise and eulogy.
2. In the context of hospitality, there springs up their common habits of drinking wine which was

regarded as a channel branching out of generosity and showing hospitality. Wine drinking was a genuine source of pride for the Arabs of the pre-Islamic period. The great poets of that era never forgot to include their suspending odes the most ornate lines pregnant with boasting and praise of drinking orgies. Even the word 'grapes' in Arabic is identical to generosity in both pronunciation and spelling. Gambling was also another practice of theirs closely associated with generosity since the proceeds would always go to charity. Even the Noble Qur'ân does not play down the benefits that derive from wine drinking and gambling, but also says,

"And the sin of them is greater than their benefit." [2:219]

3. Keeping a covenant: For the Arab, to make a promise was to run into debt. He would never grudge the death of his children or destruction of his household just to uphold the deep-rooted tradition of covenant-keeping. The literature of that period is rich in stories highlighting this merit.
4. Sense of honour and repudiation of injustice: This attribute stemmed mainly from excess courage, keen sense of self-esteem and impetuosity. The Arab was always in revolt against the least allusion to humiliation or slackness. He would never hesitate to sacrifice himself to maintain his ever alert sense of self-respect.
5. Firm will and determination: An Arab would never desist an avenue conducive to an object of pride or a standing of honour, even if it were at the expense of his life.
6. Forbearance, perseverance and mildness: The Arab regarded these traits with great admiration, no wonder, his impetuosity and courage-based life was sadly wanting in them.
7. Pure and simple bedouin life, still untarnished with accessories of deceptive urban appearances, was a driving reason to his nature of truthfulness and honesty, and detachment from intrigue and treachery.

Such priceless ethics coupled with a favourable geographical position of Arabia were in fact the factors that lay behind selecting the Arabs to undertake the burden of communicating the Message (of Islam) and leading mankind down a new course of life.

In this regard, these ethics per se, though detrimental in some areas, and in need of rectification in certain aspects, were greatly invaluable to the ultimate welfare of the human community and Islam has did it completely.

The most priceless ethics, next to covenant-keeping, were no doubt their sense of self-esteem and strong determination, two human traits indispensable in combatting evil and eliminating moral corruption on the one hand, and establishing a good and justice-orientated society, on the other.

Actually, the life of the Arabs in the pre-Islamic period was rich in other countless virtues we do not need to enumerate for the time being.

THE LINEAGE AND THE FAMILY OF MUHAMMAD (Peace be upon him)

With respect to the lineage of Prophet Muhammad (Peace be upon him), there are three versions: The first was authenticated by biographers and genealogists and states that Muhammad's genealogy has been traced to 'Adnan. The second is subject to controversies and doubt, and traces his lineage beyond 'Adnan back to Abraham. The third version, with some parts definitely incorrect, traces his lineage beyond Abraham back to Adam (Peace be upon him)

After this rapid review, now ample details are believed to be necessary.

The first part: Muhammad bin 'Abdullah bin 'Abdul-Muttalib (who was called Shaiba) bin Hashim, (named 'Amr) bin 'Abd Munaf (called Al-Mugheera) bin Qusai (also called Zaid) bin Kilab bin Murra bin Ka'b bin Lo'i bin Ghalib bin Fahr (who was called Quraish and whose tribe was called after him) bin Malik bin An-Nadr (so called Qais) bin Kinana bin Khuzaiman bin Mudrikah (who was called 'Amir) bin Elias bin Mudar bin Nizar bin Ma'ad bin 'Adnan.

The second part: 'Adnan bin Add bin Humaisi' bin Salaman bin Aws bin Buz bin Qamwal bin Obai bin 'Awwam bin Nashid bin Haza bin Bildas bin Yadlaf bin Tabikh bin Jahim bin Nahish bin Makhi bin Aid bin 'Abqar bin 'Ubaid bin Ad-Da'a bin Hamdan bin Sanbir bin Yathrabi bin Yahzin bin Yalhan bin Ar'awi bin Aid bin Deshan bin Aisar bin Afnad bin Aiham bin Muksar bin Nahith bin Zarih bin Sami bin Mazzi bin 'Awda bin Aram bin Qaidar bin Ishmael son of Abraham (Peace be upon them).

The third part: beyond Abraham (Peace be upon him) , Ibn Tarih (Azar) bin Nahur bin Saru' bin Ra'u bin Falikh bin Abir bin Shalikh bin Arfakhshad bin Sam bin Noah (Peace be upon him) , bin Lamik bin Mutwashlack bin Akhnukh [who was said to be Prophet Idris (Enoch) (Peace be upon him)   bin Yarid bin Mahla'il bin Qabin Anusha bin Shith bin Adam (Peace be upon him)

THE PROPHETIC FAMILY:

The family of Prophet Muhammad (Peace be upon him) is called the Hashimite family after his grandfather Hashim bin 'Abd Munaf. Let us now speak a little about Hashim and his descendants:

1. Hashim: As we have previously mentioned, he was the one responsible for giving food and water to the pilgrims. This had been his charge when the sons of 'Abd Munaf and those of 'Abd Ad-Dar compromised on dividing the charges between them. Hashim was wealthy and honest. He was the first to offer the pilgrims sopped bread in broth. His first name was 'Amr but he was called Hashim because he had been in the practice of crumbling bread (for the pilgrims). He was also the first man who started Quraish's two journeys of summer and winter. It was reported that he went to Syria as a merchant. In Madinah, he married Salma — the daughter of 'Amr from Bani 'Adi bin An-Najjar. He spent some time with her in Madinah then he left for Syria again while she was pregnant. He died in Ghazza in Palestine in 497 A.D. Later, his wife gave birth to 'Abdul-Muttalib and named him Shaiba for the white hair in his head , and brought him up in her father's house in Madinah. None of his family in Makkah learned of his birth. Hashim had four sons; Asad, Abu Saifi, Nadla and 'Abdul-Muttalib, and five daughters Ash-Shifa, Khalida, Da'ifa, Ruqyah and Jannah.
2. 'Abdul-Muttalib: We have already known that after the death of Hashim, the charge of pilgrims' food and water went to his brother Al-Muttalib bin 'Abd Munaf (who was honest, generous and trustworthy). When 'Abdul-Muttalib reached the age of boyhood, his uncle Al-Muttalib heard of him and went to Madinah to fetch him. When he saw him, tears filled his eyes and rolled down his cheeks, he embraced him and took him on his camel. The boy, however abstained from going with him to Makkah until he took his mother's consent. Al-Muttalib asked her to send the boy with him to Makkah, but she refused. He managed to convince her saying: "Your son is going to Makkah to restore his father's authority, and to live in the vicinity of the Sacred House." There in

Makkah, people wondered at seeing Abdul-Muttalib, and they considered him the slave of Muttalib. Al-Muttalib said: "He is my nephew, the son of my brother Hashim." The boy was brought up in Al-Muttalib's house, but later on Al-Muttalib died in Bardman in Yemen so 'Abdul-Muttalib took over and managed to maintain his people's prestige and outdo his grandfathers in his honourable behaviour which gained him Makkah's deep love and high esteem.

3. When Al-Muttalib died, Nawfal usurped 'Abdul-Muttalib of his charges, so the latter asked for help from Quraish but they abstained from extending any sort of support to either of them. Consequently, he wrote to his uncles of Bani An-Najjar (his mother's brothers) to come to his aid. His uncle, Abu Sa'd bin 'Adi (his mother's brother) marched to Makkah at the head of eighty horsemen and camped in Abtah in Makkah. 'Abdul-Muttalib received the men and invited them to go to his house but Abu Sa'd said: "Not before I meet Nawfal." He found Nawfal sitting with some old men of Quraish in the shade of Al-Ka'bah. Abu Sa'd drew his sword and said: "I swear by Allâh that if you don't restore to my nephew what you have taken, I will kill you with this sword." Nawfal was thus forced to give up what he had usurped, and the notables of Quraish were made to witness to his words. Abu Sa'd then went to 'Abdul-Muttalib's house where he stayed for three nights, made 'Umra and left back for Madinah. Later on, Nawfal entered into alliance with Bani 'Abd Shams bin 'Abd Munaf against Bani Hashim. When Khuza'a, a tribe, saw Bani An-Najjar's support to 'Abdul-Muttalib they said: "He is our son as he is yours. We have more reasons to support him than you." 'Abd Munaf's mother was one of them. They went into An-Nadwa House and entered into alliance with Bani Hashim against Bani 'Abd Shams and Nawfal. It was an alliance that was later to constitute the main reason for the conquest of Makkah. 'Abdul-Muttalib witnessed two important events in his lifetime, namely digging Zamzam well and the Elephant raid.

In brief, 'Abdul-Muttalib received an order in his dream to dig Zamzam well in a particular place. He did that and found the things that Jurhum men had buried therein when they were forced to evacuate Makkah. He found the swords, armours and the two deer of gold. The gate of Al-Ka'bah was stamped from the gold swords and the two deer and then the tradition of providing Zamzam water to pilgrims was established.

When the well of Zamzam gushed water forth, Quraish made a claim to partnership in the enterprise, but 'Abdul-Muttalib refused their demands on grounds that Allâh had singled only him out for this honourable job. To settle the dispute, they agreed to consult Bani Sa'd's diviner. On their way, Allâh showed them His Signs that confirmed 'Abdul-Muttalib's prerogative as regards the sacred spring. Only then did 'Abdul-Muttalib make a solemn vow to sacrifice one of his adult children to Al-Ka'bah if he had ten.

The second event was that of Abraha As-Sabah Al-Habashi, the Abyssinian (Ethiopian) viceroy in Yemen. He had seen that the Arabs made their pilgrimage to Al-Ka'bah so he built a large church in San'a in order to attract the Arab pilgrims to it to the exclusion of Makkah. A man from Kinana tribe understood this move, therefore he entered the church stealthily at night and besmeared its front wall with excrement. When Abraha knew of that, he got very angry and led a great army – of sixty thousand warriors – to demolish Al-Ka'bah. He chose the biggest elephant for himself. His army included nine or thirteen elephants. He continued marching until he reached a place called Al-Magmas. There, he mobilized his army, prepared his elephants and got ready to enter Makkah. When he reached Muhassar Valley, between Muzdalifah and Mina, the elephant knelt down and refused to go forward. Whenever they directed it northwards, southwards or eastwards, the elephant moved quickly but when directed westwards towards Al-Ka'bah, it knelt down. Meanwhile, Allâh loosed upon them birds in flights, hurling against them stones of baked clay and made them like green blades devoured. These birds were very much like swallows and sparrows, each carrying three stones; one in its peak and two in its claws. The stones hit Abraha's men and cut their limbs and killed them. A large number of Abraha's soldiers were killed in this way and the others fled at random and died everywhere. Abraha himself had an infection that had his fingertips amputated. When he reached San'a he was in a miserable state and died soon after.

The Quraishites on their part had fled for their lives to the hillocks and mountain tops. When the enemy had been thus routed, they returned home safely.

The Event of the Elephant took place in the month of Al-Muharram, fifty or fifty five days before the birth of Prophet Muhammad (Peace be upon him) which corresponded to late February or early March 571 A.D. It was a gift from Allâh to His Prophet and his family. It could actually be regarded as a Divine auspicious precursor of the light to come and accompany the advent of the Prophet and his family. By contrast, Jerusalem had suffered under the yoke of the atrocities of Allâh's enemies. Here we can recall Bukhtanassar in B.C. 587 and the Romans in 70 A.D. Al-Ka'bah, by Divine Grace, never came under the hold of the Christians – the Muslims of that time – although Makkah was populated by polytheists.

News of the Elephant Event reached the most distant corners of the then civilized world. Abyssinia (Ethiopia) maintained strong ties with the Romans, while the Persians on the other hand, were on the vigil with respect to any strategic changes that were looming on the socio-political horizon, and soon came to occupy Yemen. Incidentally, the Roman and Persian Empires stood for the powerful civilized world at that time. The Elephant Raid Event riveted the world's attention to the sacredness of Allâh's House, and showed that this House had been chosen by Allâh for its ho. It followed then if any of its people claimed Prophethood, it would be congruous with the outcome of the Elephant Event, and would provide a justifiable explanation for the ulterior Divine Wisdom that lay behind backing polytheists against Christians in a manner that transcended the cause-and-effect formula.

'Abdul-Muttalib had ten sons, Al-Harith, Az-Zubair, Abu Talib, 'Abdullah, Hamzah, Abu Lahab, Ghidaq, Maqwam, Safar and Al-'Abbas. He also had six daughters, who were Umm Al-Hakim – the only white one, Barrah, 'Atikah, Safiya, Arwa and Omaima.

4. 'Abdullah: The father of Prophet Muhammad (Peace be upon him). His mother was Fatimah, daughter of 'Amr bin 'A'idh bin 'Imran bin Makhzum bin Yaqdha bin Murra. 'Abdullah was the smartest of 'Abdul-Muttalib's sons, the chastest and the most loved. He was also the son whom the divination arrows pointed at to be slaughtered as a sacrifice to Al-Ka'bah. When 'Abdul-Muttalib had ten sons and they reached maturity, he divulged to them his secret vow in which they silently and obediently acquiesced. Their names were written on divination arrows and given to the guardian of their most beloved goddess, Hubal. The arrows were shuffled and drawn. An arrow showed that it was 'Abdullah to be sacrificed. 'Abdul-Muttalib then took the boy to Al-Ka'bah with a razor to slaughter the boy. Quraish, his uncles from Makhzum tribe and his brother Abu Talib, however, tried to dissuade him from consummating his purpose. He then sought their advice as regards his vow. They suggested that he summon a she-diviner to judge whereabout. She ordered that the divination arrows should be drawn with respect to 'Abdullah as well as ten camels. She added that drawing the lots should be repeated with ten more camels every time the arrow showed 'Abdullah. The operation was thus repeated until the number of the camels amounted to one hundred. At this point the arrow showed the camels, consequently they were all slaughtered (to the satisfaction of Hubal) instead of his son. The slaughtered camels were left for anyone to eat from, human or animal.

- This incident produced a change in the amount of blood-money usually accepted in Arabia. It had been ten camels, but after this event it was increased to a hundred. Islam, later on, approved of this. Another thing closely relevant to the above issue goes to the effect that the Prophet (Peace be upon him) once said:

"I am the offspring of the slaughtered two," meaning Ishmael and 'Abdullah.

'Abdul-Muttalib chose Amina, daughter of Wahab bin 'Abd Munaf bin Zahra bin Kilab, as a wife for his son, 'Abdullah. She thus, in the light of this ancestral lineage, stood eminent in respect of nobility of position and descent. Her father was the chief of Bani Zahra to whom great honour was attributed. They were married in Makkah, and soon after 'Abdullah was sent by his father to buy dates in Madinah where he died. In another version, 'Abdullah went to Syria on a trade journey and died in Madinah on his way back. He was buried in the house of An-Nabigha Al-Ju'di. He was twenty-five years old when he died. Most historians state that his death was two months before the birth of Muhammad ﷺ. Some others said that his death was two months after the Prophet's birth. When Amina was informed of her husband's death, she celebrated his memory in a most heart-touching elegy.

'Abdullah left very little wealth —five camels, a small number of goats, a she-servant, called Barakah – Umm Aiman – who would later serve as the Prophet's nursemaid.

MUHAMMAD'S BIRTH AND FORTY YEARS PRIOR TO PROPHETHOOD

HIS BIRTH:

Muhammad (Peace be upon him), the Master of Prophets, was born in Bani Hashim lane in Makkah on Monday morning, the ninth of Rabi' Al-Awwal, the same year of the Elephant Event, and forty years of the reign of Kisra (Khosru Nushirwan), i.e. the twentieth or twenty-second of April, 571 A.D., according to the scholar Muhammad Sulaimân Al-Mansourpuri, and the astrologer Mahmûd Pasha.

Ibn Sa'd reported that Muhammad's mother said: "When he was born, there was a light that issued out of my pudendum and lit the palaces of Syria." Ahmad reported on the authority of 'Arbadh bin Sariya something similar to this.

It was but controversially reported that significant precursors accompanied his birth: fourteen galleries of Kisra's palace cracked and rolled down, the Magians' sacred fire died down and some churches on Lake Sawa sank down and collapsed.

His mother immediately sent someone to inform his grandfather 'Abdul-Muttalib of the happy event. Happily he came to her, carried him to Al-Ka'bah, prayed to Allâh and thanked Him. 'Abdul-Muttalib called the baby Muhammad, a name not then common among the Arabs. He circumcised him on his seventh day as was the custom of the Arabs.

The first woman who suckled him after his mother was Thuyebah, the concubine of Abu Lahab, with her son, Masrouh. She had suckled Hamzah bin 'Abdul-Muttalib before and later Abu Salamah bin 'Abd Al-Asad Al-Makhzumi.

BABYHOOD:

It was the general custom of the Arabs living in towns to send their children away to bedouin wet nurses so that they might grow up in the free and healthy surroundings of the desert whereby they would develop a robust frame and acquire the pure speech and manners of the bedouins, who were noted both for chastity of their language and for being free from those vices which usually develop in sedentary societies.

The Prophet (Peace be upon him) was later entrusted to Haleemah bint Abi Dhuaib from Bani Sa'd bin Bakr. Her husband was Al-Harith bin 'Abdul 'Uzza called Abi Kabshah, from the same tribe.

Muhammad(Peace be upon him) had several foster brothers and sisters, 'Abdullah bin Al-Harith, Aneesah bint Al-Harith, Hudhafah or Judhamah bint Al-Harith (known as Ash-Shayma'), and she used to nurse the Prophet (Peace be upon him) and Abu Sufyan bin Al-Harith bin 'Abdul-Muttalib, the Prophet's cousin. Hamzah bin 'Abdul-Muttalib, the Prophet's uncle, was suckled by the same two wet nurses, Thuyeba and Haleemah As-Sa'diyah, who suckled the Prophet (Peace be upon him).

Traditions delightfully relate how Haleemah and the whole of her household were favoured by successive strokes of good fortune while the baby Muhammad (Peace be upon him) lived under her care. Ibn Ishaq states that Haleemah narrated that she along with her husband and a suckling babe, set out from her village in the company of some women of her clan in quest of children to suckle. She said:

It was a year of drought and famine and we had nothing to eat. I rode on a brown she-ass. We also had with us an old she-camel. By Allâh we could not get even a drop of milk. We could not have a wink of sleep during the night for the child kept crying on account of hunger. There was not enough milk in my breast and even the she-camel had nothing to feed him. We used to constantly pray for rain and immediate relief. At length we reached Makkah looking for children to suckle. Not even a single woman amongst us accepted the Messenger of Allâh (Peace be upon him) offered to her. As soon as they were told that he was an orphan, they refused him. We had fixed our eyes on the reward that we would get from the child's father. An orphan! What are his grandfather and mother likely to do? So we spurned him because of that. Every woman who came with me got a suckling and when we were about to depart, I said to my husband: "By Allâh, I do not like to go back along with the other women without any baby. I should go to that orphan and I must take him." He said, "There is no harm in doing so and perhaps Allâh might bless us through him." So I went and took him because there was simply no other alternative left for me but to take him. When I lifted him in my arms and returned to my place I put him on my breast and to my great surprise, I found enough milk in it. He drank to his heart's content, and so did his foster brother and then both of them went to sleep although my baby had not been able to sleep the previous night. My husband then went to the she-camel to milk it and, to his astonishment, he found plenty of milk in it. He milked it and we drank to our fill, and enjoyed a sound sleep during the night. The next morning, my husband said: "By Allâh Haleemah, you must understand that you have been able to get a blessed child." And I replied: "By the grace of Allâh, I hope so."

The tradition is explicit on the point that Haleemah's return journey and her subsequent life, as long as the Prophet (Peace be upon him)stayed with her, was encircled with a halo of good fortune. The donkey that she rode when she came to Makkah was lean and almost foundered; it recovered speed much to the amazement of Haleemah's fellow travellers. By the time they reached the encampments in the country of the clan of Sa'd, they found the scales of fortune turned in their favour. The barren land sprouted forth luxuriant grass and beasts came back to them satisfied and full of milk. Muhammad (Peace be upon him) stayed with Haleemah for two years until he was weaned as Haleemah said:

We then took him back to his mother requesting her earnestly to have him stay with us and benefit by the good fortune and blessings he had brought us. We persisted in our request which we substantiated by our anxiety over the child catching a certain infection peculiar to Makkah. At last, we were granted our wish and the Prophet (Peace be upon him) stayed with us until he was four or five years of age.

When, as related by Anas in *Sahih Muslim*, Gabriel came down and ripped his chest open and took out the heart. He extracted a blood-clot out of it and said: "That was the part of Satan in thee." And then he washed it with the water of Zamzam in a gold basin. After that the heart was joined together and restored to its place. The boys and playmates came running to his mother, i.e. his nurse, and said: "Verily, Muhammad (Peace be upon him) has been murdered." They all rushed towards him and found him all right only his face was white.

BACK TO HIS COMPASSIONATE MOTHER:

After this event, Haleemah was worried about the boy and returned him to his mother with whom he stayed until he was six.

In respect of the memory of her late husband, Amina decided to visit his grave in Yathrib (Madinah). She set out to cover a journey of 500 kilometers with her orphan boy, woman servant Umm Ayman and her father-in-law 'Abdul-Muttalib. She spent a month there and then took her way back to Makkah. On the way, she had a severe illness and died in Abwa on the road between Makkah and Madinah.

BACK TO HIS COMPASSIONATE GRANDFATHER:

'Abdul-Muttalib brought the boy to Makkah. He had warm passions towards the boy, his orphan grandson, whose recent disaster (his mother's death) added more to the pains of the past. 'Abdul-Muttalib was more passionate with his grandson than with his own children. He never left the boy a prey to loneliness, but always preferred him to his own kids. Ibn Hisham reported: A mattress was put in the shade of Al-Ka'bah for 'Abdul-Muttalib. His children used to sit around that mattress in honour to their father, but Muhammad (Peace be upon him) used to sit on it. His uncles would take him back, but if 'Abdul-Muttalib was present, he would say: "Leave my grandson. I swear by Allâh that this boy will hold a significant position." He used to seat the boy on his mattress, pat his back and was always pleased with what the boy did.

When Muhammad (Peace be upon him) was eight years, two months and ten days old, his grandfather 'Abdul-Muttalib passed away in Makkah. The charge of the Prophet (Peace be upon him) was now passed on to his uncle Abu Talib, who was the brother of the Prophet's father.

Abu Talib tookthe charge of his nephew in the best way. He put him with his children and preferred him to them. He singled the boy out with great respect and high esteem. Abu Talib remained for forty years cherishing his nephew and extending all possible protection and support to him. His relations with the others were determined in the light of the treatment they showed to the Prophet (Peace be upon him).

Ibn 'Asakir reported on the authority of Jalhamah bin 'Arfuta who said: "I came to Makkah when it was a rainless year, so Quraish said 'O Abu Talib, the valley has become leafless and the children hungry, let us go and pray for rain-fall.' Abu Talib went to Al-Ka'bah with a young boy who was as beautiful as the sun, and a black cloud was over his head. Abu Talib and the boy stood by the wall of Al-Ka'bah and prayed for rain. Immediately clouds from all directions gathered and rain fell heavily and caused the flow of springs and growth of plants in the town and the country.

BAHIRA, THE MONK:

When the Messenger of Allâh (Peace be upon him) was twelve years old, he went with his uncle Abu Talib on a business journey to Syria. When they reached Busra (which was a part of Syria, in the vicinity of Howran under the Roman domain) they met a monk called Bahira (his real name was Georges), who showed great kindness, and entertained them lavishly. He had never been in the habit of receiving or entertaining them before. He readily enough recognized the Prophet (Peace be upon him) and said while taking his hand: "This is the master of all humans. Allâh will send him with a Message which will be a mercy to all beings." Abu Talib asked: "How do you know that?" He replied: "When you appeared from the direction of 'Aqabah, all stones and trees prostrated themselves, which they never do except for a Prophet. I can recognize him also by the seal of Prophethood which is below his shoulder, like an apple. We have got to learn this from our books." He also asked Abu Talib to send the boy back to Makkah and not to take him to Syria for fear of the Jews. Abu Talib obeyed and sent him back to Makkah with some of his men servants.

THE 'SACRILIGIOUS' WARS:

Muhammad (Peace be upon him) was hardly fifteen when the 'sacrilegious' wars — which continued with varying fortunes and considerable loss of human life for a number of years — broke out between Quraish and Banu Kinana on the one side and Qais 'Ailan tribe on the other. It was thus called because the inviolables were made violable, the prohibited months being included. Harb bin Omaiyah, on account of his outstanding position and honourable descent, used to be the leader of Quraish and their allies. In one of those battles, the Prophet (Peace be upon him) attended on his uncles but did not raise arms against their opponents. His efforts were confined to picking up the arrows of the enemy as they fell, and handing them over to his uncles.

ALFUDOUL CONFEDERACY:

At the conclusion of these wars, when peace was restored, people felt the need for forming confederacy at Makkah for suppressing violence and injustice, and vindicating the rights of the weak and the destitute. Representatives of Banu Hashim, Banu Al-Muttalib, Asad bin 'Abd Al-'Uzza, Zahrah bin Kilab and Taim bin Murra were called to meet in the habitation of an honourable elderly man called 'Abdullah bin Jada'an At-Taimy to enter into a confederacy that would provide for the above-mentioned items. The Messenger of Allâh (Peace be upon him) shortly after he had been honoured with the ministry of Prophethood, witnessed this league and commented on it, with very positive words: "I witnessed a confederacy in the house of 'Abdullah bin Jada'an. It was more appealing to me than herds of cattle. Even now in the period of Islam I would respond positively to attending such a meeting if I were invited."

In fact, the spirit of this confederacy and the course of deliberations therein marked a complete departure from the pre-Islamic tribal-pride. The story that led to its convention says that a man from Zubaid clan came as a merchant to Makkah where he sold some commodities to Al-'As bin Wail As-Sahmy. The latter by hook or by crook tried to evade paying for the goods. The salesman sought help from the different clans in Quraish but they paid no heed to his earnest pleas. He then resorted to a mountain top and began, at the top of his voice, to recite verses of complaint giving account of the injustices he sustained. Az-Zubair bin 'Abdul-Muttalib heard of him and made inquiries into the matter. Consequently, the parties to the aforesaid confederacy convened their meeting and managed to force Az-Zubaidy's money out of Al-'As bin Wa'il.

MUHAMMAD'S EARLY JOB:

Muhammad (Peace be upon him), had no particular job at his early youth, but it was reported that he worked as a shepherd for Bani Sa'd and in Makkah. At the age of 25, he went to Syria as a merchant for Khadijah (May Allah be pleased with her) Ibn Ishaq reported that Khadijah, daughter of Khwailid was a business-woman of great honour and fortune. She used to employ men to do her business for a certain percentage of the profits. Quraish people were mostly tradespeople, so when Khadijah was informed of Muhammad (Peace be upon him), his truthful words, great honesty and kind manners, she sent for him. She offered him money to go to Syria and do her business, and she would give him a higher rate than the others. She would also send her hireling, Maisarah, with him. He agreed and went with her servant to Syria for trade.

HIS MARRIEAGE TO KHADIJAH:

When he returned to Makkah, Khadijah noticed, in her money, more profits and blessings than she used to. Her hireling also told her of Muhammad's good manners, honesty, deep thought, sincerity and faith. She realized that she homed at her target. Many prominent men had asked for her hand in marriage but she always spurned their advances. She disclosed her wish to her friend Nafisa, daughter of Maniya, who immediately went to Muhammad (Peace be upon him) and broke the good news to him. He agreed and requested his uncles to go to Khadijah's uncle and talk on this issue. Subsequently, they were married. The marriage contract was witnessed by Bani Hashim and the heads of Mudar. This took place after the Prophet's return from Syria. He gave her twenty camels as dowry. She was, then, forty years old and was considered as the best woman of her folk in lineage, fortune and wisdom. She was the first woman whom the Messenger of Allâh (Peace be upon him) married. He did not get married to any other until she had died.

Khadijah bore all his children, except Ibrahim: Al-Qasim, Zainab, Ruqaiyah, Umm Kulthum, Fatimah and 'Abdullah who was called Taiyib and Tahir. All his sons died in their childhood and all the daughters except Fatimah died during his lifetime. Fatimah died six months after his death. All his daughters witnessed Islam, embraced it, and emigrated to Madinah.

REBUILDING AL-KA'BAH AND THE ARBITRATION ISSUE:

When the Messenger of Allâh (Peace be upon him) was thirty five, Quraish started rebuilding Al-Ka'bah. That was because it was a low building of white stones no more than 6.30 metres high, from the days of Ishmael. It was also roofless and that gave the thieves easy access to its treasures inside. It was also exposed to the wearing factors of nature — because it was built a long time ago — that weakened and cracked its walls. Five years before Prophethood, there was a great flood in Makkah that swept towards Al-Ka'bah and almost demolished it. Quraish was obliged to rebuild it to safeguard its holiness and position. The chiefs of Quraish decided to use only licit money in rebuilding Al-Ka'bah, so all money that derived from harlotry, usury or unjust practices was excluded. They were, at first, too awed to knock down the wall, but Al-Waleed bin Al-Mugheerah Al-Mukhzumi started the work. Seeing that no harm had happened to him, the others participated in demolishing the walls until they reached the basis laid by Abraham. When they started rebuilding its walls, they divided the work among the tribes. Each tribe was responsible for rebuilding a part of it. The tribes collected stones and startwork. The man who laid the stones was a Roman mason called Baqum. The work went on in harmony till the time came to put the sacred Black Stone in its proper place. Then strife broke out among the chiefs, and lasted for four or five days, each contesting for the honour of placing the stone in its position. Daggers were on the point of being drawn and great bloodshed seemed imminent. Luckily, the oldest among the chiefs Abu Omaiyah bin Mugheerah Al-Makhzumi made a proposal which was accepted by all. He said: "Let him, who enters the Sanctuary first of all, decide on the point." It was then Allâh's Will that the Messenger of Allâh (Peace be upon him) should be the first to enter the Mosque. On seeing him, all the people on the scene, cried with one voice: "*Al-Ameen* (the trustworthy) has come. We are content to abide by his decision." Calm and self-possessed, Muhammad (Peace be upon him) received the commission and at once resolved upon an expedient which was to conciliate them all. He asked for a mantle which he spread on the ground and placed the stone in its centre. He then asked the representatives of the different clans among them, to lift the stone all together. When it had reached the proper place, Muhammad (Peace be upon him) laid it in the proper position with his own hands. This is how a very tense situation was eased and a grave danger averted by the wisdom of the Prophet (Peace be upon him).

Quraish ran short of the licit money, they collected, so they eliminated six yards area on the northern side of Al-Ka'bah which is called Al-Hijr or Al-Hateem. They raised its door two metres from the level ground to let in only the people whom they desired. When the structure was fifteen yards high they erected the roof which rested on six columns.

When the building of Al-Ka'bah had finished, it assumed a square form fifteen metres high. The side with the Black Stone and the one opposite were ten metres long each. The Black Stone was 1.50 metre from the circumambulation level ground. The two other sides were twelve metres long each. The door was two metres high from the level ground. A building structure of 0.25 metre high and 0.30 metre wide on the average surrounded Al-Ka'bah. It was called Ash-Shadherwan, originally an integral part of the Sacred Sanctuary, but Quraish left it out.

A RAPID REVIEW OF MUHAMMAD'S BIOGRAPHY BEFORE COMMISSIONING OF THE PROPHETHOOD:

Prophet Muhammad (Peace be upon him) was, in his youth, a combination of the best social attributes. He was an exemplary man of weighty mind and faultless insight. He was favoured with intelligence, originality of thought and accurate choice of the means leading to accurate goals. His long silence helped favourably in his habit of meditation and deep investigation into the truth. His vivid mind and pure nature were helpfully instrumental in assimilating and comprehending ways of life and people, individual and community-wise. He shunned superstitious practices but took an active part in constructive and useful dealings, otherwise, he would have recourse to his self-consecrated solitude. He kept himself aloof from drinking wine, eating meat slaughtered on stone altars, or attending idolatrous festivals. He held the idols in extreme aversion and most abhorrence. He could never tolerate someone swearing by Al-Lat and Al-'Uzza. Allâh's providence, no doubts, detached him from all abominable or evil practices. Even when he tried to obey his instinct to enjoy some life pleasures or follow some irrespectable traditions, Allâh's providence intervened to curb any lapse in this course. Ibn Al-Atheer reported Muhammad (Peace be upon him) as saying: "I have never tried to do what my people do except for two times. Every time Allâh intervened and checked me from doing so and I never did that again. Once I told my fellow-shepherd to take care of my sheep when we were in the upper part of Makkah. I wanted to go down to Makkah and entertain myself as the young men did. I went down to the first house of Makkah where I heard music. I entered and asked: 'What is this?' Someone answered: 'It is a wedding party.' I sat down and listened but soon went into deep sleep. I was awakened by the heat of the sun. I went back to my fellow-shepherd and told him of what had happened to me. I have never tried it again."

Al-Bukhari reported on the authority of Jabir bin 'Abdullah that he said: "While the people were rebuilding Al-Ka'bah, the Prophet Muhammad (Peace be upon him) went with 'Abbas to carry some stones. 'Abbas said: 'Put your loincloth round your neck to protect you from the stones.' (As he did that) the Prophet (Peace be upon him) fell to the ground and his eyes turned skyward. Later on he woke up and shouted: 'My loincloth... my loincloth.' He wrapped himself in his loincloth." In another report: "His loins were never seen afterwards."

The authorities agree in ascribing to the youth of Muhammad (Peace be upon him) modesty of deportment, virtuous behaviour and graceful manners. He proved himself to be the ideal of manhood, and to possess a spotless character. He was the most obliging to his compatriots, the most honest in his talk and the mildest in temper. He was the most gentle-hearted, chaste, hospitable and always impressed people by his piety-inspiring countenance. He was the most truthful and the best to keep covenant. His fellow-citizens, by common consent, gave him the title of *Al-'Ameen* (trustworthy). The Mother of believers, Khadijah (May Allah be pleased with her) once said: He unites uterine relations, he helps the poor and the needy, he entertains the guests and endures hardships in the path of truthfulness.

IN THE SHADE OF THE MESSAGE AND PROPHETHOOD IN THE CAVE HIRA:

When Prophet Muhammad (Peace be upon him) was nearly forty, he had been wont to pass long hours in retirement meditating and speculating over all aspects of creation around him. This meditative temperament helped to widen the mental gap between him and his compatriots. He used to provide himself with *Sawiq* (barley porridge) and water and then directly head for the hills and ravines in the neighbourhood of Makkah. One of these in particular was his favourite resort — a cave named Hira', in the Mount An-Nour. It was only two miles from Makkah, a small cave 4 yards long and 1.75 yard wide. He would always go there and invite wayfarers to share him his modest provision. He used to devote most of his time, and Ramadan in particular, to worship and meditation on the universe around him. His heart was restless about the moral evils and idolatry that were rampant among his people; he was as yet helpless because no definite course, or specific approach had been available for him to follow and rectify the ill practices around him. This solitude attended with this sort of contemplative approach must be understood in its Divine perspective. It was a preliminary stage to the period of grave responsibilities that he was to shoulder very soon.

Privacy and detachment from the impurities of life were two indispensable prerequisites for the Prophet's soul to come into close communion with the Unseen Power that lies behind all aspects of existence in this infinite universe. It was a rich period of privacy which lasted for three years and ushered in a new era, of indissoluble contact with that Power.

GAGRIEL BRINGS DOWN THE REVELATION:

When he was forty, the age of complete perfection at which Prophets were always ordered to disclose their Message, signs of his Prophethood started to appear and twinkle on the horizons of life; they were the true visions he used to experience for six months. The period of Prophethood was 23 years; so the period of these six months of true visions constituted an integral part of the forty-six parts of Prophethood. In Ramadan, in his third year of solitude in the cave of Hira', Allâh's Will desired His mercy to flow on earth and Muhammad (Peace be upon him) was honoured with Prophethood, and the light of Revelation burst upon him with some verses of the Noble Qur'ân.

As for the exact date, careful investigation into circumstantial evidence and relevant clues point directly to Monday, 21st. Ramadan at night, i.e. Au, 10, 610 A.D. with Prophet Muhammad (Peace be upon him) exactly 40 years, 6 months and 12 days of age, i.e. 39 Gregorian years, 3 months and 22 days.

'Aishah, the veracious, gave the following narration of that most significant event that brought the Divine light which would dispel the darkness of disbelief and ignorance. It led life down a new course and brought about the most serious amendment to the line of the history of mankind:

Forerunners of the Revelation assumed the form of true visions that would strikingly come true all the time. After that, solitude became dear to him and he would go to the cave, Hira', to engage in *Tahannuth* (devotion) there for a certain number of nights before returning to his family, and then he would return for provisions for a similar stay. At length, unexpectedly, the Truth (the angel) came to him and said, "Recite." "I cannot recite," he [Muhammad (Peace be upon him)] said. The Prophet (Peace be upon him) described: "Then he took me and squeezed me vehemently and then let me go and repeated the order 'Recite.' 'I cannot recite' said I, and once again he squeezed me and let me till I was exhausted. Then he said: 'Recite.' I said 'I cannot recite.' He squeezed me for a third time and then let me go and said:

- "Read! In the Name of your Lord, Who has created (all that exists), has created man from a clot (a piece of thick coagulated blood). Read! and your Lord is the Most Generous.'" [96:1-3]

The Prophet (Peace be upon him) repeated these verses. He was trembling with fear. At this stage, he came back to his wife Khadijah, and said, "Cover me, ... cover me." They covered him until he restored security. He apprised Khadijah of the incident of the cave and added that he was horrified. His wife tried to soothe him and reassured him saying, "Allâh will never disgrace you. You unite uterine relations; you bear the burden of the weak; you help the poor and the needy, you entertain the guests and endure hardships in the path of truthfulness."

She set out with the Prophet (Peace be upon him) to her cousin Waraqa bin Nawfal bin Asad bin 'Abd Al-'Uzza, who had embraced Christianity in the pre-Islamic period, and used to write the Bible in Hebrew. He was a blind old man. Khadijah said: "My cousin! Listen to your nephew!" Waraqa said: "O my nephew! What did you see?" The Messenger of Allâh (Peace be upon him) told him what had happened to him. Waraqa replied: "This is 'Namus' i.e. (the angel who is entrusted with Divine Secrets) that Allâh sent to Moses. I wish I were younger. I wish I could live up to the time when your people would turn you out." Muhammad (Peace be upon him) asked: "Will they drive me out?" Waraqa answered in the affirmative and said: "Anyone who came with something similar to what you have brought was treated with hostility; and if I should be alive till that day, then I would support you strongly." A few days later Waraqa died and the revelation also subsided.

At-Tabari and Ibn Hisham reported that the Messenger of Allâh (Peace be upon him) left the cave of Hira' after being surprised by the Revelation, but later on, returned to the cave and continued his solitude. Afterwards, he came back to Makkah. At-Tabari reported on this incident, saying:

After mentioning the coming of the Revelation, the Messenger of Allâh (Peace be upon him) said: "I have never abhorred anyone more than a poet or a mad man. I can not stand looking at either of them. I will never tell anyone of Quraish of my Revelation. I will climb a mountain and throw myself down and die. That will relieve me. I went to do that but halfway up the mountain, I heard a voice from the sky saying 'O Muhammad! You are the Messenger of Allâh (Peace be upon him) and I am Gabriel.' I looked upwards and saw Gabriel in the form of a man putting his legs on the horizon. He said: 'O Muhammad You are the Messenger of Allâh (Peace be upon him) and I am Gabriel.' I stopped and looked at him. His sight distracted my attention from what I had intended to do. I stood in my place transfixed. I tried to shift my eyes away from him. He was in every direction I looked at. I stopped in my place without any movement until Khadijah sent someone to look for me. He went down to Makkah and came back while I was standing in the same place. Gabriel then left, and I went back home. I found Khadijah at home, so I sat very close to her. She asked: 'Father of Al-Qasim! Where have you been? I sent someone to look for you. He went to Makkah and returned to me.' I told her of what I had seen. She replied: 'It is a propitious sign, O my husband. Pull yourself together, I swear by Allâh that you are a Messenger for this nation.' Then she stood up and went to Waraqa and informed him. Waraqa said: 'I swear by Allâh that he has received the same Namus, i.e. angel that was sent to Moses. He is is the Prophet of this nation. Tell him to be patient.' She came back to him and told him of Waraqa's words. When the Messenger of Allâh (Peace be upon him) finished his solitary stay and went down to Makkah, he went to Waraqa, who told him: 'You are the Prophet of this nation. I swear by Allâh that you have received the same angel that was sent to Moses.'"

<u>INTERRUPION OF REVELATION:</u>

Ibn Sa'd reported on the authority of Ibn 'Abbas that the Revelation paused for a few days. After careful study, this seems to be the most possible. To say that it lasted for three and a half years, as some scholars allege, is not correct, but here there is no room to go into more details.

Meanwhile, the Prophet (Peace be upon him), was caught in a sort of depression coupled with astonishment and perplexity. Al-Bukhari reported:

The Divine inspiration paused for a while and the Prophet (Peace be upon him) became so sad, as we have heard, that he intended several times to throw himself from the tops of high mountains, and every time he went up the top of a mountain in order to throw himself down, Gabriel would appear before him and say: "O Muhammad! You are indeed Allâh's Messenger in truth," whereupon his heart would become quiet and he would calm down and return home. Whenever the period of the coming of the Revelation used to become long, he would do as before, but Gabriel would appear again before him and say to him what he had said before.

ONCE, GABRIEL BRINGS ALLAH'S REVELATION:

Ibn Hajar said: 'That (the pause of Allâh's revelation for a few days) was to relieve the Messenger of Allâh (Peace be upon him) of the fear he experienced and to make him long for the Revelation. When the shades of puzzle receded, the flags of truth were raised, the Messenger of Allâh (Peace be upon him) knew for sure that he had become the Messenger of the Great Lord. He was also certain that what had come to him was no more than the ambassador of inspiration. His waiting and longing for the coming of the revelation constituted a good reason for his steadfastness and self-possession on the arrival of Allâh's inspiration, Al-Bukhari reported on the authority of Jabir bin 'Abdullah that he had heard the Messenger of Allâh (Peace be upon him) speak about the period of pause as follows:

"While I was walking, I heard a voice from the sky. I looked up, and surely enough, it was the same angel who had visited me in the cave of Hira'. He was sitting on a chair between the earth and the sky. I was very afraid of him and knelt on the ground. I went home saying: 'Cover me …, Cover me …'. Allâh revealed to me the verses:

- 'O you [Muhammad (Peace be upon him)] enveloped (in garments)! Arise and warn! And your Lord (Allâh) magnify! And your garments purify! And keep away from *Ar-Rujz* (the idols)!'" [74:1-5]

After that the revelation started coming strongly, frequently and regularly.

SOME DETAILS PERTINENT TO THE SUCCESSIVE STAGES OF REVELATION:

Before we go into the details of the period of communicating the Message and Prophethood, we would like to get acquainted with the stages of the Revelation which constituted the main source of the Message and the subject-matter of the Call. Ibn Al-Qayyim, mentioning the stages of the Revelation, said:

- The First: The period of true vision. It was the starting point of the Revelation to the Men of Allâh (Peace be upon him).

    The Second: What the angel invisibly cast in the Prophet's mind and heart. The Messenger of Allâh (Peace be upon him) said: "The Noble Spirit revealed to me 'No soul will perish until it exhausts its due course, so fear Allâh and gently request Him. Never get so impatient to the verge of disobedience of Allâh. What Allâh has can never be acquired but through obedience to Him.'"

    The Third: The angel used to visit the Messenger of Allâh (Peace be upon him) in the form of a human being and would speak to him directly. This would enable him to fully understand what the angel said. The angel was sometimes seen in this form by the Prophet's Companions.

    The Fourth: The angel came to him like the toll of a bell and this was the most difficult form because the angel used to seize him tightly and sweat would stream from his forehead even on the coldest day. If the Prophet (Peace be upon him) was on his camel, the camel would not withstand the weight, so it would immediately kneel down on the ground. Once the Messenger of Allâh (Peace be upon him) had such a revelation when he was sitting and his thigh was on Zaid's, Zaid felt the pressure had almost injured his thigh.

    The Fifth: The Prophet (Peace be upon him) saw the angel in his actual form. The angel would reveal to him what Allâh had ordered him to reveal. This, as mentioned in (Qur'ân), in *Sûrah An-Najm* (Chapter 53 - The Star), happened twice.

The Sixth: What Allâh Himself revealed to him in heaven i.e. when he ascended to heaven and received Allâh's behest of *Salât* (prayer).

The Seventh: Allâh's Words to His Messenger (Peace be upon him) at first hand without the mediation of an angel. It was a privilege granted to Moses (Peace be upon him) and clearly attested in the Qur'ân, as it is attested to our Prophet (Peace be upon him) in the *Sûrah Al-Isrâ'* (Chapter 17 - The Journey by Night) of the Noble Qur'ân.

Some religious scholars added a controversial eighth stage in which they state that Allâh spoke to the Prophet (Peace be upon him) directly without a curtain in between. This issue remains however unconfirmed.

PROCLAIMING ALLAH, THE ALL-HIGH; AND THE IMMEDIATE CONSTITUENTS

The first Revelation sent to the Prophet (Peace be upon him) implied several injunctions, simple in form but highly effective and of serious far-reaching ramifications. The angel communicated to him a manifest Message saying:

- "O you [Muhammad (Peace be upon him)] enveloped (in garments)! Arise and warn! And your Lord (Allâh) magnify! And your garments purify! And keep away from *Ar-Rujz* (the idols). And give not a thing in order to have more (or consider not your deeds of Allâh's obedience as a favour to Allâh). And be patient for the sake of your Lord (i.e. perform your duty to Allâh)!" [74:1-7]

For convenience and ease of understanding, we are going to segment the Message into its immediate constituents:

1. The ultimate objective of warning is to make sure that no one breaching the pleasures of Allâh in the whole universe is ignorant of the serious consequences that his behaviour entails, and to create a sort of unprecedented shock within his mind and heart.
2. 'Magnifying the Lord' dictates explicitly that the only pride allowed to nourish on the earth is exclusively Allâh's to the exclusion of all the others'.
3. 'Cleansing the garments and shunning all aspects of abomination' point directly to the indispensable need to render both the exterior and interior exceptionally chaste and pure, in addition to the prerequisite of sanctifying the soul and establishing it highly immune against the different sorts of impurities and the various kinds of pollutants. Only through this avenue can the soul of the Prophet (Peace be upon him) reach an ideal status and become eligible to enjoy the shady mercy of Allâh and His protection, security, guidance and ever-shining light; and will consequently set the highest example to the human community, attract the sound hearts and inspire awe and reverence in the stray ones in such a manner that all the world, in agreement or disagreement, will head for it and take it as the rock-bed in all facets of their welfare.
4. The Prophet (Peace be upon him) must not regard his strife in the way of Allâh as a deed of grace that entitles him to a great reward. On the contrary, he has to exert himself to the utmost, dedicate his whole efforts and be ready to offer all sacrifices in a spirit of self-fogetfulness enveloped by an ever-present awareness of Allâh, without the least sense of pride in his deeds or sacrifices.
5. The last verse of the Qur'ân revealed to the Prophet (Peace be upon him) alludes to the hostile attitude of the obdurate disbelievers, who will jeer at him and his followers. They are expected to disparage him and step up their malice to the point of scheming against his life and lives of all the believers around him. In this case he has got to be patient and is supposed to persevere and display the highest degree of stamina for the sole purpose of attaining the pleasure of Allâh.

These were the basic preliminaries that the Prophet (Peace be upon him) had to observe, very simple injunctions in appearance, greatly fascinating in their calm rhythm, but highly effective in practice. They constituted the trigger that aroused a far-ranging tempest in all the corners of the world.

The verses comprise the constituents of the new call and propagation of the new faith. A warning logically implies that there are malpractices with painful consequences to be sustained by the perpetrators, and since the present life is not necessarily the only room to bring people to account for their misdeeds or some of them, then the warning would necessarily imply calling people to account on another day, i.e. the Day of Resurrection, and this per se suggests the existence of a life other than this one we are living. All the verses of the Noble Qur'ân call people to testify explicitly to the Oneness of Allâh, to delegate all their affairs to Allâh, the All-High, and to subordinate the desires of the self and the desires of Allâh's servants to the attainment of His Pleasures.

The constituents of the call to Islam could, briefly speaking, go as follows:

1. Testimony to the Oneness of Allâh.
2. Belief in the Hereafter.
3. Sanctifying one's soul and elevating it high above evils and abominations that conduce to terrible consequences, besides this, there is the dire need for virtues and perfect manners coupled with habituating oneself to righteous deeds.
4. Committing one's all affairs to Allâh, the All-High.
5. All the foregoing should run as a natural corollary to unwavering belief in Muhammad's Message, and abidance by his noble leadership and righteous guidance.

The verses have been prefaced, in the voice of the Most High, by a heavenly call mandating the Prophet (Peace be upon him) to undertake this daunting responsibility (calling people unto Allâh). The verses meant to extract him forcibly out of his sleep, divest him of his mantle and detach him from the warmth and quiet of life, and then drive him down a new course attended with countless hardships, and requiring a great deal of strife in the way of Allâh:

- "O you [Muhammad (Peace be upon him)] enveloped (in garments)! Arise and warn." [74:1-2]

Suggesting that to live to oneself is quite easy, but it has been decided that you have to shoulder this heavy burden; consequently sleep, comfort, or warm bed are items decreed to be alien in your lexicon of life. O Muhammad, arise quickly for the strife and toil awaiting you; no time is there for sleep and such amenities; grave responsibilities have been Divinely determined to fall to your lot, and drive you into the turmoil of life to develop a new sort of precarious affinity with the conscience of people and the reality of life.

The Prophet (Peace be upon him) managed quite successfully to rise to his feet and measure up to the new task, he went ahead in a spirit of complete selflessness, relentlessly striving and never abating in carrying the burden of the great Trust, the burden of enlightening mankind, and the heavy weight of the new faith and strife for over twenty years, nothing distracting his attention from the awcommission. May Allâh reward him, for us and all humanity, the best ending. The following research at hand gives an account in miniature of his long strive and uninterrupted struggle he made after receiving the ministry of Messengership.

PHASES ANS STAGES OF THE CALL:

The Muhammadan Call could be divided into two phases distinctively demarcated:

1. The Makkan phase: nearly thirteen years.
2. The Madinese phase: fully ten years.

Each of the two phases included distinctive features easily discernible through accurate scrutiny into the circumstances that characterized each of them.

The Makkan phase can be divided into three stages:

1. The stage of the secret Call: three years.
2. The stage of the proclamation of the Call in Makkah: from the beginning of the fourth year of Prophethood to almost the end of the tenth year.
3. The stage of the call to Islam and propagating it beyond Makkah: it lasted from the end of tenth year of the Prophethood until Muhammad's (Peace be upon him) emigration to Madinah.

The Madinese phase will be considered later in its due course.

THE FIRST STAGE

STRIFE IN THE WAY OF THE CALL THREE YEARS OF SECRETE CALL:

It is well-known that Makkah was the centre for the Arabs, and housed the custodians of Al-Ka'bah. Protection and guardianship of the idols and stone graven images that received veneration on the part of all the Arabs lay in the hands of the Makkans. Hence the difficulty of hitting the target of reform and rectitude in a place considered the den of idolatry. Working in such an atmosphere no doubt requires unshakable will and determination, that is why the call unto Islam assumed a clandestine form so that the Makkans should not be enraged by the unexpected surprise.

THE EARLY CONVERTS:

The Prophet (Peace be upon him) naturally initiated his sacred mission right from home and then moved to the people closely associated with him. He called unto Islam whomsoever he thought would attest the truth which had come from his Lord. In fact, a host of people who nursed not the least seed of doubt as regards the Prophet (Peace be upon him), immediately responded and quite readily embraced the true faith. They are known in the Islamic literature as the early converts.

Khadijah, the Prophet's spouse, the mother of believers, was the first to enter the fold of Islam followed by his freed slave Zaid bin Harithah, his cousin, 'Ali bin Abi Talib, who had been living with him since his early childhood, and next came his intimate friend Abu Bakr As-Siddiq (Abu Bakr the truth verifier). All of those professed Islam on the very first day of the call. Abu Bakr, and from the first day he embraced Islam, proved to be an energetic and most zealous activist. He was wealthy, obliging, mild and upright. People used to frequent his house and draw nigh to him for his knowledge, amity, pleasant company and business. He invited whomever he had confidence in to Islam and through his personal efforts a good number of people converted to Islam, such as 'Uthman bin 'Affan Al-Umawi, Az-Zubair bin 'Awwam Al-Asadi, 'Abdur Rahman bin 'Awf, Sa'd bin Abi Waqqas, Az-Zuhri and Talhah bin 'Ubaidullah At-Tamimy. Those eight men constituted the forerunners and more specifically the vanguard of the new faith in Arabia. Among the early Muslim were Bilal bin Rabah (the Abyssinian), Abu 'Ubaidah bin Al-Jarrah from Bani Harith bin Fahr (the most trustworthy of the Muslim Nation), Abu Salamah bin 'Abd Al-Asad, Al-Arqam bin Abi Al-Arqam from the tribe of Makhzum, 'Uthman bin Maz'oun and his two brothers Qudama and 'Abdullah, 'Ubaidah bin Al-Harith bin Al-Muttalib bin 'Abd Munaf, Sa'id bin Zaid Al-'Adawi and his wife Fatimah - daughter of Al-Khattab (the sister of 'Umar bin Al-Khattab), Khabbab bin Al-Aratt, 'Abdullâh bin Mas'ud Al-Hadhali and many others. These were the Muslim predecessors. They belonged to various septs of Quraish. Ibn Hisham, a biographer, counted them to be more than forty.

Ibn Ishaq said: "Then people entered the fold of Islam in hosts, men or women and the new faith could no longer be kept secret."

The Prophet (Peace be upon him) used to meet and teach, the new converts, the religion in privacy because the call to Islam was still running on an individual and secret basis. Revelation accelerated and continued after the first verses of "*O you wrapped in garments*." The verses and pieces of *Sûrah* (chapters) revealed at this time were short ones with wonderful strong pauses and quite fascinating rhythms in full harmony with that delicate whispering setting. The central topic running through them focused on sanctifying the soul, and deterring the Muslims from falling prey to the deceptive glamour of life. The early verses used as well to give a highly accurate account of the Hell and the Garden (Paradise), leading the believers down a new course diametrically opposed to the ill practices rampant amongst their compatriots.

AS-SALAT (the Prayer):

Muqatil bin Sulaiman said: "*Salât (prayer) was established as an obligatory ritual at an early stage of the Islamic Call, a two rak' ah (unit of prayer) Salât in the morning and the same in the evening;*

"And glorify the praises of your Lord in the *'Ashi* (i.e. the time period after the mid-noon till sunset) and in the *Ibkar* (i.e. the time period from early morning or sunrise till before mid-noon)." [40:55]

Ibn Hijr said: "Definitely the Prophet (Peace be upon him) used to pray before 'The Night Journey' but it still remains a matter of controversy whether or not the prayer was established as an obligatory ritual before imposing the rules of the usual five prayers a day. It is related that obligatory prayer was established twice a day, in the morning before sunrise and after sunset. It is reported through a chain of narrators that when the Prophet (Peace be upon him) received the first Revelation, Gabriel - the angel, proceeded and taught him how to observe *Wudu* (ablution). When the Prophet (Peace be upon him) had finished, he took a handful of water and sprinkled it on his loins.

Ibn Hisham reported that when it was time for prayers, the Messenger of Allâh (Peace be upon him) and his Companions went into a mountain valley to pray secretly. Abu Talib once saw the Messenger of Allâh (Peace be upon him) and Ali praying, he asked them what they were up to. When he got to know that it was obligatory prayer, he told them to stay constant in their practice.

THE QURAISHITES LEARN ABOUT THE CALL:

This stage of the Call, even though conducted in a clandestine manner and on an individual basis, its news leaked out and assumed a public interest all over Makkah. In the beginning, the Makkan leaders did not care much about Muhammad (Peace be upon him) and took no heed of his teachings. At first, they thought that Muhammad (Peace be upon him) was merely a religious philosophist like Omaiyah bin Abi As-Salt, Quss bin Sa'idah, 'Amr bin Nufail and their ilk who used to philosophize on godship and religious obligations. But this attitude of indifference soon changed into real apprehension. The polytheists of Quraish began to watch Muhammad's movements closely and anxiously for fear of spreading his Call and producing a change in the prevalent mentality.

For three underground years of activism, a group of believers emerged stamped by a spirit of fraternity and cooperation with one definite objective in their mind: propagating and deeply establishing the call unto Islam. For full three years Muhammad (Peace be upon him) had been content to teach within a rather narrow circle. The time had, however, come to preach the faith of the Lord openly. The angel Gabriel had brought him down a further Revelation of Allâh's Will to confront his people, invalidate their falsehood and crush down their idolatrous practices.

THE SECOND PHASE OPEN PREACHING

"And warn your tribe [O Muhammad (Peace be upon him)] of near kindred." [26:214].

This was the first verse to be revealed in this concern. It is included in *Sûrah Ash-Shu'arâ* (Chapter 26 - The Poets) which relates the story of Moses (Peace be upon him) from his early days of Prophethood going through his migration with the Children of Israel, their escape from the Pharaoh and his folk, and the drowning Pharaoh and his hosts. This Chapter in fact narrates the different stages that Moses (Peace be upon him) passed through in his struggle with Pharaoh and the mission of calling his people unto Allâh. Moreover, it includes stories that speak about the terrible end in store for those who belied the Messengers such as the people of Noah, 'Ad, Thamud, Abraham, Lout and *Ahlul-Aikah* (Companions of the Wood). (A group of people who used to worship a tree called *Aikah*)

Chronologically, this Chapter belongs to the middle Makkan period, when the contact of the light of Prophecy with the cultural milieu of pagan Makkah was testing the Makkans in their most arrogant mood. The Message that this Chapter communicates is in brief: "The Truth is insurmountable. When the spirit of Prophecy came to Makkah, it was resisted by the votaries of evil; but Truth, unlike falsehood, is bound to stay, whereas falsehood is surely perishable."

CALLING THE CLOSET KINSPEOPLE:

In obedience to Allâh's Commands, Muhammad (Peace be upon him) rallied his kinsmen of Bani Hashim with a group of Bani Al-Muttalib bin 'Abd Munaf. The audience counted forty-five men.

Abu Lahab immediately took the initiative and addressed the Prophet (Peace be upon him): "These are your uncles and cousins, speak on to the point, but first of all you have got to know that your kinspeople are not in a position to withstand all the Arabs. Another point you have got to bear in mind is that your relatives are sufficient unto you. If you follow their tradition, it will be easier for them than to face the other clans of Quraish supported by the other Arabs. Verily, I have never heard of anyone who has incurred more harm on his kinspeople than you." The Messenger of Allâh (Peace be upon him) kept silent and said nothing 7in that meeting.

He invited them to another meeting and managed to secure audience. He then stood up and delivered a short speech explaining quite cogently what was at stake. He said: "I celebrate Allâh's praise, I seek His help, I believe in Him, I put my trust in Him, I bear witness that there is no god to be worshipped but Allâh with no associate. A guide can never lie to his people. I swear by Allâh, there is no god but He, that I have been sent as a Messenger to you, in particular and to all the people, in general. I swear by Allâh you will die just as you sleep, you will be resurrected just as you wake up. You will be called to account for your deeds. It is then either Hell forever or the Garden (Paradise) forever."

Abu Talib replied: "We love to help you, accept your advice and believe in your words. These are your kinspeople whom you have collected and I am one of them but I am the fastest to do what you like. Do what you have been ordered. I shall protect and defend you, but I can't quit the religion of 'Abdul-Muttalib."

Abu Lahab then said to Abu Talib: " I swear by Allâh that this is a bad thing. You must stop him before the others do." Abu Talib, however, answered: "I swear by Allâh to protect him as long as I am alive."

ON MOUNT AS-SAFA:
After the Messenger of Allâh (Peace be upon him) became sure of Abu Talib's commitment to his protection while he called the people unto Allâh, he stood up on Mount As-Safa one day and called out loudly: "O *Sabahah!* * " Septs of Quraish came to him. He called them to testify to the Oneness of Allâh and believe in his Messengership and the Day of Resurrection. Al-Bukhari reported part of this story on the authority of Ibn 'Abbas 9May Allah be pleased with him). He said: "When the

following verses were revealed:

> "And warn your tribe [O Muhammad (Peace be upon him)] of near kindred." [26:214]

The Messenger of Allâh (Peace be upon him) ascended Mount As-Safa and started to call: "O Bani Fahr! O Bani 'Adi (two septs of Quraish)." Many people gathered and those who couldn't, sent somebody to report to them. Abu Lahab was also present. The Prophet (Peace be upon him) said: "You see, if I were to tell you that there were some horsemen in the valley planning to raid you, will you believe me?" They said: "Yes, we have never experienced any lie from you." He said: "I am a warner to you before a severe torment." Abu Lahab promptly replied: "Perish you all the day! Have you summoned us for such a thing?" The verses were immediately revealed on that occasion:

> "Perish the two hands of Abi Lahab..." [111:1].

Muslim reported another part of this story on the authority of Abu Hurairah (May Alah be pleased with him) — He said: "When the following verses were revealed:

> "And warn your tribe [O Muhammad (Peace be upon him)] of near kindred." [26:214]

The Messenger of Allâh (Peace be upon him) called all the people of Quraish; so they gathered and he gave them a general warning. Then he made a particular reference to certain tribes, and said: "O Quraish, rescue yourselves from the Fire; O people of Bani Ka'b, rescue yourselves from Fire; O Fatimah, daughter of Muhammad (Peace be upon him) , rescue yourself from the Fire, for I have no power to protect you from Allâh in anything except that I would sustain relationship with you."

It was verily a loud suggestive Call stating unequivocally to the closest people that belief in his Message constituted the corner-stone of any future relation between him and them, and that the blood-relation on which the whole Arabian life was based, had ceased to exist in the light of that Divine ultimatum.

SHOUTING THE TRUTH AND THE POLYTHEISTS' REACTION:

The Prophet's voice kept reverberating in Makkah until the following verse was revealed:

> "Therefore proclaim openly (Allâh's Message — Islamic Monotheism), that which you are commanded, and turn away from Al-Mushrikûn (polytheists)." [15:94]

He then commenced discrediting the superstitious practices of idolatry, revealing its worthless reality and utter impotence, and giving concrete proofs that idolatry per se or taking it as the media through which an idolater could come in contact with Allâh, is manifest falsehood.

The Makkans, on their part, burst into outrage and disapproval. Muhammad's (Peace be upon him) words created a thunderbolt that turned the Makkan time-honoured ideological life upside down. They could ill afford to hear someone attaching to polytheists and idolaters, the description of straying people. They started to rally their resources to settle down the affair, quell the onward marching revolution and deal a pre-emptive strike to its votaries before it devours and crushes down their consecrated traditions and long standing heritage. The Makkans had the deep conviction that denying godship to anyone save Allâh and that belief in the Divine Message and the Hereafter are interpreted in terms of complete compliance and absolute commitment, and this in turn leaves no area at all for them to claim authority over themselves and over their wealth, let alone their subordinates. In short, their arrogated religiously-based supremacy and highhandedness would no longer be in effect; their pleasures would be subordinated to the pleasures of Allâh and His Messenger and lastly they would have to abstain from incurring injustices on those whom they falsely deemed to be weak, and perpetrating dreadful sins in their everyday life. They had already been fully aware of these meanings, that is why their souls would not condescend to accept this 'disgraceful' position not out of motives based on dignity and honour but rather because:

"Nay! (Man denies Resurrection and Reckoning. So) he desires to continue committing sins." [75:5]

They had been aware of all these consequences but they could afford to do nothing before an honest truthful man who was the highest example of good manners and human values. They had never known such an example in the history of theifolks or grandfathers. What would they do? They were baffled, and they had the right to be so.

Following careful deliberations, they hit upon the only target available, i.e. to contact the Messenger's uncle, Abu Talib and request him to intervene and advise his nephew to stop his activities. In order to attach a serious and earnest stamp to their demand, they chose to touch the most sensitive area in Arabian life, viz., ancestral pride. They addressed Abu Talib in the following manner: "O Abu Talib! Your nephew curses our gods; finds faults with our way of life, mocks at our religion and degrades our forefathers; either you must stop him, or you must let us get at him. For you are in the same opposition as we are in opposition to him; and we will rid you of him." Abu Talib tried to appease their wrath by giving them a polite reply. The Prophet (Peace be upon him), however, continued on his way preaching Allâh's religion and calling men hitherto, heedless of all their desperate attempts and malicious intentions

AN ADVISORY COUNCIL TO DEBAR PILGRIMS FROM MUHAMMAD'S CALl: During those days, Quraish had another serious concern; the proclamation of the Call had only been a few months old when the season of pilgrimage was soon to come. Quraish knew that the Arab delegates were coming within a short time. They agreed that it was necessary to contemplate a device that was bound to alienate the Arab pilgrims from the new faith preached by Muhammad (Peace be upon him). They went to see Al-Waleed bin Al-Mugheerah to deliberate on this issue. Al-Waleed invited them to agree on a unanimous resolution that could enjoy the approbation of them all. However, they were at variance. Some suggested that they describe him as *Kahin*, i.e., soothsayer; but this suggestion was turned down on grounds that his words were not so rhymed. Others proposed *Majnun*, i.e., possessed by jinn; this was also rejected because no insinuations peculiar to that state of mind ware detected, they claimed. "Why not say he is a poet?" Some said. Here again they could not reach a common consent, alleging that his words were totally outside the lexicon of poetry. "OK then; let us accuse him of practising witchcraft," was a fourth suggestion. Here also Al-Waleed showed some reluctance saying that the Prophet (Peace be upon him) was known to have never involved himself in the practice of blowing on the knots, and admitted that his speech was sweet tasting root and branch. He, however, found that the most plausible charge to be levelled against Muhammad (Peace be upon him) was witchcraft. The ungodly company adopted this opinion and agreed to propagate one uniform formula to the effect that he was a magician so powerful and commanding in his art that he would successfully alienate son from father, man from his brother, wife from her husband and man from his clan.

It is noteworthy in this regard to say that Allâh revealed sixteen verses as regards Al-Waleed and the cunning method he contemplated to manipulate the people expected to arrive in Makkah for pilgrimage. Allâh says:

"Verily, he thought and plotted; so let him be cursed! How he plotted! And once more let him be cursed, how he plotted! Then he thought; then he frowned and he looked in a bad tempered way; then he turned back and was proud; then he said: 'This is nothing but magic from that of old; this is nothing but the word of a human being!' " [74:18-25]

The most wicked of them was the sworn enemy of Islam and Muhammad (Peace be upon him), Abu Lahab, who would shadow the Prophet's steps crying aloud, "O men, do not listen to him for he is a liar; he is an apostate." Nevertheless, Muhammad (Peace be upon him) managed to create a stir in the whole area, and even to convince a few people to accept his Call.

THE FIRST MIGRATION TO ABYSSINIA (ETHIOPIA): The series of persecutions started late in the fourth year of Prophethood, slowly at first, but steadily accelerated and worsened day by day and month by month until the situation got so extremely grave and no longer tolerable in the middle of the fifth year, that the Muslims began to seriously think of feasible ways liable to avert the painful tortures meted out to them. It was at that gloomy and desperate time that *Sûrah Al-Kahf* (Chapter 18 — The Cave) was revealed comprising definite answers to the questions with which the polytheists of Makkah constantly pestered the Prophet (Peace be upon him). It comprises three stories that include highly suggestive parables for the true believers to assimilate. The story of the Companions of the Cave implies implicit guidance for the believers to evacuate the hot spots of disbelief and aggression pregnant with the peril of enticement away from the true religion:

> The young men said to one another): And when you withdraw from them, and that which they worship, except Allâh, then seek refuge in the Cave, your Lord will open a way for you from His Mercy and will make easy for you your affair (i.e. will give you what you will need of provision, dwelling, etc.)18:16].

Next, there is the story of Al-Khidr (The Teacher of Arabia) and Moses (Peace be upon him) in a clear and delicate reference to the vicissitudes of life. Future circumstances of life are not necessarily the products of the prevalent conditions, they might be categorically the opposite. In other words, the war waged against the Muslims would in the future assume a different turn, and the tyrannous oppressors would one day come to suffer and be subjected to the same tortures to which the Muslims were then put. Furthermore, there is the story of Dhul-Qarnain (The Two Horned One), the powerful ruler of west and east. This story says explicitly that Allâh takes His righteous servants to inherit the earth and whatever in it. It also speaks that Allâh raises a righteous man every now and then to protect the weak against the strong.

Sûrah Az-Zumar (Chapter 39 — The Crowds) was then revealed pointing directly to migration and stating that the earth is spacious enough and the believers must not consider themselves constrained by the forces of tyranny and evil:

> "Good is (the reward) for those who do good in this world, and Allâh's earth is spacious (so if you cannot worship Allâh at a place, then go to another)! Only those who are patient shall receive their rewards in full without reckoning." [39:10].

The Prophet (Peace be upon him) had already known that Ashamah Negus, king of Abyssinia (Ethiopia), was a fair ruler who would not wrong any of his subordinates, so he permitted some of his followers to seek asylum there in Abyssinia (Ethiopia).

In Rajab of the fifth year of Prophethood, a group of twelve men and four women left for Abyssinia (Ethiopia). Among the emigrants were 'Uthman bin 'Affan and his wife Ruqaiyah [the daughter of the Prophet (Peace be upon him)]. With respect to these two emigrants, the Prophet (Peace be upon him) said:

> "They are the first people to migrate in the cause of Allâh after Abraham and Lot (Peace be upon them) ."

They sneaked out of Makkah under the heavy curtain of a dark night and headed for the sea where two boats happened to be sailing for Abyssinia (Ethiopia), their destination. News of their intended departure reached the ears of Quraish, so some men were despatched in their pursuit, but the believers had already left Shuaibah Port towards their secure haven where they were received warmly and accorded due hospitality.

In Ramadan of the same year, the Prophet (Peace be upon him) went into the Holy Sanctuary where there was a large host of Quraish polytheists, including some notables and celebrities. Suddenly he began reciting *Sûrah An-Najm* (Chapter 41 — The Star). The awe-inspiring Words of Allâh descended unawares upon them and they immediately got stunned by them. It was the first time for them to be shocked by the truthful Revelation. It had formerly been the favourite trick of those people who wished to dishonour Revelation, not only not to listen to it themselves but also to talk loudly and insolently when it was being read, so that even the true listeners may not be able to hear. They used to think that they were drowning the Voice of Allâh; in fact, they were piling up misery for themselves, for Allâh's Voice can never be silenced, "And those who disbelieve say:

"Listen not to this Qur'ân, and make noise in the midst of its (recitation) that you may overcome." [41:26].

When the unspeakably fascinating Words of Allâh came into direct contact with their hearts, they were entranced and got oblivious of the materialistic world around them and were caught in a state of full attentiveness to the Divine Words to such an extent that when the Prophet (Peace be upon him) reached the stormy heart-beating ending:

"So fall you down in prostration to Allâh and worship Him (Alone)." [53:62]

The idolaters, unconsciously and with full compliance, prostrated themselves in absolute god-fearing and stainless devotion. It was in fact the wonderful moment of the Truth that cleaved through the obdurate souls of the haughty and the attitude of the scoffers. They stood aghast when they perceived that Allâh's Words had conquered their hearts and done the same thing that they had been trying hard to annihilate and exterminate. Their co-polytheists who had not been present on the scene reproached and blamed them severely; consequently they began to fabricate lies and calumniate the Prophet (Peace be upon him) alleging that he had attached to their idols great veneration and ascribed to them the power of desirable intercession. All of these were desperate attempts made to establish an excusable justification for their prostrating themselves with the Prophet (Peace be upon him) on that day. Of course, this foolish and iniquitous slanderous behaviour was in line with their life-consecrated practice of telling lies and plot hatching.

News of this incident was misreported to the Muslim emigrants in Abyssinia (Ethiopia). They were informed that the whole of Quraish had embraced Islam so they made their way back home. They arrived in Makkah in Shawwal of the same year. When they were only an hour's travel from Makkah, the reality of the situation was discovered. Some of them returned to Abyssinia (Ethiopia), others sneaked secretly into the city or went in publicly but under the tutelage of a local notable. However, due to the news that transpired to the Makkans about the good hospitality and warm welcome that the Muslims were accorded in Abyssinia (Ethiopia), the polytheists got terribly indignant and started to mete out severer and more horrible maltreatment andtortures to the Muslims. Thereupon the Messenger of Allâh (Peace be upon him) deemed it imperative to permit the helpless creatures to seek asylum in Abyssinia (Ethiopia) for the second time. Migration this time was not as easy as it was the previous time, for Quraish was on the alert to the least suspicious moves of the Muslims. In due course, however, the Muslims managed their affairs too fast for the Quraishites to thwart their attempt of escape. The group of emigrants this time comprised eighty three men and nineteen or, in some versions, eighteen women. Whether or not 'Ammar was included is still a matter of doubt.

QURAISH'S MACHINATION AGAINSTN THE EMIGRANTS: Quraish could not tolerate the prospect of a secure haven available for the Muslims in Abyssinia (Ethiopia), so they despatched two staunch envoys to demand their extradition. They were 'Amr bin Al-'As and 'Abdullah bin Abi Rabi'a — before embracing Islam. They had taken with them valuable gifts to the king and his clergy, and had been able to win some of the courtiers over to their side. The pagan envoys claimed that the Muslim refugees should be expelled from Abyssinia (Ethiopia) and made over to them, on the ground that they had abandoned the religion of their forefathers, and their leader was preaching a religion different from theirs and from that of the king.

The king summoned the Muslims to the court and asked them to explain the teachings of their religion. The Muslim emigrants had decided to tell the whole truth whatever the consequences were. Ja'far bin Abi Talib stood up and addressed the king in the following words: "O king! we were plunged in the depth of ignorance and barbarism; we adored idols, we lived in unchastity, we ate the dead bodies, and we spoke abominations, we disregarded every feeling of humanity, and the duties of hospitality and neighbourhood were neglected; we knew no law but that of the strong, when Allâh raised among us a man, of whose birth, truthfulness, honesty, and purity we were aware; and he called to the Oneness of Allâh, and taught us not to associate anything with Him. He forbade us the worship of idols; and he enjoined us to speak the truth, to be faithful to our trusts, to be merciful and to regard the rights of the neighbours and kith and kin; he forbade us to speak evil of women, or to eat the substance of orphans; he ordered us to fly from the vices, and to abstain from evil; to offer prayers, to render alms, and to observe fast. We have believed in him, we have accepted his teachings and his injunctions to worship Allâh, and not to associate anything with Him, and we have allowed what He has allowed, and prohibited what He has prohibited. For this reason, our people have risen against us, have persecuted us in order to make us forsake the worship of Allâh and return to the worship of idols and other abominations. They have tortured and injured us, until finding no safety among them, we have come to your country, and hope you will protect us from oppression."

The king was very much impressed by these words and asked the Muslims to recite some of Allâh's Revelation. Ja'far recited the opening verses of *Sûrah Maryam* (Chapter 19 — Mary) wherein is told the story of the birth of both John and Jesus Christ, down to the account of Mary having been fed with the food miraculously. Thereupon the king, along with the bishops of his realm, was moved to tears that rolled down his cheeks and even wet his beard. Here, the Negus exclaimed: "It seems as if these words and those which were revealed to Jesus are the rays of the light which have radiated from the same source." Turning to the crest-fallen envoys of Quraish, he said, "I am afraid, I cannot give you back these refugees. They are free to live and worship in my realm as they please."

On the morrow, the two envoys again went to the king and said that Muhammad (Peace be upon him) and his followers blasphemed Jesus Christ. Again the Muslims were summoned and asked what they thought of Jesus. Ja'far again stood up and replied: "We speak about Jesus as we have been taught by our Prophet (Peace be upon him) , that is, he is the servant of Allâh, His Messenger, His spirit and His Word breathed into Virgin Mary." The king at once remarked, "Even so do we believe. Blessed be you, and blessed be your master." Then turning to the frowning envoys and to his bishops who got angry, he said: "You may fret and fume as you like but Jesus is nothing more than what Ja'far has said about him." He then assured the Muslims of full protection. He returned to the envoys of Quraish, the gifts they had brought with them and sent them away. The Muslims lived in Abyssinia (Ethiopia) unmolested for a number of years till they returned to Madinah.

In this way Quraish's malicious intentions recoiled on them and their machination met with utter failure. They came to fully realize that the grudge they nursed against he Muslims would not operate but within their realm of Makkah. They consequently began to entertain a horrible idea of silencing the advocate of the new Call once and for all, through various channels of brutality, or else killing him. An obstinate difficulty, however, used to curtail any move in this direction embodied by the Prophet's uncle Abu Talib and the powerful social standing he used to enjoy as well as the full protection and support he used to lend to his nephew. The pagans of Makkah therefore decided to approach Abu Talib for the second time and insisted that he put a stop to his nephew's activities, which if allowed unchecked, they said, would involve him into severe hostility. Abu Talib was deeply distressed at this open threat and the breach with his people and their enmity, but he could not afford to desert the Messenger too. He sent for his nephew and told him what the people had said, "Spare me and yourself and put not burden on me that I can't bear." Upon this the Prophet (Peace be upon him) thought that his uncle would let him down and would no longer support him, so he replied:

> "O my uncle! by Allâh if they put the sun in my right hand and the moon in my left on condition that I abandon this course, until Allâh has made me victorious, or I perish therein, I would not abandon it." The Prophet (Peace be upon him) got up, and as he turned away, his uncle called him and said, "Come back, my nephew," and when he came back, he said, "Go and preach what you please, for by Allâh I will never forsake you."

He then recited two lines of verse pregnant with meanings of full support to the Prophet (Peace be upon him) and absolute gratification by the course that his nephew had chalked out in Arabia.

ONECE MORE QURAISH APPROACHES ABU TALIB: Quraish, seeing that the Messenger of Allâh (Peace be upon him) was still intent on his Call, realized that Abu Talib would never forsake his nephew even if this incurred their enmity. Some of them then went to see him once more taking with them a youth called 'Amarah bin Al-Waleed bin Al-Mugheerah, and said, "O Abu Talib! we have brought you a smart boy still in the bloom of his youth, to make use of his mind and strength and take him as your son in exchange for your nephew, who has run counter to your religion, brought about social discord, found fault with your way of life, so that we kill him and rid you of his endless troubles; just man for man." Abu Talib's reply was, "It is really an unfair bargain. You give me your son to bring him up and I give you my son to kill him! By Allâh, it is something incredible!!" Al-Mut'im bin 'Adi, a member of the delegation, interrupted saying that Quraish had been fair in that bargain because "they meant only to rid you of that source of hateful trouble, but as I see you are determined to refuse their favours." Abu Talib, of course, turned down all their offers and challenged them to do whatever they pleased. Historical resources do not give the exact date of these two meetings with Abu Talib. They, however, seem more likely to have taken place in the sixth year of Prophethood with a brief lapse of time in between.

THE TYRANTS' DECISION TO KILL THE PROPHET: Now that all the schemes and conspiracof Quraish had failed, they resorted to their old practices of persecution and inflicting tortures on the Muslims in a more serious and brutal manner than ever before. They also began to nurse the idea of killing the Prophet (Peace be upon him). In fact, contrary to their expectations, this new method and this very idea served indirectly to consolidate the Call to Islam and support it with the conversion of two staunch and mighty heroes of Makkah, i.e. Hamzah bin 'Abdul-Muttalib and 'Umar bin Al-Khattab (May Allah be pleased with him).

'Utaibah bin Abi Lahab once approached the Prophet (Peace be upon him) and most defiantly and brazenly shouted at him, "I disbelieve in: "By the star when it goes down." [53:1] and in "Then he (Gabriel) approached and came closer." [53:8] In other words: "I do not believe in any of the Qur'ân." He then started to deal highhandedly with Muhammad (Peace be upon him) and laid violent hand on him, tore his shirt and spat into his face but his saliva missed the Holy face of the Prophet (Peace be upon him). Thereupon, the Prophet (Peace be upon him) invoked Allâh's wrath on 'Utaibah and supplicated:

"O Allâh! Set one of Your dogs on him."

Allâh responded positively to Muhammad's supplication, and it happened in the following manner: Once 'Utaibah with some of his compatriots from Quraish set out for Syria and took accommodation in Az-Zarqa'. There a lion approached the group to the great fear of 'Utbah, who at once recalled Muhammad's words in supplication, and said: "Woe to my brother! This lion will surely devour me just as Muhammad (Peace be upon him) supplicated. He has really killed me in Syria while he is in Makkah." The lion did really rush like lightning, snatched 'Utbah from amongst his people and crushed his head.

It is also reported that a wretched idolater from Quraish, named 'Uqbah bin 'Abi Mu'ait once trod on the Prophet's neck while he was prostrating himself in prayer until his eyes protruded.

More details reported by Ibn Ishaq testify to the tyrants' deeply-established intentions of killing the Prophet (Peace be upon him). Abu Jahl, the archenemy of Islam, once addressed some of his accomplices: "O people of Quraish! It seems that Muhammad (Peace be upon him) is determined to go on finding fault with our religion, degrading our forefathers, discrediting our way of life and abusing our gods. I bear witness to our god that I will carry a too heavy rock and drop it on Muhammad's head while he is in prostration to rid you of him, once and for all. I am not afraid of whatever his sept, Banu 'Abd Munaf, might do." The terrible unfortunate audience endorsed his plan and encouraged him to translate it into a decisive deed.

In the morning of the following day, Abu Jahl lay waiting for the arrival of the Messenger of Allâh (Peace be upon him) to offer prayer. The people of Quraish were in their assembly rooms waiting for news. When the Prophet (Peace be upon him) prostrated himself, Abu Jahl proceeded carrying the big rock to fulfill his wicked intention. No sooner had he approached closer to the Prophet (Peace be upon him) than he withdraw pale-faced, shuddering with his hands strained the rock falling off. Thereupon, the people watching hurried forward asking him what the matter was. He replied: "When I approached, a male-camel unusual in figure with fearful canines intercepted and almost devoured me." Ibn Ishaq reported that the Prophet (Peace be upon him), in the context of his comment on the incident, said "It was Gabriel (Peace be upon him) , if Abu Jahl had approached closer, he would have killed him. " Even so the tyrants of Quraish would not be admonished, contrariwise, the idea of killing the Prophet (Peace be upon him) was still being nourished in their iniquitous hearts. On the authority of 'Abdullah bin 'Amr bin Al-'As, some people of Quraish were in a place called Al-Hijr complaining that they had been too patient with the Prophet (Peace be upon him), who suddenly appeared and began his usual circumambulation. They started to wink at him and utter sarcastic remarks but he remained silent for two times, then on the third, he stopped and addressed the infidels saying:

> "O people of Quraish! Hearken, I swear by Allâh in Whose Hand is my soul, that you will one day be slaughtered to pieces." As soon as the Prophet (Peace be upon him) uttered his word of slaughter, they all stood aghast and switched off to a new style of language smacking of fear and even horror trying to soothe his anger and comfort him saying: "You can leave Abul Qasim, for you have never been foolish."

'Urwa bin Az-Zubair narrated: I asked Abdullah bin 'Amr bin Al-'As to tell me of the worst thing that the pagans did to the Prophet (Peace be upon him). He said: "While the Prophet (Peace be upon him) was praying in Al-Hijr of Al-Ka'bah, 'Uqbah bin Al-Mu'ait came and put his garment around the Prophet's neck and throttled him violently. Abu Bakr came and caught him by his shoulder and pushed him away from the Prophet (Peace be upon him) and said: "Do you want to kill a man just because he says, My Lord is Allâh?"

THE CONVERSION OF HAMZAH BIN 'ABDUL-MUTTALIB: In a gloomy atmosphere infested with dark clouds of iniquity and tyranny, there shone on the horizon a promising light for the oppressed, i.e. the conversion of Hamzah bin 'Abdul-Muttalib in Dhul Hijjah, the sixth year of Prophethood. It is recorded that the Prophet (Peace be upon him) was one day seated on the hillock of Safa when Abu Jahl happened to pass by and accused the religion preached by him. Muhammad (Peace be upon him), however, kept silent and did not utter a single word. Abu Jahl went on unchecked, took a stone and cracked the Prophet's head which began to bleed. The aggressor then went to join the Quraishites in their assembly place. It so happened that shortly after that, Hamzah, while returning from a hunting expedition, passed by the same way, his bow hanging by his shoulder. A slave-girl belonging to 'Abdullah bin Jada'an, who had noted the impertinence of Abu Jahl, told him the whole story of the attack on the Prophet (Peace be upon him) . On hearing that, Hamzah was deeply offended and hurried to Al-Ka'bah and there, in the courtyard of the Holy Sanctuary, found Abu Jahl sitting with a company of Quraishites. Hamzah rushed upon him and struck his bow upon his head violently and said: "Ah! You have been abusing Muhammad (Peace be upon him); I too follow his religion and profess what he preaches." The men of Bani Makhzum came to his help, and men of Bani Hashim wanted to render help, but Abu Jahl sent them away saying: "Let Abu 'Ummarah alone, by Allâh I did revile his nephew shamelessly." In fact, Hamzah's conversion derived initially from the pride of a man who would not accept the notion of others humiliating his relative. Later on, however, Allâh purified his nature and he managed to grasp the most trustworthy hand-hold (Faith in Allâh). He proved to be a source of great strength to the Islamic Faith and its followers.

THE CONVERSION OF 'UMAR BIN AL-KHATTAB: Another significant addition to the strength of Islam was the conversion of 'Umar bin Al-Khattab in Dhul-Hijjah, the sixth year of Prophethood, three days following the conversion of Hamzah.] He was a man of dauntless courage and resolution, feared and respected in Makkah, and hitherto a bitter opponent of the new religion. The traditional account reveals that the Prophet (Peace be upon him) once raised his hands in prayer and said:

> "O Allâh! Give strength to Islam especially through either of two men you love more: 'Umar bin Al-Khattab or Abu Jahl bin Hisham."

'Umar, obviously, was the one who merited that privilege.

When we scrutinize the several versions that speak of 'Umar's conversion, we can safely conclude that various contradictory emotions used to conflict with one another within his soul. On the one hand, he used to highly regard the traditions of his people, and was habituated to the practice of indulgence in wine orgies; on the other hand, he greatly admired the stamina of the Muslims and their relentless dedication to their faith. These two extreme views created a sort of skepticism in himind and made him at times tend to believe that the doctrines of Islam could bear better and more sacred seeds of life, that is why he would always experience fits of outrage directly followed by unexpected enervation. On the whole, the account of his conversion is very interesting and requires us to go into some details.

One day, 'Umar bin Al-Khattab set out from his house, and headed for the Holy Sanctuary where he saw the Prophet (Peace be upon him) offering prayer and overheard him reciting the *Sûrah Al-Hâqqah* (Chapter 69 — The Reality) of the Noble Qur'ân. The Words of Allâh appealed to him and touched the innermost cells of his heart. He felt that they derived from unusual composition, and he began to question his people's allegations as regards the man-composed poetry or words of a soothsayer that they used to attach to the Noble Qur'ân. The Prophet (Peace be upon him) went on to recite:

> "That this is verily the word of an honoured Messenger (i.e. Gabriel or Muhammad (Peace be upon him) which he has brought from Allâh). It is not the word of a poet, little is that you believe! Nor is it the word of a soothsayer (or a foreteller), little is that you remember! This is the Revelation sent down from the Lord of the *'Alamin* (mankind, jinns and all that exists)." [69:40-43]

At that very moment, Islam permeated his heart. However, the dark layer of pre-Islamic tendencies, the deep-seated traditional bigotry as well as the blind pride in his forefathers overshadowed the essence of the great Truth that began to feel its way reluctantly into his heart. He, therefore, persisted in his atrocities against Islam and its adherents unmindful of the pure and true-to-man's nature feeling that lay behind that fragile cover of pre-Islamic ignorance and mentality. His sharp temper and excessive enmity towards the Prophet (Peace be upon him) led him one day to leave his house, sword in hand, with the intention of killing the Prophet (Peace be upon him) . He was in a fit of anger and was fretting and fuming. Nu'aim bin 'Abdullah, a friend of 'Umar's, met him accidentally half way. What had caused so much excitement in him and on whom was the fury to burst, he inquired casually. 'Umar said furiously: "To destroy the man Muhammad (Peace be upon him) this apostate, who has shattered the unity of Quraish, picked holes in their religion, found folly with their wise men and blasphemed their gods." "'Umar, I am sure, your soul has deceived you, do you think that Banu 'Abd Munaf would let you walk on earth if you slain Muhammad (Peace be upon him)? Why don't you take care of your own family first and set them right?"

"Which of the folk of my house?" asked 'Umar angrily. "Your brother-in-law and your sister have apostatized [meaning to say: They have become followers of Muhammad (Peace be upon him)] and abandoned your religion."

'Umar directed his footsteps to his sister's house. As he drew near, he heard the voice of Khabbab bin Aratt, who was reading the Qur'ânic Chapter *Tâ-Hâ* (mystic letters, T. H.) to both of them. Khabbab, perceiving the noise of his footsteps retired to a closet. Fatimah, 'Umar's sister, took hold of the leaf and hid it. But 'Umar had already heard the voice. "What sound was that I have heard just now?" shouted the son of Khattab, entering angrily. Both his sister and her husband replied, "You heard nothing." "Nay," said he swearing fiercely, "I have heard that you have apostatized." He plunged forward towards his brother-in-law and beat him severely, but Fatimah rushed to the rescue of her husband. Thereupon, 'Umar fell upon his sister and struck upon her head. The husband and wife could not contain themselves and cried aloud: "Yes, we are Muslims, we believe in Allâh and His Messenger Muhammad (Peace be upon him) so do what you will." When 'Umar saw the face of his dear sister besmeared with blood, he was softened and said: "Let me see what you were reading, so that I may see what Muhammad (Peace be upon him) has brought." Fatimah was satisfied with the assurance, but said: "O brother, you are unclean on account of your idolatry, none but the pure may touch it. So go and wash first." He did so, and took the page and read the opening verses of the Chapter *Tâ-Hâ* until he reached:

> "Verily! I am Allâh! *Lâ ilâha illa Ana* (none has the right to be worshipped but I), so worship Me and offer prayers perfectly (*Iqâmat-as-Salât*), for My Remembrance." [20:14].

'Umar read the verses with great interest and was much entranced with them. "How excellent it is, and how graceful! Please guide me to Muhammad (Peace be upon him) ." said he. And when he heard that, Khabbab came out of concealment and said, "O 'Umar, I hope that Allâh has answered the prayer of the Prophet (Peace be upon him) , for I heard him say: 'O Allâh! Strengthen Islam through either 'Umar bin

Al-Khattab or Abu Jahl bin Hisham.'" 'Umar then left for a house in Safa where Muhammad (Peace be upon him) had been holding secret meetings along with his Companions. 'Umar reached that place with the sword swinging by his arm. He knocked at the door. The Companions of the Prophet (Peace be upon him) turned to see who the intruder was. One of them peeped through a chink in the door and reeled back exclaiming: "It is 'Umar with his sword." Hamzah, dispelling the fears of his friends, said: "Let him in. As a friend he is welcome. As a foe, he will have his head cut off with his own sword." The Prophet (Peace be upon him) asked his Companions to open the door. In came the son of Khattab. The Prophet (Peace be upon him) advanced to receive the dreadful visitor, caught him by his garment and scabbard, and asked him the reason of his visit. At that 'Umar replied: "O Messenger of Allâh (Peace be upon him), I come to you in order to believe in Allâh and his Messenger and that which he has brought from his Lord." Filled with delight, Muhammad (Peace be upon him) together with his Companions, cried aloud: *'Allâhu Akbar*' (Allâh is Great).

The conversion of 'Umar was a real triumph for the cause of Islam. So great and instant was the effect of his conversion on the situation that the believers who had hitherto worshipped Allâh within their four walls in secret now assembled and performed their rites of worship openly in the Holy Sanctuary itself. This raised their spirits, and dread and uneasiness began to seize Quraish.

Ibn Ishaq narrated on the authority of 'Umar (May Allah be pleased), "When I embraced Islam, I remembered the archenemy of Muhammad (Peace be upon him), i.e. Abu Jahl. I set out, and knocked at his door. When he came out to see me, I told him directly that I had embraced Islam. He immediately slammed the door repulsively denouncing my move as infamous and my face as ugly." In fact, 'Umar's conversion created a great deal of stir in Makkah that some people denounced him as an apostate, yet he would never waver in Faith, on the contrary, he persisted in his stance even at the peril of his life. The polytheists of Quraish marched towards his house with the intention of killing him. 'Abdullah bin 'Umar (May Allah be pleased with him) narrated: While 'Umar was at home in a state of fear, there came Al-'As bin Wa'il As-Sahmy Abu 'Amr, wearing an embroidered cloak and a shirt having silk hems. He was from the tribe of Bani Sahm who were our allies during the pre-Islamic period of ignorance. Al-'As said to 'Umar: What's wrong with you? He said: Your people claim that they will kill me if I become a Muslim. Al-'As said: Nobody will harm you after I have given protection to you. So Al-'As went out and met the people streaming in the whole valley. He said: Where are you going? They replied: We want son of Al-Khattab who has embraced Islam. Al-'As said: There is no way for anybody to touch him. So the people retreated.

With respect to the Muslims in Makkah, 'Umar's conversion had a different tremendous impact. Mujahid, on the authority of Ibn Al-'Abbas (May Allah be pleased with him) related that he had asked 'Umar bin Al-Khattab why he had been given the epithet of *Al-Farouque* (he who distinguishes truth from falsehood), he replied: After I had embraced Islam, I asked the Prophet (Peace be upon him): 'Aren't we on the right path here andHereafter?' The Prophet (Peace be upon him) answered: 'Of course you are! I swear by Allâh in Whose Hand my soul is, that you are right in this world and in the hereafter.' I, therefore, asked the Prophet (Peace be upon him) 'Why we then had to conduct clandestine activism. I swear by Allâh Who has sent you with the Truth, that we will leave our concealment and proclaim our noble cause publicly.' We then went out in two groups, Hamzah leading one and I the other. We headed for the Mosque in broad daylight when the polytheists of Quraish saw us, their faces went pale and got incredibly depressed and resentful. On that very occasion, the Prophet (Peace be upon him) attached to me the epithet of Al-Farouque. Ibn Mas'ud (May Allah be pleased with him) related that they (the Muslims) had never been able to observe their religious rites inside the Holy Sanctuary except when 'Umar embraced Islam.

Suhaib bin Sinan (May Allah be pleased with him), in the same context, said that it was only after 'Umar's conversion, that we started to proclaim our Call, assemble around and circumambulate the Sacred House freely. We even dared retaliate against some of the injustices done to harm us. In the same context, Ibn Mas'ud said: We have been strengthened a lot since 'Umar embraced Islam.

QURAISH'S REPRESENTATIVE NEGOTIATES WITH THE MESSENGER OF ALLAH: Shortly after the conversion of these two powerful heroes, Hamzah bin 'Abdul-Muttalib and 'Umar bin Al-Khattab (May Allah be pleased with him), the clouds of tyranny and oppression started to clear away and the polytheists realized that it was no use meting out torture to the Muslims. They consequently began to direct their campaign to a different course. The authentic records of the biography of the Prophet (Peace be upon him) show that it had occurred to the Makkan leaders to credit Muhammad (Peace be upon him) with ambition. They, therefore, time and again plied him with temptation. One day some of the important men of Makkah gathered in the enclosure of Al-Ka'bah, and 'Utbah bin Rabi'a, a chief among them, offered to approach the Prophet (Peace be upon him) and contract a bargain with him whereby they give him whatever worldly wealth he asks for, on condition that he keep silent and no longer proclaim his new faith. The people of Quraish endorsed his proposal and requested him to undertake that task. 'Utbah came closer to Muhammad (Peace be upon him) and addressed him in the following words:

We have seen no other man of Arabia, who has brought so great a calamity to a nation, as you have done. You have outraged our gods and religion and taxed our forefathers and wise men with impiety and error and created strife amongst us. You have left no stone unturned to estrange the relations with us. If you are doing all this with a view to getting wealth, we will join together to give you greater riches than any Quraishite has possessed. If ambition moves you, we will make you our chief. If you desire kingship we will readily offer you that. If you are under the power of an evil spirit which seems to haunt and dominate you so that you cannot shake off its yoke, then we shall call in skilful physicians to cure you.

"Have you said all?" asked Muhammad (Peace be upon him); and then hearing that all had been said, he spoke forth, and said:

> "In the Name of Allâh, the Most Beneficent, the Most Merciful. *Hâ-Mîm*. [These letters are one of the miracles of the Qur'ân, and none but Allâh (Alone) knows their meanings]. A revelation from Allâh, the Most Beneficent, the Most Merciful. A Book whereof the verses are explained in detail; — a Qur'ân in Arabic for people who know. Giving glad tidings [of Paradise to the one who believes in the Oneness of Allâh (i.e. Islamic Monotheism) and fears Allâh much (abstains from all kinds of sins and evil deeds.) and loves Allâh much (performing all kinds of good deeds which He has ordained)], and warning (of punishment in the Hell-fire to the one who disbelieves in the Oneness of Allâh), but most of them turn away, so they listen not. And they say: Our hearts are under coverings (screened) from that to which you invite us ..." [41: 1-5]

The Messenger of Allâh (Peace be upon him) went on reciting the Chapter while 'Utbah sitting and listening attentively with his hand behind his back to support him. When the Messenger reached the verse that required prostration, he immediately prostrated himself. After that, he turned to 'Utbah saying: "Well Abu Al-Waleed! You have heard my reply, you are now free to do whatever you please." 'Utbah then retired to his company to apprise them of the Prophet's attitude. When his compatriots saw him, they swore that he had returned to them with a countenance unlike the one he had before meeting the Prophet (Peace be upon him) . He immediately communicated to them the details of the talk he gave and the reply he received, and appended saying: "I have never heard words similar to those ones he recited. They definitely relate neither to poetry nor to witchcraft nor do they derive from soothsaying. O people of Quraish! I request you to heed my advice and grant the man full freedom to pursue his goals, in which case you could safely detach yourselves from him. I swear that his words bear a supreme Message. Should the other Arabs rid you of him, they will then spare you the trouble, on the other hand if he accedes to power over the Arabs, then you will bask in his kingship and share him his might." These words of course fell on deaf ears, and did not appeal to the infidels, who jeered at 'Utbah and claimed that the Prophet (Peace be upon him) had bewitched him.

In another version of the same event, it is related that 'Utbah went on attentively listening to the Prophet (Peace be upon him) until the latter began to recite Allâh's Words:

> "But if they turn away, they say [O Muhammad (Peace be upon him)]: "I have warned you of a *Sa'iqa* (a destructive awful cry, torment, hit, a thunder-bolt) like the *Sa'iqa* which overtook 'Ad and Thamûd (people)." [41:13]

Here 'Utbah stood up panicked and stunned putting his hand on the Prophet's mouth beseeching him: "I beg you in the Name of Allâh and uterine ties to stop lest the calamity should befall the people of

Quraish." He then hurriedly returned to his compatriots and informed them of what he had heard.

ABU TALIB ASSEMBLES BANI HASHIM ND BANI AL-MUTTALIB: The new and welcome changes notwithstanding, Abu Talib still had a deep sensation of fear over his nephew. He deliberated on the previous series of incidents including the barter affair of 'Amarah bin Al-Waleed, Abu Jahl's rock, 'Uqbah's attempt to choke the Prophet (Peace be upon him) , and finally 'Umar's (before conversion) intention to kill Muhammad (Peace be upon him). The wise man understood that all of these unequivocally smacked of a serious plot being hatched to disregard his status as a custodian of the Prophet (Peace be upon him), and kill the latter publicly. In the event of such a thing, Abu Talib deeply believed, neither 'Umar nor Hamzah would be of any avail, socially powerful though they were.

Abu Talib was right. The polytheists had laid a carefully-studied plan to kill the Prophet (Peace be upon him), and banded together to put their plan into effect. He, therefore, assembled his kinsfolk of Bani Hashim and Bani Al-Muttalib, sons of 'Abd Munaf and exhorted them to immunize and defend his nephew. All of them, whether believers or disbelievers, responded positively except his brother Abu Lahab, who sided with the idolaters.

GENERAL SOCIAL BOYCOTT:

Four events of special significance occurred within less than four weeks — the conversion of Hamzah, the conversion of 'Umar, Muhammad's (Peace be upon him) refusal to negotiate any sort of compromise and then the pact drawn up between Banu Muttalib and Banu Hashim to immunize Muhammad (Peace be upon him) and shield him against any treacherous attempt to kill him. The polytheists were baffled and at a loss as to what course they would follow to rid themselves of this obstinate and relentless obstacle that had appeared to shatter to pieces their whole tradition of life. They had already been aware that if they killed Muhammad (Peace be upon him) theblood would surely flow profusely in the valleys of Makkah and they would certainly be exterminated. Taking this dreadful prospect into consideration, they grudgingly resorted to a different iniquitous course that would not imply murder.

A PACT OF INJUSTICE AND AGGRESSION:

The pagans of Makkah held a meeting in a place called Wadi Al-Muhassab, and formed a confederation hostile to both Bani Hashim and Bani Al-Muttalib. They decided not to have any business dealings with them nor any sort of inter-marriage. Social relations, visits and even verbal contacts with Muhammad (Peace be upon him) and his supporters would discontinue until the Prophet (Peace be upon him) was given up to them to be killed. The articles of their proclamation, which had provided for merciless measures against Bani Hashim, were committed to writing by an idolater, Bagheed bin 'Amir bin Hashim and then suspended in Al-Ka'bah. The Prophet (Peace be upon him) invoked Allâh's imprecations upon Bagheed, whose hand was later paralysed.

Abu Talib wisely and quietly took stock of the situation and decided to withdraw to a valley on the eastern outskirts of Makkah. Banu Hashim and Banu Al-Muttalib, who followed suit, were thus confined within a narrow pass (Shi'b of Abu Talib), from the beginning of Muharram, the seventh year of Muhammad's mission till the tenth year, viz., a period of three years. It was a stifling siege. The supply of food was almost stopped and the people in confinement faced great hardships. The idolaters used to buy whatever food commodities entered Makkah lest they should leak to the people in Ash-Shi'b, who were so overstrained that they had to eat leaves of trees and skins of animals. Cries of little children suffering from hunger used to be heard clearly. Nothing to eat reached them except, on few occasions, some meagre quantities of food were smuggled by some compassionate Makkans. During 'the prohibited months' — when hostilities traditionally ceased, they would leave their confinement and buy food coming from outside Makkah. Even then, the food stuff was unjustly overpriced so that their financial situation would fall short of finding access to it.

Hakeem bin Hizam was once on his way to smuggle some wheat to his aunt Khadijah (May Allah be pleased with her) when Abu Jahl intercepted and wanted to debar him. Only when Al-Bukhtari intervened, did Hakeem manage to reach his destination. Abu Talib was so much concerned about the personal safety of his nephew. Whenever people retired to sleep, he would ask the Prophet (Peace be upon him) to lie in his place, but when all the others fell asleep, he would order him to change his place and take another, all of which in an attempt to trick a potential assassin.

Despite all odds, Muhammad (Peace be upon him) persisted in his line and his determination and courage never weakened. He continued to go to Al-Ka'bah and to pray publicly. He used every opportunity to preach to outsiders who visited Makkah for business or on pilgrimage during the sacred months and special seasons of assemblies.

This situation ultimately created dissension amongst the various Makkan factions, who were tied with the besieged people by blood relations. After three years of blockade and in Muharram, the tenth year of Muhammad's mission, the pact was broken. Hisham bin 'Amr, who used to smuggle some food to Bani Hashim secretly at night, went to see Zuhair bin Abi Omaiyah Al-Makhzoumy and reproached him for resigning to that intolerable treatment meted out to his uncles in exile. The latter pleaded impotence, but agreed to work with Hisham and form a pressure group that would secure the extrication of the exiles. On the ground of motivation by uterine relations, there emerged a group of five people who set out to abrogate the pact and declare all relevant clauses null and void. They were Hisham bin 'Amr, Zuhair bin Abi Omaiya, Al-Mut'im bin 'Adi, Abu Al-Bukhtari and Zam'a bin Al-Aswad. They decided to meet in their assembly place and start their self-charged mission from the very precinct of the Sacred House. Zuhair, after circumambulating seven times, along with his colleagues approached the hosts of people there and rebuked them for indulging in the amenities of life whereas their kith and kin of Bani Hashim were perishing on account of starvation and economic boycott. They swore they would never relent until the parchment of boycott was torn to piece and the pact broken at once. Abu Jahl, standing nearby, retorted that it would never be torn. Zam'a was infuriated and accused Abu Jahl of telling lies, adding that the pact was established and the parchment was written without seeking their approval. Al-Bukhtari intervened and backed Zam'a. Al-Mut'im bin 'Adi and Hisham bin 'Amr attested to the truthfulness of their two companions. Abu Jahl, with a cunning attempt to liquidate the hot argument that was running counter to his malicious goals, answered that the issue had already been resolved sometime and somewhere before.

Abu Talib meanwhile was sitting in a corner of the Mosque. He came to communicate to them that a Revelation had been sent to his nephew, the Prophet (Peace be upon him) to the effect that ants had eaten away all their proclamation that smacked of injustice and aggression except those parts that bore the Name of Allâh. He contended that he would be ready to give Muhammad (Peace be upon him) up to them if his words proved untrue, otherwise, they would have to recant and repeal their boycott. The Makkans agreed to the soundness of his proposition. Al-Mut'im went to see the parchment and there he did discover that it was eaten away by ants and nothing was left save the part bearing (in the Name of Allâh).

The proclamation was thus abrogated, and Muhammad (Peace be upon him) and the other people were permitted to leave Ash-Sh'ib and return home. In the context of this trial to which the Muslims were subjected, the polytheists had a golden opportunity to experience a striking sign of Muhammad's Prophethood (the white ants eating away the parchment) but to their miserable lot they desisted and augmented in disbelief:

- "But if they see a Sign, they turn away, and say 'This is continuous magic." [54:2]

THE FINAL PHASE OF THE DIPLOMACY OF NEGOTIATION:

The Messenger of Allâh (Peace be upon him) left his confinement and went on preaching his Faith as usual. Quraish, likewise, repealed the boycott but went on in their atrocities and oppression on the Muslims. Abu Talib, the octogenarian notable, was still keen on shielding his nephew but by that time, and on account of the series of tremendous events and continual pains, he began to develop certain fits of weakness. No sooner had he emerged victorious from the inhuman boycott, than he was caught in a persistent illness and physical enervation. The polytheists of Makkah, seeing this serious situation and fearing that the stain of infamy that the other Arabs could attribute to them in case they took any aggressive action against the Prophet (Peace be upon him) after he had lost his main support, Abu Talib, took a decision to negotiate with the Prophet (Peace be upon him) once more and submit some concessions withheld previously. They then delegated some representatives to see Abu Talib and discuss the issue with him. Ibn Ishaq and others related: "When a serious illness caught Abu Talib, the people of Quraish began to deliberate on the situation and reviewed the main features that characterized that period and which included the conversion of 'Umar and Hamzah to Islam, coupled with the tremendous stir that Muhammad (Peace be upon him) had created amongst all the tribes of Quraish. They then deemed it imperative to see Abu Talib before he died to pressure his nephew to negotiate a compromise on the various disputed points. They were afraid that the other Arabs might attribute to them the charge of opportunism."

The delegation of Quraish comprised 25 men including notables like 'Utbah bin Rabi'a, Shaibah bin Rabi'a, Abu Jahl bin Hisham, Omaiyah bin Khalaf, Abu Sufyan bin Harb. They first paid tribute to him and confirmed their high esteem of his person and position among them. They then shifted to the newgive-and-take policy that they claimed they wanted to follow. To substantiate their argument they alleged that they would refrain from intervening in his religion if he did the same.

Abu Talib summoned his nephew and apprised him of the minutes of his meeting with them, and said: "Well, my nephew, here are the celebrities of your people. They have proposed this meeting to submit a policy of mutual concessions and peaceful coexistence." The Messenger of Allâh (Peace be upon him) turned to them saying:

- "I will guide you to the means by which you will gain sovereignty over both the Arabs and non-Arabs."

In another version, the Prophet (Peace be upon him) addressed Abu Talib in the following words: "O uncle! Why don't you call them unto something better?" Abu Talib asked him, "What is it that you invite them to?" The Prophet (Peace be upon him) replied, "I invite them to hold fast to a Message that is bound to give them access to kingship over the Arabs and non-Arabs." According to Ibn Ishaq's version, "It is just one word that will give you supremacy over the Arabs and non-Arabs." The Makkan deputies were taken by incredible surprise and began to wonder what sort of word was that which would benefit them to that extent. Abu Jahl asked, "What is that word? I swear by your father that we will surely grant you your wish followed by ten times as much." He said, "I want you to testify that there is no god worthy to be worshipped but Allâh, and then divest yourselves of any sort of worship you harbour for any deities other than Allâh." They immediately clapped their hands in ridicule, and said "How can you expect us to combine all the deities in one God. It is really something incredible." On their way out leaving, they said to one another, "By god this man [Muhammad (Peace be upon him)] will never relent, nor will he offer any concessions. Let us hold fast to the religion of our forefathers, and Allâh will in due course adjudicate and settle the dispute between us and him." As regards this incident, Allâh revealed the following verses:

- "Sâd: [These letters (Sâd, etc.) are one of the miracles of the Qur'ân and none but Allâh (Alone) knows their meanings]. By the Qur'ân full of reminding. Nay, those who disbelieve are in false pride and Apposition. How many a generation We have destroyed before them, and they cried out when there was no longer time for escape! And they (Arab pagans) wonder that a warner [Prophet Muhammad (Peace be upon him)] has come to them from among themselves! And the *disbelievers say, 'This [Prophet Muhammad (Peace be upon him)] is a sorcerer, a liar. Has he made the gods (all) into One God (Allâh). Verily, this is a curious thing!' And the leaders among them went about (saying): 'Go on, and remain constant to your gods! Verily, this is a thing designed (against you)! We have not heard (the like) of this among the people of these later days. This is nothing but an invention.'"* [38:1-7]

THE YEAR OF GRIEF

ABU TALIB'S DEATH:

In Rajab, the tenth year of the Prophethood, Abu Talib fell ill and passed away, six months after leaving the confinement at Ash-Sh'ib. In another version, Abu Talib breathed his last in Ramadan, three days prior to the death of Khadijah (May Allah be pleased with her). On the authority of Al-Musaiyab, when Abu Talib was on the death bed, the Prophet (Peace be upon him) entered the room where he saw Abu Jahl and 'Abdullah bin Abi Omaiyah. He requested his uncle:

- "My uncle, you just make a profession that there is no true god but Allâh, and I will bear testimony before Allâh (of your being a believer)".

Abu Jahl and 'Abdullah bin Abi Omaiyah addressing him said: "Abu Talib, would you abandon the religion of 'Abdul-Muttalib?" The Messenger of Allâh (Peace be upon him) constantly requested him (to accept his offer), and (on the other hand) was repeated the same statement (of Abu Jahl and 'Abdullah bin Abi Omaiyah) — till Abu Talib gave his final decision and he stuck to the religion of 'Abdul-Muttalib and refused to profess that there is no true god but Allâh. Upon this the Messenger of Allâh (Peace be upon him) remarked:

- "By Allâh, I will persistently beg pardon for you till I am forbidden to do so (by Allâh)".

It was then that Allâh, the Magnificent and Glorious revealed this verse:

- "It is not (proper) for the Prophet and those who believe to ask Allâh's forgiveness for the *Mushrikûn* (polytheists, idolaters, pagans, disbelievers in the Oneness of Allâh) even though they be of kin, after it has become clear to them that they are the dwellers of the Fire (because they died in a state of disbelief)." [9:113]

And it was said to the Messenger of Allâh (Peace be upon him):

- "Verily! You [O Muhammad (Peace be upon him)] guide not whom you like." [28:56]

It goes without saying that Abu Talib was very much attached to Muhammad (Peace be upon him) . For forty years, Abu Talib had been the faithful friend — the prop of his childhood, the guardian of his youth and in later life a very tower of defence. The sacrifices to which Abu Talib exposed himself and his family for the sake of his nephew, while yet incredulous of his mission, stamp his character as singularly noble and unselfish. The Prophet (Peace be upon him) did his best to persuade his octogenarian uncle to make profession of the true faith, but he remained obdurate and stuck to the paganism of his forefathers, and thus could not achieve complete success. Al-'Abbas bin 'Abdul-Muttalib narrated that he said to the Prophet (Peace be upon him) "You have not been of any avail to your uncle (Abu Talib) (though) by Allâh, he used to protect you and get angry on your behalf." The Prophet (Peace be upon him) said: "He is in a shallow fire, and had it not been for me, he would have been at the bottom of the (Hell) Fire."

Abu Sa'id Al-Khudri narrated that he heard the Prophet (Peace be upon him) say, when the mention of his uncle was made, "I hope that my intercession may avail him, and he be placed in a shallow fire that rises up only to his heels."

KHADIJAH PASSES AWAY TO THE MERCY OF ALLAH:

Only two months after the death of his uncle, did the Messenger of Allâh (Peace be upon him) experience another great personal loss viz., the Mother of believers, his wife Khadijah passed away in Ramadan of the tenth year of his Prophethood, when she was sixty-five years old, and he was fifty. Khadijah was in fact a blessing of Allâh for the Prophet (Peace be upon him). She, for twenty-five years, shared with him the toils and trials of life, especially in the first ten years of his ministry of Prophethood. He deeply mourned over her death, and once he replied in an honest burst of tender emotions:

- "She believed in me when none else did. She embraced Islam when people disbelieved me. And she helped and comforted me in her person and wealth when there was none else to lend me a helping hand. I had children from her only."

Abu Hurairah reported that Gabriel came to Allâh's Messenger (Peace be upon him) and said: "Allâh's Messenger, lo, Khadijah is coming to you with a vessel of seasoned food or drink. When she comes to you, offer her greetings from her Lord, and give her glad tidings of a palace of jewels in Paradise where there is no noise and no toil."

These two painful events took place within a short lapse of time and added a lot to his grief and suffering. The Makkans now openly declared their campaign of torture and oppression. The Prophet (Peace be upon him) lost all hope of bringing them back to the right path, so he set out for Al-Ta'if seeking a supportive atmosphere. But there too, he was disappointed and he sustained unbearable tortures and maltreatment that far outweighed his miserable situation in his native town.

His Companions were on equal footing subjected to unspeakable torture and unbearable oppression to such an extent that his closest friend, Abu Bakr, to escape pressure, fled out of Makkah and wanted to leave for Abyssinia (Ethiopia) if it were not for Ibn Ad-Daghanah who met him at Bark Al-Ghamad and managed to dissuade him from completing his journey of escape and brought him back under his protection.

Tdeath of Abu Talib rendered the Prophet (Peace be upon him) vulnerable, and the polytheists availed them of that opportunity to give free rein to their hatred and highhandedness and to translate them in terms of oppression and physical tortures. Once an insolent Quraishite intercepted him and sprinkled sand on his head. When he arrived home, a daughter of his washed the sand away and wept. "Do not weep, my daughter. Allâh will verily protect your father." The Prophet (Peace be upon him) said.

Rapid succession of misfortunes, led the Prophet (Peace be upon him) to call that period, 'the year of grief and mourning'. Thenceforth, that year bore that appellation.

HIS MARRIAGE TO SAWDA IN SHAWWAL, THE TENTH YEAR OF PROPHETHOOD :

The death of Khadijah left the Prophet (Peace be upon him) lonely. The name of Sawdah was suggested to him for marriage which he accepted. This lady had suffered many hardships for the sake of Islam. She was an early convert to the Islamic Faith and it was by her persuasion that her husband had embraced Islam. On the second emigration to Abyssinia (Ethiopia), Sawdah had accompanied her husband As-Sakran bin 'Amr. He died on their way back to Makkah leaving her in a terrible state of destitution. She was the first woman for the Prophet (Peace be upon him) to marry after the death of Khadijah. Some years later she granted her turn with the Prophet (Peace be upon him) to her co-wife, 'Aishah.

FACTORS INSPIRING PATIENCE AND PERSERVANCE

It is natural for sensible and mild-tempered people to meditate deeply on the factors that inspired those early Muslims that miraculous constancy and perseverance. It is normal to wonder how those people managed to tolerate unspeakable persecutions, and stand fast in the face of tyrannical tortures. With respect to these questions, we deem it wise just to touch on those underlying reasons:

1. Unshakable Belief in Allâh. The first and foremost factor is no doubt, unshakable Belief in Allâh Alone coupled with a wonderful degree of perception of His Attributes. A man with this Belief deeply averred in his heart will look at those foreseen difficulties as triflings and can under no circumstance compare with the sweetness of Belief:

- "Then, as for the foam, it passes away as scum upon the banks, while that which is for the good of mankind remains in the earth." [13:17]

Other sub-factors that branch out from that Belief and assist in strengthening it and promoting long amity are:

2. Wholeheartedly-loved leadership. Muhammad (Peace be upon him) the great leader of the Muslim community, and mankind at large, was an exemplary man in his perfect manners and noble attributes; no one could measure up to his endowments of nobility, honesty, trustworthiness and abstinence; unanimously and uncontestedly acknowledged even by his enemies. Abu Jahl himself, the great enemy of Islam, used repeatedly to say: "O Muhammad (Peace be upon him), we are in no position to belie you, we rather disbelieve what you have brought us (Islam)." It is narrated that three people of Quraish each separately and secretly listened to some verses of the Noble Qur'ân. Later, this secret was uncovered and one of them asked Abu Jahl (one of the three) what he thought of what he heard from Muhammad (Peace be upon him). He answered: We contested the honour of leadership and generosity with Banu 'Abd Munaf and shared equal privileges competitively. They then began to boast saying that a Prophet rose among them whom Revelation came down upon from heavens. I swear we will never believe in him.

- So Allâh said:
"... It is not you that they deny, but it is the Verses (the Qur'ân) of Allâh that the Zâlimûn (polytheists and wrong-doers) deny." [6:33]

One day, the disbelievers of Quraish leveled to him a cynical remark three times. He remained silent but for the third one he remarked, "O Quraish! Slaughter is in store for you." They were taken aback and ulterior fear filled their hearts to such an extent that the most hostile among them began to make up for their insult by the best friendly terms they could afford. When they slung the entrails of a camel on him while prostrating himself in prayer, he invoked Allâh's wrath on them, and they immediately were caught in an inexpressible state of worry and were almost convinced that they would be destroyed. Ubai bin Khalaf used always to threaten he would kill Muhammad (Peace be upon him). One day the Prophet (Peace be upon him) retorted that he would kill him by Allâh's Will. When Ubai received a scratch in his neck, on the day of Uhud, he, under the sense of horror, remembered the Prophet's words and remarked, "I am convinced he would be able to kill me even if he spat on me. " Sa'd bin Mu'adh said to Omaiyah bin Khalaf in Makkah, "I heard the Messenger of Allâh (Peace be upon him) one day say that the Muslims would surely kill you." Omaiyah was extremely panicked and swore he would never step out of Makkah. Even when Abu Jahl obliged him to march with them to fight the Prophet (Peace be upon him) on the day of Badr, he bought the best and swift camels in Makkah in order that they hasten his escape. Even his wife warned him against going out reminding him of Sa'd's words, his reply was "By Allâh, I have no intention of going out with Quraish, I will disengage from them after a short distance."

That was the clear sense of horror and terror haunting his enemies wherever they were. His friends and companions, on the other hand, held him dearest to them, and he occupied the innermost cells of their hearts. They were always ready to defend him and secure his well-being even at the risk of their lives. One day, Abu Bakr bin Abi Quhafa was severely beaten by 'Utbah bin Rabi'a, a terrible polytheist. His whole body was almost bleeding and he was on the verge of death, yet when his people took him back home extremely indignant at his misfortune, he swore he would never eat or drink anything until they had told him about the well-being of his noble Companion, Muhammad (Peace be upon him). That was the spirit of selflessness and sacrifice that characterized the behaviour of those early Companions.

3. The sense of responsibility. The early Companions were fully aware of the daunting responsibility they were expected to shoulder. They were also convinced that those charges were inescapable even though they were being persecuted for fear of the far-reaching ramifications, and the horrible impact that humanity would suffer in case they shirked their obligations.

4. Unwavering Belief in the truth of the Hereafter. This was the corner-stone that strengthened their sense of responsibility. There was a deep certainty established through the light of their religion that one day they would have to rise on the Day of Resurrection and account for all worldly deeds, small or big. They were sure that their future in the other world would depend wholly on their acts in their provisional life on earth, either to everlasting Garden (Paradise) or perpetual chastisement in Hell. Their whole life was divided between hope for Allâh's mercy and fear of His punishment.

- "... Who give that (their charity) which they give (and also do other good deeds) with their hearts full of fear (whether their alms and charities, etc., have been accepted or not), because they are sure to return to their Lord." [23:60]

They had already known that life with all its amenities and pains was worthless when compared with the Hereafter. Such deep convictions brought about in them a sense of indifference to all troubles and hardships that attended their life.

5. The Qur'ân. The verses and chapters of the Noble Qur'ân were attractively, forcefully and successively revealed at that gloomy and critical stage, supporting and advancing arguments on the truth and soundness of the principles of Islam, round whose axis the whole Call of Muhammad صلى الله عليه وسلم was revolving. They constituted the immune basis upon which the best and most wonderful Divinely decreed society was to be established. The Qur'ânic verses served also to excite the feelings of the believers, strengthen their selves on their course of patience and endurance and introduce them to the most purposeful examples and suggestive instructions:

- "Or think you that you will enter Paradise without such (trials) as came to those who passed away before you? They were afflicted with severe poverty and ailments and were so shaken that even the Messenger and those who believed along with him said, 'When (will come) the Help of Allâh?' Yes! Certainly, the Help of Allâh is near!" [2:214]

"Alif-Lam-Mim. Do people think that they will be left alone because they say: 'We believe', and will not be tested. And We indeed tested those who were before them. And Allâh will certainly make (it) known (the truth of) those who are true, and will certainly make (it) known (the falsehood of) those who are liars, (although Allâh knows all that before putting them to test)." [29: 1-3]

Mere lip profession of Faith is not enough. It must be tried and tested in the real turmoil of life. The test will be applied in all kinds of circumstances, in individual life and in relation to the environment around us to see whether we can strive constantly and put the Lord above self. Much pain, sorrow and self-sacrifice may be necessary, not because they are good in themselves, but because they will purify us, like fire applied to a goldsmith's crucible to burn out the dross.

These verses also constituted an irrefutable answer to the false allegations of the disbelievers, and a clear ultimatum that smacked of the horrible consequethat would ensue in case they persisted in their disbelief. On the other hand, the Noble Qur'ân was leading the Muslims to a new world and enlightening them as to its features, the beauty of Lordship, the perfection of Godship, the impact of kindness and mercy and the manifestations of the yearned for Allâh's pleasure. They implicitly connoted meaningful messages carrying glad tidings of definitely approaching Divine Mercy leading to eternal bliss in a blissful Garden (Paradise). They, at the same time, envisaged the end of the tyrants and disbelievers who would be brought to Divine Justice and then dragged through the Fire where they would taste the touch of Hell.

6. Glad tidings of success. Ever since the time they experienced the adversities of life, the Muslims had been certain that entrance into the fold of Islam did not entail involvement into hardships or digging one's own grave. They had been aware that the Islamic Call had one goal, viz extermination of pre-Islamic tradition and destroying its iniquitous system, to go on parallel lines with extending its influence allover the earth and holding in firm control the political situation worldwide to lead humanity along a course conducive to Allâh's Pleasure, and perfect enough to rid people of worshipping Allâh's servant to worshipping Allâh, Himself. Glad tidings of this sort were being revealed sometimes explicitly and at other times implicitly, in a manner relevant to the situation. When the Muslims were forced to undergo constraints, or when their life was kept under continual restraint, there would be revealed verses telling identical stories of past Prophets with their people and the sufferings and pains they had experienced. The verses would also include suggestive clues to the final tragic end of the Makkan disbelievers envisaging their final perdition, yet and at the same time, bearing glad tidings to the believers and promising the true servants of vicegerency on earth to go with absolute success, and victory to attend the Islamic Call and its proponents.

- Here we could adduce some of the verses of this category pregnant with glad tidings referring to the final victory that would crown the perseverance and patience of the Muslims:
    - "And, verily, Our Word has gone forth of old for Our slaves, — the Messengers, that they verily would be made triumphant. And that Our hosts, they verily would be the victors. So turn away [O Muhammad (Peace be upon him)] from them for a while, and watch them and they shall see (the punishment)! Do they seek to hasten on Our torment? Then, when it descends into their courtyard (i.e. near to them), evil will be the morning for those who had been warned." [37:171-177]

In the same context, Allâh told His Prophet (Peace be upon him):

- "Their multitude will be put to flight, and they will show their backs." [54:45]

He also said:

- "They will be a defeated host like the confederates of the old times." [38:11]

The Muslims who migrated to Abyssinia (Ethiopia) had the following:

- "And as for those who emigrated for the cause of Allâh, after suffering oppression, We will certainly give them goodly residence in this world, but indeed the reward of the Hereafter will be greater, if they but knew." [16:41]

In the context of the story of Joseph, there was:

- "Verily, in Joseph and his brethren there were *Ayât* (proofs, evidences, verses, lessons, signs, revelations, etc.) for those who ask." [12:7] i.e., the Makkans will receive the same fate that befell Joseph's brothers, viz, failure and surrender. In another instance, Allâh speaks about the Messengers:

- "And those who disbelieved, said to their Messengers: 'Surely, we shall drive you out of our land, or you shall return to our religion!' So their Lord inspired them: 'Truly, We shall destroy the Zâlimûn (polytheists, disbelievers and wrong-doers). And indeed, We shall make you dwell in the land after them. This is for him who fears standing before Me (on the Day of Resurrection or fears My punishment) and also fears My threat." [14:13,14]

During the war between the Persians and the Romans, the disbelievers had a sincere wish that victory be the former's lot, because both parties professed polytheism, whereas the Muslims prayed for a Roman victory because both groups believed in Allâh, His Messengers, Books, the Revelation and the Hereafter.

The war resulted in the overthrow of Rome by Persia. They were pro-Persian, as we have said, and in their hearts they hoped that the nascent movement of Islam, which at that time was, from a worldly point of view, very weak and helpless, would collapse under their persecution. But they misread the true signs of the times. They were told that they would soon be disillusioned in both their calculations, and it actually so happened when Heraclius carried his campaign into the heart of Persia and the Makkan Quraish were beaten off at Badr:

- "And on that Day, the believers (i.e. Muslims) will rejoice (at the victory given by Allâh to the Romans against the Persians) with the help of Allâh." [30:4,5]

During the season of 'Ukaz forum, and other such occasions, the Messenger of Allâh (Peace be upon him) himself would communicate not only glad tidings pertinent to the Garden (Paradise) but also news of promising prospects for the true believers in the Call of Islam. He would openly tell them that they would surely prosper, rule the whole of Arabia and subdue Persia if they professed the most serious pillar of Islam, i.e. the Oneness of Allâh.

Khabbab bin Al-Aratt once urged the Messenger to call upon Allâh to shield him against the adversities he was suffering at the hand of the polytheists. The Prophet's face reddened and he remarked that the true believer must not precipitate things, it was incumbent upon a believer to undergo all the odds of life as much as he could, fearing nobody except Allâh until the religion was established, which would surely happen. The Prophet (Peace be upon him) in this regard, referred to the perseverance that the Muslims had to show and the hardships they had to undergo in order to establish the land of Islam where peace and security would prevail all over it.

Glad tidings of better prospects for Islam and the Muslims were not confined to Muhammad's followers, in fact they were being disclosed time and again to both believers and disbelievers. Whenever the two parties met, the latter would jeer at the former and mockingly say "Here are the sovereigns of earth who will defeat Chosroes and Caesar." But the believers, in anticipation of that shining and Godly-orientated future, would always persevere and tolerate all sorts of persecution and humiliation regarding them as summer clouds that would soon clear away.

The Prophet (Peace be upon him), on his part, would always maintain and sustain his followers' souls with the light of belief, sanctify them through inculcating the Qur'ânic wisdom in their hearts and cultivate their minds deeply with the spirit of Islam that would elevate them to a state of noble spirituality, pure heartedness and an absolute degree of freedom from the yoke of materialism, a high morale powerful enough to resist worldly lusts and consequently lead them from darkness to light. He would constantly teach them to be tolerant, forgiving and overpowering over their selves in order to get well established in their religion, disdain lust, and devote themselves to attaining the Pleasure of Allâh, yearning for the Garden (Paradise), enthusiasm in sciences relating to their faith, calling themselves to account, subordinating fleeing whims, holding under firm control all rage-provoking incidents and finally observing sobriety, patience and gravity.

THE THIRD PHASE CALLING UNTO ISLAM BEYOND MAKKAH

In Shawwal (in the last of May or in the beginning of June 619 A.D.), ten years after receiving his mission from his Lord, the Prophet (Peace be upon him) set out towards At-Ta'if, about 60 kilometres from Makkah, in the company of his freed slave Zaid bin Haritha inviting people to Islam. But contrary to his expectations, the general atmosphere was terribly hostile. He approached the family of 'Umair, who were reckoned amongst the nobility of the town. But, to his disappointment, all of them turned deaf ear to his message and used abusive language as regards the noble cause he had been striving for. Three brothers from the chieftains of Thaqeef —'Abd Yaleel, Mas'ud and Habeeb — sons of 'Amr bin 'Umair Ath-Thaqafy met the Prophet (Peace be upon him), who invited them to embrace Islam and worship Allâh, but they impudently jeered at him and refused his invitation. "He is tearing the cloths of Al-Ka'bah; is it true that Allâh has sent you as a Messenger?" said one of them. "Has not Allâh found someone else to entrust him with His Message?" said the second. "I swear by Allâh that I will never have any contact with you. If you are really the Messenger of Allâh, then you are too serious to retort back; and if you are belying Allâh, then I feel it is imperative not to speak to." said the third. The Messenger of Allâh (Peace be upon him), finding that they were hopeless cases, stood up and left them saying: "Should you indulge in these practices of yours, never divulge them to me."

For ten days he stayed there delivering his message to several people, one after another, but all to no purpose. Stirred up to hasten the departure of the unwelcome visitor, the people hooted him through the alley-ways, pelted him with stones and obliged him to flee from the city pursued by a relentless rabble. Blood flowed down both his legs; and Zaid, endeavouring to shield him, was wounded in the head. The mob did not desist until they had chased him two or three miles across the sandy plains to the foot of the surrounding hills. There, wearied and exhausted, he took refuge in one of the numerous orchards, and rested against the wall of a vineyard. At a time when the whole world seemed to have turned against him, Muhammad (Peace be upon him) turned to his Lord and betook himself to prayer and the following touching words are still preserved as those through which his oppressed soul gave vent to its distress. He was weary and wounded but confident of the help of his Lord:

- "O Allâh! To You alone I make complaint of my helplessness, the paucity of my resources and my insignificance before mankind. You are the most Merciful of the mercifuls. You are the Lord of the helpless and the weak, O Lord of mine! Into whose hands would You abandon me: into the hands of an unsympathetic distant relative who would sullenly frown at me, or to the enemy who has been given control over my affairs? But if Your wrath does not fall on me, there is nothing for me to worry about."

"I seek protection in the light of Your Countenance, which illuminates the heavens and dispels darkness, and which controls all affairs in this world as well as in the Hereafter. May it never be that I should incur Your wrath, or that You should be wrathful to me. And there is no power nor resource, but Yours alone."

Seeing him in this helpless situation, Rabi'a's two sons, wealthy Makkans, were moved on grounds of kinship and compassion, and sent to him one of their Christian servants with a tray of grapes. The Prophet (Peace be upon him) accepted the fruit with pious invocation: "In the Name of the Allâh." The Christian servant 'Addas was greatly impressed by these words and said: "These are words which people in this land do not generally use." The Prophet (Peace be upon him) inquired of him whence he came and what religion he professed. 'Addas replied: "I am a Christian by faith and come from Nineveh." The Prophet (Peace be upon him) then said: "You belong to the city of the righteous Jonah, son of Matta." 'Addas asked him anxiously if he knew anything about Jonah. The Prophet (Peace be upon him) significantly remarked: "He is my brother. He was a Prophet and so am I." Thereupon 'Addas paid homage to Muhammad (Peace be upon him) and kissed his hands. His masters admonished him at this act but he replied: "None on the earth is better than he is. He has revealed to me a truth which only a Prophet can do." They again reprimanded him and said: "We forewarn you against the consequences of abandoning the faith of your forefathers. The religion which you profess is far better than the one you feel inclined to."

Heart-broken and depressed, Muhammad (Peace be upon him) set out on the way back to Makkah. When he reached Qarn Al-Manazil, Allâh, the Almighty sent him Gabriel together with the angel of mountains. The latter asked the Prophet (Peace be upon him) for permission to bury Makkah between Al–Akhshabain —Abu Qubais and Qu'ayqa'an mountains. Full narration of this event was given by 'Aishah (May be pleased with her) (the Prophet's spouse). She said: "I asked the Prophet (Peace be upon him) if he had ever experienced a worse day than Uhud. He answered that he had suffered a lot from those people (the idolaters) but the most painful was on the day of 'Aqabah. I went seeking support from Ibn 'Abd Yalil bin 'Abd Kalal, but he spurned me. I set out wearied and grieved heedless of anything around me until I suddenly realized I was in Qarn Ath-Tha'alib, called Qarn Al-Manazil. There, I looked up and saw a cloud casting its shade on me, and Gabriel addressing me: Allâh has heard your people's words and sent you the angel of mountains to your aid. The latter called and gave me his greetings and asked for my permission to bury Makkah between Al-Akhshabain, the two mountains flanking Makkah. I said in reply that I would rather have someone from their loins who will worship Allâh, the All–Mighty with no associate." A concise meaningful answer fully indicative of the Prophet's matchless character and the fathomless magnanimous manners.

The Messenger of Allâh (Peace be upon him) then came back to wakefulness and his heart was set at rest in the light of that invisible Divinely provided aid. He proceeded to Wadi Nakhlah where he stayed for a few days.

During his stay there, Allâh sent him a company of jinns who listened to him reciting the Noble Qur'ân:

- "And (remember) when We sent towards you [Muhammad (Peace be upon him)] *Nafran* (three to ten persons) of the jinns, (quietly) listening to the Qur'ân, when they stood in the presence thereof, they said: 'Listen in silence!' And when it was finished, they returned to their people, as warners. They said: 'O our people! Verily! We have heard a Book (this Qur'ân) sent down after Moses, confirming what came before it, it guides to the Truth and to a Straight Path (i.e. Islam). O our people! Respond (with obedience) to Allâh's Caller [i.e. Allâh's Messenger Muhammad (Peace be upon him)], and believe in him (i.e. believe in that which Muhammad (Peace be upon him) has brought from Allâh and follow him). He (Allâh) will forgive you of your sins, and will save you from a painful torment (i.e. Hell-fire).'" [46:29-31]

The same incident is referred to in *Sûrah Al-Jinn*:

- "Say [O Muhammad (Peace be upon him)]: "It has been revealed to me that a group (from three to ten in number) of jinns listened (to this Qur'ân). They said: 'Verily! We have heard a wonderful Recital (this Qur'ân)! It guides to the Right Path, and we have believed therein, and we shall never join (in worship) anything with our Lord (Allâh).'" [72:1,2] ... Till the end of the 15th verse.

From the context of these verses and their relevant interpretation, we can safely establish it that the Prophet (Peace be upon him) was not aware of the presence of that group of jinns. It was only when Allâh revealed those verses that he came to know of it. The verses also confirm that it was the first time they came. However, the context of the different versions suggests that the jinns repeated their visits later on. The presence of that company of jinns comes in the context of the Divine support givto His Messenger, and constitutes a propitious sign of ultimate victory and success for the Call of Islam. It provides an unshakable proof that no power however mighty could alter what is wrought by Allâh:

- "And whosoever does not respond to Allâh's Caller, he cannot escape on earth, and there will be no *Auliyâ* (protectors) from him besides Allâh (from Allâh's punishment). Those are in manifest error." [46:32]

"And we think that we cannot escape (from the punishment of) Allâ h in the earth, nor can we escape (from the punishment) by flight." [72:12]

Given this support and auspicious start, depression, dismay and sadness that used to beset him since he was driven out of At-Ta'if, he turned his face towards Makkah with fresh determination to resume his earlier plan to expose people to Islam and communicate his Message in a great spirit of zeal and matchless enthusiasm.

Zaid bin Harithah, his companion, addressing the Prophet (Peace be upon him) said, "How dare you step into Makkah after they (Quraish) have expatriated you?" The Prophet (Peace be upon him) answered: "Hearken Zaid, Allâh will surely provide relief and He will verily support His religion and Prophet."

When he was a short distance from Makkah, he retired to Hira' Cave. Whence he despatched a man from Khuza'ah tribe to Al-Akhnas bin Shuraiq seeking his protection. The latter answered that he was Quraish's ally and in no position to offer protection. He despatched the messenger to Suhail bin 'Amr, but to no avail, either. Al-Mut'im bin 'Adi, a notable in Makkah, however, volunteered to respond to the Prophet's appeal for shelter. He asked his people to prepare themselves fully armed and then asked Muhammad (Peace be upon him) to enter into the town and directly into the Holy Sanctuary. The Prophet (Peace be upon him) observed a two-*Rak'a* prayer and left for his house guarded by the heavily-armed vigilant 'Adi's.

It has been reported that later Abu Jahl, the archenemy of Islam, asked Mut'im if his behaviour suggested protection or conversion, the latter replied it was merely protection. Abu Jahl was relieved and said that he would give Muhammad protection for his sake.

The Messenger of Allâh (Peace be upon him) never forgot Mut'im's favour. At the conclusion of the battle of Badr, he declared publicly that if Mut'im had been still alive and asked for the release of the Quraishite captives, he would not deny him his request.

ISLAM BEING INTRODUCED TO ARABIAN TRIBES AND INDIVIDUALS

In Dhul Qa'dah, the tenth year of Prophethood, i.e. July 619, the Prophet (Peace be upon him), returned to Makkah to resume his activities. The time for pilgrimage to Makkah was approaching so he hastened to introduce people both tribes and individuals to Islam and call upon them to embrace it, just as it was his practice since the fourth year of his Prophethood.

On the authority of Az-Zuhri, of the tribes that Islam was introduced to, we could speak of Banu 'Amir bin Sa'sa'ah, Muharib bin Khasfa, Fazarah, Ghassan, Murrah, Haneefah, Saleem, 'Abs, Banu Nasr, Banu Al-Buka', Kindah, Kalb, Al-Harith bin Ka'b, Udhrah and people of Hadrmout. Islam was not introduced to them in one single year but rather repeatedly from the fourth year till the last pre-migration season of pilgrimage. They however, remained obdurate and none of them responded positively.

The following is a resume of aspects relating to the Prophet's appeals as regards the new faith he was preaching:

1. He visited a sept of Banu Kalb known as Banu 'Abdullah. He called them to Allâh's Message and entreated them to accept it for the sake of Allâh Who had chosen a beautiful name for their father, but without avail.
2. He called on Bani Haneefah in their habitation, but received very repugnant treatment.
3. He addressed Bani 'Amir bin Sa'sa'ah in their encampment, calling them to abandon idolatry and join him. One of them called Buhairah bin Firras, answered him back: "Should we give you allegiance and Allâh give you power over your opponents, will you give us right to inheritance and succeed you in power?" The Prophet replied: "The whole affair lies in Allâh's Hands. He gives the power to whomever He desires." The man commented: "Do you expect us to incur the wrath and vengeance of the Arabs without the least hope of leadership? We can in fact readily dispense with your offers."

When Banu 'Amir returned to their habitations, they narrated the story to an elderly man who had lingered behind because he was too old. They told him, "A young man of Quraish of Bani 'Abdul Muttalib, claiming that he is a Prophet, contacted us, asked for support and invited us to embrace his religion." The old sheikh was struck by the news, and wondered if there was no way of making amends for the loss of that opportunity and swore, "He is really Ishmaelite (he descends from Ishmael). He is the Truth (he is a real Prophet). How did it happen that you misjudged his words?"

The Prophet (Peace be upon him) was not dismayed at all. He persisted in his mission for the fulfillment of which he had been commissioned to strive despite all odds. He did not confine his efforts to the tribes but also conducted contacts with individuals from some of whom he was able to receive a favourable response. Moreover, later in the same season, some of them did believe in his Prophethood and entered the fold of Islam. The following list included some of those early converts:

1. Swaid bin Samit. He was an intelligent discreet poet from Yathrib (Madinah). During his stay in Makkah for pilgrimage (or lesser pilgrimage), he encountered the Prophet (Peace be upon him) who invited him to embrace Islam. At this invitation, Swaid imparted to the Prophet some sound words from Luqman's wisdom. The Prophet approved of that wisdom but told the man that he had something far better. He recited some verses from the Qur'ân, the man listened meditatively and the words appealed to his originally pure nature and accepted Islam as his faith at once. He was killed in the battle of Bu'ath. That was in the eleventh year of the Prophethood.
2. Eyas bin Mu'adh. He was still a youth from Aws tribe. He came as a member of delegation seeking alliance with Quraish against another rival tribe dwelling in Madinah, Al-Khazraj. The Prophet (Peace be upon him) met them and advised them to follow a better course than that they had in mind. He introduced himself and Islam to them, apprised them of his mission and narrated some verses from the Noble Qur'ân. Eyas's heart immediately absorbed the Divine Message and agreed with the Prophet (Peace be upon him). Abul Haisar Anas bin Rafi', a member of the delegation disapproved of the boy's behaviour and silenced him by hurling some dust into his face. The people then left Madinah after having failed in establishing alliance with

Quraish. Shortly after arrival in Madinah, the boy breathed his last acclaiming Allâh's Name and celebrating His Glory.
3. Abu Dhar Al-Ghifari. He used to live in the suburbs of Yathrib. News of the Islamization of Swaid bin Samit and Eyas bin Mu'adh reached him and constituted a turning point in his life per se. He sent his brother to Makkah for more details about the Prophet's intentions. The man came back and reported to Abu Dhar that the 'said man' enjoined good and forbade evil. Abu Dhar was not satisfied and decided that he himself should go out and probe the real situation. After some attempts to identify the person of the Prophet(Peace be upon him) , he managed to meet him though not without some difficulties due to the antagonistic atmosphere within which the proponents of the new faith were trying to work their way. No sooner than Abu Dhar was exposed to the real nature of Islam, he embraced it. Despite the Prophet's earnest plea not to divulge his new move, Abu Dhar went directly to the Holy Sanctuary where he publicly declared that he had testified to the Oneness of Allâh and Prophethood of Muhammad. The heathens all around hurried and began beating him. He almost died when Al-'Abbas intervened warning against killing someone whose tribe was in full command of the strategic commercial caravan routes leading to Makkah. Thevent recurred in the following morning with the same man to come to the scene and rescue him.
4. Tufail bin 'Amr Ad-Dausi. He was an honest poet and chief of Ad-Daus tribe inhabiting an area close to Yemen in South Arabia. He arrived in Makkah in the eleventh year of Prophethood. Great reception ceremonies were accorded to him on his advent. The Makkans soon started to inculcate in his ears all sorts of antipathy against the Prophet (Peace be upon him) . They even alleged that he had caused the most horrible societal schism, dividing all sorts of social life even the family ties were subject to his schemes and plans of dissension. They even warned him against speaking or even listening to him. The man overpowered by these pleas, complied by their requests. He even stuffed his ears with a piece of cotton in order not to hear any word of his. However, when this tribesman entered the mosque, he saw Muhammad (Peace be upon him) observing his prayer and out of curiosity, he approached him for it was a Divine Will to hear the Prophet's sound and appealing words. The temptation to hear more was irresistible so he followed the Prophet (Peace be upon him) into his house, briefed him on his advent and all the story of the people of Quraish. The Messenger of Allâh (Peace be upon him) recited some verses of the Noble Qur'ân and the man managed to taste something exceptionally beautiful and discern the truth latent within. He embraced Islam and testified that there was no god but Allâh and that Muhammad was His Messenger. He then said that he was an influential man among his people and that he would call them to profess Islam, yet he wanted the Prophet (Peace be upon him) to equip him with a supportive sign that would ease his future task. It was in fact a Divinely bestowed light in his whip. He called his father and wife to embrace Islam and they did respond. His people lagged a little but he exhorted them fervently and was fully successful. He and seventy or eighty of his followers emigrated to Madinah after the Trench Battle. He was a perfect fighter in the cause of Allâh and was martyred in Al-Yamama events.
5. Dhumad Al-Azdi. He came from Azd Shanu'a in Yemen, specialist in incantation. He arrived in Makkah to hear the fools there say that Muhammad (Peace be upon him) was out of his mind. He decided to practise his craft on the Prophet (Peace be upon him) , who on seeing him said: "Praise is to Allâh, we entertain His praise and seek His help. Whomsoever Allâh guides, none will lead astray, and whomsoever Allâh leads astray, none will guide. I testify there is no god but Allâh and Muhammad is His servant and Messenger." Dhumad heard the words and requested the Prophet (Peace be upon him) to echo them again, and he was granted his wish thrice. Here he said: "I have heard the soothsayers, sorcerers and poets, but never have I experienced the sweetness of your words." He then gave a pledge of a sincere convert.

HOPE INSPIRING BREEZES FROM THE MADINESE:

It was during the pilgrimage season, in the eleventh year of Prophethood, that the Islamic Call found the righteous seeds through which it would grow up to constitute tall trees whose leaves would foster the new faith and shelter the new vulnerable converts from the blows of injustices and high-handness of Quraish. It was the Prophet's wise practice to meet the delegates of the Arabian tribes by night so that the hostile Makkans would not debar him from achieving his objectives. In the company of his two truthful Companions 'Ali and Abu Bakr, he had an interesting talk regarding Islamization with Bani Dhuhal, but the latter suspended their conversion. In pursuit of the same objective, the Prophet and his

Companions passed by 'Aqabat Mina where they heard people talking. They went at their heels until they encountered six men from Yathrib, all of whom from Khazraj tribe: As'ad bin Zurarah, 'Awf bin Harith, Rafi' bin Malik, Qutbah bin 'Amir, 'Uqbah bin 'Amir and Jabir bin 'Abdullah. The last two being from Aws and the former four from Khazraj.

The Madinese always heard the Jews say that a Prophet was about to rise, for the time for a new dispensation had arrived. Him they would follow and then smite their enemies as the children of 'Ad and Iram had been smitten.

"Of what tribe are you?" asked the Prophet. "Of the tribe of Khazraj," they replied. "Are you the allies of the Jews?" The Prophet enquired. They said: "Yes." "Then why not sit down for a little and I will speak to you." The offer was readily accepted for the fame of Muhammad (Peace be upon him) had spread to Madinah and the strangers were curious to see more of the man who had created a stir in the whole area. The Prophet (Peace be upon him) presented to them an expose of Islam, explained its implications, and the responsibilities that fell upon the men who accepted it. When the Prophet (Peace be upon him) concluded his talk, they exchanged among themselves ideas to the following effect: "Know surely, this is the Prophet with whom the Jews are ever threatening us; wherefore let us make haste and be the first to join him."

They, therefore, embraced Islam, and said to the Prophet, "We have left our community for no tribe is so divided by hatred and rancour as they are. Allâh may cement our ties through you. So let us go and invite them to this religion of yours; and if Allâh unites them in it, no man will be dearer than you."

The handful of Madinese converts remained steady to the cause and they preached the Islam with full zeal and devotion with the result that they succeeded in winning adherents for Islam from amongst their fellow citizens and hardly was there a house in Madinah not talking curiously and enthusiastically about the Messenger of Allâh (Peace be upon him) .

MARRIAGE OF THE PROPHET (Peace be upon him) to 'Aishah (May Allah be pleased her):

In Shawwal of the same year, the Prophet (Peace be upon him) concluded a marriage contract with 'Aishah (May Allah be pleased with her) *'the truth verifier'*, when she was six of age and consummated his marriage with her in Shawwal, the year 1 A.H. in Madinah when she was nine.

AL-ISRA' AND Al-MI'RAJ (The Miraculous Night Journey from Makkah to the Farthest Mosque in Jerusalem, and the Ascent through the Spheres of Heavens)

The last days of the Makkan phase of the Prophet's life are noted for alternate fortunes ranging between two extremes: gradual success and continual persecution. However, glimpses of propitious lights were looming on the distant horizon, to ultimately materialize in the event of the Prophet's Night Journey to Jerusalem and then Ascension through the spheres of the heavens.

As for its exact date, it is still controversial and no common consent has been reached. However, the majority of jurists is in favour of a date between 16-12 months prior to migration to Madinah. The following is a epitome of the details of that miraculous event narrated on the authority of Ibn Al-Qayyim.

The Messenger of Allâh (Peace be upon him) was carried in body from the Sacred Mosque in Makkah to the Distant Mosque in Jerusalem on a horse called Al-Buraq in the company of Gabriel, the archangel. There he alighted, tethered the horse to a ring in the gate of the Mosque and led the Prophets in prayer. After that Gabriel took him to the heavens on the same horse. When they reached the first heaven Gabriel asked the guardian angel to open the door of heaven. It was opened and he saw Adam, the progenitor of mankind. The Prophet (Peace be upon him) saluted him and the other welcomed him and expressed his faith in Muhammad's Prophethood. He saw the souls of martyrs on his right and those of the wretched on his left.

Gabriel then ascended with the Prophet to the second heaven, asked for opening the gate and there he saw and saluted John, son of Zachariya (Yahya bin Zakariya) and Jesus, son of Mary. They returned the salutation, welcomed him and expressed their faith in his Prophethood. Then they reached the third heaven where they saw Joseph (Yusuf) and saluted him. The latter welcomed the Prophet and expressed faith in his Prophethood. The Prophet, in the company of Gabriel, then reached the fourth heaven where he met the Prophet (Idris) and saluted him. Prophet Enoch returned the salutation and expressed faith in his Prophethood. Then he was carried to the fifth heaven where he met the Prophet Aaron (Harun) and saluted him. The latter returned the salutation and expressed faith in his Prophethood. In the sixth heaven he met Moses (Musa) and saluted him. The latter returned the salutation and expressed faith in his Prophethood. Muhammad (Peace be upon him) on leaving, saw that Moses began to weep. He asked about the reason. Moses answered that he was weeping because he witnessed a man sent after him as a Messenger (Muhammad) who was able to lead more of his people to the Paradise than he himself did. Then Prophet Muhammad (Peace be upon him) reached the seventh heaven and met Abraham (Ibrahim) (Peace be upon him) and saluted him. The latter returned the salutation and expressed faith in his Prophethood. Then he was carried to *Sidrat-al-Muntaha* (the remotest lote tree) and was shown *Al-Bait-al-Ma'mûr* [(the much frequented house) which is like the Ka'bah (Sacred House) encompassed daily by seventy thousand angels, so that the angels who once encompassed it would not have their turn again till the Resurrection]. He was then presented to the Divine Presence and experienced the thrill of witnessing the Divine Glory and Manifestation at the closest possible propinquity. There the Lord revealed unto His servant that which He revealed, and ordained fifty daily prayers for him. On his return, he spoke to Moses that his followers had been enjoined to pray fifty times a day. Moses addressing the Prophet (Peace be upon him) said: "Your followers cannot perform so many prayers. Go back to your Lord and ask for a remission in number." The Prophet (Peace be upon him) turned to Gabriel as if holding counsel with him. Gabriel nodded, "Yes, if you desire," and ascended with him to the Presence of Allâh. The All-Mighty Allâh, Glory is to Him, made a reduction of ten prayers. He then descended and reported that to Moses, who again urged him to request for a further reduction. Muhammad (Peace be upon him) once more begged his Lord to reduce the number still further. He went again and again in the Presence of Allâh at the suggestion of Moses for reduction in the number of prayers till these were reduced to five only. Moses again asked him to implore for more reduction, but he said: "I feel ashamed now of repeatedly asking my Lord for reduction. I accept and resign to His Will." When Muhammad(Peace be upon him) went farther, a Caller was heard saying: "I have imposed My Ordinance and alleviated the burden of My servants."

There is however some difference as regards the issue whether the Prophet saw Allâh with his physical eye or not. Some interpreters say that seeing Allâh with his naked eyes was not confirmed. Ibn 'Abbas, on the other hand, says that the word *Ru'ya* as used in the Noble Qur'ân signifies the observation with the help of the eye.

In *Sûrah An–Najm* (Chapter —The Star) we read:

- "Then he approached and came closer." [53:8]

Here (he) refers to archangel Gabriel, and this context is completely different from that in the Prophetic tradition of *Isra'* and *Mi'raj*, where 'the approach' relates to that of the Lord, Glory is to Him.

Some significant suggestive incidents featured the 'Night Journey' of the Prophet, of which we could mention:

1. The Prophet's breast was cleft by Gabriel, his heart extracted and washed with the water of Zamzam —a sacred spring in Makkah.
2. In the same context, there were brought to him two gold vessels. There was milk in one, while the other was full of wine. He was asked to choose either of them, so he selected the vessel containing milk and drank it. He (the angel) said: "You have been guided on *Al-Fitrah* or you have attained *Al-Fitrah*. Had you selected wine, your nation would have been misled." [It is a symbolic way of saying that good and evil in the form of milk and wine were brought before the Prophet and he instinctively made a choice for the good. It is very difficult to render the Arabic term '*Fitrah'* into English. It denotes the original constitution or disposition, with which a child comes into this world, as contrasted with qualities or inclinations acquired during life; besides it refers to the spiritual inclination inherent in man in his unspoilt state].
3. The Prophet صلى الله عليه وسلم told that he saw two manifest rivers, — the Nile and the Euphrates — and two hidden ones. It appears that the two manifest rivers, the Nile and the Euphrates, symbolically describe the area in whose fertile valleys, Muhammad's Message will settle, and the people whereof will always remain the adherent bearers of Islam that will be passed on from generation to another. They can by no means suggest that they well up from the Garden.
4. He had the opportunity to see Malik, the guardian of Hell, with a cheerless frowning face. Therein, he saw the Hell dwellers, of whom were those who unjustly eat up the property of the orphans. They have flews similar to those of camels, swallowing red-hot stones and then issuing out of their backs. There were also the people who take usury with bellies too big to be able to move around; they are trodden by the people of Pharaoh when these are admitted into Hell. In the same abode, he saw the adulterers offered tasty fatty meat and rotten smelly one but they make option for the latter. The licentious women were also there hanging from their breasts.
5. The 'Night Journey' raised a good deal of stir among the people and the sceptical audience plied Muhammad with all sorts of questions. He told them that he saw the camels of Makkan merchants to and fro. He also guided them to some of their animals that went astray. He informed them that he had drunk some of their water while they were fast asleep and left the container covered.

The disbelievers, however, found it a suitable opportunity to jeer at the Muslims and their creed. They pestered the Prophet (Peace be upon him) with questions as to the description of the Mosque at Jerusalem, where he had never gone before and, to the astonishment of many, the Prophet's replies furnished the most accurate information about that city. He supplied them with all the news about their caravans and the routes of their camels. However, all this increased in them nothing but flight from the Truth, and they accepted nothing but disbelief.

For the true Muslims, however there was nothing unusual about the Night Journey. The All-Mighty Allâh, Who is Powerful enough to have created the heavens and the earth by an act of His Will, is surely Powerful enough to take His Messenger beyond the heavens and show him those signs of His at firsthand which are inaccessible to man otherwise. The disbelievers on their part went to see Abu Bakr on account of this event, and he readily said: "Yes, I do verify it." It was on this occasion that he earned the title of *As-Siddiq* (the verifier of the truth).

The most eloquent and most concise justification of this 'Journey' is expressed in Allâh's Words:

- "… in order that We might show him (Muhammad) of Our *Ayât* (proofs, evidences, signs, etc.)" [17:1].

The Divine rules as regards the Prophets goes as follows:

- "Thus did We show Abraham the kingdom of the heavens and the earth that he be one of those who have Faith with certainty." [6:75]

To Moses, his Lord said:

- "That We may show you (some) of Our Greater Signs." [20:23]

In order that:

- "He be of those who have Faith with certainty."

The Prophets, after seeing Allâh's Signs, will establish their Faith on solid certainty too immune to be parted with. They are in fact eligible for this Divine privilege because they are the ones who will bear burdens too heavy for other ordinary people to carry, and in the process of their mission, they will regard all worldly ordeals and agonies too small to care about.

There are simple facts that emanate from this blessed Journey, and flow along into the flowery garden of the Prophetic biography; peace and blessings of Allâh be upon its author, Muhammad. The story of 'the Night Journey' as we see in the Noble Qur'ân is epitomised in the first verse of the *Sûrah Isra'*(Chapter 17 — The Jourby Night) then there is a quick shift to uncover the shameful deeds and crimes of the Jews, followed by an admonition saying that the Qur'ân guides to that which is most just and right. This arrangement is not in fact a mere coincidence. Jerusalem was the first scene of the Night Journey, and here lies the message directed to the Jews and which explicitly suggested that they would be discharged of the office of leadership of mankind due to the crimes they had perpetrated and which no longer justified their occupation of that office. The message suggested explicitly that the office of leadership would be reinstituted by the Messenger of Allâh (Peace be upon him) to hold in his hand both headquarters of the Abrahamic Faith, the Holy Sanctuary in Makkah and the Farthest Mosque in Jerusalem. It was high time for the spiritual authority to be transferred from a nation whose history got pregnant with treachery, covenant-breaching and aggression to another nation blessed with piety, and dutifulness to Allâh, with a Messenger who enjoys the privilege of the Qur'ânic Revelation, which leads to that which is best and right.

There, however, remains a crucial question waiting to be answered: How could this foreseen transition of authority be effected while the champion himself (Muhammad) was left deserted and forsaken stumbling in the hillocks of Makkah? This question per se uncovered the secrets of another issue which referred to a phase of the Islamic Call and the appearance of another role it was about to take up, different in its course and noble in its approaches. The forerunners of that new task took the shape of Qur'ânic verses smacking of direct and unequivocal warning accompanied by a severe ultimatum directed to the polytheists and their agents:

- "And when We decide to destroy a town (population), We (first) send a definite order (to obey Allâh and be righteous) to those among them [or We (first) increase in number those of its population] who are given the good things of this life. Then, they transgress therein, and thus the word (of torment) is justified against it (them). Then We destroy it with complete destruction. And how many generations (past nations) have We destroyed after Noah! And Sufficient is your Lord as an All-Knower and All-Beholder of the sins of His slaves." [17:16, 17]

Together with these verses, there were others revealed to show the Muslims the rules and items of the civilization upon which they could erect their Muslim community, and foreshadowing their ownership of a piece of land, exercising full freedom over it and establishing a coherent society around whose axis the whole humanity would rotate. Those verses in reality implied better prospects for the Prophet (Peace be upon him) comprising a secure shelter to settle in, and headquarters safe enough to empower and embolden him to communicate his Message to all the world at large; that was in fact the inner secret of that blessed journey. For this very wisdom and the like we deem it appropriate to suggest that 'the Night Journey' took place either before the First Pledge of 'Aqabah or between the two; after all, Allâh knows best.

THE FIRST 'AQABAH PLEDGE

We have already spoken about six Madinese who embraced Islam in the pilgrimage season in the eleventh year of Prophethood. They promised to communicate the Message of Islam to their townsfolk.

The following year, on the occasion of the pilgrimage, there came a group of twelve disciples ready to acknowledge Muhammad as their Prophet. The group of men comprised five of the six who had met the Prophet (Peace be upon him) the year before, the sixth who stayed away was Jabir bin 'Abdullah bin Reyab, the other seven were:

1. Mu'adh bin Al-Harith, Ibn 'Afra, from Khazraj.
2. Dhakwan bin 'Abd Al-Qais, from Khazraj.
3. 'Ubadah bin As-Samit, from Khazraj.
4. Yazeed bin Tha'labah, from Khazraj.
5. 'Al-'Abbas bin 'Ubadah bin Nadalah, from Khazraj.
6. Abul Haitham bin At-Taihan, from Aws.
7. 'Uwaim bin Sa'idah, from Aws.

They avowed their faith in Muhammad (Peace be upon him) as a Prophet and swore: "We will not worship any one but one Allah; we will not steal; neither will we commit adultery, nor kill our children; we will not utter slander, intentionally forging falsehood and we will not disobey you in any just matter." When they had taken the pledge, Muhammad (Peace be upon him) said: "He who carries it out, Allâh will reward him; and who neglects anything and is afflicted in this world, it may prove redemption for him in the Hereafter; and if the sin remains hidden from the eyes of the men and no grief comes to him, then his affair is with Allâh. He may forgive him or He may not."

THE MUSLIM ENVOY IN MADINAH:

After the Pledge (in the form of an oath had been taken) the Prophet (Peace be upon him) sent to Yathrib (Madinah) Mus'ab bin 'Umair Al-'Abdari, (May Allah be pleased with him) the first Muslim 'ambassador' to teach the people there the doctrines of Islam, give them practical guidance and make attempts at propagating the Islam among those who still professed polytheism. As'ad bin Zurarah hosted him in Madinah. So prepared was the ground, and so zealous the propagation that the Islam spread rapidly from house to house and from tribe to tribe. There were various cheerful and promising aspects of success that characterized Mus'ab's task. One day Mus'ab and As'ad were on their way to the habitations of Bani 'Abd Al-Ashhal and Bani Zafar, when they went into the premises of the latter clan. There they sat near a well conversing with some new converts. Sa'd bin Mu'adh and Usaid bin Hudair, chiefs of the two clans heard of this meeting, so Usaid approached the Muslims armed with his lance while the other Sa'd excused himself on grounds that As'ad was his maternal cousin. Usaid came closer cursing and swearing and accused the two men of befooling people weak of heart, and ordered that they stop it altogether. Mus'ab calmly invited him to sit saying, "If you are pleased with our talk, you can accept it; should you hold it in abhorrence, you could freely immunize yourself against what you hate." "That's fair," said Usaid, pierced his lance in the sand, listened to Mus'ab and then heard some verses of the Noble Qur'ân. His face bespoke satisfaction and pleasure before uttering any words of approval. He asked the two men about the procedures pertinent to embracing Islam. They asked him to observe washing, purge his garment, bear witness to the Truth and then perform two *Rak'a*. He responded and did exactly what he was asked to do, and then said there was a man (Sa'd bin Mu'adh) whose people would never hang back if he followed the Islam. He then left to see Sa'd and his people. Sa'd could immediately understand that Usaid had changed. To a question posed by Sa'd, Usaid said that two men were ready to comply with whatever orders they received. He then managed a certain situation that provided the two men with a chance to talk with Sa'd privately. The previous scene with Usaid recurred and Sa'd embraced Islam, and directly turned to his people swearing that he would never talk with them until they had believed in Allâh, and in His Messenger. Hardly did the evening of that day arrive when all the men and women of that sept of Arabians embraced Islam with the exception of one, Al-Usairim, who hung back until the Day of Uhud. On that day he embraced Islam and fought the polytheists but was eventually killed before observing any prostration in the way of prayer. The Prophet (Peace be upon him) commented saying: "He has done a little but his reward is great."

Mus'ab stayed in Madinah carrying out his mission diligently and successfully until all the houses of *Al-Ansar* (the future Helpers) had Muslims elements, men and women. One family only stood obdurate to the Islamic *Da'wah* (Call). They were under the influence of the poet Qais bin Al-Aslat, who managed to hold them at bay and screen off the Call of Islam from their ears until the year 5 A.H.

Shortly before the approach of the following pilgrimage season, i.e. the thirteenth year of Prophethood, Mus'ab bin 'Umair returned to Makkah carrying to the Prophet (Peace be upon him) glad tidings about the new fertile soil of Islam in Madinah, and its environment rich in the prospects of good, and the power and immunity that that city was bound to provide to the cause of Islam.

THE SECOND 'AQABAH PLEDGE

The next year, thirteenth of Prophethood, June 622 A.D., during the pilgrimage season, over seventy converts from Madinah came in the trail of their polytheist people to perform the rituals of pilgrimage in Makkah. The oft-repeated question amongst them was "Isn't it high time we protect Muhammad instead of leaving him forsaken, deserted and stumbling in the hillocks of Makkah?"

Shortly after arrival, they conducted clandestine contacts with the Prophet (Peace be upon him) and agreed to meet him secretly at night in mid *Tashreeq* Days (the 11th, 12th and 13th days of Dhul Hijja) in a hillock at Al-'Aqabah, the last year's meeting place.

One of the leaders of the *Ansâr* (Helpers), Ka'b bin Malik Al-Ansari (May Allah be pleased with him), gave an account of the historic meeting which changed the whole course of the struggle between Islam and paganism, he said:

We set out for pilgrimage and struck a rendezvous in mid *Tashreeq* Days. We were accompanied by a celebrity and a notable of ours called 'Abdullah bin 'Amr bin Haram, who was still a polytheist. We disclosed to him our intention of meeting Muhammad (Peace be upon him) and exhorted him to join our ranks and give up polytheism lest he should serve as wood for Hell in the Hereafter. He promptly embraced Islam and witnessed the serious meeting at Al-'Aqabah.

That very night we slept with our people in our camps. After a third of the night had elapsed, we began to leave stealthily and met in a hillock nearby. We were seventy three men and two women Nusaibah bint Ka'b from the Najjars and Asma' bint 'Amr from Bani Salamah. We waited for the Messenger of Allâh (Peace be upon him) until he came in the company of his uncle Al-'Abbas bin 'Abdul Muttalib who (though himself not a Muslim), adjured us not to draw his nephew away from the protection of his own kindred unless we were fully prepared to defend him even at the risk of our lives. He was the first to speak:

"O you people of the Khazraj — the Arabs used to call the *Ansâr* (Helpers) Khazraj, whether from Khazraj or Aws — you all know the position that Muhammad holds among us. We have protected him from our people as much as we could. He is honoured and respected among his people. He refuses to join any party except you. So if you think you can carry out what you promise while inviting him to your town, and if you can defend him against the enemies, then assume the burden that you have taken. But if you are going to surrender him and betray him after having taken him away with you, you had better leave him now because he is respected and well defended in his own place."

Ka'b replied: "We have heard your words, and now O Messenger of Allâh, it is for you to speak and take from us any pledge that you want regarding your Lord and yourself."

It was a definite stance showing full determination, courage and deep faith to shoulder the daunting responsibility and bear its serious consequences.

The Messenger of Allâh then preached the Faith, and the pledge was taken. Al-Imam Ahmad, on the authority of Jabir, gave the following details:

The *Ansâr* (Helpers) asked the Messenger of Allâh about the principles over which they would take a pledge. The Prophet answered:

1. To listen and obey in all sets of circumstances.
2. To spend in plenty as well as in scarcity.
3. To enjoin good and forbid evil.
4. In Allâh's service, you will fear the censure of none.
5. To defend me in case I seek your help, and debar me from anything you debar yourself, your spouses and children from. And if you observe those precepts, Paradise is in store for you.

In another version narrated by Ka'b, he said:

The Prophet (Peace be upon him) began to speak, recited some Qur'ânic verses, called people unto Allâh, exhorted them to enter the fold of Islam and concluded saying: "I give you my pledge that you debar me from whatever you debar your women and children from." Here Al-Bara' bin Ma'rur, caught him by hand, and said: "Oh yes, we swear by Allâh, Who sent you as a Prophet in Truth, that we will debar you from whatever we debar our women from. Have confidence in us, O Messenger of Allâh. By Allâh, we are genuine fighters and quite reliable in war, it is a trait passed down to us from our ancestors."

Then 'Abul Haitham At-Taihan interrupted and said: "O Prophet of Allâh! Between us and the Jews, there are agreements which we would then sever. If Allâh grants you power and victory, should we expect that you would not leave us, and join the ranks of your people (meaning Quraish)?" The Prophet (Peace be upon him) smiled and replied:

- "Nay, it would never be; your blood will be my blood. In life and death I will be with you and you with me. I will fight whom you fight and I will make peace with those with whom you make peace."

After the negotiations concerning the conditions of allegiance had ended, and all of the audience were unanimously agreed to ratify it, two men of the early generation of converts who had embraced Islam in the eleventh and twelfth years rose to their feet to apprise the others of the serious step they were about to take so that they could give their pledge fully aware of the whole affair and consequently be ready for the sacrifice they were expected to make. Al 'Abbas bin Ubada bin Nadlah, in this context, remarked: "O you people of Khazraj! Do you know the significance of the pact that you are entering into with this man? You are in fact avowing that you will fight against all and sundry. If you fear that your property will be at stake or the lives of your nobles will be endangered, then leave him now, because if you do this after the pledge, it will be degrading for you both in this world and the world to come. But if you think that you can carry out what you are called upon to do in spite of the loss of precious lives and property, then undertake this heavy responsibility, and I swear by Allâh, that herein lies the good of this world and that of the next."

They replied, "We have already considered the loss of property and the murder of our notables, yet we pay him allegiance. But what is our reward if we observe all the items of this pact?" The Prophet replied: "Paradise is in store for you." Then they asked him to stretch out his hand, and they all stretched out their hands and took the pledge. Only at that time did As'ad bin Zurarah come to realize the people's readiness for sacrifice in the cause of Allâh.

On the authority of Jabir, who said: "When we started to pay allegiance to the Prophet (Peace be upon him) , As'ad bin Zurarah stood up and gave the following short address: "Take it easy people of Yathrib! We have not covered that long distance except because we have had deep belief that he (Muhammad

(Peace be upon him)) is the Messenger of Allâh. We are already convinced that following him entails departure from the pagan Arabs even if it were at the risk of our life. Should you preserve in this course, holdfast to it, and your great reward is placed in the Hand of Allâh, but if you are caught in fear, I admonish you to give it up just now, and then you would be more excusable by Allâh."

With respect to the two women, the pledge was taken orally for the Prophet (Peace be upon him) had never shaken hands with a strange lady.

The Prophet (Peace be upon him) then asked the group to appoint twelve deputies to preach Islam to their people in Madinah, to shoulder the responsibility of implementing the articles of this pledge and to guide the respective men of their own tribes in matters relating to the propagation of Islam. The deputies elected were nine from Al-Khazraj: As'ad bin Zurarah bin 'Ads, Sa'd bin Ar-Rabi' bin 'Amr, 'Abdullah bin Rawahah bin Tha'labah, Rafi' bin Malik bin Al-'Ajlan, Al-Bara' bin Ma'rur bin Sakhr,

'Abdullah bin 'Amr bin Haram, 'Ubadah bin As-Samit bin Qais, Sa'd bin 'Ubadah bin Dulaim and Al-Mundhir bin 'Amr bin Khunais. Three others were from Al-Aws: Usaid bin Hudair bin Sammak, Sa'd bin Khaithamah bin Al-Harith and Rifa'a bin 'Abdul Mundhir bin Zubair. Once again, those twelvemen were sworn to act as surety over the affairs of their people just as the Christ's disciples did, and the Prophet would act as surety over his people, meaning all the Muslims.

Somehow or other, the news of these secret desert meetings with the Madinese leaked out. The Prophet immediately knew that it was a certain pudgy ugly devil, inhabited in Al-'Aqabah, who discovered their meeting, and he threatened to settle his account with him as soon as possible.

On hearing this, Al-'Abbas bin Nadlah said "By Allâh, Who has sent you in Truth, we are powerful enough to put the people of Mina (the Quraishites) to our swords tomorrow, if you desire." The Prophet (Peace be upon him) said "We have not been commanded to follow that course. Now, back to your camps." They went back to sleep till morning.

No sooner did Quraish hear of this treaty than a kind of trouble-provoking tumult began to mushroom in all directions. They realized quite fully that an allegiance of this sort is bound to produce far-reaching ramifications of direct impact on their lives and wealth. The following day, a large delegation comprising the leaders and arch-criminals of Makkah set out for the camp of the Madinese to protest severely against the treaty. They addressed the Madinese: "O people of Khazraj, it transpired to us that you have come here to conclude a treaty with this man (Muhammad) and evacuate him out of Makkah. By Allâh, we do really hold in abhorrence any sort of fight between you and us."

The Madinese polytheists having known nothing about the secretly taken pledge, began to swear by Allâh and answered in good faith that there was no truth in the report. 'Abdullah bin Ubai bin Salul, a Madinese polytheist, refuted their allegations denouncing them as null and void, claiming that his people would never initiate anything unless he gave them clear orders.

The Madinese Muslims, however, remained silent neither negating nor confirming. The Quraishite leaders seemed to be almost convinced by the arguments presented by the polytheists, and went back home frustrated. However, they did not fully acquiesce in the words they heard. They began to scrutinize the smallest details, and trace the minutest news till it was established beyond a shadow of doubt that the pact did take place, but that was after the Madinese pilgrims had left Makkah. In a fit of rage, they pursued the pilgrims but did not succeed in catching hold of anyone except Sa'd bin 'Ubadah. They subjected him to unspeakable tortures, but he was later rescued by Al-Mut'im bin 'Adi and Harith bin Harb bin Omaiya with whom he had trade relations.

That is the story of the Second 'Aqabah Pledge, later known as the Great 'Aqabah Pledge, effected in an atmosphere of love, allegiance and mutual support between Madinese believers and weak Makkan Muslims. This new spirit of affection, rapport and cooperation could never be attributable to a fleeing whim, on the contrary, it totally derived from an already deeply-established approach, viz. Belief in Allâh, His Messenger and His Book. It was a Belief so rooted in the selves that it managed to stand immune to all powers of injustice and aggression, and could be translated into miracles in the practical aspects of action and ideology pursuit. That sort of Belief was the real instrument for the Muslims to record in the annals of history unprecedented breakthroughs. We are also sure that the future will always remain wanting as regards those great achievements carried out by those great men.

THE VANGUAD OF MIGRATION (in the Cause of Allâh)

After the endorsement of the Second 'Aqabah Pledge and the establishment of a petite Muslim state in a vast desert surging with disbelief and ignorance — the most serious gain in terms of Islam —, the Prophet (Peace be upon him) gave his leave for the Muslims to migrate to Madinah, the nascent Muslim state.

Migration to Madinah, in terms of personal interests, was no more than material waste and sacrifice of wealth, all in return for personal safety only. Even here, the migrant could not expect full security; he was liable to be robbed or even killed either at the beginning or end of his departure. The future was foggy, pregnant with various unpredictable sorts of sorrows and crises.

Bearing all this in mind, the Muslims began to migrate, while the polytheists spared no effort in hindering and debarring them, knowing beforehand that such a move implied unimaginable threats and unthinkable destructive dangers to their whole society:

1. The first one to migrate was Abu Salamah, a year before the Great 'Aqabah Pledge. When he had made up his mind to leave Makkah, his in-laws, in a desperate attempt to raise obstacles, detained his wife and snatched his son and dislocated his hand. Umm Salamah, after the departure of her husband and the loss of her son spent a year by herself weeping and lamenting. A relative of hers eventually had pity on her and exhorted the others to release her son and let her join her husband. She then set out on a journey of 500 kilometres with no help whatsoever. At a spot called At-Tan'im, 'Uthman bin Talhah came across her and offered to give her a ride to Madinah. She, along with her son, joined Abu Salamah in the village of Quba', a suburb of Madinah.
2. Another instance of the atrocities of the polytheist Makkans, as regards migration, is Suhaib. This man expressed his wish to migrate and of course this was a source of indignation to the disbelievers. They began to insult him claiming that he had come into Makkah as a worthless tramp, but their town was gracious enough and thanks to them he managed to make a lot of money and become wealthy. They gave orders that he would not leave. Seeing this, he offered to give away all his wealth to them. They eventually agreed to release him on that condition. The Prophet heard this story and commented on it saying:

- "Suhaib is the winner, after all."

3. Then, there was the story of 'Umar bin Al-Khattab, 'Ayyash bin Abi Rabi'a and Hisham bin Al-'Asi, who agreed to meet at a certain place one morning in order to leave for Madinah; 'Umar and 'Ayyash came but Hisham was detained by the Makkans.

Shortly afterwards Abu Jahl, and his brother Al-Harith came to Madinah to see their third brother 'Ayyash. They cunningly tried to touch the most sensitive area in man, i.e. his relation with his mother.

They addressed him claiming that his mother had sworn she would never comb her hair, nor shade herself off the sun unless she had seen him. 'Ayyash took pity on his mother, but 'Umar was intelligent enough to understand that they wanted to entice 'Ayyash away from Islam so he cautioned him against their tricks, and added "your mother would comb her hair if lice pestered her, and would shade herself off if the sun of Makkah got too hot for her." These words notwithstanding, 'Ayyash was determined to go and see his mother, so 'Umar gave him his manageable docile camel advising him to stick to its back because it would provide rescue for him if he perceived anything suspicious on their part. The party of three then set forth towards Makkah. As soon as they covered part of the distance, Abu Jahl complained about his camel and requested 'Ayyash to allow him to ride behind him on his camel. When they knelt down to the level of the ground, the two polytheists fell upon 'Ayyash and tied him. They rode on into Makkah shouting at people to follow their example with respect to 'fools'

These are just three self-explanatory models of the Makkans' reaction towards anyone intending to migrate. Nevertheless, the believers still managed to escape in successive groups and so rapidly that within two months of the Second 'Aqabah Pledge, entire quarters of Makkah were deserted. Almost all the followers of Muhammad had migrated to their new abode, except Abu Bakr, 'Ali, the Prophet (Peace be upon him) himself, and those helpless noble souls who had been detained in confinement or were unable to escape. The Prophet (Peace be upon him), together with Abu Bakr and 'Ali, had made all the necessary preparations for migration but was waiting for leave from his Lord.

It is noteworthy that most of the Mwho had migrated to Abyssinia (Ethiopia), came back to Madinah to join the rest of the Muslims there.

The situation was no doubt critical in Makkah but Muhammad (Peace be upon him) was not at all perturbed. Abu Bakr was, however, urging the Prophet to depart from that town. He was also eagerly waiting for an opportunity to accompany Muhammad (Peace be upon him) on this eventful journey. But the Prophet told him that the time had not yet come; the Lord had not given him the command to migrate. In anticipation of the Command of Allâh, Abu Bakr had made preparations for the journey. He had purchased two swift camels and had fed them properly for four months so that they could successively stand the ordeals of the long desert journey.

IN AN-NADWAH (COUNCIL) HOUSE THE PARLIAMENT OF QURAISH

The polytheists were paralysed by the carefully planned and speedy movement of Muhammad's followers towards their new abode in Madinah. They were caught in unprecedented anxiety and got deeply worried over their whole pagan and economic entity. They already experienced Muhammad (Peace be upon him) as an influential leader; and his followers as determined, decent and always ready to sacrifice all they had for the sake of the Messenger of Allâh (Peace be upon him). Al-Aws and Al-Khazraj tribes, the would-be-hosts of the Makkan Muslims, were also known in Arabia for their might and power in war, and judicious and sensible approach in peace. They were also averse to rancour and prejudice for they themselves had had bitter days of inter-tribal warfare. Madinah, itself, the prospective headquarters of the ever-growing Islamic Call, enjoyed the most serious strategic position. It commanded the commercial routes leading to Makkah whose people used to deal in about a quarter of a million gold dinar-worth commodities every year. Security of the caravan routes was crucial for the perpetuity of prosperous economic life. All those factors borne in mind, the polytheists felt they were in the grip of a serious threat. They, therefore, began to seek the most effective method that could avert this imminent danger. They convened a meeting on Thursday, 26th Safar, the year fourteen of Prophethood / 12th September 622 A.D., i.e. two and a half months after the Great 'Aqabah Pledge. On that day, "the Parliament of Makkah" held the most serious meeting ever, with one item on the agenda: How to take effective measures with a view to stopping that tidal wave. Delegates representing all the Quraishite tribes attended the meeting, the most significant of whom were:

1. Abu Jahl bin Hisham, from Bani Makhzum;
2. Jubair bin Mut'im, Tuaima bin 'Adi, and Al-Harith bin 'Amir representing Bani Naufal bin 'Abd Munaf;
3. Rabi'a's two sons Shaibah and 'Utbah besides Abu Sufyan bin Harb from Bani 'Abd Shams bin 'Abd Munaf;
4. An-Nadr bin Al-Harith (who had besmeared the Prophet (Peace be upon him) with animal entrails) to speak for Bani 'Abd Ad-Dar;
5. Abul Bukhtary bin Hisham, Zama'a bin Al-Aswad and Hakeem bin Hizam to represent Bani Asad bin 'Abd Al-'Uzza;
6. Al-Hajjaj's two sons Nabih and Munbih from Bani Sahm;
7. Omaiyah bin Khalaf from Bani Jumah.

On their way to An-Nadwah House, *Iblis* (Satan) in the guise of a venerable elderly man standing at the door interrupted their talk and introduced himself as a man from Najd curious enough to attend the meeting, listen to the debate and wish them success to reach a sound opinion. He was readily admitted in.

There was a lengthy debate and several proposals were put forward. Expulsion from Makkah was proposed and debated in turn but finally turned down on grounds that his sweet and heart-touching words could entice the other Arabs to attack them in their own city. Imprisonment for life was also debated but also refused for fear that his followers might increase in number, overpower them and release him by force. At this point, the arch-criminal of Makkah, Abu Jahl bin Hisham suggested that they assassinate him. But assassination by one man would have exposed him and his family to the vengeance of blood. The difficulty was at last solved by Abu Jahl himself, who suggested that a band of young men, one from each tribe, should strike Muhammad simultaneously with their swords so that the blood-money would be spread over them all and therefore could not be exacted, and his people would seek a mind-based recourse for settlement. The sinful proposal was unanimously accepted, and the representatives broke up the meeting and went back home with full determination for immediate implementation.

MIGRATION OF THE PROPHET (Peace be upon him) :

When the iniquitous decision had been made, Gabriel was sent down to Muhammad (Peace be upon him) to reveal to him Quraish's plot and give him his Lord's Permission to leave Makkah. He fixed to him the time of migration and asked him not to sleep that night in his usual bed. At noon, the Prophet (Peace be upon him) went to see his Companion Abu Bakr and arranged with him everything for the intended migration. Abu Bakr was surprised to see the Prophet (Peace be upon him) masked coming to visit him at that unusual time, but he soon learned that Allâh's Command had arrived, and he proposed that they should migrate together, to which the Prophet (Peace be upon him) gave his consent.

To make the necessary preparations for the implementation of their devilish plan, the chiefs of Makkah had chosen eleven men: Abu Jahl, Hakam bin Abil Al-'As, 'Uqbah bin Abi Mu'ait, An-Nadr bin Harith, Omaiyah bin Khalaf, Zama'a bin Al-Aswad, Tu'aima bin 'Adi, Abu Lahab, Ubai bin Khalaf, Nabih bin Al-Hajjaj and his brother Munbih bin Al-Hajjaj. All were on the alert. As night advanced, they posted assassins around the Prophet's house. Thus they kept vigil all night long, waiting to kill him the moment he left his house early in the morning, peeping now and then through a hole in the door to make sure that he was still lying in his bed. Abu Jahl, the great enemy of Islam, used to walk about haughtily and arrogantly jeering at Muhammad's words, saying to the people around him: "Muhammad claims that if you follow him, he will appoint you rulers over the Arabs and non-Arabs and in the Hereafter your reward will be Gardens similar to those in Jordan, otherwise, he will slaughter you and after death you will be burnt in fire." He was too confident of the success of his devilish plan. Allâh, the All-Mighty, however, in Whose Hands lie the sovereignty of the heavens and earth, does what He desires; He renders succour and can never be overpowered. He did exactly what He later said to His Prophet:

- "And (remember) when the disbelievers plotted against you [O Muhammad (Peace be upon him)] to imprison you, or to kill you, or to get you out (from your home, i.e. Makkah); they were plotting and Allâh too was planning, and Allâh is the Best of the planners." [8:30]

At that critical time the plans of Quraish utterly failed despite the tight siege they laid to the Prophet's house, the Prophet (Peace be upon him) and 'Ali were inside the house. The Prophet (Peace be upon him) told 'Ali to sleep in his bed and cover himself with his green mantle and assured him full security under Allâh's protection and told him that no harm would come to him. The Prophet (Peace be upon him) then came out of the room and cast a handful of dust at the assassins and managed to work his way through them reciting verses of the Noble Qur'ân:

- "And We have put a barrier before them, and a barrier behind them, and We have covered them up, so that they cannot see." [36:9]

He proceeded direct to the house of Abu Bakr who, immediately accompanied him and both set out southwards, clambered up the lofty peak of Mountain Thawr, and decided to take refuge in a cave.

The assassins who laid siege to the house were waiting for the zero hour when someone came and informed them that the Prophet (Peace be upon him) had already left. They rushed in and to their utter surprise, found that the person lying in the Prophet's bed was 'Ali not Muhammad (Peace be upon him). This created a stir in the whole town. The Prophet (Peace be upon him) had thus left his house on Safar 27th, the fourteenth year of Prophethood, i.e. 12/13 September 622 A.D.

Knowing already that Quraish would mobilize all its potentials to find him, he played a clever trick on them and instead of taking the road to Madinah in north side of Makkah as the polythiest would expect, he walked along a road least expected lying south of Makkah and leading to Yemen. He walked for 5 miles until he reached a rough rocky mountain called Thawr. There his shoes were worn out, some said he used to walk tiptoe in order not to leave a trail behind him. Abu Bakr (May Allah be pleased with him) carried him up the mountain to a cave called after the name of the mountain, Cave Thawr. Abu Bakr first entered to explore the cave and be sure that it was safe, closed all holes with pieces torn off from his clothes, cleaned it and then asked the Prophet (Peace be upon him) to step in. The Prophet

(Peace be upon him) went in and immediately laid his head in Abu Bakr's lap and fell asleep. Suddenly Abu Bakr's foot was stung by a poisonous insect. It hurt so much that his tears fell on the Prophet's face. The Prophet (Peace be upon him) immediately applied his saliva on Abu Bakr's foot and the pain went off on the spot. They confined themselves to this cave for three nights, Friday, Saturday and Sunday. 'Abdullah, the son of Abu Bakr would go to see them after dusk, stay the night there, apprise them of the latest situation in Makkah, and then leave in the early morning to mix with the Makkans as usual and not to draw the least attention to his clandestine activities. 'Amir bin Fuhairah, while in the company of other shepherds of Makkah tending his master Abu Bakr's flock, used to stole away unobserved every evening with a few goats to the cave and furnished its inmates with a plentiful supply of milk.

Quraish, on the other hand, were quite baffled and exasperated when the news of the escape of the two companions was confirmed. They brought 'Ali to Al-Ka'bah, beat him brutally and confined him there for an hour attempting desperately to make him divulge the secret of the disappearance of the two 'fugitives', but to no avail. They then went to see Asma', Abu Bakr's daughter, but here also their attempts went in vain. While at her door Abu Jahl slapped the girl so severely that her earring broke up.

The notables of Makkah convened an emergency session to determine the future course of action and explore all areas that could help arrest the two men. They decided to block all avenues leading out of Makkah and imposed heavy armed surveillance over all potential exits. A price of 100 camels was set upon the head of each one. Horsemen, infantry and tracers of tracks scoured the country. Once they even reached the mouth of the cave where the Prophet (Peace be upon him) and Abu Bakr were hiding. When he saw the enemy at a very close distance, Abu Bakr whispered to the Prophet (Peace be upon him): "What, if they were to look through the crevice and detect us?" The Prophet (Peace be upon him) in his God-inspired calm replied:

- "Silence Abu Bakr! What do you think of those two with whom the Third is Allâh."

It was really a Divine miracle, the chasers were only a few steps from the cave.

For three days Muhammad (Peace be upon him) and Abu Bakr lived in the cave and Quraish continued their frantic efforts to get hold of them.

Someone called 'Abdullah bin Uraiqit, who had as yet not embraced Islam, but was trusted by Abu Bakr, and had been hired by him as a guide, reached the cave after three nights according to a plan bringing with him Abu Bakr's two camels. His report satisfied the noble 'fugitives' that the search had slackened. The opportunity to depart was come. Here Abu Bakr offered the Prophet (Peace be upon him) the swift animal to ride on. The latter agreed provided that he would pay its price. They took with them the food provisions that Asma', daughter of Abu Bakr, brought and tied in a bundle of her waistband, after tearing it into two parts, hence the appellation attached to her: "Asma' of the two waistbands." The Prophet (Peace be upon him), Abu Bakr and 'Amir bin Fuhairah departed, and their guide 'Abdullah bin Uraiqit led them on hardly ever trodden ways along the coastal route. That was in Rabi' Al-Awwal, 1st year A.H., i.e. September 622 A.D. The little caravan travelled through many villages on their way to Quba'. In this context, it is relevant to introduce some interesting incidents that featured their wearying journey:

1. One day they could find no shelter from the scorching heat so Abu Bakr (May Allah be pleased with him) cast a glance and found a little shade beside a rock. He cleaned the ground, spread his mantle for the Prophet (Peace be upon him) to lie on and himself went off in search of food. He came across a shepherd, a bedouin boy, who was also seeking a shelter. Abu Bakr asked him for some milk and took it to the Prophet (Peace be upon him), cooled it with some water and waited till the Prophet (Peace be upon him) woke up and quenched his thirst.
2. Whoever asked Abu Bakr (May Allah be pleased with him) about the identity of his honourable companion, he would reply that he was a man who guided him on his way. The questioner would think that Muhammad (Peace be upon him) was a guide, in terms of roads, whereas Abu Bakr

used to mean guide to the way of righteousness.
3. Quraish, as we have already mentioned, had declared that whoever would seize Muhammad (Peace be upon him) would receive a hundred camels as reward. This had spurred many persons to try their luck. Among those who were on the lookout for the Prophet (Peace be upon him) and his companion in order to win the reward was Suraqah, the son of Malik. He, on receiving information that a party of four, had been spotted on a certain route, decided to pursue it secretly so that he alone should be the winner of the reward. He mounted a swift horse and went in hot pursuit of them. On the way the horse stumbled and he fell on the ground. On drawing a lot so as to divine whether he should continue the chase or not, as the Arabs used to do in such circumstances, he found the omens unpropitious. But the lust for material wealth blinded him altogether and he resumed the chase. Once more he met with the same fate but paid no heed to it. Again he jumped onto the saddle and galloped at a break-neck speed till he came quite close to the Prophet (Peace be upon him). Abu Bakr's heart agitated and he kept looking back while the Prophet (Peace be upon him) remained steadfast and continued reciting verses of the Qur'ân.

   - The repeated stumbling of Suraqah's horse and his falling off awakened him to the situation, and he realized that it was a constant warning of Allâh for his evil design which he contemplated against the Prophet (Peace be upon him). He approached the travelling group with a penitent heart and begged of the Prophet (Peace be upon him) forgiveness in all humility. He addressed the Prophet (Peace be upon him) and his companion, saying: "Your people (the Quraishites) have promised a generous reward to anyone who captures you." He added that he offered them provision but they declined his offer. They only asked him to screen off their departure and blind the polytheists to their hiding place. Then the Prophet (Peace be upon him) forgave him and confirmed it with a token written by 'Amir bin Fuhairah on a piece of parchment. Suraqah hurried back to Makkah and tried to foil the attempts of those who were in pursuit of Muhammad (Peace be upon him) and his noble companions. The sworn enemy was converted into an honest believer.

   In a version by Abu Bakr (May Allah be pleased with him), he said: "We emigrated while the Makkans were in pursuit of us. None caught up with us except Suraqah bin Malik bin Ju'sham on a horse. I said: 'O Messenger of Allâh, this one has caught up with us.' The Prophet (Peace be upon him) replied:

     - 'Don't be cast down, verily, Allâh is with us.'"

4. The party continued its journey until it reached to solitary tents belonging to a woman called Umm Ma'bad Al-Khuza'iyah. She was a gracious lady who sat at her tent-door with a mat spread out for any chance traveller that might pass by the way. Fatigued and thirsty, the Prophet (Peace be upon him) and his companions wanted to refresh themselves with food and some milk. The lady told them that the flock was out in the pasture and the goat standing nearby was almost dry. It was a rainless year. The Prophet (Peace be upon him), with her permission, touched its udders, reciting over them the Name of Allâh, and to their great joy, there flowed plenty of milk out of them. The Prophet (Peace be upon him) first offered that to the lady of the house, and he shared what was left with the members of the party. Before he left, he milked the goat, filled the container and gave it to Umm Ma'bad. Later on, her husband arrived with slender goats hardly having any milk in their udders. He was astonished to see milk in the house. His wife told him that a blessed man passed by the way, and then she gavedetails about his physical appearance and manner of talk. Here Abu Ma'bad realized on the spot that the man was the one whom Quraish were searching for and asked her to give full description of him. She gave a wonderful account of his physique and manners, to which we will go in detail later in the process of talking about his attributes and merits.

   - Abu Ma'bad, after listening to his wife's account, expressed a sincere wish to accompany the Prophet (Peace be upon him) whenever that was possible, and reiterated his admiration in verses of poetry that echoed all over Makkah to such an extent that the people therein thought it was a jinn inculcating words in their ears. Asma', daughter of Abu Bakr, on hearing those lines, got to know that the two companions were heading for Madinah . The short poem opened with thanks giving to Allâh having given them (the Ma'bads) the chance to host the Prophet (Peace be upon him) for a while. It then gave an account of the bliss that would settle in the heart of the Prophet's companion whosoever he was; it closed with an invitation to all mankind to come and see by themselves Umm Ma'bad, her goat and the container of milk that would all testify to the truthfulness of the Prophet (Peace be upon him).

5. On his way to Madinah, the Prophet (Peace be upon him) met Abu Buraidah, one of those driven by their lust for the reward of Quraish. No sooner did he face the Prophet (Peace be upon him) and talk with him, than he embraced Islam along with seventy of his men. He took off his turban, tied it round his lance and took it as a banner bearing witness that the angel of security and peace had come to imbue the whole world with justice and fairness.
6. The two Emigrants resumed their journey. It was during this time that they met Az-Zubair at the head of a caravan returning from Syria. There was warm greeting and Az-Zubair presented to them two white garments which they thankfully accepted.

On Monday, 8th Rabi' Al-Awwal, the fourteenth year of Prophethood, i.e. September 23rd. 622, the Messenger of Allâh arrived at Quba'.

As soon as the news of Muhammad's arrival began to spread, crowds came flocking out of Madinah. They would come every morning and wait eagerly for his appearance until forced by the unbearable heat of the midday sun to return. One day they had gone as usual, and after a long wait and watch they retired to the city when a Jew, catching a glimpse of three travellers clad in white winding their way to Madinah, shouted from the top of a hillock: "O you people of Arabia! Your grandfather has come! He, whom you have been eagerly waiting for, has come!" The Muslims immediately rushed holding their weapons, (to defend him). The joyful news soon spread through the city and people marched forward to greet their noble guest.

Ibn Al-Qayyim said: "The shouts of '*Allâhu Akbar*' (Allâh is Great) resounded in Banu 'Amr bin 'Auf. Muhammad's (Peace be upon him) elation correspondingly increased, but with rare sense of timing and propriety, called a halt. Serenity enveloped him and the 'evelation was sent down:

- "... then verily, Allâh is his Maula (Lord, Master or Protector), and Gabriel, and the righteous among the believers, - and furthermore, the angels - are his helpers." [66:4]

'Urwah bin Az-Zubair said: They received the Messenger of Allâh (Peace be upon him), and went with them to the right. There Banu 'Amr bin 'Awf hosted him. That was on Monday, Rabi' Al-Awwal. He sat down silent, and *Al-Ansar* (the Helpers), who had not had the opportunity to see him before, came in to greet him: It is said that the sun became too hot so Abu Bakr stood up to shade him from the hot sun rays. It was really an unprecedented day in Madinah. The Jews could perceive concretely the veracity of their Prophet Habquq, who said: 'God has come from At-Taiman, and the Qudus one from Faran Mount.'

Muhammad (Peace be upon him) stayed in Quba' with Kulthum bin Al-Hadm, a hospitable chief of the tribe of 'Amr bin 'Awf. Here he spent four days: Monday, Tuesday, Wednesday and Thursday. It was during this period that the foundation of Quba' Mosque was laid on the basis of pure piety. 'Ali hung back in Makkah for three days to return the trusts, on behalf of the Prophet (Peace be upon him), to their respective owners. After that he started his emigration journey to catch up with him at Quba'.

On Friday morning, the Prophet (Peace be upon him), sent for Bani An-Najjar, his maternal uncles, to come and escort him and Abu Bakr to Madinah. He rode towards the new headquarters amidst the cordial greetings of his Madinese followers who had lined his path. He halted at a place in the vale of Banu Salim and there he performed his Friday prayer with a hundred others. Meanwhile the tribes and families of Madinah, the new name for Yathrib and a short form of 'The Messenger's *Madinah* (City)', came streaming forth, and vied with one another in inviting the noble visitor to their homes. The girls of the Madinese used to chant beautiful verses of welcome rich in all meanings of obedience and dutifulness to the new Messenger.

Though not wealthy, every *Ansar* (Helper) was wholeheartedly eager and anxious to receive the Messenger in his house. It was indeed a triumphal procession. Around the camel of Muhammad (Peace be upon him) and his immediate followers, rode the chiefs of the city in their best raiment and in glittering armour, everyone saying: "Alight here O Messenger of Allâh, abide by us." Muhammad (Peace be upon him) used to answer everyone courteously and kindly: "This camel is commanded by Allâh, wherever it stops, that will be my abode."

The camel moved onward with slackened rein, reached the site of the Prophetic Mosque and knelt down. He did not dismount until it rose up again, went on forward, turned back and then returned to kneel down in the very former spot. Here, he alighted in a quarter inhabited by Banu Najjar, a tribe related to the Prophet (Peace be upon him) from the maternal side. In fact, it was his wish to honour his maternal uncles and live among them. The fortunate host, Abu Ayyub Al-Ansari, stepped forward with unbounded joy for the Divine blessing appropriated to him, welcomed the Noble Guest and solicited him to enter his house.

A few days later, there arrived the Prophet's spouse Sawdah, his two daughters Fatimah and Umm Kulthum, Usama bin Zaid, Umm Aiman, 'Abdullah — son of Abu Bakr with Abu Bakr's house-hold including 'Aishah (May Allah be pleased with her). Zainab was not able to emigrate and stayed with her husband Abi Al-'As till Badr Battle.

'Aishah (May Allah be pleased with her) said: "When the Messenger of Allâh (Peace be upon him) arrived in Madinah , both Abu Bakr and Bilal fell ill. I used to attend to their needs. When the fever took firm grip of Abu Bakr he used to recite verses of poetry that smacked of near death; Bilal, when the fit of fever alleviated, would also recite verses of poetry that pointed to clear homesickness." 'Aishah (May Allah be pleased with her) added:

"I briefed the Prophet (Peace be upon him) on their grave situation, and he replied: O Allâh, we entreat You to establish in our hearts a strong love for Madinah equal to that we used to have for Makkah, or even more. O Allâh, bless and increase the wealth of Madinah and we beseech You to transmute its rotten mud into wholesome edible fat."

LIFE IN MADINAH:

The Madinese era could be divided into three phases:

1. The first phase was characterized by too much trouble and discord, and too many obstacles from within coupled by a hostile wave from without aiming at total extermination of the rising faith. It ended with Al-Hudaibiyah Peace Treaty in Dhul Qa'da 6 A.H.
2. The second phase featured a truce with the pagan leadership and ended in the conquest of Makkah in Ramadan 8 A.H. It also witnessed the Prophet (Peace be upon him) inviting kings beyond Arabia to enter the fold of Islam.
3. In the third phase, people came to embrace Islam in hosts. Tribes and other folks arrived in Madinah to pay homage to the Prophet (Peace be upon him). It ended at the death of the Prophet (Peace be upon him) in Rabi' Al-Awwal 11 A.H.

THE FIRST PHASE THE STATUS QUO IN MADINAH AT THE TIME OF EMIGRATION

Emigration to Madinah could never be attributable to attempts to escape from jeers and oppression only, but it also constituted a sort of cooperation with the aim of erecting the pillars of a new society in a secure place. Hence it was incumbent upon every capable Muslim to contribute to building this new homeland, immunizing it and holding up its prop. As a leader and spiritual guide, there was no doubt the Noble Messenger (Peace be upon him), in whose hands exclusively all affairs would be resolved.

In Madinah, the Prophet (Peace be upon him) had to deal with three distinctively different categories of people with different respective problems:

1. His Companions, the noble and Allâh fearing elite (May Allah be pleased with them).
2. Polytheists still detached from the Islam and were purely Madinese tribes.
3. The Jews.

   1. As for his Companions, the conditions of life in Madinah were totally different from those they experienced in Makkah. There, in Makkah, they used to strive for one corporate target, but physically, they were scattered, overpowered and forsaken. They were helpless in terms of pursuing their new course of orientation. Their means, socially and materially, fell short of establishing a new Muslim community. In parallel lines, the Makkan Chapters of the Noble Qur'ân were confined to delineating the Islamic precepts, enacting legislations pertaining to the believers individually and enjoining good and piety and forbidding evils and vices.

   In Madinah , things were otherwise; here all the affairs of their life rested in their hands. Now, they were at ease and could quite confidently handle the challenges of civilization, construction, means of living, economics, politics, government administration, war and peace, codification of the questions of the allowed and prohibited, worship, ethics and all the relevant issues. In a nutshell, they were in Madinah at full liberty to erect the pillars of a new Muslim community not only utterly different from that pre-Islamic code of life, but also distinctive in its features in the world at large. It was a society that could stand for the Islamic Call for whose sake the Muslims had been put to unspeakable tortures for 10 years. No doubt, the construction of a society that runs in line with this type of ethics cannot be accomplished overnight, within a month or a year. It requires a long time to build during which legislation and legalization will run gradually in a complementary process with mind cultivation, training and education. Allâh, the All-Knowing, of course undertook legislation and His Prophet Muhammad (Peace be upon him), implementation and orientation:

   o "He it is Who sent among the unlettered ones a Messenger [Muhammad (Peace be upon him) from among themselves, reciting to them His Verses, purifying them (from the filth of disbelief and polytheism), and teaching them the Book (this Qur'ân, Islamic laws and Islamic Jurisprudence) and Al-Hikmah [As-Sunna: legal ways, orders, acts of worship, etc. of the Prophet Muhammad (Peace be upon him)]." [62:2]

   The Prophet's Companion (May Allah be pleased with), rushed enthusiastically to assimilate these Qur'ânic rules and fill their hearts joyfully with them:

   o "And when His Verses (this Qur'ân) are recited unto them, they (i.e. the Verses) increase their Faith." [8:2]

   With respect to the Muslims, this task constituted the greatest challenge for the Messenger of Allâh (Peace be upon him). In fact, this very purpose lay at the heart of the Islamic Call and the Muhammadan mission; it was never an incidental issue though there were the matters that required urgent addressing.

The Muslims in Madinah consisted virtually of two parties: The first one already settled down in their abode, land and wealth, fully at ease, but seeds of discord amongst them were deeply seated and chronic enmity continually evoked; they were *Al-Ansar* (the Helpers). The second party were *Al-Muhajirun* (the Emigrants), homeless, jobless and penniless. Their number was not small, on the contrary, it was increasing day by day after the Prophet (Peace be upon him) had given them the green light to leave for Madinah whose economic structure, originally not that prosperous one, began to show signs of imbalance aggravated by the economic boycott that the anti-Islamic groups imposed and consequently imports diminished and living conditions worsened.

2. The purely Madinese polytheists constituted the second sector with whom the Prophet (Peace be upon him) had to deal. Those people had no control at all over the Muslim. Some of them nursed no grudge against the Muslims, but were rather skeptical of their ancestors' religious practices, and developed tentative inclination towards Islam and before long they embraced the new faith and were truly devoted to Allâh. However, some others harboured evil intentions against the Prophet (Peace be upon him) and his followers but were too cowardly to resist them publicly, they were rather, under those Islamically favourable conditions, obliged to fake amicability and friendliness. 'Abdullah bin Ubai, who had almost been given presidency over Al-Khazraj and Al-Aws tribes in the wake of Bu'ath War between the two tribes, came at the head of that group of hypocrites. The Prophet's advent and the vigorous rise of the new spirit of Islam foiled that orientation and the idea soon went into oblivion. He, seeing another one, Muhammad (Peace be upon him), coming to deprive him and his agents of the prospective temporal privileges, could not be pleased, and for overriding reasons he showed pretension to Islam but with horrible disbelief deeply-rooted in his heart. He also used to exploit some events and weak-hearted new converts in scheming malevolently against the true believers.

3. The Jews (the Hebrews), who had migrated to Al-Hijaz from Syria following the Byzantine and Assyrian persecution campaigns, were the third category existent on the demographic scene in Madinah. In their new abode they assumed the Arabian stamp in dress, language and manner of life and there were instances of intermarriage with the local Arabs, however they retained their ethnic particularism and detached themselves from amalgamation with the immediate environment. They even used to pride in their Jewish-Israeli origin, and spurn the Arabs around designating them as illiterate meaning brutal, naïve and backward. They desired the wealth of their neighbours to be made lawful to them and they could thus appropriate it the way they liked.

- "... because they say: "There is no blame on us to betray and take the properties of the illiterates (Arabs)" [3:75]

Religiously, they showed no zeal; their most obvious religious commodity was fortunetelling, witchcraft and the secret arts (blowing on knots), for which they used to attach to themselves advantages of science and spiritual precedence.

They excelled at the arts of earning money and trading. They in fact monopolized trading in cereals, dates, wine, clothes, export and import. For the services they offered to the Arabs, the latter paid heavily. Usury was a common practice amongst them, lending the Arab notables great sums to be squandered on mercenary poets, and in vanity avenues, and in return seizing their fertile land given as surety.

They were very good at corrupting and scheming. They used to sow seeds of discord between adjacent tribes and entice each one to hatch plots against the other with the natural corollary of continual exhaustive bloody fighting. Whenever they felt that fire of hatred was about to subside, they would nourish it with new means of perpetuity so that they could always have the upper hand, and at the same time gain heavy interest rates on loans spent on inter-tribal warfare.

Three famous tribes of Jews constituted the demographic presence in Yathrib (now Madinah): Banu Qainuqua`, allies of Al-Khazraj tribe, Banu An-Nadir and Banu Quraizah who allied Al-Aws and inhabited the suburbs of Madinah.

Naturally they held the new changes with abhorrence and were terribly hateful to them, simply because the Messenger of Allâh was of a different race, and this point was in itself too repugnant for them to reconcile with. Second, Islam came to brabout a spirit of rapport, to terminate the state of enmity and hatred, and to establish a social regime based on denunciation of the prohibited and promotion of the allowed. Adherence to these canons of life implied paving the way for an Arab unity that could work to the prejudice of the Jews and their interests at both the social and economic levels; the Arab tribes would then try to restore their wealth and land misappropriated by the Jews through usurious practices.

The Jews of course deeply considered all these things ever since they had known that the Islamic Call would try to settle in Yathrib, and it was no surprise to discover that they harboured the most enmity and hatred to Islam and the Messenger (Peace be upon him) even though they did not have the courage to uncover their feelings in the beginning.

The following incident could attest clearly to that abominable antipathy that the Jews harboured towards the new political and religious changes that came to stamp the life of Madinah. Ibn Ishaq, on the authority of the Mother of believers Safiyah (May Allah be pleased her) narrated: Safiyah, daughter of Huyayi bin Akhtab said: I was the closest child to my father and my uncle Abi Yasir's heart. Whenever they saw me with a child of theirs, they should pamper me so tenderly to the exclusion of anyone else. However, with the advent of the Messenger of Allâh (Peace be upon him) and setting in Quba' with Bani 'Amr bin 'Awf, my father, Huyayi bin Akhtab and my uncle Abu Yasir bin Akhtab went to see him and did not return until sunset when they came back walking lazily and fully dejected. I, as usually, hurried to meet them smiling, but they would not turn to me for the grief that caught them. I heard my uncle Abu Yasir say to Ubai and Huyayi: "Is it really he [i.e. Muhammad (Peace be upon him)]?" The former said: "It is he, I swear by Allâh!" "Did you really recognize him?" they asked. He answered: "Yes, and my heart is burning with enmity towards him"

An interesting story that took place on the first day, the Prophet (Peace be upon him) stepped in Madinah, could be quoted to illustrate the mental disturbance and deep anxiety that beset the Jews. 'Abdullah bin Salam, the most learned rabbi among the Jews came to see the Prophet (Peace be upon him) when he arrived, and asked him certain questions to ascertain his real Prophethood. No sooner did he hear the Prophet's answers than he embraced Islam, but added that if his people knew of his Islamization they would advance false arguments against me. The Prophet (Peace be upon him) sent for some Jews and asked them about 'Abdullah bin Salam, they testified to his scholarly aptitude and virtuous standing. Here it was divulged to them that he had embraced Islam and on the spot, they imparted categorically opposite testimonies and described him as the most evil of all evils. In another narration 'Abdullah bin Salam said, "O Jews! Be Allâh fearing. By Allâh, the only One, you know that he is the Messenger of Allâh sent to people with the Truth." They replied, "You are lying." ... That was the Prophet's first experience with the Jews.

That was the demo-political picture within Madinah. Five hundred kilometres away in Makkah, there still lay another source of detrimental threat, the archenemy of Islam, Quraish. For ten years, while at the mercy of Quraish, the Muslims were subjected to all sorts of terrorism, boycott, harassment and starvation coupled by a large scale painstaking psychological war and aggressive organized propaganda. When they had emigrated to Madinah, their land, wealth and property were seized, wives detained and the socially humble in rank brutally tortured. Quraish also schemed and made attempts on the life of the first figure of the Call, Muhammad (Peace be upon him) . Due to their acknowledged temporal leadership and religious supremacy among the pagan Arabs, given the custodianship of the Sacred Sanctuary, the Quraishites spared no effort in enticing the Arabians against Madinah and boycotting the Madinese socially and economically. To quote Muhammad Al-Ghazali: "A state of war virtually existed between the Makkan tyrants and the Muslims in their abode. It is foolish to blame the Muslims for the horrible consequences that were bound to ensue in the light of that long-standing feud."

The Muslims in Madinah were completely eligible then to confiscate the wealth of those tyrants, mete out for them exemplary punishment and bring twofold retaliation on them in order to deter them from committing any folly against the Muslims and their sanctities.

That was a resume of the major problems that the Prophet Muhammad (Peace be upon him) had to face, and the complicated issues he was supposed to resolve.

In full acknowledgment, we could safely say that he quite honestly shouldered the responsibilities of Messengership, and cleverly discharged the liabilities of both temporal and religious leadership in Madinah. He accorded to everyone his due portion whether of mercy or punishment, with the former usually seasoning the latter in the overall process of establishing Islam on firm grounds among its faithful adherents.

A NEW SOCIETY BEING BUILT

We have already mentioned that the Messenger of Allâh (Peace be upon him) arrived in Madinah on Friday, 12th Rabi` Al-Awwal 1 A.H., i.e. September 27th. 622 A.D. and took the downstairs of Abi Ayyub's house as a temporary residence.

The first task to which the Prophet (Peace be upon him) attended on his arrival in Madinah was the construction of a Mosque, in the very site where his camel knelt down. The land, which belonged to two orphans, was purchased. The Prophet (Peace be upon him) himself contributed to building the Mosque by carrying adobe bricks and stones while reciting verses:

- "O Allâh! no bliss is there but that of the Hereafter, I beseech you to forgive the Emigrants and Helpers."

The ground was cleared, of weeds and shrubs, palm trees and rubbish, the graves of the polytheists dug up and then levelled and the trees planted around. The *Qiblah* (the direction in which the Muslims turn their faces in prayer) was constructed to face Jerusalem; two beams were also erected to hold the ceiling up. It was square in form, each side measuring approximately 100 yards, facing towards the north and having three gates on each of the remaining sides. Nearby, rooms reserved for the Prophet's household were built of stones and adobe bricks with ceilings of palm leaves. To the north of the Mosque a place was reserved for the Muslims who had neither family nor home. The *Adhân* (summoning the Muslims to the Mosque by the Call for prayer) was initiated at this early stage of post-migration era. The Mosque was not merely a locus to perform prayers, but rather an Islamic league where the Muslim's were instructed in Islam and its doctrines. It served as an assembly place where the conflicting pre-Islamic trends used to come to terms; it was the headquarter wherein all the affairs of the Muslims were administered, and consultative and executive councils held.

The Mosque being thus constructed, the Prophet (Peace be upon him) next turned his attention to cementing the ties of mutual brotherhood amongst the Muslims of Madinah, *Al-Ansar* (the Helpers) and *Al-Muhajirun* (the Emigrants). It was indeed unique in the history of the world. A gathering of 90 men, half of whom Emigrants and the others Helpers assembled in the house of Anas bin Malik where the Prophet (Peace be upon him) gave the spirit of brotherhood his official blessing. When either of the two persons who had been paired as brothers, passed away, his property was inherited by his brother-in-faith. This practice continued till the following verse was revealed at the time of the battle of Badr, and the regular rule of inheritance was allowed to take its usual course:

- "But kindred by blood are nearer to one another regarding inheritance." [8:75]

"Brotherhood-in-faith" to quote Muhammad Al-Ghazali again, "was holding subordinate every distinction of race and kindred and supporting the Islamic precept: none is superior to the other except on the basis of piety and God-fearing."

The Prophet (Peace be upon him) attached to that brotherhood a valid contract; it was not just meaningless words but rather a valid practice relating to blood and wealth rather than a passing whim taking the form of accidental greeting.

The atmosphere of brotherhood and fellow-feeling created a spirit of selflessness infused deeply in the hearts of his followers, and produced very healthy results. For example, Sa`d bin Ar-Rabi`, a Helper, said to his fellow brother `Abdur Rahman bin `Awf, "I am the richest man amongst the Helpers. I am glad to share my property half and half with you. I have two wives, I am ready to divorce one and after the expiry of her *'Iddah*, (the prescribed period for a woman divorcee to stay within her house unmarried) you may marry her." But `Abdur Rahman bin `Awf was not prepared to accept anything: neither property nor home. So he blessed his brother and said: "Kindly direct me to the market so that I may make my fortune with my own hands." And he did prosper and got married.

The Helpers were extremely generous to their brethren-in-faith. Abu Hurairah reported that they once approached the Prophet (Peace be upon him) with the request that their orchards of palm trees should be distributed equally between the Muslims of Madinah and their brethren from Makkah. But the Prophet (Peace be upon him) was reluctant to put this heavy burden upon them. It was, however, decided that the Emigrants would work in the orchards alongwith the Helpers and the yield would be divided equally amongst them.

Such examples point directly to the spirit of sacrifice, altruism and cordiality on the part of the Helpers, and also to the feeling of appreciation, gratitude and self-respect that the Emigrants held dear to their hearts. They took only what helped them eke a reasonable living. In short, this policy of mutual brotherhood was so wise and timely that many obstinate problems were resolved wonderfully and reasonably.

A CHARTER OF ISLAMIC ALLIANCE:

Just as the Prophet (Peace be upon him) had established a code of brotherhood amongst the believers, so too he was keen on establishing friendly relations between the Muslims and non-Muslim tribes of Arabia. He established a sort of treaty aiming at ruling out all pre-Islamic rancour and inter-tribal feuds. He was so meticulous not to leave any area in the charter that would allow pre-Islamic traditions to sneak in or violate the new environment he wanted to establish. Herein, we look over some of its provisions.

- In the Name of Allâh, the Most Beneficent, the Most Merciful.

    This is a document from Muhammad, the Messenger of Allâh, concerning Emigrants and Helpers and those who followed and strove with them.

1. They are one nation to the exclusion of other people.
2. The Emigrants of Quraish unite together and shall pay blood money among themselves, and shall ransom honourably their prisoners. Every tribe of the Helpers unite together, as they were at first, and every section among them will pay a ransom for acquitting its relative prisoners.
3. Believers shall not leave anyone destitute among them by not paying his redemption money or blood money in kind.
4. Whoever is rebellious or whoever seeks to spread enmity and sedition, the hand of every God-fearing Muslim shall be against him, even if he be his son.
5. A believer shall not kill another believer, nor shall support a disbeliever against a believer.
6. The protection of Allâh is one (and is equally) extended to the humblest of the believers.
7. The believers are supported by each other.
8. Whosoever of the Jews follows us shall have aid and succour; they shall not be injured, nor any enemy be aided against them.
9. The peace of the believers is indivisible. No separate peace shall be made when believers are fighting in the way of Allâh. Conditions must be fair and equitable to all.
10. It shall not be lawful for a believer, who holds by what is in this document and believes in Allâh and the Day of Judgement, to help a criminal nor give him refuge. Those who give him refuge and render him help shall have the curse and anger of Allâh on the Day of Resurrection. Their indemnity is not accepted.
11. Whenever you differ about a matter, it must be referred to Allâh and to Muhammad.
12. Killing a believer deliberately with no good reason entails killing the killer unless the sponsor deems it otherwise.

It was solely by his wisdom and dexterity, that the Prophet (Peace be upon him) erected the pillars of the new society. This phenomenon no doubt left its mark on the virtuous Muslims. He used to bring them up in the light of the Islamic education, he sanctified their selves, enjoined them to observe righteousness and praiseworthy manners and was keen on infusing into them the ethics of amity, glory, honour, worship and first and foremost obedience to Allâh and His Messenger.

The following is a cluster of the virtues he used to inculcate in the minds of his followers:

- A man asked the Messenger of Allâh (Peace be upon him) which of the merits is superior in Islam. He [the Prophet (Peace be upon him)] remarked:
  - "That you provide food and extend greetings to one whom you know or do not know."

'Abdubin Salâm said: When the Prophet (Peace be upon him) arrived in Madinah, I went to see him and I immediately recognized through his features that he would never be a liar. The first things he (the Prophet [Peace be upon him]) said was:

  - "Extend peace greetings amongst yourselves, provide food to the needy, maintain uterine relations, observe prayer at night while people are asleep, then you will peacefully enter the Garden (Paradise)."

And he said:

- "The Muslim is that one from whose tongue and hand the Muslims are safe."

And said:

- "None amongst you believes (truly) till one likes for his brother that which he loves for himself."

And said:

- "He will not enter Paradise, he whose neighbour is not secure from his wrongful conduct."

And said:

- "A Muslim is the brother of a Muslim; he neither oppresses him nor does he fail him. Whosoever removes a worldly grief from a believer, Allâh will remove from him one of the griefs of the Day of Judgement. Whosoever shields a Muslim, Allâh will shield him on the Day of Resurrection."

And said:

- "Abusing a Muslim is an outrage and fighting against him is disbelief."

And said:

- "To remove something harmful from the road, is charity."

And said:

- "Charity erases sins just as water extinguishes fire."

And said:

- "He is not a perfect believer, who goes to bed full and knows that his neighbour is hungry."

And said:

- "Show mercy to people on earth so that Allâh will have mercy on you in heaven."

And said:

- "Try to avert fire even by half a date (in charity) if not by tendering a good word."

And said:

- "Clothing an under-clad Muslim, entitles you to a garment from the Paradise; feeding a hungry Muslim will make you eligible (by Allâh's Will) for the fruit of the Paradise, and if you provide water to a thirsty Muslim, Allâh will provide you with a drink from 'the Sealed Nectar'."

He used as well to exhort the believers to spend in charity reminding them of relevant virtues for which the hearts yearn.

He said:

- "The believers in their mutual love, are like the human body where when the eye is in agony, the entire body feels the pain; when the head aches, all the body will suffer."

And said:

- "The bonds of brotherhood between two Muslims are like parts of a house, one part strengthens and holds the other."

And said:

- "Do not have malice against a Muslim; do not be envious of other Muslims; do not go against a Muslim and forsake him. O the slaves of Allâh! Be like brothers with each other. It is not violable for a Muslim to desert his brother for over three days."

The Prophet (Peace be upon him) used as well to promote that habit of abstention from asking the others for help unless one is totally helpless. He used to talk to his companions a lot about the merits, virtues and Divine reward implied in observing the prescribed worships and rituals. He would always bring forth corroborated proofs in order to link them physically and spiritually to the Revelation sent to him, hence he would apprise them of their duties and responsibilities in terms of the consequences of the Call of Islam, and at the same time emphasize the exigencies of comprehension and contemplation.

That was his practice of maximizing their morale and imbuing them with the noble values and ideals so that they could become models of virtue to be copied by subsequent generations.

'Abdullah bin Mas'ud (May Allah be pleased with him) once said: If you are willing to follow a good example, then you can have a recourse in the tradition of the deceased, because the living are likely to fall an easy victim to oppression (so they might waver in faith). Follow the steps of Muhammad's Companions. They were the best in this nation, the most pious, the most learned and the least pretentious. Allâh chose them to accompany the Prophet (Peace be upon him) and establish His religion. Therefore, it is imperative to get to know their grace, follow their righteous way and adhere as much as you can to their manners and assimilate their biography. They were always on the orthodox path. There is then the great Messenger of Allâh (Peace be upon him) whose moral visible attributes, aspects of perfection, talents, virtues, noble manners and praiseworthy deeds, entitle him to occupy the innermost cells of our hearts, and become the dearest target that the self yearns for. Hardly did he utter a word when his Companions would race to assimilate it and work in its light.

Those were the attributes and qualities on whose basis the Prophet (Peace be upon him) wanted to build a new society, the most wonderful and the most honourable society ever known in history. On these grounds, he strove to resolve the longstanding problems, and later gave mankind the chance to breathe a sigh of relief after a long wearying journey in dark and gloomy avenues. Such lofty morale lay at the very basis of creating a new society with integrated components immune to all fluctuations of time, and powerful enough to change the whole course of humanity.

A COOPEARATION AND NON-AGGRESSION PACT WITH THE JEWS

Soon after emigrating to Madinah and making sure that the pillars of the new Islamic community were well established on strong bases of administrative, political and ideological unity, the Prophet (Peace be upon him) commenced to establish regular and clearly-defined relations with non-Muslims. All of these efforts were exerted solely to provide peace, security, and prosperity to all mankind at large, and to bring about a spirit of rapport and harmony within his region, in particular.

Geographically, the closest people to Madinah were the Jews. Whilst harbouring evil intentions, and nursing bitter grudge, they showed not the least resistance nor the slightest animosity. The Prophet decided to ratify a treaty with them with clauses that provided full freedom in faith and wealth. He had no intention whatsoever of following severe policies involving banishment, seizure of wealth and land or hostility.

The treaty came within the context of another one of a larger framework relating to inter-Muslim relationships.

The most important provisions of the treaty are the following:

1. The Jews of Bani 'Awf are one community with the believers. The Jews will profess their religion, and the Muslims theirs.
2. The Jews shall be responsible for their expenditure, and the Muslims for theirs.
3. If attacked by a third party, each shall come to the assistance of the other.
4. Each party shall hold counsel with the other. Mutual relation shall be founded on righteousness; sin is totally excluded.
5. Neither shall commit sins to the prejudice of the other.
6. The wronged party shall be aided.
7. The Jews shall contribute to the cost of war so long as they are fighting alongside the believers.
8. Madinah shall remain sacred and inviolable for all that join this treaty.
9. Should any disagreement arise between the signatories to this treaty, then Allâh, the All-High and His Messenger shall settle the dispute.
10. The signatories to this treaty shall boycott Quraish commercially; they shall also abstain from extending any support to them.
11. Each shall contribute to defending Madinah, in case of a foreign attack, in its respective area.
12. This treaty shall not hinder either party from seeking lawful revenge.

Madinah and its suburbs, after the ratification of this treaty, turned into a coalition state, with Madinah proper as capital and Muhammad (Peace be upon him) as 'president'; authorities lay mainly in the hand of the Muslims, and consequently it was a real capital of Islam. To expand the zone of peace and security the Prophet (Peace be upon him) started to enter into similar treaties with other tribes living around 'his state'.

THE PROPHET ON THE BATTLEFIELD

The Quraishites, mortified at the escape of the Prophet (Peace be upon him) along with his devoted companions, and jealous of his growing power in Madinah, kept a stringent watch over the Muslims left behind and persecuted them in every possible way. They also initiated clandestine contacts with 'Abdullah bin Uabi bin Salul, chief of Madinese polytheists, and president designate of the tribes 'Aws and Khazraj before the Prophet's emigration. They senthim a strongly-worded ultimatum ordering him to fight or expel the Prophet, otherwise they would launch a widespread military campaign that would exterminate his people and proscribe his women.

His pride wounded and kingship no longer his, 'Abdullah bin Uabi bin Salul, a priori responded positively to his Quraishite co-polytheists. He mobilized his supporters to counteract the Muslims. The Prophet (Peace be upon him) on hearing about this unholy alliance, summoned 'Abdullah and admonished him to be more sensible and thoughtful and cautioned his men against being snared in malicious tricks. The men, on grounds of cowardice, or reason, gave up the idea. Their chief, however, seemingly complied, but at heart, he remained a wicked unpredictable accomplice with Quraish and the envious Jews. Skirmishes and provocations started to pave the way for a major confrontation between the Muslims and polytheists. Sa'd bin Mu'adh, an outstanding Helper, announced his intention to observe *'Umrah* (lesser pilgrimage) and headed for Makkah. There Omaiya bin Khalaf provided tutelage for him to observe the ritual circumambulation. Abu Jahl, an archenemy of Islam saw him in the Sacred Sanctuary and threatened he would have killed him if he had not been in the company of Omaiya. Sa'd, fearlessly and defiantly, challenged him to committing any folly at the risk of cutting their caravans off.

Provocative actions continued and Quraish sent the Muslims a note threatening to put them to death in their own homeland. Those were not mere words, for the Prophet (Peace be upon him) received information from reliable sources attesting to real intrigues and plots being hatched by the enemies of Islam. Precautionary measures were taken and a state of alertness was called for, including the positioning of security guards around the house of the Prophet (Peace be upon him) and strategic junctures. 'Aishah (May Allah be pleased with her) reported that Allâh's Messenger (Peace be upon him) lay down on bed during one night on his arrival in Madinah and said: Were there a pious person from amongst my Companions who should keep a watch for me during the night? She ['Aishah (May Allah be pleased with her)] said: We were in this state when we heard the clanging noise of arms. He [the Prophet (Peace be upon him)] said: Who is it? He said: This is Sa'd bin Abi Waqqas. Allâh's Messenger (Peace be upon him) said to him: What brings you here? Thereupon he said: I harboured fear (lest any harm should come to) Allâh's Messenger (Peace be upon him), so I came to serve as your sentinel. Allâh's Messenger (Peace be upon him) invoked blessings upon him and then he slept.

This state of close vigilance continued ceaselessly until the Words of Allâh were revealed saying:

- "Allâh will protect you from mankind."[5:67]

Here, the Prophet (Peace be upon him) peeped from the dome of his house asking his people to go away, and making it clear that Allâh would take the charge of protecting him.

The Prophet's life was not the only target of the wicked schemes, but rather the lives and the whole entity of the Muslims. When the Madinese provided the Prophet (Peace be upon him) and his Companions with safe refuge, the desert bedouins began to look at them all in the same perspective, and outlawed all the Muslims.

At this precarious juncture with Quraish, intent on pursuing their aggressive and devilish plans, Allâh, the All-High, gave the Muslims the permission to take arms against the disbelievers:

- "Permission to fight is given to those (i.e. believers against those disbelievers), who are fighting them, (and) because they (believers) have been wronged, and surely Allâh is Able to give them (believers) victory." [22:39]

This verse was revealed in a larger context of Divine instructions to eradicate all aspects of falsehood, and hold in honour the symbols and rites of Allâh:

- "Those (Muslim rulers) who, if We give them power in the land, (they) order for *Iqamat-as-Salât*: [i.e. to perform *Salât* (prayer) — the five compulsory, congregational prayers (the males in Mosques)], to pay the *Zakat* (obligatory charity), and they enjoin *Al-Ma'ruf* (i.e. Islamic Monotheism and all that Islam orders one to do), and forbid *Al-Munkar* (i.e. disbelief, polytheism and all that Islam has forbidden) [i.e. they make the Qur'ân as the Law of their country in all the spheres of life]." [22:41].

Doubtlessly, the permission to fight was revealed in Madinah after emigration, not in Makkah, still the exact date where of is in doubt.

The permission to fight was already there, but in the light of the status quo, it was wise for the Muslims to bring the commercial routes leading to Makkah under their control. To realize this strategic objective, the Prophet (Peace be upon him) had to choose either of two options:

1. Entering into non-aggression pacts with the tribes inhabiting either the areas adjacent to the routes or between these routes and Madinah. With respect to this course of action, the Prophet (Peace be upon him) had already signed, together with the Jews and other neighbouring tribes, the aforementioned pact of cooperation and good neighbourliness.
2. Despatching successive armed missions for harassment along the strategic commercial routs.

PRE-BADR MISSIONS AND INVASIONS:

With a view to implementing these plans, the Muslims commenced real military activities, which at first took the form of reconnaissance patrols delegated to explore the geopolitical features of the roads surrounding Madinah and others leading to Makkah, and building alliances with the tribes nearby. The Prophet wanted to impress upon the polytheists and Jews of Madinah as well as the bedouins in its vicinity, that the Muslims had smashed their old fears, and had been too strong to be attacked with impunity. He also wanted to display the power of his followers in order to deter Quraish from committing any military folly against him which might jeopardize their economic life and means of living, and to stop them from persecuting the helpless Muslims detained in Makkah, consequently he would avail himself of this opportunity and resume his job of propagating the Divine Call freely.

The following is a resume of these missions and errands:

1. Saif Al-Bahr Platoon sent in Ramadan 1 A.H., i.e. 623 A.D. led by Hamzah bin 'Abdul Muttalib and comprising 30 Emigrants with a definite task of intercepting a caravan belonging to Quraish. It was a caravan of 300 people including Abu Jahl bin Hisham. The two parties encountered each other and aligned in preparation for fighting. Majdi bin 'Amr, on good terms with both sides, happened to be there and managed to prevent an imminent clash.

- On that occasion, the Prophet (Peace be upon him) accredited the first flag in the history of Muslims. It was white in colour and was entrusted to Kinaz bin Husain Al-Ghanawi, to carry.

2. In Shawwal, 1 A.H., i.e. April 623 A.D. The Messenger of Allâh (Peace be upon him) despatched 'Ubaidah bin Al-Harith bin Al-Muttalib at the head of 60 horsemen of Emigrants to a spot called Batn Rabegh where they encountered Abu Sufyan at the head of a caravan of 200 men. There was arrow shooting but no actual fighting.

- It is interesting to note that two Muslims, Al-Miqdad bin 'Amr Al-Bahrani and 'Utbah bin Ghazwan Al-Mazini, defected from the caravan of Quraish and joined the ranks of 'Ubaidah. The Muslims had a white flag carried by Mistah bin Athatha bin Al-Muttalib bin 'Abd Munaf.

3. In Dhul Qa'dah 1 A.H., i.e. May 623 A.D. the Prophet (Peace be upon him) despatched Sa'd bin Abi Waqqas at the head of 20 horsemen, and instructed them not to go beyond Al-Kharrar. After a five-day march they reached the spot to discover that the camels of Quraish had left the day before; their flag, as usual, was white and carried by Al-Miqdad bin 'Amr.
4. Ghazwa Al-Abwa' or Waddan. It was in Safar 2 A.H., i.e. 623 A.D. The Messenger of Allâh (Peace be upon him) set out himself at the head of 70 men, mostly Emigrants, to intercept a camel caravan belonging to Quraish, leaving behind Sa'd bin 'Ubadah to dispose the affairs in Madinah. When he reached Waddan, a place between Makkah and Madinah, he found none.

- In the process of this campaign, he contracted a non-aggressiopact with 'Amr bin Makhshi Ad-Damari. The provisions of the pact go as follows:
    - "This is a document from Muhammad, the Messenger of Allâh concerning Bani Damrah in which he established them safe and secure in their wealth and lives. They can expect support from the Muslims unless they oppose the religion of Allâh. They are also expected to respond positively in case the Prophet sought their help."

This was the first invasion under the leadership of the Messenger of Allâh. It took fifteen days, with a white flag carried by Hamzah bin 'Abdul Muttalib.

5. Buwat Invasion. It took place in Rabi' Al-Awwal 2 A.H., i.e. 623 A.D. The Prophet (Peace be upon him), at the head of 200 companions, marched for Buwat to intercept a caravan belonging to Quraish comprising 100 Quraishites, Omaiya bin Khalaf among them, and 2500 camels. When he reached Buwat, the caravan had left. Before leaving Madinah, he mandated Sa'd bin Mu'adh to dispose the affairs until his return.
6. Safwan Invasion. In Rabi' Al-Awwal 2 A.H., i.e. 623 A.D. Karz bin Jabir at the head of a small group of polytheists raided the pastures of Madinah and looted some animals. The Prophet (Peace be upon him) at the head of 70 men left Madinah to fight the aggressors. He went in their pursuit till he reached a place called Safwan near Badr but could not catch up with them. This invasion came to be known as the preliminary Badr Invasion. During his absence, the Prophet (Peace be upon him) entrusted Zaid bin Harithah with the disposition of the affairs in Madinah. The standard was white in colour and entrusted to 'Ali bin Abi Talib to carry.
7. Dhil 'Ushairah Invasion. It was in Jumada-al-Ula and Jumada-al-Akhirah the first or second 2 A.H., i.e. November-December 623 A.D. The Prophet (Peace be upon him) at the head of 150-200 Muslim volunteers, with 30 camels which they rode turn by turn, set out to intercept a Quraishite caravan. He reached Dhil 'Ushairah but the camels had left some days before. These camels were the same that he went out to intercept on their return from Syria, and were the direct reason for the break out of the battle of Badr. In the process of this campaign, the Prophet صلى الله عليه وسلم contracted a non-aggression pact with Bani Madlij and their allies Bani Dhumrah. Abu Salama bin 'Abd Al-Asad Al-Makhzumi was mandated to rule Madinah in his absence.
8. The Platoon of Nakhlah. It took place in Rajab 2 A.H., i.e. January 624 A.H. The Messenger of Allâh (Peace be upon him) despatched 'Abdullah bin Jahsh Asadi to Nakhlah at the head of 12 Emigrants with six camels. 'Abdullah was given a letter by the Prophet (Peace be upon him) but was instructed to read it only after two days. He followed the instructions and discovered that he was asked to go on to a place called Nakhlah standing between Makkah and At-Ta'if, intercept a caravan for Quraish and collect news about their intentions. He disclosed the contents of the letters to his fellows who blindly obeyed the orders. At Nakhlah, the caravan passed carrying loads of raisins (dried grapes), food stuff and other commodities. Notable polytheists were also there such as 'Amr bin Al-Hadrami, 'Uthman and Naufal, sons of 'Abdullah bin Al-Mugheerah and others... The Muslims held consultations among themselves with respect to fighting them taking into account Rajab which was a sacred month (during which, along with Dhul Hijja, Dhul Qa'da and Muharram, war activities were suspended as was the custom in Arabia then). At last they agreed to engage with them in fighting. 'Amr bin Al-Hadrami was shot dead by an arrow, 'Uthman and Al-Hakam were captured whereas Naufal escaped. They came back with the booty and the two prisoners. They set aside one-fifth of the booty assigned to Allâh and His Messenger, and took the rest. The Messenger disapproved of that act and suspended any action as regards

the camels and the two captives on account of the prohibited months already mentioned. The polytheists, on their part, exploited this golden opportunity to calumniate the Muslims and accuse them of violating what is Divinely inviolable. This idle talk brought about a painful headache to Muhammad's Companions, until at last they were relieved when the Revelation came down giving a decisive answer and stating quite explicitly that the behaviour of the polytheists in the whole process was much more heinous and far more serious than the act of the Muslims:

- "They ask you concerning fighting in the sacred months (i.e. 1st, 7th, 11th and 12th months of the Islamic calendar). Say, 'Fighting therein is a great (transgression) but a greater (transgression) with Allâh is to prevent mankind from following the way of Allâh, to disbelieve in Him, to prevent access to *Al-Masjid-Al-Harâm* (at Makkah), and to drive out its inhabitants, and *Al-Fitnah* is worse than killing." [2:217]

The Words of Allâh were quite clear and said that the tumult created by the polytheists was groundless. The sacred inviolable sanctities had been repeatedly violated in the long process of fighting Islam and persecuting its adherents. The wealth of the Muslims as well as their homes had already been violated and their Prophet (Peace be upon him) had been the target of repeated attempts on his life. In short, that sort of propaganda could deservedly be described as impudence and prostitution. This has been a resume of pre-Badr platoons and invasions. None of them witnessed any sort of looting property or killing people except when the polytheists had committed such crimes under the leadership of Karz bin Jabir Al-Fahri. It was, in fact, the polytheists who had initiated such acts. No wonder, for such ill-behaviour is immanent in their natural disposition.

Shortly afterwards, the two captives were released and blood money was given to the killed man's father.

After this event, Quraish began to realize the real danger that Madinah could present with. They came to know that Madinah had always been on the alert, watching closely their commercial caravans. It was then common knowledge to them that the Muslims in their new abode could span and extend their military activities over an area of 300 miles. and bring it under full control. However, the new situation borne in mind, the Makkans could not be deterred and were too obstinate to come to terms with the new rising power of Islam. They were determined to bring their fall by their own hands and with this recklessness they precipitated the great battle of Badr.

The Muslims, on the other hand, and at the behest of their Lord, were ordered to go to war in Sha'ban 2 A.H:

- "And fight, in the way of Allâh those who fight you; but transgress not the limits. Truly, Allâh likes not the transgressors. And kill them wherever you find them, and turn them out from where they have turned you out. And *Al-Fitnah* (polytheism or calamity) is worse than killing. And fight not with them at *Al-Masjid-Al-Harâm* (the Sanctuary at Makkah), unless they (first) fight you there. But if they attack you, then kill them. Such is the recompense of the disbelievers. But if they cease, then Allâh is Oft-Forgiving, Most Merciful. And fight them until there is no more *Fitnah* (disbelief and worshipping of others along with Allâh) and (all and every kind of) worship is for Allâh (Alone). But if they cease, let there be no transgression except against *Az-Zalimûn* (polytheists, and wrong-doers, etc.)" [2:190-193]

Before long, Allâh again sent the Muslims a different sort of verses whereby teaching them ways of fighting, urging them to go to war and demonstrating relevant rules:

- "So, when you meet (in fight - *Jihâd* in Allâh's cause), those who disbelieve smite at their necks till when you have killed and wounded many of them, then bind a bond firmly (on them, i.e. take them as captives). Thereafter (is the time) either for generosity (i.e. free them without ransom), or ransom (according to what benefits Islam), until the war lays down its burden. Thus [you are ordered by Allâh to continue in carrying out *Jihâd* against the disbelievers till they embrace Islam (i.e. are saved from the punishment in the Hell-fire) or at least come under your protection], but if it had been Allâh's Will, He Himself could certainly have punished them (without you). But (He lets you fight), in order to test you, some with others. But those who are killed in the way of Allâh, He will never let their deeds be lost. He will guide them and set right their state. And admit them to Paradise which He has made known to them (i.e. they will know their places in Paradise more than they used to know their houses in the world). O you who believe! If you help (in the cause of) Allâh, He will help you, and make your foothold firm." [47:4-7]

Shortly afterwards, Allâh began to dispraise the hypocrites, the weak at heart and cowardly elements:

- "But when a decisive *Sûrah* (explaining and ordering things) is sent down, and fighting (*Jihâd* — the holy fighting) is mentioned (i.e. ordained) therein, you will see those in whose hearts is a disease (of hypocrisy) looking at you with a look of one fainting to death. " [47:20]

The prevalent exigencies required as a top priority exhorting the Muslims to fight. Any leader with a deep insight would order his soldiers to get ready for any sort of emergency, let alone the All-Knowing Exalted Lord, Who is at all times omniscient of the minutest details of affairs. The event of that skirmish with the polytheists dealt a heavy blow to the pride of Quraish and created a sort of horrible restlessness amongst them.

The aforementioned Qur'ânic verses, enjoining the Muslims to strive in the cause of Allâh, betrayed the proximity of blood clashes that would be crowned by a decisive victory for the Muslims, and final expulsion of polytheists out of the Sacred City, Makkah. They referred to rules pertinent to the treatment of captives and slaughtering the pagan soldiers till the war ended and laid down its burdens. All of these could act as clues to a final triumph that would envelop the strife of the Muslims towards their noble objectives.

Another event of great significance featured the same month Sha'ban 2 A.H., i.e. February 624 A.D., which was a Divine injunction ordering that *Al-Qiblah* be changed from Jerusalem to the Sacred Mosque in Makkah. That was of a great advantage to the Muslims at two levels. First, it brought about a kind of social sifting, so to speak, in terms of the hypocrites of the Jews and others weak at heart, and revealed their true nature and inclinations; the ranks of the Muslims were thereby purged from those discord-prone elements. Second, facing a new *Qiblah*, the Sacred Mosque in Makkah, refers gently to a new role awaiting the Muslims to take up, and would start only after the repatriation of the Muslims to their Sacred City, Makkah for it is not logical for the Muslims to leave their *Qiblah* at the mercy of non-Muslims.

The Muslims, therefore, at the behest of Allâh and on account of those Divine clues, augmented their activities and their tendency towards striving in the cause of Allâh and encountering His enemies in a decisive battle were greatly intensified.

THE BATTLE OF BADR THE FIRST DECISIVE BATTLE IN THE HISTORY OF ISLAM REASON OF THE BATTLE:

We have already spoken about Al-'Ushairah Invasion when a caravan belonging to Quraish had escaped an imminent military encounter with the Prophet (Peace be upon him) and his men. When their return from Syria approached, the Prophet (Peace be upon him) despatched Talhah bin 'Ubaidullâh and Sa'id bin Zaid northward to scout around for any movements of this sort. The two scouts stayed at Al-Hawra' for some days until Abu Sufyan, the leader of the caravan, passed by them. The two men hurried back to Madinah and reported to the Prophet (Peace be upon him) their findings. Great wealth amounting to 50 thousand gold Dinars guarded by 40 men moving relatively close to Madinah constituted a tempting target for the Muslim military, and provided a potentially heavy economic, political and military strike that was bound to shake the entire structure of the Makkan polytheists.

The Prophet (Peace be upon him) immediately exhorted the Muslims to rush out and waylay the caravan to make up for their property and wealth they were forced to give up in Makkah. He did not give orders binding to everyone, but rather gave them full liberty to go out or stay back, thinking that it would be just an errand on a small scale.

The Muslim army was made up of 300-317 men, 82-86 Emigrants, 61 from Aws and 170 from Khazraj. They were not well-equipped nor adequately prepared. They had only two horses belonging to Az-Zubair bin Al-'Awwam and Al-Miqdad bin Al-Aswad Al-Kindi, 70 camels, one for two or three men to ride alternatively. The Messenger of Allâh (Peace be upon him) himself, 'Ali and Murthid bin Abi Murthid Al-Ghanawi had only one camel. Disposition of the affairs of Madinah was entrusted to Ibn Umm Maktum but later to Abu Lubabah bin 'Abdul Mundhir. The general leadership was given to Mus'ab bin 'Umair Al-Qurashi Al-'Abdari, and their standard was white in colour. The little army was divided into two battalions, the Emigrants with a standard raised by 'Ali bin Abi Talib, and the Helpers whose standard was in the hand of Sa'd bin Mu'adh. Az-Zubair bin Al-'Awwam was appointed to the leadership of the right flank, Al-Miqdad bin 'Amr to lead the left flank, and the rear of the army was at the command of Qais bin Abi Sa'sa'ah. The General Commander-in-Chief was the Prophet (Peace be upon him), of course.

The Prophet (Peace be upon him), at the head of his army, marched out along the main road leading to Makkah. He then turned left towards Badr and when he reached As-Safrâ', he despatched two men to scout about for the camels of Quraish.

Abu Sufyan, on the other hand, was on the utmost alert. He had already been aware that the route he was following was attended with dangers. He was also anxious to know about the movements of Muhammad (Peace be upon him). His scouting men submitted to him reports to the effect that the Muslims were lying in ambush for his caravan. To be on the safe side, he hired Damdam bin 'Amr Al-Ghifari to communicate a message asking for help from the Quraishites. The messenger rode fast and reached Makkah in frenzy. Felling himself from his camel, he stood dramatically before Al-Ka'bah, cut off the nose and the ears of the camel, turned its saddle upside down, tore off his own shirt from front and behind, and cried: "O Quraish! Your merchandise! It is with Abu Sufyan. The caravan is being intercepted by Muhammad (Peace be upon him) and his companions. I cannot say what would have happened to them. Help! Help!"

The effect of this hue and cry was instantaneous and the news stunned Quraish and they immediately remembered their pride that was wounded when the Muslims had intercepted Al-Hadrami caravan. They therefore swiftly mustered almost all of their forces and none stayed behind except Abu Lahab, who delegated someone who owed him some money. They also mobilized some Arab tribes to contribute to the war against the Prophet (Peace be upon him). All the clans of Quraish gave their consent except Banu 'Adi. Soon an excited throng of 1300 soldiers including 100 horsemen and 600 mailed soldiers with a large number of camels, was clamouring to proceed to fight the Muslims. For food supplies, they used to slaughter an alternate number of camels of ten and nine every day. They were however afraid that Banu Bakr, on account of old long deep-seated animosity, would attack their rear. At that critical moment, *Iblis* (Satan) appeared to them in the guise of Suraqa bin Malik bin Ju'sham Al-Mudlaji — chief of Bani Kinana — saying to them: "I guarantee that no harm will happen from behind."

They set out burning with indignation, motivated by a horrible desire for revenge and exterminating anyone that might jeopardize the routes of their caravans:

- "...boastfully and to be seen of men, and hinder (men) from the path of Allâh. " [8:47]

Or as the Prophet (Peace be upon him) said:

- "O Allâh these are the haughty and conceited; they have come defying Allâh and defying His Messenger."

They moved swiftly northward to Badr. On the way they received another message from Abu Sufyan asking them to go back home because the caravan had escaped the Muslims. Incidentally, Abu Sufyan, on learning the intention of the Muslims, led his caravan off the main route, and inclined it towards the Red Sea. By this manoeuvre, he was able to slip past the Madinese ambush and was out of their reach.

On receiving Abu Sufyan's message, the Makkan army showed a desire to return home. The tyrant Abu Jahl, however haughtily and arrogantly insisted that they proceed to Badr, stay three nights there for making festivities. Now they wanted to punish the Muslims and prevent them from intercepting their caravans, and impress on the Arabs that Quraish still had the upper hand and enjoyed supremacy in that area.

Abu Jahl's threats and insistence notwithstanding, Banu Zahrah, acting on the advice of Al-Akhnas bin Shuraiq, broke away and returned to Makkah. Thenceforth Al-Akhnas remained 'the well-rubbed palm tree' for Bani Zahrah and was blindly obeyed in all relevant matters.

Banu Hashim were also inclined to break away, but Abu Jahl's threats made them desist from that idea.

The rest of the army, now 1000 soldiers, approached Badr and encamped themselves beyond a sand dune at Al-'Udwat Al-Quswa.

'The intelligence corps' of the Madinese army reported to the Prophet (Peace be upon him) that a bloody encounter with the Makkans was inescapable, and that a daring step in this context had to be taken, or else the forces of evil would violate the inviolable and would consequently manage to undermine the noble cause of the Islam and tread upon its faithful adherents. The Muslims were afraid that the pagan Makkans would march on and start the war activities within the headquarters of Islam, Madinah. A move of such nature would certainly damage and produce an infamous impact on the dignity and stance of the Muslims.

On account of the new grave developments, the Prophet (Peace be upon him) held an advisory military emergency meeting to review the ongoing situation and exchange viewpoints with the army leaders. Admittedly, some Muslims feared the horrible encounter and their courage began to waver; in this regard, Allâh says:

- "As your Lord caused you (O Muhammad [Peace be upon him]) to go out from your home with the Truth, and verily, a party among the believers disliked it, disputing with you concerning the Truth after it was made manifest, as if they were being driven to death while they were looking (at it)." [8:5, 6]

The Prophet (Peace be upon him) apprised his men of the gravity of the situation and asked for their advice. Abu Bakr was the first who spoke on the occasion and assured the Prophet (Peace be upon him) of the unreserved obedience to his command. 'Umar was the next to stand up and supported the views expressed by his noble friend. Then Al-Miqdad bin 'Amr got up and said: "O Messenger of Allâh! Proceed where Allâh directs you to, for we are with you. We will not say as the Children of Israel said to Moses (Peace be upon him):

- "Go you and your Lord and fight and we will stay here;"

Rather we shall say:

- "Go you and yourLord and fight and we will fight along with you."

By Allâh! If you were to take us to Bark Al-Ghimad, we will still fight resolutely with you against its defenders until you gained it."

The Prophet (Peace be upon him) thanked him and blessed him.

The three leaders who spoke were from the Emigrants, who only constituted a minor section of the army. The Prophet (Peace be upon him) wanted, and for the more reason, to hear the Helpers' view because they were the majority of the soldiers and were expected to shoulder the brunt of the war activities. Moreover, the clauses of Al-'Aqabah Pledge did not commit them to fighting beyond their territories.

The Prophet (Peace be upon him) then said: "Advise me my men!"

by which he meant the Helpers, in particular. Upon this Sa'd bin Mu'adh stood up and said: "By Allâh, I feel you want us (the Helpers) to speak." The Prophet (Peace be upon him) directly said: "Oh, yes!" Sa'd said: "O Prophet of Allâh! We believe in you and we bear witness to what you have vouchsafed to us and we declare in unequivocal terms that what you have brought is the Truth. We give you our firm pledge of obedience and sacrifice. We will obey you most willingly in whatever you command us, and by Allâh, Who has sent you with the Truth, if you were to ask us to plunge into the sea, we will do that most readily and not a man of us will stay behind. We do not grudge the idea of encounter with the enemy. We are experienced in war and we are trustworthy in combat. We hope that Allâh will show you through our hands those deeds of valour which will please your eyes. Kindly lead us to the battlefield in the Name of Allâh."

The Prophet (Peace be upon him) was impressed with the fidelity and the spirit of sacrifice which his companions showed at this critical juncture. Then he said to them: "Forward and be of cheer, for Allâh has promised me one of the two (the lucrative course through capturing the booty or strife in the cause of Allâh against the polytheists), and by Allâh it is as if I now saw the enemy lying prostrate."

In the immediate vicinity of Badr, the Prophet (Peace be upon him) and his cavemate Abu Bakr conducted a scouting operation during which they managed to locate the camp of Quraish. They came across an old bedouin nearby whom they manipulated and managed to extract from him the exact location of the army of the polytheists. In the evening of the same day, he despatched three Emigrant leaders, 'Ali bin Abi Talib, Az-Zubair bin Al-'Awwam and Sa'd bin Abi Waqqas to scout about for news about the enemy. They saw two men drawing water for the Makkan army. On interrogation, they admitted that they were water carriers working for Quraish. But that answer did not please some Muslims and they beat the two boys severely in order to exact from them an answer, even if it isn't true, alluding to the caravan laden with wealth. The two boys thus lied, and so they were released. The Prophet (Peace be upon him) was angry with those men and censured them saying: "On telling the truth, you beat them, and on telling a lie, you released them!" He then addressed the two boys and after a little conversation with them he learned a lot about the enemy: number of soldiers, their exact location and names of some of their notables. He then turned to the Muslims and said: "Hearken, Quraish has sent you their most precious lives."

The same night it rained on both sides. For the polytheists it obstructed further progress, whereas it was a blessing for the Muslims. It cleaned them and removed from them the stain of Satan. Allâh sent rain to strengthen their hearts and to plant their feet firmly therewith. They marched a little forward and encamped at the farther bank of the valley. Muhammad (Peace be upon him) stopped at the nearest spring of Badr. Al-Hubab bin Mundhir asked him, "Has Allâh inspired you to choose this very spot or is it stratagem of war and the product of consultation?" The Prophet (Peace be upon him) replied "It is stratagem of war and consultation." Al-Hubab said: "This place is no good; let us go and encamp on the nearest water well and make a basin or reservoir full of water, then destroy all the other wells so that they will be deprived of the water." The Prophet (Peace be upon him) approved of his plan and agreed to carry it out, which they actually did at midnight.

Sa'd bin Mu'adh suggested that a trellis be built for the Prophet (Peace be upon him) to function as headquarters for the Muslim army and a place providing reasonable protection for the leader. Sa'd began to justify his proposal and said that if they had been victorious, then everything would be satisfactory. In case of defeat, the Prophet (Peace be upon him) would not be harmed and he could go back to Madinah where there were more people who loved him and who would have come for help if they had known that he was in that difficult situation, so that he would resume his job, hold counsel with them and they would strive in the cause of Allâh with him again and again.

A squad of guards was also chosen from amongst the Helpers under the leadership of the same man, Sa'd bin Mu'adh, in order to defend the Prophet (Peace be upon him) in his headquarters.

The Prophet (Peace be upon him) spent the whole night preceding the day of the battle in prayer and supplication. The Muslim army, wearied with their long march, enjoyed sound and refreshing sleep, a mark of the Divine favour and of the state of their undisturbed minds.

- "(Remember) when He covered you with a slumber as a security from Him, and He caused rain to descend on you from the sky, to clean you thereby and to remove from you the *Rijz* (whispering, evil suggestions, etc.) of Satan, and to strengthen your hearts, and make your feet firm thereby." [8:11]

That was Friday night, Ramadan 17th., the year 2 A.H.

In the morning, the Prophet (Peace be upon him) called his men to offer the prayers and then urged them to fight in the way of Allâh. As the sun rose over the desert, the Prophet(Peace be upon him) drew up his little army, and pointing with an arrow which he held in his hand, arranged the ranks.

Quraish, on the other hand, positioned their forces in Al-'Udwat Al-Quswa opposite the Muslim lines. A few of them approached, in a provocative deed, to draw water from the wells of Badr, but were all shot dead except one, Hakeem bin Hizam, who later became a devoted Muslim. 'Umair bin Wahab Al-Jumahi, in an attempt to reconnoiter the power of the Muslims, made a scouting errand and submitted a report saying that the Muslim army numbered as many as 300 men keen on fighting to the last man. On another reconnaissance mission he came to the conclusion that neither reinforcements were coming nor ambushes laid. He understood that they were too brave to surrender and too intent on carrying out their military duties to withdraw without slaying the largest number possible of the polytheists. This report as well as kindred relations binding the two belligerent parties together, slackened the desire to fight among some of the Quraishites. To counteract this reason-based opposition advocated by a rival of his, 'Utbah bin Rabi'a and others, Abu Jahl started an anti-campaign seeking vengeance on Muhammad's followers for the Quraishites killed at Nakhlah. In this way, he managed to thwart the opposite orientation, and manipulated the people to see his evil views only.

When the two parties approached closer and were visible to each other, the Prophet (Peace be upon him) began supplicating Allâh "O Allâh! The conceited and haughty Quraishites are already here defying You and belying Your Messenger. O Allâh! I am waiting for Your victory which You have promised me. I beseech You Allâh to defeat them (the enemies)." He also gave strict orders that his men would not start fighting until he gave them his final word. He recommended that they use their arrows sparingly and never resort to sword unless the enemies came too close.

Abu Jahl also prayed for victory, saying: "Our Lord, whichever of the two parties was less kind to his relatives, and brought us what we do not know, then destroy him tomorrow.". They were confident ththeir superior number, equipment and experience would be decisive. The Noble Qur'ân, with a play on the word, told them that the decision had come, and the victory — but not in the sense they had hoped for:

- "(O disbelievers) if you ask for a judgement, now has the judgement come unto you and if you cease (to do wrong), it will be better for you, and if you return (to the attack), so shall we return, and your forces will be of no avail to you, however numerous it be, and verily, Allâh is with the believers." [8:19]

The first disbeliever to trigger the fire of the battle and be its first victim was Al-Aswad bin 'Abdul Asad Al-Makhzumi, a fierce bad-tempered idolater. He stepped out swearing he would drink from the water basin of the Muslims, otherwise, destroy it or die for it. He engaged with Hamzah bin 'Abdul Muttalib, who struck his leg with his sword and dealt him another blow that finished him off inside the basin.

The battle had actually started. Protected by armour and shields, 'Utbah bin Rabi'a stepped forth between his brother Shaibah and his son Al-Waleed bin 'Utbah from the lines of Quraish and hurled maledictions at the Muslims. Three young men of the Helpers came out against them: 'Awf and Mu'wwadh — the sons of Harith, and 'Abdullah bin Rawaha. But the Makkans yelled that they had nothing to do with them. They wanted the heads of their cousins. Upon this the Prophet (Peace be upon him) asked 'Ubaidah bin Al-Harith, Hamzah — his uncle, and his cousin 'Ali (May Allah be pleased with him) to go forward for the combat. The three duels were rapid. Hamzah killed Shaibah, while 'Ali killed Al-Waleed. 'Ubaidah was seriously wounded but, before he fell, Hamzah fell upon 'Utbah and with a sweep of his sword, cut off his head. 'Ali and Hamzah carried 'Ubaidah back with his leg cut off. He died four or five days later of a disease in the bile duct.

'Ali was possessed of a deep conviction that Allâh's Words were revealed:

- "These two opponents (believers and disbelievers) dispute with each other about their Lord." [22:19]

These verses were revealed in connection with men of Faith who confess their Lord and seek to carry out His Will (i.e. Muhammad 's followers at Badr Battle), and men who deny their Lord and defy Him (the people of Quraish).

The duel was followed by a few more duels but the Makkans suffered terrible defeats in all the combats and lost some of their most precious lives. They were too much exasperated and enraged and fell upon the Muslims to exterminate them once and for all. The Muslims, however, after supplicating their Lord, calling upon Him for assistance, were made to hold to their position and conduct a defensive war plan that was successful enough to inflict heavy losses on the attackers. The Prophet (Peace be upon him) used to pray to his Lord ceaselessly persistently and day and night to come to their succour. When the fierce engagement grew too hot he again began to supplicate his Lord saying:

- "O Allâh! Should this group (of Muslims) be defeated today, You will no longer be worshipped."

He continued to call out to his Lord, stretching forth his hands and facing *Al-Qiblah*, until his cloak fell off his shoulders. Then Abu Bakr came, picked up the cloak, and put it back on his shoulders and said: "O Prophet of Allâh, you have cried out enough to your Lord. He will surely fulfill what He has promised you."

Immediate was the response from Allâh, Who sent down angels from the heavens for the help and assistance of the Prophet (Peace be upon him) and his companions. The Noble Qur'ân observes:

- "Verily, I am with you, so keep firm those who have believed. I will cast terror into the hearts of those who have disbelieved." [8:12]

Allâh, the All-Mighty, also inspired another message to His Messenger, saying:

- "I will help you with a thousand of the angels each behind the other (following one another) in succession." [8:9]

The Prophet (Peace be upon him), in his trellis, dozed off a little and then raised his head joyfully crying:

- "O Abu Bakr, glad tidings are there for you: Allâh's victory has approached, by Allâh, I can see Gabriel on his mare in the thick of a sandstorm."

He then jumped out crying:

- "Their multitude will be put to flight, and they will show their backs." [54:45]

At the instance of Gabriel, the Prophet (Peace be upon him) took a handful of gravel, cast it at the enemy and said: "Confusion seize their faces!" As he flung the dust, a violent sandstorm blew like furnace blast into the eyes of the enemies. With respect to this, Allâh says:

- "And you [i.e. Muhammad (Peace be upon him)] threw not when you did throw but Allâh threw." [8:17]

Only then did he give clear orders to launch a counter-attack. He was commanding the army, inspiring confidence among his men and exhorting them to fight manfully for the sake of their Lord, reciting the Words of Allâh:

- "And be quick for forgiveness from your Lord, and for Paradise as wide as are the heavens and the earth." [3:133]

The spirit he infused into his men was clearly witnessed by the valour of 'Umair, a lad of sixteen, who flung away some dates he was eating crying out: "These (the dates) are holding me back from Paradise." So saying he plunged into the thick of the battle and died fighting bravely. Unique deeds of valour, deep devotion and full obedience to the Prophet (Peace be upon him) were exhibited in the process of the battle. The army of the faithfuls was borne forward by the power of enthusiasm which the half-hearted warriors of Makkah miserably lacked. A large number of the polytheists were killed and the others began to waver. No wonder! The standard-bearers of Truth were given immediate help, and supernatural agencies (the angels), were sent to their assistance by their Lord to help them defeat the forces of evil.

The records of *Hadith* speak eloquently of the fact that the angels did appear on that day and fought on the side of the Muslims. Ibn 'Abbas said: "While on that day a Muslim was chasing a disbeliever and he heard over him the swashing of a whip and the voice of the rider saying: 'Go ahead Haizum'. He glanced at the polytheist who had (now) fallen down on his back. The Helper came to the Messenger of Allâh (Peace be upon him) and related that event to him. The Prophet (Peace be upon him) replied: 'You have told the truth. This was the help from the third heaven.'"

One of the Helpers captured 'Abbas bin 'Abdul Muttalib, who said: "O Messenger of Allâh, by Allâh this man did not capture me. I was captured by a man who was bald and had the most handsome face, and who was riding a piebald horse, I cannot see him here among the people." The Helper interrupted: "I captured him, O Messenger of Allâh." The Prophet (Peace be upon him) replied:

- "Be quiet, Allâh the All-Mighty strengthened you with the help of a noble angel."

Iblîs, the archsatan, in the guise of Suraqah bin Malik bin Ju'sham Al-Mudlaji, on seeing angels working in favour of the Muslims, and Quraish rapidly losing ground on the battlefield, made a quick retreat despite the polytheists' pleas to stay on. He ran off and plunged into the sea.

The ranks of Quraish began to give way and their numbers added nothing but confusion. The Muslims followed eagerly their retreating steps, slaying or taking captive all that fell within their reach. Retreat soon turned into ignominious rout; and they flied in haste, casting away their armour, abandoned beasts of burden, camp and equipage.

The great tyrant Abu Jahl, however, on seeing the adverse course of the battle, tried to stop the tidal wave of the Islamic victory by nerving the polytheists and encouraging them by all means available and adjuring them by Al-Lat and 'Uzza and all symbols of paganism to stand firm in place and retaliate against the Muslims, but to no avail. Their morale had already been drastically reduced to zero, and their lines broken down. He then began to realize the reality of his arrogance and haughtiness. None remained around him except a gang of doomed polytheists whose resistance was also quelled by an Islamic irresistible storm of true devotion-based valour and Islam-orientated pursuit of martyrdom. Jahl was deserted and left by himself on his horse waiting for death at the hand of two courageous lads of the Helpers.

'Abdur-Rahman bin 'Awf related the following interesting story in this regard: I was in the thick of the battle when two youths, still seemingly inexperienced in the art of fighting, one on the right and the second on the left. One of them spoke in a secret voice asking me to show him Abu Jahl. I asked about his intention, to which he replied, that he had a strong desire to engage with him in a combat until either of them was killed. It was something incredible to me. I turned left and the other said something to the same effect and showed a similar desire. I acceded to their earnest pleas and pointed directly at their target. They both rushed swiftly towards the spot, and without a moment's hesitation struck him simultaneously with their swords and finished him off. They went back to the Messenger of Allâh (Peace be upon him), each claiming that he had killed Abu Jahl to the exclusion of the other. The Prophet (Peace be upon him)asked if they had wiped the blood off their swords and they answered that they had not. He then examined both swords and assured them that they both had killed him. When the battle concluded, Abu Jahl's spoils were given to Mu'adh bin 'Amr bin Al-Jumuh, because the other Mu'awwadh bin Al-'Afrâ' was later killed in the course of the same battle. At the termination of the battle, the Prophet (Peace be upon him) wanted to look for this archenemy of Islam, Abu Jahl. 'Abdullah bin Mas'ud found him on the verge of death breathing his last. He stepped on his neck addressing him: "Have you seen how Allâh has disgraced you?" The enemy of Islam still defiantly answered: "I am not disgraced. I am no more than a man killed by his own people on the battlefield." And then inquired "Who has won the battle?" Ibn Mas'ud replied "Allâh and His Messenger." Abu Jahl then said with a heart full of grudge "You have followed difficult ways, you shepherd!" Ibn Mas'ud used to be a shepherd working for the Makkan aristocrats.

Ibn Mas'ud then cut off his head and took it to the Messenger of Allâh (Peace be upon him) who, on seeing it, began to entertain Allâh's praise:

- "Allâh is Great, praise is to Allâh, Who has fulfilled His Promise, assisted His servant and defeated the confederates alone."

He then set out to have a look at the corpse. There he said: "This is the Pharaoh of this nation."

SOME SIGNIFICANT INSTANCES OF DEVOTION:

1. The Prophet (Peace be upon him) advised his companions to preserve the lives of Banu Hashim who had gone out to Badr with the polytheists unwillingly because they had feared the censure of their people. Among them, he named Al-'Abbas bin 'Abdul Muttalib and Abu Bukhtari bin Hisham. He ordered the Muslims to capture, but not to kill them. Abu Hudhaifah bin 'Utbah showed great surprise and commented saying: "We kill our fathers, children, brothers and members of our clan, and then come to spare Al-'Abbas? By Allâh! If I see him I will surely strike him with my sword." On hearing these words, the Messenger of Allâh (Peace be upon him), addressing 'Umar bin Al-Khattab, said "Is it fair that the face of the Messenger's uncle be struck with sword?" 'Umar got indignant and threatened to kill Abu Hudhaifah; the latter later said that extreme fear had taken firm grip of him and felt that nothing except martyrdom could expiate for his mistake. He was actually killed later on during Al-Yamamah events.
2. Abu Al-Bukhtari bin Hisham had already done his best to restrain his people, the Makkans, from committing any act of folly against the Prophet (Peace be upon him) while the latter was still in Makkah. He also neither hurt nor was reported to have uttered anything repugnant with regard to the Prophet (Peace be upon him). He had as well been among the people who tried to invalidate the boycott alliance taken against Banu Hashim and Banu 'Abdul Muttalib.

- Here, however, in the battle of Badr he insisted on fighting unless his compatriot was spared. Al-Mujdhir bin Ziyad Al-Balwi, with whom he was engaged in combat, replied that the other was not included in the Prophet 's recommendation. The combat went on to end in Al-Bukhtari's death.

3. 'Abdur-Rahman bin 'Awf and Omaiyah bin Khalaf had been close friends during the pre-Islamic era. When the battle of Badr ended, 'Abdur-Rahman saw Omaiyah and his son among the captives. He threw away the armour he had as spoils, and walked with them both. Bilal, the Prophet's caller for prayer, saw Omaiyah and soon all the torture he had been put to at the hand of this man dawned upon him, and swore he would have revenge on Omaiyah. 'Abdur-Rahman tried to ease the tension and address embarrassing situation amicably but with no success. The Muslims gathered around and struck Omaiyah's son with swords. At this point, 'Abdur-Rahman called upon his old friend to run for his life but he was put to swords from different people and lay down dead. 'Abdur-Rahman, completely helpless and resigned said: May Allâh have mercy on Bilal, for he deprived me of the spoils, and I have been stricken by the death of my two captives.
4. On the moral level, the battle of Badr was an inescapable conflict between the forces of good and those of evil. In this context, 'Umar bin Al-Khattab did not spare the life of any polytheist even his uncle on the maternal side Al-'As bin Hisham bin Al-Mugheerah.
5. Abu Bakr shouted at his son 'Abdur-Rahman, still a polytheist and fighting with them, "Where is my wealth, you wicked boy?" The son answered that it was gone with the wind.
6. When the battle ended, the Muslims began to hold some polytheists in captivity. The Prophet (Peace be upon him) looked into the face of Sa'd bin Mu'adh, the Head of the Prophet's guards, and understood that he was hateful to taking the enemy elements as prisoners. Sa'd agreed to what the Prophet (Peace be upon him) said and added that it was the first victory for the Muslims over the forces of polytheism, and he had more liking for slaying them than sparing their lives.
7. On the day of Badr, the sword of 'Ukashah bin Mihsan Al-Asdi broke down so the Prophet (Peace be upon him) gave him a log of wood which he shook and it immediately turned into a long strong white sword. 'Ukashah went on using that same sword in most of the Islamic conquests until he died in the process of the apostasy wars.
8. When the war activities had been concluded, Mus'ab bin 'Umair Al-'Abdari saw his brother, still a polytheist, being handcuffed by a Ansari. Mus'ab recommended that the Helper tighten the knot for the prisoner's mother was wealthy enough to ransom her son. 'Abu 'Aziz, Mus'ab's brother, tried to appeal to his brother through the family ties, but the latter firmly replied that the Helper was more eligible for brotherhood than him.
9. When the Prophet (Peace be upon him) ordered that the corpses of the polytheists be dropped into an empty well, Abu Hudhaifah bin 'Utbah looked sadly at his dead father, who fought on the side of the polytheists. The Prophet (Peace be upon him) noticed that and asked him about it. Hudhaifah said that he had never held the least doubt that his father met his fate deservedly, but added that he wished he had been guided to the path of Islam, and that is why he felt sad. The Prophet (Peace be upon him) whispered in his ears some comforting words.

The outcome of the battle was as aforementioned an ignominious rout for the polytheists and a manifest victory for the Muslims. Fourteen Muslims were killed, of whom six were from the Emigrants and eight from the Helpers. The polytheists sustained heavy casualties, seventy were killed and a like number taken prisoners. Many of the principal men of Makkah, and some of Muhammad 's bitterest opponents, were among the slain. Chief of these was Abu Jahl.

On the third day, the Messenger of Allâh (Peace be upon him) went out to look at the slain polytheists, and said:

- "What an evil tribe you were as regards your Prophet, you belied me but the others have believed; you let me down while the others have supported me; you expelled m, whereas the others have sheltered me."

He stood over the bodies of twenty-four leaders of Quraish who had been thrown into one of the wells, and started to call them by name and by the names of their fathers, saying: "Would it not have been much better for you if you had obeyed Allâh and His Messenger? Behold, we have found that our Lord's promise do come true; did you (also) find that the promises of your Lord came true?" Thereupon, 'Umar bin Al-Khattab said: "O Messenger of Allâh! Why you speak to bodies that have no souls in them?" The Prophet (Peace be upon him) answered: "By Him in Whose hand is Muhammad 's soul! You do not hear better what I am saying than they do."

REACTION IN MAKKAH:

The polytheists having received a large dose of disciplining and heavy defeat, fled away in great disorder in the vales and hillocks heading for Makkah panicked and too ashamed to see their people.

Ibn Ishaq related that the first herald of bad tidings was Al-Haisaman bin 'Abdullah Al-Khuza'i. He narrated to them how their notables were killed. People there did not believe him at first and thought that he had gone mad, but soon the news was confirmed and a state of incredible bewilderment overwhelmed the whole Makkan scene. Abu Sufyan bin Al-Harith gave Abu Lahab a full account of the massacre and the disgraceful rout they sustained, with emphasis on the role that the angels played in bringing about their tragic end. Abu Lahab could not contain himself and gave vent to his feelings of resentment in beating, abusing and slapping Abu Rafi', a Muslim, but reticent on his conversion, for reiterating the role of the angels. Umm Al-Fadl, another Muslim woman, greatly exasperated by Abu Lahab's thoughtless behaviour, struck him with a log and cracked his head. Seven days later, he died of an ominous ulcer and was left for three days unburied. His sons, however, for fear of shameful rumours, drove him to a pit and keeping their distance, hurled stones and dust at him.

The defeat was a matter of great shame and grief for the Makkans. In almost every house there were silent tears for the dead and the captives. They were burning with humiliation and were thirsting for revenge. Wailing, lamenting and crying however were decreed strictly forbidden lest the Muslims should rejoice at their affliction.

MADINAH RECEIVES THE NEWS OF VICTORY:

Two heralds, 'Abdullah bin Rawahah and Zaid bin Harithah were despatched to Madinah, to convey the glad tidings of victory to the Muslims there.

The multi-ethnic and ideological structure of Madinah featured different respective reactions. Rumour-mongers amongst the Jews and hypocrites spread news to the effect that the Prophet (Peace be upon him) had been killed, and tried to impress their false assumption on the fact that Zaid bin Harithah was riding Al-Qaswâ', the Prophet's she-camel. Having reached, the two messengers imparted to the Muslims the happy news of victory, and furnished accurate information about the course of events in order to establish the sense of reassurance deep in the hearts of the anxious, but now, joyous Muslims. They immediately started acclaiming Allâh's Name and entertaining His praise at the top of their voices. Their chiefs went out of the city to wait and receive the Prophet (pbuh) on the road leading to Badr.

Usamah bin Zaid related that they received the news of the manifest victory shortly after Ruqaiyah, the Prophet 's daughter, and the wife of 'Uthman bin 'Affan had been committed to earth. She had been terminally ill and the Prophet (Peace be upon him) had asked 'Uthman to stay in Madinah and look after her.

Before leaving the scene of the battle, dispute concerning the spoils of war arose among the Muslim warriors, as the rule relating to their distribution had not yet been legislated. When the difference grew wider, the Messenger of Allâh (Peace be upon him) suspended any solution whereof until the Revelation was sent down.

'Ubadah bin As-Samit said: "We went out with the Messenger of Allâh (Peace be upon him) and I witnessed Badr with him. The battle started and Allâh, the Exalted, defeated the enemy. Some of the Muslims sought and pursued the enemy, some were intent on collecting the spoils from the enemy camp, and others were guarding the Messenger of Allâh (Peace be upon him) and were on the alert for any emergency or surprise attack. When night came and the Muslims gathered together, those who had collected the booty said: "We collected it, so no one else has any right to it." Those who had pursued the enemy said: "You do not have more right to it than we do; we held the enemy at bay and then defeated them." As for the men who had been guarding the Prophet (Peace be upon him), they also made similar claims to the spoils.

At that very time, a Qur'ânic verse was revealed saying:

- "They ask you [O Muhammad (Peace be upon him)] about the spoils of war. Say: 'The spoils are for Allâh and the Messenger.' So fear Allâh and adjust all matters of difference among you, and obey Allâh and His Messenger [Muhammad (Peace be upon him)], if you are believers." [8:1]

On their way back to Madinah, at a large sand hill, the Prophet (Peace be upon him) divided the spoils equally among the fighters after he had taken *Al-Khums* (one-fifth). When they reached As-Safra', he ordered that two of the prisoners should be killed. They were An-Nadr bin Al-Harith and 'Uqbah bin Abi Muait, because they had persecuted the Muslims in Makkah, and harboured deep hatred towards Allâh and His Messenger (Peace be upon him). In a nutshell, they were criminals of war in modern terminology, and their execution was an awesome lesson to oppressors. 'Uqbah forgot his pride and cried out, "Who will look after my children O Messenger of Allâh?" The Prophet (Peace be upon him) answered, "The fire (of Hell). " Did 'Uqbah not remember the day when he had thrown the entrails of a sheep onto the head of the Prophet (Peace be upon him) while he was prostrating himself in prayer, and Fatimah had come and washed it off him? He had also strangled the Prophet (Peace be upon him) with his cloak if it had not been for Abu Bakr to intervene and release the Prophet (Peace be upon him). The heads of both criminals were struck off by 'Ali bin Abi Talib.

At Ar-Rawhâ', a suburb of Madinah, the Muslim army was received by the joyous Madinese who had come to congratulate the Prophet (Peace be upon him) on the manifest victory that Allâh had granted him. Usaid bin Hudair, acting as a mouthpiece of the other true believers, after entertaining Allâh's praise, he excused himself for not having joined them on grounds that the Prophet 's intention was presumably, an errand aiming to intercept a caravan of camels only, he added that if it had occurred to him that it would be real war, he would have never tarried. The Prophet (Peace be upon him) assured Usaid that he had believed him.

The Prophet now entered Madinah as a man to be counted for in a new dimension — the military field. In consequence, a large number of the people of Madinah embraced Islam, which added a lot to the strength, power and moral standing of the true religion.

The Prophet exhorted the Muslims to treat the prisoners so well to such an extent that the captors used to give the captives their bread and keep the dates for themselves.

Prisoners of war constituted a problem awaiting resolution because it was a new phenomenon in the history of Islam. The Prophet (Peace be upon him) consulted Abu Bakr and 'Umar bin Al-Khattab as to what he should do with the prisoners. Abu Bakr suggested that he should ransom them, explaining this by saying: "They are after all our relatives, and this money would give us strength against the disbelievers, moreover, Allâh could guide them to Islam." 'Umar advised killing them, saying, "They are the leaders of *Kufr* (disbelief)." The Prophet (Peace be upon him) preferred Abu Bakr's suggestion to that of 'Umar's. The following day, 'Umar called on the Prophet (Peace be upon him) and Abu Bakr to see them weeping. He shextreme astonishment and inquired about the situation so that he might weep if it was worth weeping for, or else he would feign weeping.

The Prophet (Peace be upon him) said that a Qur'ânic verse had been revealed rebuking them for taking ransom from the captives rather than slaying them:

- "It is not for a Prophet that he should have prisoners of war (and free them with ransom) until he had made a great slaughter (among his enemies) in the land. You desire the good of this world (i.e. the money of ransom for freeing the captives), but Allâh desires (for you) the Hereafter. And Allâh is All-Mighty, All-Wise. Were it not a previous ordainment from Allâh, a severe torment would have touched you for what you took." [8:67,68]

The previous Divine ordainment went as follows,

- "Thereafter (is the time) either for generosity (i.e. free them without ransom) or ransom." [47:4]

Which included an area providing permission to take ransom, that is why no penalty was imposed. They were rebuked only for taking prisoners before subduing all the land of disbelief. Apart from this, the polytheists taken to Madinah were not only prisoners of war but rather archcriminals of war whom modern war penal law brings to justice to receive their due sentence of death or prison for life.

The ransom for the prisoners ranged between 4000 and 1000 Dirhams in accordance with the captive's financial situation. Another form of ransom assumed an educational dimension; most of the Makkans, unlike the Madinese, were literate and so each prisoner who could not afford the ransom was entrusted with ten children to teach them the art of writing and reading. Once the child had been proficient enough, the instructor would be set free. Another clan of prisoners were released unransomed on grounds of being hard up. Zainab, the daughter of the Prophet (Peace be upon him), paid the ransom of her husband Abul-'As with a necklace. The Muslims released her prisoner and returned the necklace in deference to the Prophet (Peace be upon him) but on condition that Abul-'As allow Zainab to migrate to Madinah, which he actually did.

In captivity, there was also an eloquent orator called Suhail bin 'Amr. 'Umar suggested that they pull out his front teeth to disable him from speaking, but the Prophet (Peace be upon him) turned down his suggestion for fear Quraish should retaliate in the same manner on one hand, and on the other for fear of Allâh's wrath on the Day of Resurrection.

Sa'd bin An-Nu'man, a lesser pilgrim detained in Makkah, was released in return for setting Abu Sufyan's son, a captive, free.

THE BATTLE OF BADR IN ITS QUR'ANIC CONTEXT:

The Chapter of *Al-Anfal* (spoils of war) was revealed on the occasion of the battle of Badr, Ramadan 17th 2 A.H. It constituted a unique Divine commentary on this battle.

Allâh, the All-High, in the context of this Chapter draws on major issues relating to the whole process of

Islamization. Allâh, here draws the attention of the Muslims to the still lingering moral shortcomings in their character. He wants them to build an integrated, purified society. He speaks about the invisible assistance he sent down to His obedient servants to enable them to accomplish their noble objectives. He wants the Muslims to rid themselves of any trait of haughtiness or arrogance that might sneak in. He wants them to turn to Him for help, obey Him and His Messenger (Peace be upon him).

After that He delineated the noble objectives for which the Messenger (Peace be upon him) launched that bloody battle, and directed them to the merits and qualities that brought about the great victory.The polytheists, hypocrites, the Jews and prisoners of war were also mentioned, being admonished to surrender to the Truth and adhere to it only. The question of the spoils of war was resolved and the principles and basics relevant to this issue were clearly defined.

The laws and rules pertinent to war and peace were legalized and codified, especially at this advanced stage of the Islamic action. Allâh wanted the Muslims to follow war ethics dissimilar to those of pre-Islamic practices. The Muslims are deemed to outdo the others in ethics, values and fine ideals. He wants to impress on the world that Islam is not merely a theoretical code of life, it is rather mind cultivation-orientated practical principles. In this context, He established inter and intra-state relations.

The fast of Ramadan was established as an obligatory observance in the year 2 A.H., appended by the duty imposed upon Muslims of paying *Zakat* (alms tax, poor-due) in order to alleviate the burden of the needy Emigrants.

A wonderful and striking coincidence was the establishment of Shawwal *'Eid* (the Festival of the Fast-Breaking) directly after the manifest victory of Badr. It was actually the finest spectacle ever witnessed of Muslims leaving their houses praying, acclaiming Allâh's Name and entertaining His praise at the top of their voices in recognition of His favour and grace, and last but not least, the support He rendered them and through which the forces of the Truth overpowered those of evil.

- "And remember when you were few and were reckoned weak in the land, and were afraid that men might kidnap you, but He provided a safe place for you, strengthened you with His help, and provided you with good things so that you might be grateful." [8:26]

THE MILITARY ACTIVITIES BETWEEN BADR AND UHUD

The battle of Badr was the first armed encounter between the Muslims and Quraish. It was in fact a decisive battle that gained the Muslims a historic victory acknowledged by all the Arabs, and dealt a heavy blow to the religious and economic interests of the polytheists. There were also the Jews who also used to regard each . Islamic victory as a heavy blow to their religioeconomic entity. Both parties were burning with rage and fury since the Muslims had achieved that great victory:

- "Verily, you will find the strongest among men in enmity to the believers (Muslims) the Jews and *Al-Mushrikûn* (polytheists, pagans, idolators and disbelievers, etc.)." [5:82]

Both resentful parties had their much more indignant suite in the form of hypocrites who faked Islam just to save their faces; at the head of whom came 'Abdullah bin Ubai and his retinue. The desert bedouins living in tents pitched in the vicinity of Madinah, who depended on plundering and looting as a means of living, were totally indifferent to this axial question of belief and disbelief. Their worry derived from fear of losing their perverted avenues of subsistence in case a powerful nascent Muslim state should rise up and put an end to such ill-practices, hence the grudge they nursed against Islam and the Muslims, in general, and the person of Muhammad (Peace be upon him) in particular.

The whole cause of Faith was thus at stake with four furious parties laying ambushes against the new religion, each in its style: Pretension to Islam embedded with conspiracy plots and provocative deeds within Madinah, explicitly uncovered animosity pregnant with indignation and fire of rage on the part of the Jews, and there in Makkah open and persistent calls for vengeance coupled with open intentions to mobilize all potential resources available to silence the voice of Islam once and for all. This was later translated into military action, Uhud Invasion, which left a very bad impression on the good name and esteem that the Muslims were painstakingly working to merit and preserve.

The Muslims were always obliged to be on the lookout for any hostile movements, and it was imperative on them to launch pre-emptive strikes in all directions in order to enjoy a reasonable degree of security in this great instability-provoking ocean of unrest. The following is a list of military activities conducted in the post-Badr era:

ALKUDR INVASION

The scouting body of Madinah reported that Banu Saleem of Ghatafan were engaged in mustering troops to invade the Muslims. The Prophet (Peace be upon him) took the initiative himself and mounted a surprise attack on them in their own homeland at a watering place called Al-Kudr. Banu Saleem, on receiving the news, had fled before he arrived. He stayed there for three days, took their 500 camels as booty and distributed them to the fighters after he had set aside the usual one-fifth; each one gained two camels.

This invasion took place in Shawwal in the year 2 A.H., seven days after the event of Badr.

AN ATTEMP ON THE LIFE OF THE PROPHET (Peace be upon him)

The impact of defeat at Badr was so great that the Makkans began to burn with indignation and resentment over their horrible losses. To resolve this situation two polytheists volunteered to quench their thirst and muffle the source of that humiliation i.e. the Prophet (Peace be upon him).

'Umair bin Wahab Al-Jumahi, a terrible polytheist, and an archenemy Safwan bin Omaiyah sat together privately lamenting their loss and remembering their dead and captives. 'Umair expressed a fervent desire to kill the Prophet (Peace be upon him) and release his captured son in Madinah, if it was not for the yoke of debts he was under and the large family he had to support. Safwan, also had his good reasons to see the Prophet (Peace be upon him) killed, so he offered to discharge 'Umair's debts and support his family if he went on with his plan.

'Umair agreed and asked Safwan to be reticent on the whole scheme. He left for Madinah, having with him a sword to which he applied some kind of lethal poison. 'Umar bin Al-Khattab saw him at the door of the Mosque and understood that he had come with evil intentions. He immediately went into the Mosque and informed the Prophet (Peace be upon him). He was let in looped by the sling of his sword and in greeting he said "good morning", to which the Prophet (Peace be upon him) replied that Allâh had been Gracious and taught them the greeting of the dwellers of the Paradise: "peace be upon you!" To a question raised by the Prophet (Peace be upon him), about his object, 'Umair said that he had come to see that his captured son was well treated. As for the sword, which the Prophet (Peace be upon him) asked him about, he cursed it and said that it gained them nothing. On exhorting him to tell his real goal, he remained obdurate and did not divulge the secret meeting with Safwan. Here the Prophet (Peace be upon him) got impatient and he himself revealed to 'Umair his secret mission. 'Umair was taken by surprise, and incredible astonishment seized him, and immediately bore witness to the Messengership of Muhammad (Peace be upon him) He then began to entertain Allâh's praise for having been guided to the 'Straight Path'. The Prophet (Peace be upon him) was pleased and asked his Companions to teach 'Umair the principles of Islam, recite to him the Noble Qur'ân and release his son from captivity.

Safwan, meanwhile, was still entertaining false illusions as to the approaching redemption of honour, and burying the memory of Badr into oblivion. He was impatiently awaiting 'Umair's news but to his great surprise, he was told that the man had embraced Islam and changed into a devoted believer. 'Umair later came back to Makkah where he started to call people unto Islam and he did actually manage to convert a lot of Makkans into Islam.

INVASION OF BANI QAYNUQA:

We have already spoken about the treaty that the Prophet (Peace be upon him) signed with the Jews. He was very careful to abide by it to the letter and the Muslims did not show the least violation of any of its provisions. The Jews, however, whose natural disposition is closely linked to treachery, betrayal and covenant-breaching, could not rid themselves of the tradition of theirs, and started a process of intrigues and troublemaking with the aim of producing schism in the growing solid Muslim ranks. Here is a relevant model of their behaviour: Shas bin Qais, an elderly Jew, a terrible disbeliever and a greatly envious man of the Muslims, passed by a group of Muhammad (Peace be upon him) followers of Aws and Khazraj. He perceived a prevalent spirit of reconciliation and an atmosphere of rapport and amity enveloping the whole group; an unusual scene categorically in conflict with the animosity and hatred that characterized their pre-Islam behaviour. He, therefore, sent a youth of his to sit among them, remind them of Bu'ath war between them and recite some of their verses which they used to compose satirizing each other; all of this with the intention of sowing the seeds of discord and disagreement and undermining the new Islamically-orientated inter-tribal relations. The youth did in fact succeed and the two parties at no time recalled the old days and pre-Islam tribal fanaticism sprang to the front to bring about a state of war.

The Prophet (Peace be upon him) was reported of this account, and immediately, at the head of some Emigrants, set out to see to the situation. He began to rebuke them but in the manner of the great instructor and the tolerant spirit of the understanding guide: "O, Muslims! Do you still advance pre-Islamic arguments after I have been sent to you (as a Messenger). Remember that it is not rightful for you to turn backward after Allâh has guided you to the Straight Path, delivered you from disbelief and created amity between you." The Muslims readily realized that it was a Satanic whim and a plot hatched by the enemies. They directly embraced each other and went back home quite satisfied and in full obedience to the Messenger of Allâh (Peace be upon him).

Such were the practices of the , trouble-making, dissension-sowing, falsehood-fabrication, faking belief in the day, and practising disbelief at night. In everyday life, they used to tighten the ropes of financial dealings on the Muslims. If they happened to owe a Muslim something, they would shirk their obligations on grounds that he had converted into a new religion and they would allege the basis of agreement was no longer valid. If it was the other way, they would never cease to harass him day and night to pay back the debt, all of which in a desperate attempt to demolish the great edifice of the new religion that was rapidly gaining ground and speedily towering up skyward.

THE QAINUQA' JEWS BREACH THE COVENANT:

Seeing that Allâh sided with the believers and granted them a manifest victory and perceiving the Muslims' awesome presence in Madinah, the Jews could no longer contain themselves or conceal indignation. They started a series of provocative and harmful deeds publicly. The most wicked amongst them were the tribe of Banu Qainuqa', who lived in quarters within Madinah named after them. As for jobs, they took up goldsmithery, blacksmithing and crafts of making household instruments, that is why war weaponry was available in large quantities in their houses. They counted 700 warriors, and were the most daring amongst the Jewish community in Arabia, and now the first to breach the covenant of cooperation and non-aggression which they had already countersigned with the Prophet (Peace be upon him). Their behaviour grew too impolite and unbearable. They started a process of trouble-making, jeering at the Muslims, hurting those who frequented their bazaars, and even intimidating their women. Such things began to aggravate the general situation, so the Prophet(Peace be upon him) gathered them in assemblage, admonished and called them to be rational, sensible and guided and cautioned against further transgression. Nevertheless they remained obdurate and paid no heed to his warning, and said: "Don't be deluded on account of defeating some Quraishites inexperienced in the art of war. If you were to engage us in fight, you will realize that we are genuine war experts."

In this regard, the Words of Allâh were revealed saying:

- "Say [O Muhammad (Peace be upon him)] to those who disbelieve: 'You will be defeated and gathered together to Hell, and worst indeed is that place to rest.' There has already been a Sign for you (O Jews) in the two armies that met (in combat — i.e. the battle of Badr): One was fighting in the cause of Allâh, and as for the other (they) were disbelievers. They (the believers) saw them (the disbelievers) with their own eyes twice their number (although they were thrice their number). And Allâh supports with His Victory whom He pleases. Verily, in this is a lesson for those who understand." [3:12,13]

The answer of Banu Qainuqa' amounted, as seen, to war declaration. The Prophet (Peace be upon him) suppressed his anger and advised the Muslims to be patient and forbearing and wait for what time might reveal.

The Jews, went too far in their transgression, presumptuous behaviour and licentious practices. One day a Jewish goldsmith provoked a Muslim woman whose genitals become uncovered when he had tied the edge of the garment to her back. A Muslim man happened to be there and killed the man; the Jews retaliated by killing that Muslim. The man's family called the Muslims for help and war started.

On Saturday, Shawwal 15th, 2 A.H., the Prophet (Peace be upon him) marched out with his soldiers, Hamzah bin 'Abdul Muttalib, carrying the standard of the Muslims and laid siege to the Jews' forts for 15 days. Allâh cast fear into their hearts, and they were obliged to defer to the Messenger (Peace be upon him) judgement on their lives, wealth, women and children; their hands were tied behind their backs.

At this point, 'Abdullah bin Ubai bin Salul started his hypocritical role and began to intercede for them persistently on grounds of former alliance between those Jews and His tribe Khazraj. Muhammad (Peace be upon him) dealt with this man as being a Muslim -- He had faked conversion into Islam for only one month, by that time -- and so he granted him his request; for Islam accepts people at their face value. Banu Qainuqa' handed over all materials, wealth and war equipage to the Prophet (Peace be upon him), who set aside one fifth and distributed the rest to his men. After that they were banished out of all Arabia to Azru'a in Syria where they stayed for a while and soon perished away.

AS-SAWIQ INVASION:

Two-pronged hostile activities were being independently conducted against the Prophet (Peace be upon him) ; plots and intrigues being hatched by Safwan bin Omaiyah, the hypocrites and Jews on the one hand, going on and on parallel lines with military hostilities being prepared by Abu Sufyan aiming at saving the face of his people and impressing on the other Arabs that Quraish was still a military power to be counted for. In the aftermath of Badr, Abu Sufyan was burning for revenge and took a solemn vow he would never bathe off impurity unless he had avenged himself on Muhammad (Peace be upon him) and his followers. He set out at the head of 200 men towards Madinah but was not brave enough to attack it in broad daylight. He, instead resorted to acts of piracy that are performed in the dark. He infiltrated into the Prophet 's town and went to see an old ally Huyai bin Akhtab, who was too cowardly to let him in, so he left for Salam bin Mashkam, chief of Bani Nadeer, a tribe of Jews. The Jew entertained and gave him a full account of the situation therein. Late at night he despatched a group of his men to raid Al-'Uraid, a suburb of Madinah. There, the men felled and burnt the palm trees, killed two Muslims and then took swiftly to their heels.

On hearing the news, the Prophet (Peace be upon him) gathered his men and set out at their heels, but could not catch them. The Muslims brought back the provisions (*Sawiq*, a kind of barley porridge) which the polytheists had thrown aside in order to lighten their loads and hasten their escape; hence this campaign was called As-Sawiq Invasion. It took place in Dhul-Hijjah 2 A.H., two months after the event of Badr.

DHI AMR INVASION, MUHARRAM, 3 A.H:

The Prophet 's intelligence personnel reported that Banu Tha'labah and Banu Muhârib were mustering troops with the aim of raiding the outskirts of Madinah. The Prophet (Peace be upon him) at the head of 450 horsemen and footmen set out to handle this new situation. 'Uthman bin 'Affan was asked to dispose the affairs of the Muslims in Madinah. On their way, they captured a man who embraced Islam and acted as a guide for the army. When the enemies heard of the approach of the Muslims, they hurriedly dispersed in the mountains and disappeared. The Muslims encamped at a watering place called "Dhi Amr" for the whole of Safar 3 A.H. The Prophet (Peace be upon him) aimed to impress upon the desert bedouins in the area, that the Muslims were then powerful enough to cast fear and awe into the hearts of their enemies.

KA'B BIN AL-ASHRAF, KILLED:

Ka'b bin Al-Ashraf was the most resentful Jew at Islam and the Muslims, the keenest on inflicting harm on the Messenger of Allâh (Peace be upon him) and the most zealous advocate of waging war against him. He belonged to Tai' tribe but his mother to Banu Nadeer. He was a wealthy man known for his handsomeness, and a poet living in luxury in his fort south east of Madinah at the rear of Banu Nadeer's habitations.

On hearing the news of Badr, he got terribly exasperated and swore that he would prefer death to life if the news was true. When this was confirmed he wrote poems satirizing Muhammad (Peace be upon him), eulogizing Quraish and enticing them against the Prophet (Peace be upon him). He then rode to Makkah where he started to trigger the fire of war, and kindle rancour against the Muslims in Madinah. When Abu Sufyan asked him which religion he was more inclined to, the religion of the Makkans or that of Muhammad (Peace be upon him) and his companions, he replied that the pagans were better guided. Wrespect to this situation, Allâh revealed His Words:

- "Have you not seen those who were given a portion of the Scripture? They believe in *Jibt* and *Taghût*, and say to the disbelievers that they are better guided as regards the way than the believers (Muslims)." [4:51]

He then returned to Madinah to start a fresh campaign of slanderous propaganda that took the form of obscene songs and amatory sonnets with a view to defaming the Muslim women.

At this stage, the situation became unbearable and could no longer be put up with. The Prophet (Peace be upon him) gathered his men and said: "Who will kill Ka'b bin Al-Ashraf? He had maligned Allâh, and His Messenger." Thereupon, Muhammad bin Maslamah, 'Abbad bin Bishr, Al-Harith bin Aws, Abu 'Abs bin Hibr and Salkan bin Salamah, Ka'b's foster brother, volunteered to do the job.

Muhammad bin Maslamah said: "O Messenger of Allâh, do you wish that I should kill him?" He said: "Yes." He said: "Permit me to talk (to him in the way I deem fit)." He said: "Talk (as you like)." So, Muhammad bin Maslamah came to Ka'b and talked to him, saying: "This man (i.e. the Prophet (Peace be upon him)) has made up his mind to collect charity (from us) and this has put us to a great hardship." When he heard this, Ka'b said: "By Allâh you will be put to more trouble by him." Muhammad bin Maslamah answered: "No doubt, now we have become his followers and we do not like to forsake him until we see what turn his affairs will take. I want that you should give me a loan." He said: "What will you mortgage?" Muhammad answered: "What do you want?" The immoral and heartless Jew demanded women and children as articles of security against the debt. Muhammad said: "Should we pledge our women whereas you are the most handsome of the Arabs; and the son of one of us may be abused by saying that he was pledged for two *wasq* (measurement unit of weight) of dates but we can pledge you (our) weapons." Ka'b agreed. Salkan bin Salamah, Abu Na'ilah, at another time, went to see Ka'b for the same purpose and there were more or less the same subjects, only that Abu Na'ilah would bring him some companions. The plan was successful and provided for the presence of both men and weapons. On Rabi' Al-Awwal 14th, at night, the year 3 A.H. the people said good bye to the Prophet (Peace be upon him) and set out in the Name of Allâh to implement the carefully drawn plan. The Prophet (Peace be upon him) stayed back praying for them and supplicating Allâh to render them success. The men went and called upon him at night. He came down although his wife warned him not to meet them alleging that: "I hear a voice which sounds like the voice of murder." He said: "It is only Muhammad bin Maslamah and my foster brother Abu Na'ilah. When a gentleman is called at night even if he be pierced with a spear, he should respond to the call." Abu Na'ilah said to his companions: "As he comes down, I will extend my hand towards his head to smell and when I hold him fast, you should do your job." So when he came down, they talked together for about an hour. They then invited him to go out and spend a nice time in the moonlight. On the way out, Abu Na'ilah remarked: "I smell the nicest perfume from you." Ka'b said: "Yes, I have with me a mistress who is the most scented of the women of Arabia." Abu Na'ilah again said: "Allow me to smell (the scent on your head)". He said: "Yes, you may smell." So he caught it and smelt. Then he said: "Allow me to do so (once again)." He then held his head fast and said to his companions: "Do your job." And they killed him. The group of men came back after fulfilling their mission. One of them Al-Harith bin Aws was wounded by mistake with the swords of his men, and was bleeding badly. When they reached Baqee' Al-Gharqad, they shouted, "Allâh is Great". The Prophet (Peace be upon him) heard them and realized that they had killed the enemy of Allâh. As they saw him, he said: "Cheerful faces are yours." In reply, they said: "And yours O Messenger of Allâh." They handed the head of the tyrant over to him. He entertained Allâh's praise for their success. He then applied his saliva to Al-Harith's wound and it healed on the spot.

When the Jews learned about the death of their tyrant, Ka'b bin Al-Ashraf, they were scared and even their stonelike hearts were in the grip of inexpressible panic. They realized that the Messenger of Allâh (Peace be upon him) would thenceforth never hesitate to use force when good words and admonition failed. They remained silent and resigned, and faked adherence to covenants.

Now the Prophet (Peace be upon him) was free to collect his thoughts and give himself up to resolving foreign affairs, and facing dangers that could be carried with hostile wind blowing again from Makkah.

THE INVASION OF BUHRAN:

In Rabi' Ath-Thani, the year 3 A.H. the Prophet (Peace be upon him) led a campaign comprising 300 warriors to Buhran in the area of Al-Furu'. He stayed there till Jumada Al-Ula, 3 A.H. No fighting took place in the process of this patrolling invasion.

ZAID BIN HARITHAH LEADS A CAMPAIGN ON THE TRADE ROUTES OF QURAISH:

This was the most successful campaign prior to Uhud Battle. It took place in Jumada Ath-Thaniyah, the year 3 A.H.

Summer approached and it was high time for the Makkan trade caravans to leave for Syria. The people of Quraish whose lives depended mainly on a mercantile economy consisting of summer caravans to Syria and winter caravans to Abyssinia (Ethiopia), were now at a loss as to what route they would have to follow in order to avoid the backbreaking military strikes that the Muslims successfully inflicted on the polytheists.

They held a meeting to discuss the chances of escaping the economic blockade and decided to go along a trade route across Najd to Iraq. Furat bin Haiyan was appointed as a guide for the caravan. Safwan bin Omaiyah led the caravan along the new route. News of the meeting leaked out through Na'im bin Mas'ud Al-Ashja'i under the effect of wine, and it flew fast to Madinah by Sulit bin An-Nu'man. The Prophet (Peace be upon him) immediately mustered 100 horsemen under the leadership of Zaid bin Harithah Al-Kalbi and despatched them to intercept and capture the caravan. They caught up with the camels at a place called Al-Qardah. They took the polytheists by surprise and arrested their guide and two other men. Safwan and his guards fled away without showing the least resistance. The caravan was carrying silver and wares whose value amounted to 100 thousand dirhams. The booty was distributed among the Muslim warriors after one-fifth had been set aside for the Prophet (Peace be upon him). Furat bin Haiyan embraced Islam out of his own sweet free will.

As a result of this episode, the Muslims foiled Quraish's plans to find a new trade route. The economic siege laid to Makkah was thus consolidated and had a great impact on the mercantile economy of Makkah. The Makkans were terribly anxious and worried about their prospects of life now at stake with no hope whatsoever for any possible rehabilitation of commercial life or redemption of former prestige at the socio-political level except through two avenues categorically contrasting: Relinquishing all symbols of arrogance and all attitudes of haughtiness through reconciliation with the new status quo, and peaceableness with the Muslims; or launching a decisive overwhelming war with the aim of crushing down the military forces of Madinah. It was apparent through the process of events that Quraish had opted for the second alternative. Loud cries were being heard everywhere in Makkah demanding immediate vengeance and quick retaliatory action. These movements on all levels constituted the direct preliminaries to the battle of Uhud.

MILITARY PLATOONS AND MISSIONS BETWEEN THE BATTEL OF UHUD AND THE BATTLE OF THE CONFEDERATES

Uhud's misfortune left a bad impact on both the credibility and military reputation of the Muslims. Their dignity and power in people's eyes were impaired. Troubles and dangers spread everywhere in and out of Madinah. The Jews, hypocrites and bedouins declared publicly their enmity to the Muslims and each party was keen on degrading and, in the final place, exterminating their whole existence.

Two months had almost passed after this battle, when Banu Asad made preparations to raid Madinah, 'Udal and Qarah tribes conspired against the Muslims in the month of Safar, 4 A.H. and killed ten of the Prophet 's Companions. Similarly Banu 'Amir plotted against them too, and seventy Companions were killed in the battle of Ma'una Well. During that period, Banu Nadeer kept on announcing their enmity and were involved in a plot to kill the Prophet Muhammad (Peace be upon him) in Rabi' Al-Awwal in 4 A.H. Banu Ghatfan were about to attack Madinah in Jumada Al-Ula in 4 A.H.

Thus we see that the Muslims turned into an attractive target of several potential dangers after they had lost their military credibility in the battle of Uhud. Muhammad (Peace be upon him) most wisely managed to hold all those hostile currents at bay, and even redeem the lost dignity of the Muslims and gain them anew fresh glory and noble standing. The first initiative he took in this process was Hamra' Al-Asad pursuit operation, whereby he could retain the Muslim military reputation. He succeeded in recovering his followers' dignity and awe-inspiring position in such a manner that astonished or even astounded both the Jews and hypocrites, alike, then he proceeded to crown his successful attempts by despatching military errands and missions:

ABI SALAMAH MISSION:

The first people to take up arms against the Muslims in the aftermath of Uhud reverse were Banu Asad bin Khuzaimah. "The Intelligence Corps" of Madinah reported that Talhah and Salamah, sons of Khuwailid have mustered some volunteers to fight the Messenger of Allâh (Peace b upon him). The Prophet (Peace be upon him) immediately despatched a 150-man-platoon of Helpers and Emigrants headed by Abu Salamah. The Muslim leader took Bani Asad bin Khuzaimah by surprise in their own homeland, neutralized their attempts, dispersed them and captured their cattle. On his return, Abu Salamah had an inflammation of a previous wound he sustained in Uhud, and caused him to die soon after. This expedition took place on Muharram 1st, 4 A.H.

AN ERRAND LED BY 'ABDALLAH BIN UNAIS:

On the fifth day of the same month Muharram, 4 A.H., it was reported that Khalid bin Sufyan Al-Hudhali was gathering some mob to raid the Muslim positions. 'Abdullah bin Unais, at the behest of the Prophet (Peace be upon him) set out to destroy the enemies.

The Muslim military leader stayed away for eighteen days during which he successfully fulfilled his task, killed the head of the rebels and brought his head back to Madinah on Saturday, seven days before the end of Muharram. The Prophet (Peace be upon him), as a reward, gave him a stick saying "This will function as a sign of recognition for you and me on the Day of Resurrection." On his death bed, 'Abdullah requested that the log be with him in his shroud.

THE EVENT OF AR-RAJI:

In Safar of the fourth year A.H., a delegation from the tribes of 'Udal and Qarah came to Madinah and asked the Prophet (Peace be upon him) to send a group of Companions to instruct them in religion, claiming the existence of some Muslims among them. He sent six of his Companions, in another version, ten headed by Murthid bin Abi Murthid Al-Ghanawi, or, according to Al-Bukhari, 'Asim bin Thabit, the grandfather of 'Asim bin 'Umar bin Al-Khattab. When they reached a spot called Ar-Raji' between Rabigh and Jeddah, a hundred archers of Banu Lihyan clan surrounded the place and attacked them. The delegation of Muslims took shelter on some high ground, Fudfud, and the bedouins offered them a pledge that they would not be killed. 'Asim refused to come down, instead he fought them until he and six of his companions were killed. Three men were left, Khubaib, Zaid bin Ad-Dathna and another one. Once again, the bedouins offered them a guarantee of safety and they accepted. When they descended, the bedouins treacherously bound them. The third man rebuked them for their insincerity and resisted them so they killed him. The other two men who had killed some notables of Quraish at Badr were taken and sold in Makkah. The first was Khubaib who was detained for some time and then it was unanimously decided to crucify him. He was taken from the Holy Sanctuary to At-Tan'im for crucifixion. He requested a respite to offer a two-*Rak'a* prayer. After the final greeting, he turned to his executioners, and said: "Had I not been afraid that you would think that I was afraid of death, I would have prayed for a long time." It was then that Khubaib first set the tradition of praying two *Rak'a* before being executed. He then said:

- O Lord! Count them one by one, exterminate them to the last one."

He then recited some verses of poetry which speak eloquently of the atrocities borne by him, and testify to his Faith in Allâh at this hour of suffering:

The confederates have gathered their tribes around me,
And summoned all of them who could come.
They have gathered their women and children,
I am bound fastly to a lofty trunk.
To Allâh alone I complain of my helplessness and sufferings,
And of the death, the confederates have prepared for me.
Lord of the Throne! Give me endurance against their design,
They have cut my flesh bit by bit, and I have been deprived of sustenance.
They let me choose infidelity but death is preferable,
Tears roll out of my eyes, though not of fear.
By Allâh! I fear not if I die a Muslim,
On what side I fall for the sake of Allâh.
I will not show subservience to the enemy,
If Lord so desires, He will bless my torn limbs and broken joints.

Abu Sufyan then addressed him saying: "I adjure you by Allâh, don't you wish that Muhammad (Peace be upon him) were here in your place so that we might cut off his head, and that you were with your family?" Khubaib answered, "By Allâh, I do not wish that Muhammad (Peace be upon him) now were in the place I occupy or that a thorn could hurt him, and that I were sitting with my family." Quraish ordered 'Uqbah bin Al-Harith, whose father had been killed by Khubaib himself, to crucify him. They also appointed someone to guard his corpse. 'Amr bin Omaiyah Ad-Damari played a cunning trick and carried the corpse stealthily at night to bury it somewhere. It was later reported that shortly before his crucifixion, he was seen eating a bunch of grapes although there was not even one date available in Makkah at that time. [In fact, it was nothing but sustenance bestowed upon him by Allâh.

Safwan bin Omaiyah purchased the second man, Zaid bin Ad-Dathna, and killed him as an act of vengeance for his father's murder.

Quraish, whom 'Asim had killed one of their notables, sent someone to fetch a portion of his body, but to their disappointment, his corpse was inaccessible because a large swarm of hornets had been shielding him against any malicious tampering. 'Asim had already given his Lord a pledge to remain immune against any polytheist tampering with respect to his body, and also stay detached from any contact with the enemies of Allâh. 'Umar bin Al-Khattab, when hearing this piece of news exclaimed, "Allâh verily protects His believing slave after death just as He does during his lifespan.

THE TRAGEDY OF MA'UNA WELL:

Ma'una Well tragedy, which was even more horrible than that of Ar-Raji', took place in the same month.

Abu Bara' — 'Amir bin Malik — nicknamed '*Spear Player*' came to the Messenger of Allâh (Peace be upon him) in Madinah. The Messenger of Allâh (Peace be upon him) called him to embrace Islam but he neither agreed nor refused. He said: "O Messenger of Allâh, if you dispatch some of your Companions to the people of Najd to call them to Islam, I expect them to accept." "I am afraid the people of Najd willkill them." Said the Messenger. But he replied, "I will protect them." Ibn Ishaq confirms that forty men were sent to them; but *As-Sahih* states that they were seventy — Al-Mundhir bin 'Amr, one of Bani Sa'ida, nicknamed '*Freed to die*' — commanded that group, who were the best and most learned in the Qur'ân and jurisprudence.

On their way to Najd they used to gather firewood to buy food for the people of '*Ahl As-Suffah*' as charity by day and study, meditate on the meanings of the Qur'ân by night. They kept on doing that till they arrived at Ma'una Well — which was a well in between Bani 'Amir, Harrah and Bani Saleem. They stayed there and sent the Message of the Prophet (Peace be upon him) with Haram bin Milhan, the brother of Umm Sulaim to the enemy of Allâh 'Amir bin At-Tufail. 'Amir did not heed the Message but rather ordered a man to spear Haram in the back. When the spear penetrated Haram's body, he saw the blood and said: "*Allâhu Akbar! (i.e. Allâh is the Greatest) By Lord of Al-Ka'bah I have won!*"

Then the enemy of Allâh, promptly, called out Bani 'Amir to fight the rest. Bani 'Amir refused because they were under the protection of Abu Bara'. Therefore he turned to Bani Saleem for help. The people of 'Usaiyah, Ri'al and Dhakwan, who were folks of Bani Saleem, responded to his call. The Companions of the Prophet (Peace be upon him), who were encompassed by idolaters, kept on fighting till they were all killed. The only survivor was Ka'b bin Zaid bin An-Najjar who was carried wounded from among the dead. It was in *Al-Khandaq* (the trench) Battle that he was killed.

'Amr bin Omaiyah Ad-Damari and Al-Mundhir bin 'Uqbah bin 'Amir, who were entrusted with the Muslims' animals far from them, saw the birds circling in the air over the battleground. Al-Mundhir rushed to share in the fight till he was killed. But 'Amr bin Omaiyah was captured. 'Amir set him free when he knew that he was of Mudar tribe but that was after he had cut his hair. He did that to fulfil a pledge of his mother's to set a slave free.

Returning to the Prophet (Peace be upon him) 'Amr bin Omaiyah conveyed the news of the painful disaster, which resulted in the murder of seventy of the best believers, and recalled the tragedy of Uhud but with the difference that those of Uhud were killed in a clear war but those of Ma'una were killed in a disgraceful treachery. On his way back to Qarqara, 'Amr bin Omaiyah rested in the shade of a tree, and there two men of Bani Kilab joined him. When they slept, 'Amr killed them both, thinking that by doing that he would avenge some of his killed companions. Then he found out that they had been given a pledge of protection by the Prophet (Peace be upon him). He told the Messenger of Allâh (Peace be upon him) what he had done. The Messenger of Allâh (Peace be upon him) said to 'Amr: "You have killed two people; their blood-money shall be a debt I have to discharge." He then engaged himself collecting their blood-money from the Muslims and their allies, the Jews. This very act was later to trigger the invasion of Bani An-Nadeer.

The Prophet (Peace be upon him) was so deeply moved by this tragedy and that of Ar-Raji' that he used to invoke Allâh's wrath against those people and tribes who killed his Companions. Anas reported that for thirty days the Prophet (Peace be upon him) supplicated Allâh against those who killed his Companions at Ma'una Well. Every dawn prayer he would invoke Allâh's wrath against Ri'l, Dhakwan, Lihyan and 'Usaiyah. He would say, " 'Usaiyah disobeyed Allâh and His Messenger." Therefore Allâh عز وجل, sent down unto His Messenger a Qur'ânic verse that we kept on reciting till it was abrogated later on: 'Inform our folk that we have encountered our Lord and He is satisfied with us and we are satisfied with Him.' So the Messenger of Allâh (Peace be upon him) stopped his invocation.

BANI AN-NADEER INVASION:

We have already spoken about the disgraceful behaviour of the Jews and how they were always thirsting to shed the blood of the Muslims and undermine the cause of Islam despite all the covenants and pledges they had given to the Prophet (Peace be upon him). Their behaviour fluctuated between resignation and slackness after the Banu Qainuqa' event and the murder of Ka'b bin Al-Ashraf, and rebellion coupled with treacherous clandestine contacts with Quraish and the hypocrites in order to establish an alliance against the Muslims after the battle of Uhud. Being inexperienced in war tactics, they resorted to conspiracy and intrigue hatching. They first of all declared open hatred and enmity, and chose to play all sorts of tricks that might harm the Muslims, but were very careful not to initiate any sort of hostilities that might involve them in open war.

The Prophet (Peace be upon him), on his part, exercised the highest degree of patience with them but they went too far in their provocative deeds, especially after Ar-Raji' and Ma'una Well events; they even made an attempt on his life.

Once the Prophet (Peace be upon him) with some of his Companions set out to see Banu Nadeer and seek their help in raising the blood-money he had to pay to Bani Kalb for the two men that 'Amr bin Omaiyah Ad-Damari had killed by mistake. All of that was in accordance with the clauses of the treaty that both parties had already signed. On hearing his story they said they would share in paying the blood-money and asked him and his Companions Abu Bakr, 'Umar, 'Ali and others to sit under a wall of their houses and wait. The Jews held a short private meeting and conspired to kill the Prophet (Peace be upon him). The most wicked among them, 'Amr bin Jahsh, volunteered to climb up the wall and drop a large millstone on his head. One of them, Salam bin Mashkam, cautioned them against perpetrating such a crime, predicting that Allâh would divulge their plot to him, and added that such an act would constitute a manifest violation of the pact concluded with the Muslims.

In fact, Gabriel did come down to reveal to the Prophet (Peace be upon him) their wicked criminal intention, so he, with his Companions, hurried off back to Madinah. On their way, he told his Companions of the Divine Revelation.

Soon after, the Prophet (Peace be upon him) delegated Muhammad bin Maslamah to communicate an ultimatum to Bani Nadeer to the effect that they should evacuate Madinah within ten days, otherwise, their heads would be cut off. The chief of the hypocrites, 'Abdullah bin Ubai, urged the Jews not to pay heed to the Prophet 's words and to stay in their habitations, offering to run to their support with two thousands of his followers, and assuring them of help to come from Quraizah tribe and former allies Banu Ghatfan. In this regards, Allâh says:

- "If you are expelled, we (too) indeed will go out with you, and we shall never obey anyone against you, and if you are attacked (in fight), we shall indeed help you." [59:11]

The Jews regained their confidence and were determined to fight. Their chief Huyai bin Akhtab relied hopefully on what the chief of the hypocrites said. So he sent to the Messenger of Allâh (Peace be upon him) saying: "We will not leave our houses. Do whatever you like to do."

Undoubtedly the situation was awkward for the Muslims. Launching a war against their opponents at this critical stage could entail terrible far reaching ramifications in the light of the unfavourable conditions they were passing through, besides the hostile environment growing in power and hatred around them, the harbinger of which assumed the form of killing the Muslim missions, as it has been already introduced.

The Jews of Bani Nadeer were also a power to count for, and the prospects of inflicting a military defeat on them was precarious; consequently forcing them into war engagement would be attended with unpredictable risks. On the other hand, the continual state of repeated assassinations and acts of treachery carried out against the Muslims individually and collectively brought about unbearable headache to Muhammad 's followers. Having judged all the prevalent status quo in this perspective, and in the light of the disgraceful attempt on thlife of the Prophet (Peace be upon him), the Muslims made the decisive decisions of taking up arms whatever turn the consequences could assume.

When the Messenger of Allâh (Peace be upon him) received the reply of Huyai bin Akhtab he said: "*Allâhu Akbar, Allâhu Akbar.*" (Allâh is the Greatest of all) and his Companions repeated after him. Then he set out to fight them after appointing Ibn Umm Maktum to dispose the affairs of Madinah during his absence. The standard was entrusted to 'Ali bin Abi Talib. He laid siege to their forts for six nights — in another version, fifteen.

Banu Nadeer resorted to their castles, mounted them and started shooting arrows and pelting stones at the Muslims enjoying the strategic advantage that their thick fields of palm trees provided. The Muslims were therefore ordered to fell and burn those trees. In this respect, Allâh, the All-Mighty, states in the Qur'ân:

- "What you (O Muslims) cut down of the palm-trees (of the enemy), or you left them standing on their stems, it was by leave of Allâh." [59:5]

Quraizah tribe remained neutral, and the hypocrite 'Abdullah bin Ubai as well as Ghatfan failed to keep their promises of support. In this regard Allâh says:

- "(Their allies deceived them) like Satan, when he says to man: 'Disbelieve in Allâh.' But when (man) disbelieves in Allâh, Satan says: 'I am free of you.'" [59:16]

The siege did not last long for Allâh, the All-Mighty, cast horror into the hearts of the Jews, and they willingly offered to comply with the Prophet 's order and leave Madinah. The Prophet (Peace be upon him) accepted their request and allowed them to carry as much luggage as their camels could lift, arms were excepted. Of course, they had no choice but to carry out the orders, so they took with them everything they could carry even the pegs and beams of ceilings. Their caravan counted 600 loaded camels including their chiefs, Huyai bin Akhtab and Salam bin Abi Al-Huqaiq, who left for Khaibar whereas another party shifted to Syria. Two of them embraced Islam, Yameen bin 'Amr and Abu Sa'd bin Wahab, and so they retained their personal wealth.

The Messenger of Allâh (Peace be upon him) seized their weapons, land, houses, and wealth. Amongst the other booty he managed to capture, there were 50 armours, 50 helmets, and 340 swords.

This booty was exclusively the Prophet 's because no fighting was involved in capturing it. He divided the booty at his own discretion among the early Emigrants and two poor Helpers, Abu Dujana and Suhail bin Haneef. Anyway the Messenger of Allâh (Peace be upon him) spent a portion of this wealth on his family to sustain their living the year around. The rest was expended to provide the Muslim army with equipment for further wars in the way of Allâh.

The invasion of Bani An-Nadeer took place in Rabi' Al-Awwal, 4 A.H. i.e. in August 625 A.D. Almost all the verses of *Sûrah Al-Hashr* (Chapter 59 - The Gathering) describe the banishment of the Jews and reveal the disgraceful manners of the hypocrites. The verses manifest the rules relevant to the booty. In this Chapter, Allâh, the All-Mighty, praises the Emigrants and Helpers. This Chapter also shows the legitimacy of cutting down and burning the enemy's land and trees for military purposes. Such acts cannot be regarded as phenomena of corruption so long that they are in the way of Allâh.

In this very Chapter, Allâh recommends the believers to be pious and prepare themselves for the world to come and He ends it with a compliment upon Himself and a manifestation of His Holy Names and Attributes.

As this Chapter concentrates on Bani An-Nadeer and their banishment, Ibn 'Abbas used to describe it as 'An-Nadeer Chapter'.

THE INVASION OF NAJD:

With the peaceful victory that the Muslims achieved at Bani An-Nadeer invasion, their control over Madinah was undisputedly established, and the hypocrites receded to a state of silence and stopped their artful machinations publicly. Consequently the Prophet (Peace be upon him) had ample time to direct all his energies and human resources towards suppressing the desert bedouins and curbing their harmful provocations and wicked malicious practices of killing his missionaries and even contemplating an invasion of Madinah itself. Meanwhile, the Muslim scouting groups reported building up of bedouin troops of Bani Muharib and Tha'labah of Ghatfan around Madinah. The Prophet (Peace be upon him), with the Muslims, hurriedly set out to discipline those new outlaws, cast fear into their hearts and deter them from perpetrating further wicked practices. These deterring operations were carried out repeatedly and did produce effective results. The rebellious hard-hearted desert bedouins were terrorized into the mountains, and Madinah remained completely immune against their raids.

In the context of these invasions, it is interesting to draw some prominence to a significant one ¾ *Dhat Ar-Riqa'* (rags) campaign ¾ which some scholars claim, took place in Najd (a large area of tableland in the Arabian Peninsula) in Rabi' Ath-Thani or Jumada Al-Ula, 4 A.H. They substantiate their claim by saying that it was strategically necessary to carry out this campaign in order to quell the rebellious bedouins in order to meet the exigencies of the agreed upon encounter with the polytheists, i.e. minor Badr Battle in Sha'ban, 4 A.H. The most authentic opinion, however, is that *Dhat Ar-Riqa'* campaign took place after the fall of Khaibar. This is supported by the fact that Abu Hurairah and Abu Musa Al-Ash'ari (May Allah be pleased with her) witnessed the battle. Abu Hurairah embraced Islam only some days before Khaibar, and Abu Musa Al-Ash'ari came back from Abyssinia (Ethiopia) and joined the Prophet (Peace be upon him) at Khaibar. The rules relating to the prayer of fear which the Prophet (Peace be upon him) observed at *Dhat Ar-Riqa'* campaign, were revealed at 'Asfan Invasion and this beyond a shadow of doubt took place after *Al-Khandaq* (the trench) Battle in late 5 A.H.

THE INVASION OF BADR, THE SECOND:

When the Muslims destroyed the power of the Arab-desert tribes and guarded themselves against their evils, they started preparations to encounter their great enemy. A year elapsed since they fought Quraish at Uhud. So it was due time to meet them and start war again in order to determine which of the two parties was worthy of survival.

In Sha'ban 4 A.H., January 626 A.D., the Messenger of Allâh (Peace be upon him) set out to Badr accompanied by one thousand and five hundred fighters and ten mounted horsemen, and with 'Ali bin Abi Talib as standard bearer. 'Abdullah bin Rawahah was given authority over Madinah during the Prophet 's absence. Reaching Badr, the Muslims stayed there waiting for the idolaters to come.

Abu Sufyan's forces comprised two thousand footmen and fifty horsemen. They reached Mar Az-Zahran, some distance form Makkah, and camped at a water place called Mijannah. Being reluctant, discouraged and extremely terrified of the consequences of the approaching fight, Abu Sufyan turned to his people and began to introduce cowardice-based flimsy pretexts in order to dissuade his men from going to war, saying: "O tribe of Quraish! Nothing will improve the condition you are in but a fruitful year — a year during which your animals feed on plants and bushes and give you milk to drink. And I see that this is a rainless year, therefore I am returning now and I recommend you to return with me."

It seems that his army were also possessed of the same fears and apprehensions, for they readily obeyed him without the least hesitation.

The Muslims, who were then at Badr, stayed for eight days waiting for their enemy. They took advantage of their stay by selling goods and earning double as much the price out of it. When the idolaters declined to fight, the balance of powers shifted to rest in favour of the Muslims, who thus regained their military reputation, their dignity and managed to impose their awe-inspiring presence over the whole of Arabia. In brief, they mastered and controlled the whole situation.

This invasion had many a name. It is called 'Badr the Appointment', 'Badr, Second', 'Badr, the Latter', and 'Badr Minor'.

THE INVASION OF DOUMAT AL-JANDAL:

With the Messenger's return from Badr, peace and security prevailed the whole area; and the Islamic headquarters, Madinah, enjoyed full security. The Prophet (Peace be upon him) then deemed it fit and appropriate to head for the most distant areas of Arabia in order to subdue all hostile elements in order to force undisputed recognition out of friend and enemy alike.

After a six-month lull of military activities, the Prophet (Peace be upon him) was reported that some tribes, in the vicinity of Doumat Al-Jandal, on the borders of Syria, were involved in highway robbery and plundering, and were on their way to muster troops and raid Madinah itself. He immediately appointed Siba' bin 'Arfatah Al-Ghifari to dispose the affairs of Madinah during his absence, and set out at the head of 1000 Muslims in late Rabi' Al-Awwal, 5 A.H. taking with him a man, named Madhkur, from Bani 'Udhrah, as a guide.

On their way to Doumat Al-Jandal, they used to march by night and hide by day, so that they might take the enemy by surprise. When they drew near their destination, the Muslims discovered that the highway men had moved to another place, so they captured their cattle and shepherds. The inhabitants of Doumat Al-Jandal had also fled in all directions for their lives and evacuated their habitations. The Prophet (Peace be upon him) stayed there for 5 days during which he despatched expeditionary forces to hunt for the enemy personnel but they detected none. He then returned to Madinah but en route he entered into a peace treaty with 'Uyainah bin Hisn. Doumat Al-Jandal is located at about a distance of fifteen days march from Madinah and five from Damascus.

With this decisive and steady progress and wise strict plans, the Prophet (Peace be upon him) managed to spread security, control the situation and make peace prevail the whole area. He also succeeded in shifting the course of events for the welfare of the Muslims by reducing the incessant internal and external troubles. The hypocrites were silenced, a tribe of the Jews evacuated while the other continued to fake good neighbourliness and seemingly faithful adherence to the covenants, the desert bedouins subdued and finally the archenemy Quraish no longer keen on attacking the Muslims. This secure strategic attitude created optimum circumstances for the Muslims to resume their logical course in propagating Islam and communicating the Messages of the Lord to all worlds.

THE BATTLE OF UHUD

The defeat at Badr was an ignominy which the Quraishites pride could not leave unavenged. Revenge was, therefore, the catchword all over Makkah. The Makkans even forbade lamenting over their murdered people, or ransoming their captives at Badr Battle lest the Muslims should realize the grave degree of sadness and feeling of tragedy they were experiencing.

In the wake of Badr event, Quraish was in common consent and started fresh preparations to launch an overall war against the Muslims in order to restore their blemished prestige and wounded pride. The most enthusiastic polytheists desiring to go into a new battle were 'Ikrimah bin Abi Jahl, Safwan bin Omaiyah, Abu Sufyan bin Harb, and 'Abdullah bin Abi Rabi'a. They were determined to crush the commonwealth of Islam once and for all. Emissaries were sent to all the tribes to make common cause against the rising Faith. As a consequence of this, they managed to enlist the support of two well-known tribes Kinana and Tihamah besides some desert bedouins *Ahabish*. It was also decided that the profits of the escaped caravan headed by Abu Sufyan, which amounted to 1000 camels and 50 thousand Dinars, should be devoted for providing equipment to the army. The Noble Qur'ân has alluded to this decision of theirs in the following words:

- "Verily, those who disbelieve spend their wealth to hinder (men) from the path of Allâh, and so will they continue to spend it; but in the end it will become an anguish for them. Then they will be overcomed." [8:36]

They also devised other ways of recruitment including hiring poets to entice the tribes into fighting the Muslims. Safwan bin Omaiyah allured Abu 'Azza, the poet to work in this context in return for riches after the war or supporting his daughters if killed. Incidentally, this poet was prisoner of war (in the context of the Badr events) in the hands of the Muslims and the Prophet (Peace be upon him) was gracious enough to release him unransomed provided he would not engage in fight against him.

Abu Sufyan nursed the most grudge against Muslims because he had lost most of his supplies in As-Sawiq invasion, let alone the heavy economic losses that Quraish had sustained in the aftermath of the events that featured the platoon of Zaid bin Harithah.

In the light of these successive failures, Quraish precipitated and accelerated their preparations for a decisive battle with the Muslims. At the turn of the year everything was ready for the move. The Makkans also decided to take their women along with them for they might arouse them to fight manfully. Thus a contingent of three thousand pitched warriors, of whom seven hundred were mailed soldiers and two hundred well-mounted cavalry with three thousand camels and fifteen women marched towards Madinah. The general leader was Abu Sufyan bin Harb, the cavalry under the leadership of Khalid bin Al-Waleed assisted by 'Ikrimah bin Abi Jahl, and Bani 'Abd Ad-Dar were entrusted with the flag.

Old deep-seated feelings of hatred, with heart-based grudge enveloped the whole process foreshadowing bitter, bloody revenge-instigated fighting between the two parties.

Meanwhile Al-'Abbas bin 'Abdul Muttalib, was closely watching the military movements and preparations for war, and these were all included in an urgent message sent by him to Prophet (Peace be upon him) who received it while he was in Qubâ' Mosque. Ubai bin Ka'b read the letter to the Prophet (Peace be upon him), who asked him to be reticent with respect to its serious contents. He hurried back to Madinah, convened a meeting with the Helpers and Emigrants and conducted with them serious consultations as regards the measures to be taken.

The whole of Madinah was put on the alert and all men were heavily armed even during prayer in anticipation of any emergency. A group of Helpers volunteered to guard the Prophet(Peace be upon him) and kept watchful eye all night at his door, amongst whom there were Sa'd bin Mu'adh, Usaid bin Hudair and Sa'd bin 'Ubadah. Lest they should be taken by surprise, armed groups of the Madinese began to police the entrances and roads leading to the city. To reconnoitre the movements of the polytheists, Muslim platoons began to patrol the routes for any probable enemy raids.

The Makkan army, on the other hand, continued the march along the usual western road. On reaching Al-Abwâ', Hind bint 'Utbah, Abu Sufyan's wife, suggested that they dig up the grave of the Prophet's mother, but the leaders of the army refused to do so for fear of the consequent results. The army then followed Wadi Al-'Aqeeq and turned right to encamp themselves at a place called 'Ainain near Uhud Mountain. That was on Friday, 6th Shawwal, 3 A.H.

A CONSULTANT ASSEMBLY FOR A DEFENCE PLAN:

The scouting party of Madinah conveyed the news of the Makkan army step by step. Then the Messenger of Allâh (Peace be upon him) held a head military consultation assembly to exchange views about the situation. He told them about a dream he had. He said: "By Allâh, I have dreamt of — I implore Allâh to be a dream of bounty — cows slaughtered and that there was a groove at the pointed top of my sword, and that I had inserted my hand into an immune armour."

The interpretation of 'the cows' was that some of his men were killed, and 'the groove at the pointed top of his sword' was that a member of his House would be hurt. As for 'the armour' it was Madinah. Then he offered a suggestion that his Companions should not go out of Madinah and that they should encamp themselves within the city. He was of the opinion that the enemies should be left in the open to exhaust themselves and thus the Muslims would not risk a battle. But if they thought of attacking Madinah, Muslim men would be ready to fight them at the mouths of lanes; whereas Muslim-women would help from over the house roofs." 'Abdullah bin Ubai bin Salul — the head of the hypocrites; who attended the meeting as a chief of Al-Khazraj — supported the Prophet 's plan.

As a matter of fact his agreement was not based on the righteousness of the plan but rather on personal benefit. He did not want to fight. On the contrary he secretly aimed at being far away from fight. However it was Allâh's Will that he should be disclosed and disgraced in public — for the first time. It was His Will that the curtain which concealed their disbelief behind should be uncovered and pulled down. Allâh's Will enabled the Muslims to recognize the reality of those snakes that were creeping within their garments and inside the sleeves of their clothes. Thanks to Allâh they recognized them in one of the most critical times of their lives.

Some of the best honourable Companions, who had missed *Al-Jihâd* in Badr invasion, suggested that the Prophet (Peace be upon him) should go out of Madinah and urged him to accept their point of view. One of them said: "O, Messenger of Allâh (Peace be upon him), for long time we have been looking forward to this day; and we have implored Allâh to make such a day draw near. Thanks to Allâh it is time to fight. So let us go out and fight our enemies lest they should think that we have lost heart and do not dare to fight them." Hamza bin Abdul Muttalib the paternal uncle of the Prophet (Peace be upon him), who had already covered the ornaments of his sword with idolaters' blood in Badr Battle, was ahead of those enthusiastics who urged him to go out and meet the disbelievers. He said to the Prophet (Peace be upon him): "By Allâh, Who has sent the Book down unto you, I will not taste food till I fight them with my sword outside Madinah."

After weighing carefull the pros and cons of the issue, it was decided that the enemy should be resisted outside the city at Uhud.

DIVIDING THE ISLAMIC ARMY INTO PHALANXES DEPARTURE TO THE BATTLE-FIELD:

Ascending the pulpit at the Friday congregational prayer, the Prophet (Peace be upon him) urged the people in his sermon to fight courageously. "If you remain steadfast," he said "you will be helped by the Power of the All- Mighty." Then he commanded his men to make ready for the battle. Most of them rejoiced greatly.

He led the afternoon prwith crowds of people. Then he entered his house accompanied by his two friends Abu Bakr and 'Umar. They helped him dress and wear his headcloth. He armed himself and wore two armours one over the other. He wore his sword and went out to meet people.

People were waiting for him impatiently. Sa'd bin Mu'adh and Usaid bin Hudair blamed people for pressing on the Prophet (Peace be upon him). They said: "You have forced the Messenger of Allâh (Peace be upon him) to fight the enemy outside Madinah." Therefore they were determined to leave the whole matter to the Prophet (Peace be upon him), and blamed themselves for what they had already done. When the Prophet (Peace be upon him) came out, they said: "O Messenger of Allâh, we should have not disagreed with you. So, you are free to do what you desire. If you prefer to stay inside Madinah we will stay with you. Upon this the Messenger of Allâh (Peace be upon him) remarked: "It does not become a Prophet that once he had put on armour, he should take it off, until Allâh has decided between him and the enemy."

THE PROPHET (Peace be upon him) DIVIDED HIS ARMY INTO THREE BATTALIONS:

1. Al-Muhajireen battalion, under the command of Mus'ab bin 'Umair Al-'Abdari.
2. Al-Ansari-Aws battalion was commanded by Usaid bin Hudair.
3. Al-Ansari-Khazraj battalion with Al-Hubab bin Al-Mundhir to lead it.

The army consisted of a thousand fighters; a hundred of them armoured; another fifty horsemen. He appointed Ibn Umm Maktum to lead the people in prayer in Madinah. Departure was announced and the army moved northwards with the two Sa'ds, who were armoured, running in front of the army.

Upon passing along Al-Wada' mountain trail he saw a well-armed battalion, which were detached from the main body of the army. The Prophet (Peace be upon him) inquired who they were and he was told that they were Jews and were allies of Al-Khazraj. They told him that they wanted to contribute to the fight against the idolaters. "Have they embraced Islam?" The Prophet (Peace be upon him) asked. "No," they said. So he refused admitting them and said that he would not seek the assistance of disbelievers against the idolaters.

PARADING THE ARMY:

As soon as he reached a location called Ash-Shaikhan, he paraded his army. He dismissed those whom he considered to be disabled or too young to stand the fight. Among them were 'Abdullah bin 'Umar bin Al-Khattab. Usama bin Zaid; Usaid bin Zaheer, Zaid bin Thabit, Zaid bin Arqam. 'Araba bin Aws, 'Amr bin Hazm, Abu Sa'eed Al-Khudri, Zaid bin Haritha Al-Ansari, Sa'd bin Habba and Al-Barâ' bin 'Azib, Sahih Al-Bukhari pointed out that he had shared in the fight that day.

The Messenger of Allâh (Peace be upon him) allowed both Rafi' bin Khadaij and Samura bin Jundub to join the army — though they were too young. The former proved to be skillful at shooting arrows; the latter wrestled the former and beat him. The admission of Rafi' made Samura say: "I am stronger than him, I can overcome him." When the Prophet (Peace be upon him) heard this saying he ordered them to wrestle. They did. Samura won so he was also admitted.

PASSING THE NIGHT BETWEEN UHUD AND MADINAH:

As night fell upon them there, they performed both the sunset and the evening prayers and spent the night there as well. Fifty people were chosen to guard the camp and go round it. Muhammad bin Maslama Al-Ansari, the hero of the brigade of Ka'b bin Al-Ashraf, was in charge of the guards. Whereas Dhakwan bin 'Abd Qais undertook the responsibility of guarding the Prophet (Peace be upon him), in particular.

THE REBELLION OF 'ABDALLAH BIN UBAI AND HIS FOLLOWERS:

At the end of the night and just before it was daybreak, the Prophet (Peace be upon him) moved and when he got to Ash-Shawt he observed the dawn prayer. There he was close enough to the enemy that they could see one another. It was there that 'Abdullah bin Ubai — the hypocrite — rebelled against the Muslims. One-third of the army withdrew with him — that is to say three hundred fighters. He said, "We do not know why we shall kill ourselves." He claimed that his withdrawal was no more than showing protest against the Messenger of Allâh (Peace be upon him) who had already refused his opinion and accepted that of the others.

Undoubtedly that was not the real cause of his detachment. If it had been the refusal of his opinion — as the hypocrite claimed — there would have no sense whatsoever for his joining the Prophetic army. If it had been so, he would have refused to go out with the army from the very beginning of the march. As a matter of fact the real purpose of this rebellion, withdrawal and detachment — at this delicate and awkward position and time — was to produce bewilderment, confusion of mind, and disorder in the Muslims army who were within the sight and hear range of the enemy who were also looking forward to seeing more and more dissension on the side of the Muslims, like themselves. They also aimed at breaking the high morale of the believers. That would accelerate — in their opinion — the breakdown and consequently the death of Muhammad, his faithful Companions and Islam as a whole. The way would then be clear for the reclaim of presidency, which that hypocrite had lost on the advent of Islam into Madinah.

Short of Allâh's Care, the hypocrite's plot would have been successful. Banu Haritha of Al-Aws and Banu Salama of Al-Khazraj were partially impressed by the hypocrite's behaviour. Both of them were overwhelmed by confusion and they had almost started to withdraw, but Allâh's Care saved them from that disgrace. About their incident Allâh says:

- "When two parties from among you were about to lose their heart, but Allâh was their *Wali* (Supporter and Protector). And in Allâh should the believers put their trust." [3:122]

'Abdullah bin Haram — the father of Jabir bin 'Abdullah — attempted to stop their withdrawal. He reminded the hypocrites of their duty at this delicate and awkward condition, but in vain. He followed them, reproached them and urged them to go back saying: "Come and fight in the way of Allâh or at least be defenders." They said: "If we had known that you would really fight we would have not gone back." Having despaired of them, he addressed them saying: "May Allâh cast you away, you enemies of Allâh. Allâh will certainly suffice His Prophet." Allâh says about those hypocrites:

- "And that He might test the hypocrites, it was said to them: 'Come, fight in the way of Allâh or (at least) defend yourselves.' They said: 'Had we known that fighting will take place, we would certainly have followed you.' They were that day, nearer to disbelief than to Faith, saying with their mouths what was not in their hearts. And Allâh has full knowledge of what they conceal." [3:167]

THE REMINDER OF THE ISLAMIC ARMY ARE ON THE MOVE TO UHUD:

With the remainder of fighters, the Messenger of Allâh (Peace be upon him) moved towards the enemy. After the rebellion and withdrawal of the hypocrites, the number of soldiers was reduced to seven hundred only.

The camp of idolaters was situated in such a place that the many roads leading to Uhud were almost blocked by them. So the Messenger of Allâh (Peace be upon him) said to his men: "Which man of you can lead us to where the people (i.e. the idolaters) are, along a short track that does not pass by them?" Abu Khaithama said: "O Messenger of Allâh (Peace be upon him), I am the man you need." Then he chose a short track that led to Uhud passing by Harrah Bani Harithah and their farms, leaving the idolaters' army westwards.

On their way they passed by *Ha'it* (i.e. the field) of Marba' bin Qaizi, who was a blind hypocrite. When Marba' felt and realized that they were the Prophetic army, he started throwing earth at their faces, so they rushed to kill him, but the Prophet (Peace be upon him) said:

- "Do not kill him. He is blind in heart and eyes."

The Messenger of Allâh (Peace be upon him) went along till climbed down the hillock of Uhud at the slope of the valley. He camped there with his army facing Madinah while their backs were to the hills of Uhud mountain. So the army of the enemy stood a barrier between the Muslims and Madinah.

THE DEFENCE PLAN:

TheMessenger of Allâh (Peace be upon him) mobilized his army. He arranged them into two rows to prepare them for fight. He selected fifty skillful archers that formed a squad and made them under the command of 'Abdullah bin Jubair bin An-Nu'man Al-Ansari Al-Awsi Al-Badri. He issued his orders to them to stay where they were — on a mountain(side) at the south bank of Qanat Al-Wadi (i.e. a canal of the valley), south east of Muslims camp at about one hundred and fifty metres from the Islamic army. Later on this mountain was called the Mountain of Archers.

The Messenger of Allâh (Peace be upon him) clarified the mission of this squad in words he directed to them. He said to their leader: "Drive off the horses from us by means of arrows, lest they should attack us from behind (the rear). Whether we win the battle or lose it, stand steadily in your position and mind that we are not attacked from your side."

He added:

- "Defend our backs! If you see us slain. Do not come to assist us; and if you see gaining grounds, do not share us."

In a version by Al-Bukhâri the Prophet (Peace be upon him) said:

- "If you see us snatched into pieces by birds, do not leave this position of yours till I send for you. And if you see that we have defeated the enemy and trodden on them do not desert your position till I send for you."

With the assignment of this squad and locating it on the mountainside and the issuance of those strict military orders, the Messenger of Allâh (Peace be upon him) blocked the only groove that might lead the idolaters stealthily to the rear of Muslim ranks and might even enable them to encircle them in an encompassment procedure.

The assignments of posts and responsibilities for the rest of the army were performed by the Prophet (Peace be upon him) as follows: On the right wing, he appointed Al-Mundhir bin 'Amr. On the left he appointed Az-Zubair bin Al-'Awwam, and made Al-Miqdad bin Al-Aswad his assistant and supporter. Az-Zubair's function was to standfast in the face of Khalid bin Al-Waleed's horsemen. The Messenger of Allâh (Peace be upon him) selected the top and the most courageous group to be in the vanguard of the army. They were notable for their readiness, alertness and bravery and estimated to be equal to thousands of men.

It was a wise and carefully-laid plan which revealed the genius of military leadership that the Prophet (Peace be upon him) possessed. No other leader could have drawn a more accurate or wise plan. Although he approached the site later than the enemy, he managed to occupy better positions. He made the rocky mountainside to function as shield for the army's rear and right flank. He was able, by blocking the only vulnerable gap on the side, to provide additional maximum protection for the rear as well as the left wing. For fear of possible defeat, and to deter the Muslims from fleeing, in which case they would fall easy prisoners in the hands of the enemy, he chose a high place for encampment. Moreover a strategic site of this sort would surely inflict heavy losses on the polytheists if they thought of approaching or occupying his positions. In a further step, he reduced the enemy to a narrow scope of choice when they were cornered for encampment in geographically low positions that would avail them nothing of the benefits of any possible victory; at the same time they would not be able to escape the pursuit of the Muslims in case victory sided with the latter. To make up for the quantitative shortage in fighting personnel, he chose a picked body of fighters to stand at the front.

The army of the Prophet (Peace be upon him) was thus fully mobilized on Shawwal 7th, 3 A.H.

THE MESSENGER OF ALLAH IMPLANTS THE SPIRIT OF BRAVERY AMONG HIS ARMED FORCES:

The Messenger of Allâh (Peace be upon him) forbade the Muslims to start the fight without having an order from him. He, then, wore two armours — a front armour and a back one. He urged his Companions to fight and spurred them to show stamina and steadfastness at fight. He started to implant the spirit of boldness and bravery in them. To wage and inflame his Companions and in order to standfast in the fight, he took a sharp sword, held it in his hand and called out unto his Companions and said: "Who is ready to take this sword and give it its proper due?" Many a man set out to take it. Some of them were 'Ali bin Abi Talib, Az-Zubair bin Al-'Awwam and 'Umar bin Al-Khattab. But it was granted to none. Abu Dujana Sammak bin Kharsha inquired: "O Messenger of Allâh, what is its price?" The Prophet (Peace be upon him) said: "It is to strike the enemy's faces with it till it was bent." So Abu Dujana said: "O Messenger of Allâh I will take it for that price." and he was given the sword.

Abu Dujana was a man of courage who used to swagger at war. He had a red band which he wore round his head. Whenever he was head-banded everybody knew that he was determined to fight to death. Therefore as soon as Abu Dujana took the Prophet 's sword, he banded his head and started strutting amongst the fighters.

Watching him doing that, the Messenger of Allâh (Peace be upon him) said: "This is a sort of walking that Allâh detests except in such a situation."

RECRUITMENT OF THE MAKKAN ARMY:

The idolaters applied the rows system in the mobilization of their army. The general leadership of the army was entrusted to Abu Sufyan Sakhr bin Harb, who would be in the centre-position of the army. Khalid bin Al-Waleed was on the right wing; whereas 'Ikrima, the son of Abu Jahl was on the left. Safwan bin Omaiya was in charge of infantry men. The archers were under the command of 'Abdullah bin Abi Rabi'a.

As for the standard, a squad of Bani 'Abd Ad-Dar were in charge to bear it. Thus was the distribution of the posts of the army ever since 'Abd Munaf had already assigned them. This assignment had been inherited from Qusai bin Kilab — as we have previously alluded to in an early phase of this book. No one had the right to compete them with it. It was consistent with their traditions that they had inherited from their ancestors.

Abu Sufyan, the general leader, reminded his men — the standard bearers — of what had happened to Quraish on Badr Day (i.e. battle) when their standard bearer, An-Nadr bin Al-Harith, was captured. In an attempt to wage their anger and enmity to the Muslims he said: "O Bani 'Abd Ad-Dar! You have been assigned bearers of our standard and you know that the standard is the first thing that the enemy attacks. Should it fall, we fall down too. Therefore, I say either you guarantee its safety or leave it for us, and we will certainly suffice you that task."

Abu Sufyan's attempt seemed to be fruitful. For his speech made Bani 'Abd Ad-Dar so extremely angry that they threatened him and almost attacked him for that. Addressing him, they said: "You want us to deliver you the custodianship of the standard? Tomorrow when we fight them, you will witness our deeds." As a matter of fact, they fought bravely and stoodfast in defence of the standard till they were all killed.

POLITICAL MANOEUVERS OF QURAISH:

A little time before the break out of the battle, Quraish made some endeavours to sow the seeds of discord and dispute among the Muslims. First, Abu Sufyan sent to the Helpers a message saying: "Leave us alone to fight our cousins and do not interfere. If you stand aside, we will not fight you; for fighting you is not a target of ours." But that attempt proved to be fruitless. What could such a wicked scheme do to those whose Faith was as solid and firm as mountains?! The Helpers reply was undoubtedly disappointing and contrary to Abu Sufyan's expectations.

The zero-hour was due. The two parties drew nearer. Undespaired by the first failure, Quraish made another attempt, for the same purport but now with the assistance of a traitor called Abu 'Amir Al-Fasiq, whose name was 'Abd 'Amr bin Saifi. He was called a monk, but the Messenger of Allâh (Peace be upon him) nicknamed him *Al-Fâsiq* (i.e. perverted transgressor; dissolute). As he was the head of Aws in *Al-Jahiliya*, he could not tolerate Islam when it came. He announced his enmity to the Messenger of Allâh (Peace be upon him) in public. He left Madinah for the Quraishites in Makkah to rally them against the Messenger of Allâh (Peace be upon him) and to urge them to start the fight against him. He claimed that he was obeyed and esteemed by his people and that as soon as they saw him come they would join him immediately.

So he was the first one among the mob and slaves of Quraish to show resistance. He called out unto his people, recognized them and said: "O kinfolk of Aws! I am Abu 'Amir." Their reply was "No eyes of anybody shall be consoled by viewing you, O *Fâsiq*." Hearing them say so, he said: "My people must have been afflicted by an evil after my departure." Therefore when the fight broke out, he fought them fiercely and pelted his people with stones, as well.

That was how the second attempt of Quraish to sow the seeds of discord among people of Faith. This, however, revealed the great terror of the Quraishites cast in their hearts in spite of their supremacy in number and equipment.

THE EFFORT OF THE QURAISHITE WOMEN AT WAGING THE ZEAL OF MEN:

Quraishi-women participated in the battle led by the wife of Abu Sufyan, Hind bint 'Utbah. They wandered among the rows of the idolaters, tapped on tambourines, encouraged men to fight, inflamed the emotions of heroes, lancers, swordsmen and brave fighters. At one time they addressed the standard-bearers:

- "O Bani 'Abd Ad-Dar!

    O home defenders,

    Strike with your sharp swords ..."

And at another time they would wage people's zeal by singing:

- "If you fight (bravely), we will embrace

    and unfold mats to welcome you.

    But if you flee from the battlefield, we leave you,

    Desert you and no more love you."

THE COMBAT:

The two parties approached and grew very close to each another. The phases of fight started. The first combatant was the standard-bearer, Talha bin Abi Talha Al-'Abdari, who was the most distinguished idolater. He was one of the bravest men of Quraish fighters. Muslims nicknamed him 'the ram of the battalion.' He came forth riding a camel and challenged the Muslims to a single combat. People refrained from fighting him due to his bravery; but Az-Zubair bin Al-'Awwam advanced for the fight. He did not give the 'Ram' any chance to fight but fell on him like a lion on his camel's back, pulled him down to the ground and slaughtered him with his sword.

The Messenger of Allâh (Peace be upon him) who was watching that wonderful incident exclaimed: *Allâhu Akbar* that is 'Allâh is the Greatest' and the Muslims exclaimed *Allâhu Akbar* too. He praised Az-Zubair when he said:

- "Every Prophet has a disciple and Az-Zubair is a disciple of mine."

Soon the general engagement ensued and the fight of the two parties grew fierce everywhere on the battlefield. The strain of the fight was centred round the carriers of the standard. After the death of their leader Talha bin Abi Talha, Banu 'Abd Ad-Dar alternated the mission successively. Talha's brother, 'Uthman, ran forward and seized the standard which lay by the lifeless body of his brother, chanting: "The standard-bearer has the right to dye its shaft in blood, till it be beaten in his hand." Hamzah bin 'Abdul Muttalib attacked and dealt him a blow that cut his arm and shoulder and went down to his navel to uncover his lung.

The standard was raised up again by Abu Sa'd bin Abi Talha; but Sa'd bin Abi Waqqas shot him with a deadly arrow that hit him at his throat and made his tongue hang out breathing his last.

In another version it was narrated that Abu Sa'd lifted the standard up and challenged the Muslims to fight him. 'Ali bin Abi Talib went forth. They exchanged two blows. Then 'Ali gave him a terminal blow that finished him off.

Musafi' bin Talha bin Abi Talha then hoisted the standard, but was soon shot with an arrow by 'Asim bin Thabit bin Abi Al-Aqlah. His brother Kilab bin Talha bin Abi Talha followed him picked the banner and lifted it up; but Az-Zubair bin Al-'Awwam attacked him and managed to kill him. Their brother Al-Jallas bin Talha bin Abi Talha lifted the banner up but Talha bin 'Ubaidu-Allâh stabbed him to death. They also said that it was 'Asim bin Thabit who managed to deal a terminal blow to him.

All those six people killed round and in defence of the standard, belonged to one house, the house of Abi Talha 'Abdullah bin 'Uthman bin 'Abd Ad-Dar. Another man from Bani 'Abd Ad-Dar, called Artat bin Sharhabeel carried the standard but he also was killed by 'Ali bin Abi Talib. Others said it was Hamzah who killed him not 'Ali.

Then it was Shuraih bin Qariz who was killed by Quzman — he was a hypocrite who fought for prestige only, not in defence of Islam. Abu Zaid 'Amr bin 'Abd Munaf Al-'Abdari lifted the standard up but he was killed by Quzman too. A son of Sharhabeel bin Hashim Al-'Abdari hoisted it again and was also killed by Quzman.

So we see that ten fighters of Bani 'Abd Ad-Dar — the standard-bearers — were annihilated. Seeing that none of 'Abd Ad-Dars survived to carry the standard, a slave of theirs — called Sawab — came to raise it. The slave showed more admirable sorts of bravery and steadfastness than his former masters. Sawab, the slave went on fighting till his hand was cut off. So he knelt down and embraced the banner, leant it against his chest and neck lest it should fall down to the ground. He remained fighting steadily and steadfastly till he was killed. In the meanwhile he did not stop saying: "O Allâh, have I been excused?" After the death of the slave Sawab, the standard fell down to the ground, and remained there as there was no one to carry it.

Whilst the brunt of the battle centred around the standard, bitter fighting was going on everywhere on the battlefield. The spirit of Faith overwhelmed the Muslims' ranks; so they rushed among the idolaters as if they had been an outbreak of a destructive flood that overflowed and knocked down all dams and barriers standing in its way "I seek death, I seek death." That was their announced motto on Uhud Day.

Abu Dujana, recognized by the red band worn round his head, came forth, fighting with the sword of the Messenger of Allâh (Peace be upon him). He was determined to pay its price at all costs. He killed all the idolaters that stood on his way splitting and dispersing their ranks. Az-Zubair bin Al-'Awwam said:

"I felt angry and discouraged when the Messenger of Allâh (Peace be upon him) refused to give me the sword but gave it to Abu Dujana. I said to myself: 'I am his paternal cousin — the cousin of his aunt Safiya — a Quraishite, besides, I was the first who demanded it and yet he favoured him to me. By Allâh, I will watch how he will use it.' So I followed him, I saw him take out his red band and wear it round his head. Seeing him like that, the Helpers said, 'Abu Dujana had worn the band of death.' Then he set out saying loudly:

- 'I am the one whom my intimate friend made covenant with, when we were under the palm-trees on the mountain side.
The covenant that we made was that I should not fight at the rear.
But fight at the front heroically with the sword of Allâh and His Messenger.'

No one stood the way of Abu Dujana but was killed. There was a man among the idolaters whose only target was to finish off the wounded Muslims. During the fight Abu Dujana drew near that man; so I implored Allâh that they might engage in combat. They in fact did and exchanged two sword-strokes. The idolater struck Abu Dujana, but he escaped it and it pierced into his leather shield. The idolater's sword now stuck to it, Abu Dujana struck him with the sword and killed him. Into the thick of the battle, he rushed to kill a person who was inciting the enemy to fight the Muslims. Upon this the person shrieked and lo! it was a woman. Abu Dujana spared her saying: 'I respect the Prophet 's sword too much to use it on a woman.' The woman was Hind bint 'Utbah."

Describing the same incident, Az-Zubair bin Al-'Awwam said: "I saw Abu Dujana raising a sword over the parting part of Hind bint 'Utba's head then he moved it off. I said to myself: 'Allâh and His Messenger know best.' (i.e. know why he acted like that)."

Hamzah bin 'Abdul Muttalib displayed wonderful feats of gallantry againstthe overwhelming odds which stood unparalled and created consternation and confusion in the disbelieving hosts. Heroes dispersed off his way as if they had been tree-leaves blown away by strong wind. In addition to his effective contribution to the annihilation of the idolaters who stood in defence of the standard, he was even of much greater effect at fighting against men of bravery and distinguished horsemen. It was Allâh's Will that he be murdered when he was at the top. He was not killed in a face-to-face fight on the battlefield — in the normal way by which heroes die — but rather assassinated in the dead-dark as was the custom of killing generous and noble men that were impossible to kill in an honourable fight.

<u>Assassination of Asadullâh (the Lion of Allâh) Hamzah bin 'Abdul Muttalib:</u>

Hamzah's assassin, Wahshi bin Harb, described how he killed Hamzah. He said:

"I was a slave working to Jubair bin Mut'im, whose paternal uncle Tu'aimah bin 'Adi was injured at Badr Battle. So when Quraish marched to Uhud, Jubair said to me: 'If you kill Hamzah, the uncle of Muhammad, stealthily you shall be manumitted.' "

"So I marched with the people to Uhud." He used to describe himself as, "I am a picaro good at spearing." "So when the two parties fought, I set out seeking Hamzah. I saw him amidst people fighting. He was like a white and black striped camel, striking severely with his sword and no one could stand on his way. By Allâh! When I was getting ready and trying to seize the fit opportunity to spear him, hiding sometimes behind a tree or a rock hoping that he might draw nearer and be within range — at that moment I caught sight of Siba' bin 'Abd Al-'Uzza going closer towards him. When Hamzah observed him, he said: 'Come on! O son of the 'clitoris-cutter.' — for his mother used to be a circumciser. Then he struck one strong stroke that could hardly miss his head."

Wahshi said: "Then I balanced my spear and shook it till I was content with it, then I speared him and it went down into his stomach and issued out between his legs. He attempted moving towards me but he was overcome by his wound. I left him there with the spear in his entrails till he died. Then I came to him, pulled out my spear and returned to the encampment place. I stayed there and did not go out, for he was the only one I sought. I only killed him to free myself. So as soon as I got back to Makkah, I became a free man."

BRINGING THE SITUATION UNDER CONTROL:

Although the death of Asad (Lion) of Allâh and His Messenger — Hamzah bin 'Abdul Muttalib — was a great loss, the Muslims maintained full control over the whole situation on the battlefield. On that day, Abu Bakr, 'Umar bin Al-Khattab, 'Ali bin Abi Talib, Az-Zubair bin Al-'Awwam, Mus'ab bin 'Umair, Talha bin 'Ubaidullâh, 'Abdullah bin Jahsh, Sa'd bin Ar-Rabî' and Anas bin An-Nadr and others — all of them fought so fiercely, effectively and efficiently that they broke the strong will of the idolaters and scattered them.

FROM HIS WIFE'S LAP TO SWORD-FIGHTS AND SORROWS:

One of the brave adventurers of that day was Hanzala Al-Ghaseel — He was Hanzala bin Abu 'Amir. Abu 'Amir was the very monk that was nicknamed '*Al-Fâsiq*' (i.e. the dissolute, evildoer). He is the very one that we have recently mentioned. Hanzala, who was newly married, left his wife's bed for *Al-Jihâd* (Fight in the cause of Allâh). He set out the moment he heard of the call to *Al-Jihâd*. When he faced the idolaters on the battlefield, he made his way through their ranks till he reached their leader Abu Sufyan Sakhr bin Harb and had almost killed him, if he had not been ordained to be a martyr. For at that moment he was seen by Shaddad bin Al-Aswad who struck him to death.

THE CONTRIBUTION OF THE ARCHERS SQUAD TO THE BATTLE:

The archers squad whom the Messenger of Allâh (Peace be upon him) located on the Archers Mountain, had the upper hand in administering the war activities to go in favour of the Muslim army. The Makkan horsemen — commanded by Khalid bin Al-Waleed, supported by Abu 'Amir Al-Fâsiq — had for three times attacked the left wing of the Muslim army with the aim of crushing it and then infiltrating into the rear to create a sort of confusion and disorder in the ranks of the Muslims and subsequently inflict heavy defeat on them. But thanks to the dexterity and great efforts of the archers, the three assaults were thwarted.

War activities went on and on fiercely with the Muslims in full command of the whole military developments until the idolaters finally staggered and retreated, leaving all motives of alleged pride, and affected dignity in oblivion, and their standard trodden by the feet of the fighters with none ever courageous enough to approach it. It seemed as if the three thousand idolaters had been fighting thirty thousand Muslims and not merely several hundreds.

Ibn Ishaq said: "Then Allâh sent down His Help unto the Muslims and verified His Promise to them. They chased the idolaters and evacuated them from their camp. No doubt it was a certain defeat." In a version by 'Abdullah bin Az-Zubair that his father had said: "By Allâh, I was watching the servants of Hind bint 'Utbah and her women friends fleeing with their garments gathered up. No one was there to prevent us from capturing them."

In another version by Al-Barâ' bin 'Azib — mentioned in *Sahih Al-Bukhâri* — he said: "When we fought them, they fled, and their women could be seen fleeing in the mountains with their anklets and legs revealed." The Muslims pursued the enemies putting them to sword and collecting the spoils.

THE ARCHERS' FATAL MISTAKE:

While the small army of Islam were recording the second absolute and clear victory over the Makkans — which was no less in splendour and glory than the first one at Badr — the majority of the archers on the mountainside committed a fatal mistake that turned the whole situation upside down, and constituted a source of heavy losses amongst the Muslims. It has almost brought about the murder of the Prophet (Peace be upon him), and left a very bad impression on the fame and dignity they deservedly earned at Badr Battle.

We have already spoken about the positive orders given to the archers to hold on to their position whatever the course of the main engagement. In spite of those strict orders, and their leader's — 'Abdullah bin Jubair — warning, forty archers deserted their posts, enticed by the too soon roar of victory as well as worldly avarice for the spoils of war. The others, however, nine in number and 'Abdullah, their leader, decided to abide by the Prophet 's order and stay where they were until they were given leave or killed to the last. Consequently the cleft was left inadequately defended .

The shrewd Khalid bin Al-Waleed seized this golden opportunity to turn swiftly round to the rear of the Muslim army and encompass them. Exterminating Ibn Jubair and his group, they fell promptly upon the rear of the Muslims and his horsemen uttered a shout that signalled the new military developments. The polytheists returned once again to counterattack the Muslims. An idolist woman — called 'Umra bint 'Alqama Al-Harithiyah — rushed to the lying-on-earth standard, picked it up and hoisted it. The idolaters gathered together around the standard and called out unto one another till they encircled the Muslims and stoodfast to fight again.

THE MUSLIMS CONSEQUENTLY GOT ENTRAPPED BETWEEN TWO MILLSTONES.

The Messenger of Allâh (Peace be upon him) was then among a small group of fighters — nine in number at the rear of the army, watching the engagement and braving the Muslim fighters. Khalid and his men took him by utter surprise, and obliged him to follow either of two options:

1. To flee for his life and abandon his army to its doomed end, or
2. To take action at the risk of his life, rally the ranks of the Muslims again and work their way through the hills of Uhud towards the encompassed army.

The genius of the Messenger of Allâh (Peace be upon him), his peerless and matchless courage made him opt for the second course. He raised his voice calling out unto his Companions: "Slaves of Allâh." He did that though he knew that hisloud voice would be heard by the idolaters before it was heard by the Muslims. He called out unto them risking his life in this delicate situation.

The idolaters, indeed, recognized him and reached his position even before the other Muslims could do so.

The encompassment of the Muslims revealed three categories of people: The first group were those who were only interested in themselves and they went so mad that they fled. They left the battlefield and did not know what happened to the others. Some of this group fled as far as Madinah. Some others went up the mountain.

The second Muslim group were those who returned to the battle, but mixed with the idolaters in such a way that they could not recognize one another. Consequently some of them were killed by mistake. On the authority of Al-Bukhari, he states that 'Aishah (May Allah be pleased with her) said: "When it was Uhud Battle, the idolaters were utterly defeated. Satan then called out: 'O slaves of Allâh. Beware the rear (i.e. the enemy is approaching from behind)'. So those who were at the front turned back and fought the ones who were behind."

Then Hudhaifah caught sight of his father 'Al-Yaman' about to be killed by other Muslims. So he said: "O servants of Allâh! Beware! This is my father. This is my father." 'Aishah (May Allah be pleased with her) said: "But they did not part with him till he was killed." Hudhaifah then said: "May Allâh forgive you." And 'Urwa said: "By Allâh, from that time on Hudhaifah has always been blessed and wealthy till he died." That was because he forgave them and refused to take any blood-money for his father's murder but recommended that it be spent in charity.

This Muslim group suffered from great bewilderment, and disorder prevailed among them. A lot of them got lost and did not know where to go. At this awkward time they heard someone calling: "Muhammad is killed." This news made them even more bewildered and almost out of sense. Their morale broke down, or almost did in a great number of individuals. Some of them stopped fighting, slackened, and cast down their weapons. Others thought of getting in touch with 'Abdullah bin Ubai — the head of the hypocrites — and seeking his assistance to fetch them a security pledge from Abu Sufyan.

Anas bin An-Nadr passed by those people who were shuddering of fear and panic, and inquired: "What are you waiting for?" They said: "The Messenger of Allâh (Peace be upon him) has been killed." "What do you live for after Muhammad (Peace be upon him)? Come on and die for what the Messenger of Allâh (Peace be upon him) has died for." Then he said: "O Allâh I apologize for what these people (i.e. the Muslims) have done; and I swear disavowal of what the idolaters have perpetrated." Then he moved on till he was encountered by Sa'd bin Mu'adh who asked him: "Where to, Abu 'Umar?" Anas replied: "Ah, how fine the scent of the Paradise is! I smell it here in Uhud." He went on and fought against the idolaters till he was killed. Nobody but his sister could recognize his dead body. It had been cut and stabbed by over eighty swords, arrows or spears. It was by the tip of his finger that she — after the battle — recognized him.

Thabit bin Ad-Dahdah called unto his people saying:

"O kinfolk of Helpers, if Muhammad (Peace be upon him) were killed, Allâh is Everlasting and He never dies. Fight in defence of your Faith. Allâh will help you and so you will be victorious." A group of Helpers joined him and all set out and attacked a battalion of Khalid's horsemen. He kept on fighting till he and his friends were killed.

An Emigrant passed by a Helper who was besmeared by blood. He said: "O fellow! Have you heard of Muhammad 's murder?" The Helper answered: "If Muhammad (Peace be upon him) were killed, then he must have completed the delivery of the Message. So fight in defence of your religion!"

With such boldness and encouragement, the Muslims soon recovered their spirits, came round to senses and desisted the idea of surrender or contacting the hypocrite 'Abdullah bin Ubai. They took up arms and resumed the fight attempting to make way to the headquarters, particularly after the news of the Prophet 's death had been falsified. The glad tidings nerved them, and helped them to manage quite successfully the break of the military blockade, and concentrate their forces in an immune place to resume a relentless and fierce fight against the polytheists.

The third group of Muslims were those who cared for nothing except the Prophet (Peace be upon him). At the head of them were notable Companions like Abu Bakr, 'Umar bin Al-Khattab, 'Ali bin Abi Talib and others (May Allah be pleased with them), who hastened to protect the Prophet (Peace be upon him) through unrivalled devotion.

As those groups of Muslims were receiving the blows of the idolaters and resisting instantly, the fight flared up around the Messenger of Allâh (Peace be upon him), who had only nine people around him. We have already mentioned that when the idolaters started their encompassment there were only nine persons around the Messenger of Allâh (Peace be upon him); and that as soon as he called out unto the Muslims: "Come on! I am the Messenger of Allâh (Peace be upon him)," the idolaters heard his voice and recognized him. So they turned back and attacked him with all their power before any of his Companions ran to his aid.

A violent raging struggle broke out between the nine Muslims and the idolaters during which peerless sort of love, self-sacrifice, bravery and heroism were revealed.

Muslim, on the authority of Anas bin Malik narrated that the Messenger of Allâh (Peace be upon him) along with seven Helpers and two Emigrants, was confined to a trap when the idolaters attacked him. The Messenger of Allâh (Peace be upon him) then said: " He who pushes back those idolaters, will be housed in Paradise." or "He will be my Companion in Paradise." One of the Helpers stepped forward and fought the idolaters in defence of the Prophet (Peace be upon him) till he was killed. Then they attacked the Messenger (Peace be upon him) again. The same process was repeated again and again till all the seven Helpers were killed. Then the Messenger of Allâh (Peace be upon him) said to his two Quraishite Companions: "We have not done justice to our Companions."

The last of those seven Helpers was 'Amara bin Yazeed bin As-Sakan, who kept on fighting till his wounds neutralized him and he fell dead.

THE MOST AWKWARD HOUR IN THE MESSENGER'S LIFE:

After the fall of Ibn Sakan, the Messenger of Allâh (Peace be upon him) remained alone with only those two Quraishites. In a version by Abu 'Uthman — authorized in *As-Sahihain*— he said: "At that time, there were none with the Prophet (Peace be upon him) except Talha bin 'Ubaidullâh and Sa'd bin Abi Waqqas. That was the most awkward and dangerous hour for the Prophet (Peace be upon him), but it was a golden opportunity for the idolaters who promptly took advantage of it. They concentrated their attack on the Prophet (Peace be upon him) and looked forward to killing him.

'Utbah bin Abi Waqqas pelted him with stones. One of the stones fell on his face. His lower right incisor *Ruba'iya* (i.e. the tooth that is between a canine and a front tooth) was injured. His lower lip was wounded. He was also attacked by 'Abdullah bin Shihab Az-Zuhri who cleaved his forehead. 'Abdullah bin Qami'a (*Qami'a* means 'a humiliated woman'), who was an obstinate strong horseman, struck him violently on his shoulder with his sword; and that stroke hurt the Messenger of Allâh (Peace be upon him) for over a month — though it was not strong enough to break his two armours. He dealt a heavy blow on his cheek. It was so strong that two rings of his iron-ringed helmet penetrated into his holy cheek. "Take this stroke from me, I am Ibn Qami'a." He said while striking the Messenger with his sword. The Messenger of Allâh (Peace be upon him) replied — while he was wiping the blood flowing on his face: "I implore Allâh to humiliate you." (i.e. *Aqma'aka Allâh*). In *Al-Bukhâri* it is stated his incisor broke, his head was cleaved, and that he started wiping the blood off it and saying: "(I wonder) how can peopwho cut the face of their Prophet (Peace be upon him) and break the incisor of his — he who calls them to worship Allâh. How can such people thrive or be successful?" About that incident, Allâh, Glory is to Him, sent down a Qur'ânic verse saying:

- "Not for you [O Muhammad (Peace be upon him) but for Allâh] is the decision; whether He turns in mercy to (pardons) them or punishes them; verily, they are the *Zâlimûn* (polytheists, disobedients, and wrong-doers)." [3:128]

At-Tabarani states that the Prophet (Peace be upon him) said: "Allâh's Wrath is great on those who besmear the face of His Messenger," observed silence for a short while and then resumed saying:

- "O Allâh, forgive my people for they have no knowledge."

In *Sahih Muslim* it is stated that the Messenger of Allâh (Peace be upon him) said:

- "My Lord, forgive my people for they have no knowledge."

In *Ash-Shifa* — a book by 'Ayad Al-Qadi — it is related that the Prophet (Peace be upon him) said:

- "O Allâh, guide my people for they have no knowledge."

It is quite certain that killing the Prophet (Peace be upon him) was their primary aim, but the two Quraishites — Sa'd bin Abi Waqqas and Talha bin 'Ubaidullâh, who showed great and rare courage and fought so fiercely and boldly that — though they were only two — were able to stop the idolaters short of realizing their aim. They were of the best skillful Arab archers and kept on militating in defence of the Messenger of Allâh (Peace be upon him) till the whole squad of idolaters was driven off him (Peace be upon him).

The Messenger of Allâh (Peace be upon him) emptied his quiver of arrows and said to Sa'd bin Abi Waqqas: "Shoot, an arrow Sa'd. May my father and mother be sacrificed for you." The Prophet (Peace be upon him) had never gathered his parents except in the case of Sa'd — a privilege granted to him for his efficiency.

In a version by Jabir — authorized by An-Nasa'i — concerning the attitude of Talha bin 'Ubaidullâh towards the gathering of idolaters around the Messenger of Allâh (Peace be upon him) — when there were only some Helpers with him — Jabir said: "When the idolaters reached him, the Messenger of Allâh (Peace be upon him) said: 'Who will suffice us their evils (i.e. fight them back)?' Talha said: 'I will.'" Then Jabir mentioned the advance of the Helpers to fight and how they were killed one after the other in a similar way to Muslim's narration — "When all the Helpers were killed, Talha proceeded forward to fight as much as the other eleven ones did till his hand was hurt and his fingers were cut off. So he said: 'Be they cut off!' The Prophet (Peace be upon him) said: 'If you had said: In the Name of Allâh, the angels would have raised you up before the people's very eyes.'" Then he said: "Allâh drove the idolaters off them." In *Al-Ikleel* — a book by Hakim — it is stated that Talha had sustained thirty-nine or thirty-five wounds, and his fingers (i.e. the forefinger and the one next to it — got paralyzed.

In a version by Qais bin Abi Hâzim — authorized by Al-Bukhari, he said: "I saw the hand of Talha paralyzed. That was because he protected the Prophet (Peace be upon him) with it in Uhud Battle."

At-Tirmidhi stated that the Prophet (Peace be upon him) then said about Talha: "He who desires to see a martyr walking on the ground, let him look at Talha bin 'Ubaidullâh."

Abu Da'ûd At-Tayalisi on the authority of 'Aishah (May Allah be pleased with her), said: "Whenever Uhud Day (i.e. battle) was mentioned, Abu Bakr used to say: 'That was Talha's day (i.e. battle)'. Abu Bakr recited a verse of poetry about him: 'O Talha bin 'Ubaidullâh! Paradise is due to you as water-springs are due to deer to drink out of.' At the awkward and most delicate circumstances, Allâh, Glory is to Him, sent down His invisible Help. In a version by Sa'd — cleared and authorized in *Sahih Al-Bukhari* and *Muslim* — he said: "I saw the Messenger of Allâh (Peace be upon him) on Uhud Day with two men — dressed in white defending him fiercely — I have never seen similar to them neither before Uhud nor after it." In another version: "He means to say that they were Gabriel and Michael".

All those events happened in no time. If the Prophet 's elite Companions had realized the grave situation immediately, they would have rushed on the spot and would not have left him sustain these wounds. Unfortunately, they got there after the Messenger of Allâh (Peace be upon him) had been wounded and six of the Helpers killed, the seventh was staggering under the brunt of wounds and desperately militating in defence of the Prophet (Peace be upon him). However as soon as they arrived they encircled the Messenger with their bodies and weapons and were alert enough to prevent the enemies from reaching him. The first one who returned to give help, was his cavemate Abu Bakr As-Siddiq (May Allah be pleased with him).

In a version by 'Aishah (May Allah be pleased with her) recorded in Ibn Hibban's *Sahih*, she narrated that Abu Bakr had said:

"When it was Uhud Day and at the time that the Prophet (Peace be upon him) was left behind, I was the first to go back and see him. Before him I saw a man fighting to shield him from the enemies. I said to myself: 'I wish he were Talha. Let my father and mother be sacrificed for you. (O Allâh) Let him be Talha! Let my parents be sacrificed for you!' On the way, I was overtaken by Abu 'Ubaidah bin Al-Jarrah, who was then moving as swiftly as a bird. We both rushed to dress the Prophet 's wounds. There we found Talha suffering from serious wounds before the Messenger of Allâh (Peace be upon him). The Prophet (Peace be upon him) said: 'See to your brother. His deed entitled him for an abode in Paradise.' I noticed that two rings of the iron-ringed helmet had penetrated his cheek. So I set out to take them out; but Abu 'Ubaidah demanded: 'By Allâh, O Abu Bakr — I beseech you, let me do it myself.' Fearing to hurt the Prophet (Peace be upon him) he started pulling one of the two rings out very slowly and carefully with his mouth. Then he pulled the arrow out by his mouth, too. Consequently, his front tooth fell. Then I proceeded to pull the second out; but Abu 'Ubaidah besought me to leave it: 'O, Abu Bakr, I adjure you by Allâh to let me do it.' He pulled the second ring very slowly and carefully with his mouth — till it came out. The Messenger of Allâh (Peace be upon him) said: 'See to your brother. He has proved to be worthy of being housed in Paradise.' We approached Talha to cure him but found out that he had had some ten sword-strokes in his body. (This showed how efficiently Talha had fought and struggled on that day)."

At those awkward moments of that day, a group of Muslim heroes gathered around the Prophet (Peace be upon him) forming a shield to protect him from the idolaters. Some of them were Abu Dujana, Mus'ab bin 'Umair, 'Ali bin Abi Talib, Sahl bin Haneef, Malik bin — Sinan the father of Abu Sa'îd Al-Khudri, Umm'Amara, Nusaiba bint Ka'b Al-Mâziniya, Qatada bin An-Nu'man, 'Umar bin Al-Khattab, Hatib bin Abi Balta'a and Abu Talha.

The number of idolaters was steadily increasing; and their attacks, naturally, got severer. Their press had increased to an extent that the Messenger of Allâh (Peace be upon him) fell into one of the holes dug and designed by Abu 'Amir Al-Fasiq to be used as traps. His knee scratched and 'Ali helped him by grasping his hand up. Talha bin 'Ubaidullâh took him in his lap till he could stand upright. Nafi' bin Jubair said: I heard an Emigrant say: "I have witnessed Uhud Battle and watched how arrows had been hurled from all directions at the Prophet (Peace be upon him). None of them however hit him. 'Abdullah, bin Shihab Az-Zuhri said: 'Guide me to Muhammad (Peace be upon him)! By Allâh, If I didn't kill him, I would not hope to live.' Although the Messenger of Allâh (Peace be upon him) was next to him, alone — but he did not observe him. Safwan, a co-polytheist of his, blamed him (for not translating his words into deeds), but 'Abdullah swore that he did not see him [the Prophet (Peace be upon him)] and added that he might be immune to our attempts on his life. He also said that four of them pledged to maa fresh attempt and kill him, but also to no avail.

The Muslims showed unprecedented rare heroism and marvellous sacrifices. Abu Talha — for instance — shielded the Messenger of Allâh (Peace be upon him) by his body and used his chest to protect him against the enemy arrows. Anas related that on Uhud Day when people dispersed off the Prophet (Peace be upon him), Abu Talhah was a skillful sort of archer who would pull arrows so much that he broke two or three bows that day. When a man passed along with a quiver full of arrows, the Prophet (Peace be upon him) would say: "Spread the arrows to Abu Talhah!" Then when the Prophet (Peace be upon him) watched people shooting, Abu Talhah would say: "I sacrifice my father and mother for your safety. Do not go too close lest an arrow of theirs should hit you. I would rather die than see you hurt."

Abu Dujana stood before the Messenger of Allâh (Peace be upon him) and used to protect him from the arrows by his back. Hatib bin Balta'a followed 'Utbah bin Abi Waqqas — who broke the honourable incisor [of the Prophet (Peace be upon him)] — struck him with the sword, cracked his head and took his mare and sword. Sa'd bin Abi Waqqas was so keen to kill his brother 'Utbah, but he could not; however, Hatib could.

Sahl bin Haneef — a hero archer — who had pledged to die in the cause of Allâh, also played a prominent part in Uhud hostilities.

The Messenger of Allâh (Peace be upon him) himself was involved in shooting arrows. In a version by

Qatadah bin An-Nu'man that the Messenger of Allâh (Peace be upon him) shot so many arrows that the two ends of his bow were flattened. So Qatadah bin An-Nu'man took it to remain with him for good. On that day his eye was so hurt that it fell down onto his cheek; but the Messenger of Allâh (Peace be upon him) reput it in its socket with his hand and it became the better and the more sharp-sighted of the two.

On that day 'Abdur Rahman bin 'Awf kept on fighting till his mouth was hurt and got broken. He sustained over twenty wounds, some in his leg, and that lamed him.

Malik bin Sinan, the father of Abi Sa'eed Al-Khudri sucked the blood out of the Prophet 's cheek till he cleaned it. The Prophet (Peace be upon him) said: "Spit it!". But Malik said: "By Allâh, I will never spit it". Then he set out to fight. The Prophet (Peace be upon him) then said: "He who wants to see a man of the people of Paradise, let him look at this one." No sooner had he resumed fighting than he was martyred in the thick of the battle.

Umm 'Amarah participated in the fight too. She encountered Ibn Qami'a in combat, and sustained a slight wound on her shoulder, but she herself also struck him with her sword several times but he survived because he was wearing two armours. She, however, went on striking until her wounds counted twelve.

Mus'ab bin 'Umair, in his turn, fought fiercely and violently defending the Prophet (Peace be upon him) against the attacks of Ibn Qami'a and his fellows. He was carrying the standard with his right hand. In the process of fighting, it was cut off, so he grabbed the standard in his left hand till this was also amputated so he knelt down and shielded it with his chest and neck. Ibn Qami'a then killed him, mistaking him for the Messenger of Allâh (Peace be upon him) on account of resemblance in appearance. Only then did Ibn Qami'a shout 'Muhammad (Peace be upon him) has been killed.'

No sooner had Ibn Qami'a uttered that ominous sentence than consternation spread among Muhammad's followers, and their morale was drastically reduced. Consequently, confusion and a miserable state of disorder prevailed amongst them. Whilst the rumours managed to adversely act amongst the Muslims, it alleviated the sharp impact of the assaults of the polytheists who came to believe that they did really achieve their final objective and so they turned towards mutilating the dead bodies.

When Mus'ab was killed, the Messenger of Allâh (Peace be upon him) delivered the standard to 'Ali bin Abi Talib. 'Ali, in conjunction with the other Companions, went on fighting bravely and set marvellous examples of heroism, courage and endurance in both defence and attack.

Then the Messenger of Allâh (Peace be upon him) made his way to his encircled army. Ka'b bin Malik, who was the first one to recognize the approaching Prophet (Peace be upon him), shouted as loudly as he could: "O folks of Muslims, be cherished! The Messenger of Allâh (Peace be upon him) is here." But the Messenger of Allâh (Peace be upon him) signed to him to stop lest his position should be located by the idolaters. Upon hearing the shout, the Muslims immediately raced towards the source of the shout which brought about thirty Companions to gather around the Prophet (Peace be upon him). With this assembled number of his Companions, the Messenger of Allâh (Peace be upon him) started drawing a planned withdrawal to the hillocks nearby.

Hostilities of the enemy grew fiercer than ever with the aim of foiling the plan of withdrawal of the Muslims. Their attempts however proved to be fruitless due to the heroic steadfastness of the lions of Islam.

'Uthman bin 'Abdullah bin Al-Mugheerah — one of the enemy horsemen — progressed towards the Messenger of Allâh (Peace be upon him) while saying: "Either I kill him [i.e. Muhammad (Peace be upon him)] or I will be killed." The Messenger of Allâh (Peace be upon him) moved to encounter him but his mare tripped into some holes. So Al-Harith bin As-Simma combated with the enemy, and struck him on his leg so he went lame, then he finished him off, took his arm and overtook the Messenger of Allâh .

But later on another Makkan horseman, called 'Abdullah bin Jabir, attacked Al-Harith bin As-Simma, and struck him on the shoulder with his sword and he was carried to the camp of the Muslims suffering from serious wounds. Anyway that very idolater did not escape death, for Abu Dujana — the red headbanded hero and adventurer — struck him heavily and cut his head off.

During this bitter fight, a desire to sleep overwhelmed the Muslims — that was a security and tranquillity to help His slave Muslims as the Qur'ân spoke in this context. Abu Talhah said: "I was one of those who were possessed by a desire to sleep on Uhud Day. On that day my sword fell off my hand several times. Again and again it fell down and again and again I picked it up."

In a regular withdrawal and with great bravery and boldness, the Muslims finally retreated to the cover of Mountain Uhud. Then, the rest of the army followed them to that safe position. In this manner, the genius of Muhammad (Peace be upon him) foiled that of Khalid bin Al-Waleed.

Ibn Ishaq related that: "When the Messenger of Allâh (Peace be upon him) was going up the hillock, he was followed by Ubai bin Khalaf who was saying: 'Where is Muhammad (Peace be upon him)? Either I kill him or I will be killed.' The Companions of Muhammad (Peace be upon him) said: 'O Messenger of Allâh, do you mind if one of us combats with him?' But the Messenger of Allâh (Peace be upon him) said: 'Leave him!' So when he drew nearer, the Messenger of Allâh (Peace be upon him) took the spear from Al-Harith bin As-Simma. He shivered violently in such a way that made all of them scatter in all directions violently and impulsively. Then he faced him, observed his clavicle through a gap between the wide opening of the armour and the part of his neck enclosed by. He speared him in that spot. The effect of the stroke was so strong that it made him roll off his horse over and over. When he returned to Quraish, they found that he had only had a small scratch in his neck. So when blood became congested he said: 'By Allâh, Muhammad has killed me.' Hearing him say so, they said: 'By Allâh you are afraid to death. By Allâh, you are possessed by a devil.' He replied: 'He had already told me when we were in Makkah: 'I will kill you.' By Allâh, had he spate on me, he would have killed me.' Eventually, the enemy of Allâh breathed his last at a place called Sarif, while they were taking him back to Makkah." In a version by Abul-Aswad, on the authority of 'Urwa: He was lowinglike a bull and saying: "By the One in Whose Hand is my soul, if (the pain) I am suffering from now were distributed among the people of Al-Majaz, it would cause them to die."

During the withdrawal of the Messenger of Allâh (Peace be upon him) up to the cover of the mountain, a big rock blocked his way. The Prophet (Peace be upon him) tried to mount it, but having worn a short heavy armour, and being seriously wounded — he could not ascend it. Readily enough Talha sat in a position that enabled the Prophet (Peace be upon him) to stand on his back. Then he lifted him up till he stood on it. The Prophet (Peace be upon him) then said: "Talha, after this job, is eligible for the Garden (Paradise)."

When the Messenger of Allâh (Peace be upon him) settled down in his head quarters in the hillock, the idolaters started their last attack upon the Muslims. Ibn Ishaq related that: "While the Prophet (Peace be upon him) was on the way to the hillock, a group of Quraishite elite ascended the mountain. They were led by Khalid bin Al-Waleed and Abu Sufyan. So the Messenger of Allâh (Peace be upon him) implored his Lord saying: 'O Allâh, they (i.e. the idolaters) should not be higher (i.e. in position or in power) than us (i.e. the Muslims). Therefore 'Umar bin Al-Khattab and some of the Emigrants fought the idolaters till they drove them down the mountain.

In *Al-Maghazi* — a book by Al-Umawi — it is stated that the idolaters went up the mountain. So the Messenger of Allâh (Peace be upon him) said to Sa'd: "Drive them off." "How can I drive them off by myself (i.e. without anyone to assist)." But the Messenger of Allâh (Peace be upon him) repeated the phrase three times. Sa'd then took an arrow out of his quiver, shot it at one of them and killed him. He said: "Then I took another one I know (to be good) and I shot with it another man. Then I took a third I know and killed a third one. Consequently they climbed down the mountain. I said to myself, 'this must be a blessed arrow.' I put it in my quiver." He kept it with him till he died. His children kept it with them ever after.

MUTILATION OF THE MARTYRS:

That was the last attack made by the idolaters against the Prophet (Peace be upon him). Being almost certain of his death, the idolaters returned to their camp and started preparations to go back to Makkah. Some of them involved themselves in mutilating the killed Muslims, and so did their women. Women and men cut off the ears, the noses, the genitals of the martyrs. They even cut open their bellies. Hind bin 'Utbah — for instance — ripped open the liver of Hamzah and chewed it; but finding it unpleasant, she spat it out. She even made the ears and noses of Muslims into anklets and necklaces.

Two incidents occurred during the last hours of the fight. Which revealed for certain how far the Muslims were ready to fight and sacrifice in the way of Allâh:

1. Ka'b bin Malik said: I was one of those Muslims who fought in Uhud and witnessed the polytheists' act of barbarity in mutilating the dead bodies, but I passed them because I couldn't stand it. Then I saw an armed stout idolater pass through the Muslims and say: "Gather them up and combine them in the way that sheep are gathered and slaughtered." Similarly I saw an armed Muslim waiting for him. I walked towards them till I stood behind him. Comparing both of them, I found that the disbeliever was better than the other in arms and figure. I kept on watching them till they were engaged in single combat. The Muslim thrust at the disbeliever with his sword that went down his hip and split it into two. When the Muslim unveiled his face, he said: "What about that, Ka'b. I am Abu Dujana."
2. Some Muslim women came to the battlefield when the fight was over. Anas said: I saw 'Aishah bint Abu Bakr (May Allah be pleased with him) with Umm Sulaim. Their garments were gathered up so I could see their anklets. They carried water bags on their shoulders and emptied them into the mouths of people. Then they would go back to fill them and come back to do the same. 'Umar said: "Umm Saleet used to carry water bags to us on Uhud Day."

When Umm Aiman, who was one of those Muslim women who saw the defeated Muslim fighters entering Madinah, she started throwing dust at their faces rebukingly saying: "Here is a spinning wheel, take it! and give up carrying swords." Then she raced to the battlefield. There she watered the wounded. Hibban bin Al-'Arqa shot an arrow at her, she fell down and her clothes were lifted up. Seeing that, the enemy of Allâh, burst into laughter. That sight upset the Messenger of Allâh (Peace be upon him), so he gave Sa'd bin Abi Waqqas an arrow lacking an arrow-head and said "Shoot it". Sa'd shot it, it pierced the idolater's throat. He fell down and some parts of his body were revealed. The Messenger of Allâh (Peace be upon him) then laughed so much that his molars could be seen. Sa'd avenged her and Allâh responded to her supplication.

As soon as the Messenger of Allâh (Peace be upon him) reached the defile, 'Ali bin Abu Talib went out and filled his water container with water from Al-Mihras. 'Al-Mihras' is said to be hollow (concaved) rock containing plenty of water. It was also said that it is a water spring in Uhud mountain. Anyway, 'Ali brought that water to the Messenger of Allâh (Peace be upon him) to drink. Finding that it smelt bad he refused to drink it, but only washed the blood off his face and poured some of it over his head saying: Allâh's Wrath is great on those who besmeared His Messenger's face with blood.

Sahl said: "By Allâh, I know who washed the wound of the Messenger of Allâh (Peace be upon him) and who poured out water for him and what (substances) his wound was treated with: His daughter Fatimah washed it, whereas 'Ali poured water out of the container. When Fatimah realized that water increased the flow of blood, she took a piece of straw mat, burnt it a little and stuck it to the wound so blood ceased flowing."

Muhammad bin Maslamah brought him fresh water to drink. The Prophet (Peace be upon him) drank and supplicated Allâh to provide him with good things. Owing to the wounds and their bad effects on his body, the Messenger of Allâh (Peace be upon him) led his followers in prayer in a sitting posture and so did the Muslims.

When the preparations of the idolaters for departure came to an end, Abu Sufyan went up the mountain and called out: "Is Muhammad (Peace be upon him) among you?" They did not answer him. Then he asked "Is Ibn Abi Quhafah (i.e. Abu Bakr) among you?" They did not answer. He asked again: "Is 'Umar bin Al-Khattab among you?" They did not answer him; for the Prophet (Peace be upon him) forbade them answering him. He only asked about those three. That is because he and his people knew quite well that the call to Islam depended to a large degree on those men. Abu Sufyan then said: "As for those three, we have relieved you of." 'Umar could not help but talking, so he said, "O enemy of Allâh, those whom you have just mentioned, I tell you that they are still alive. Allâh has maintained what you hate." Abu Sufyan answered: "The mutilation of your killed is something I did not order it; but it did not displease me." Then he shouted: "Hubal (an idol), let it be sublime!" The Prophet (Peace be upon him) said: "Why do you not reply?" "What shall we say?" They asked him. "Say: Allâh is more Sublime and Exalted and Mightier as well."

He said: "Al-'Uzza (i.e. an idol) is ours but you have no 'Uzza." "Why do you not reply?" The Prophet (Peace be upon him) said. "What shall we say?" They inquired. He said: "Say Allâh is our Protector, but you have no protector."

Abu Sufyan said: "Well deeds! Today is a vengeance for Badr Day. This for that. War is attended with alternate success." 'Umar's reply was: "No. They are not the same. Our killed men are housed in Paradise; but yours are in Fire."

Then Abu Sufyan said: "Come on, 'Umar!" The Messenger of Allâh (Peace be upon him) said: "Go and see what the matter is." He went there. Abu Sufyan asked him: "I beseech you by Allâh's Name to tell me the truth: Have we killed Muhammad (Peace be upon him)?" 'Umar said: "O Allâh, 'No' and now he islistening to you words." He said: "For me, you are more truthful than Ibn Qami'a, and even more reliable."

Ibn Ishaq said: When Abu Sufyan and those who were with him were leaving he called out notifying: "We will meet again at Badr next year." The Messenger of Allâh (Peace be upon him) said to one of his men: "Say: 'Yes, it is an appointment for both of us.'"

Later on, the Messenger of Allâh (Peace be upon him) dispatched 'Ali bin Abi Talib to trace them out. He said to him: "Pursue them and see what they are going to do, and what they aim at. If they dismount horses and ride on camels' back, this means that they are heading for Makkah; but if they ride horses and lead camels unmounted, they are leaving for Madinah. By the One, in Whose Hand my soul is, if they attacked Madinah I would march to them there and I would fight them." 'Ali said: "I went out and traced them to see what they were up to. I saw them mounting camels and leaving the horses unmounted. They were heading for Makkah."

After the departure of the Quraishites, people went out to check the identity of the killed and the wounded. Zaid bin Thabit said: "The Messenger of Allâh (Peace be upon him) sent me on Uhud Day to seek Sa'd bin Ar-Rabî' and said: "When you see him, say: 'peace be upon you from me.' and say to him 'the Messenger of Allâh (Peace be upon him) says: How do you feel?'" Zaid said: "I started wandering about checking the killed till I came across Sa'd when he was dying — with about seventy strokes or stabs of a sword, a spear and an arrow in his body.So I said: "O Sa'd, the Messenger of Allâh (Peace be upon him) sends you his greetings. and says 'peace be upon you, tell me how do you feel?'" Sa'd said: "And let peace be upon the Messenger of Allâh (Peace be upon him), too. Tell him, I smell the scent of the Paradise. And tell the Helpers, my people, 'you shall not be excused before Allâh if the Messenger of Allâh (Peace be upon him) is hurt and your eyes are blinking' (i.e. you are still alive and not dead)." Then he died.

They came across Al-Usairim — 'Amr bin Thabit, whom they had already urged to embrace Islam but refused. They saw him among the wounded on the verge of close death. "What has he come here for? We have parted with him and he was still too obdurate to accept Islam as his religion". They asked him: "What made you come here? Is it out of zeal to defend your people or is it because of an inclination to Islam?" He said: "It is (certainly) an inclination to Islam. I believe in Allâh and in His Messenger. I have fought with the Messenger of Allâh (Peace be upon him) till I have got what you see," and then he immediately died. They told the Messenger of Allâh (Peace be upon him) about him. Hearing that, he said: "He is one of the inhabitants of Paradise." "Although he had not offered one single prayer," narrated Abu Hurairah.

Qazman, who was found among the wounded, fought heroically, and killed seven or eight idolaters. He was weakened by the wounds he had sustained, they carried him to the habitation of Bani Zufr. The Muslims gave him glad tidings of the Paradise. But he said: "By Allâh I have fought out of a zeal to my people. Had it not been for that I would have never fought." When his wounds worsened he committed suicide. The Messenger of Allâh (Peace be upon him) had already said whenever he was mentioned to him: "He is an inhabitant of Fire." This is the end of those who fight for a national cause or in a way other than that of raising up the Word of Allâh, though they fought under the banner of Islam or even in the army of the Messenger of Allâh (Peace be upon him) or of his Companions.

Contrary to Qazman there was a Jew of Bani Tha'labah among the killed. He said to his people, "O folk people of Jews! By Allâh you have already known that it is imperative to support Muhammad (Peace be upon him)." They said: "Today is Saturday." He said: "There is no Saturday for you." He took his sword and the war equipment and said: "If I were killed, my property should be put at Muhammad's disposal". Then next morning he kept on fighting till he was killed. The Messenger of Allâh (Peace be upon him) said about him, "Mukhaireeq is the best Jew."

BURIAL OF THE MARTYRS:

The Messenger of Allâh (Peace be upon him) supervised the martyrs' burial and said: "I bear witness that anyone who is wounded in the way of Allâh, Allâh will resurrect him with his wound bleeding a liquid which is blood-like in colour but musk-like in scent."

Some of the Companions carried their men killed in the war to Madinah, but the Messenger of Allâh (Peace be upon him) ordered that they should be sent back in order to be buried where they were killed. He ordered that they should not be washed but buried as they were after stripping them off their armours and leather clothes. He used to bury every two or three martyrs together in one grave and even join two men in one garment while saying: "Who is the more learned of the Qur'ân?" and he would commit him to earth first. He would say: "I bear witness to those on the Day of Resurrection." He buried both 'Abdullah bin 'Amr bin Haram and 'Amr bin Al-Jamuh in one grave due to the affection they used to possess to each other.

They missed the coffin of Hanzalah, they sought it and found that it was on a spot nearby with water dripping off it. The Messenger of Allâh (Peace be upon him) told his Companions that the angels were washing him and said: "Ask his wife". They asked her and she confirmed that he had been in a state of ceremonial impurity. That was why Hanzalah was called 'Ghaseel Al-Malâ'ikah' (i.e. the one washed by the angels).

When the Messenger of Allâh (Peace be upon him) saw how his uncle and foster brother, Hamzah, was mutilated, he was extremely grieved. When his aunt Safiyah came to see her brother Hamzah, the Messenger of Allâh (Peace be upon him) ordered her son Az-Zubair to dismiss her in order not to see what happened to her brother. She refused and said, "But why should I go away. I have been informed that they have mutilated him. But so long as it is in the way of Allâh, whatever happens to him satisfies us. I say: Allâh is Sufficient and I will be patient if Allâh wills." She approached, looked at him and supplicated Allâh for him and said: "To Allâh we all belong and to Him we will verily return." and she implored Allâh to forgive him. Then the Messenger of Allâh (Peace be upon him) ordered that he should be buried with 'Abdullah bin Jahsh — who was his nephew as well as his foster brother.

Ibn Mas'ud said: We have never seen the Messenger of Allâh (Peace be upon him) weeping so much as he was for Hamzah bin 'Abdul Muttalib. He directed him towards Al-Qiblah, then he stood at his funeral and sobbed his heart out.

The sight of the martyrs was extremely horrible and heart-breaking. Describing Hamzah's funeral,

Khabbab said: "No shroud long enough was available for Hamzah except a white-darkish garment. When they covered his head with it, it was too short to cover his feet. Similarly if they covered his feet his head would be revealed. Finally they covered his head with it and put some plant called 'Al-Idhkhir' to cover his feet."

Al-Imam Ahmad reported that when it was Uhud Day and the time that the idolaters returned, the Messenger of Allâh (Peace be upon him) said:

- *"Istawoo (i.e. form rows as for prayer) so that I offer thanks and praise to my Lord, the Great and the All-Mighty."*

So they stood in rows behind him. Then he said:

- "O Allâh, no one can withhold what You permit or permit what You withhold. No one can guide whom You decree to go astray or make go astray the one whom You guide. No one can grant provisions you have withheld and no one can withhold what you grant. No one can near what You ordained to be distant, or detach what You decree to be close. O Allâh, spread onto all of us Your Mercy, Your Grace, and Provisions."

"O Allâh, I implore You to grant me permanent bliss that neither changes nor vanishes. O Allâh, You Alone we seek for Help at hardships. You Alone we resort to for security on a day of terror. O Allâh, to You Alone I resort to protect us frthe evils of Your grants (i.e. the evils they may lead us to) and from the evils of Your deprivation. O Allâh, make us love Faith and make it pleasant and beloved wholeheartedly by us! Make disbelief, ungodliness and disobedience detestable to us. Let us be among those who are rightly guided. O Allâh, make us live as Muslims and cause us to die as Muslims; and make us join with the righteous but not with the disgraced and misled ones. O Allâh, make Your enmity befall the disbelievers, who belie Your Messenger and divert from Your righteous way. O Allâh, let Your wrath, Your chastisement and Your enmity befall the disbelievers, and those on whom You sent down the Book. Let them be afflicted with war decreed by You. O Allâh, the Author of Truth."

After committing all the martyrs to earth, and after offering praise and supplication to Allâh, the Messenger of Allâh (Peace be upon him) went back to Madinah.

On his way back, matchless examples of love and devotion were revealed by the truthful women believers; in no way less great than the men's heroic deeds in the fight.

Hamnah bint Jahsh met the Messenger of Allâh (Peace be upon him) on the way back, and he announced the death of her brother — 'Abdullah bin Jahsh — to her. She said: "To Allâh we belong and to Him we will verily return. I ask Allâh's forgiveness." Then he announced the death of her maternal uncle Hamzah bin 'Abdul Muttalib. She said: "To Allâh we belong and to Him we will verily return. I ask Allâh's forgiveness." But when he announced the death of her husband Mus'ab bin 'Umair to her, she shouted and woed. Seeing her doing so, the Messenger of Allâh (Peace be upon him) said: "The woman's husband is extremely dear to her."

He passed by a woman of Bani Dinar whose husband, father and brother were all killed at Uhud. When their death announced, she said: "How is the Messenger of Allâh (Peace be upon him)?" They said: "Well indeed. O mother of so... Thanks for Allâh; he is well and as good as you desire." She said: "Let me see him." They pointed at him. Seeing him she said: "All misfortunes are nothing so long as you are safe."

Umm Sa'd bin Mu'adh came running to see the Prophet (Peace be upon him). At that time her son was holding the rein of his mare. Seeing his mother, he said to the Prophet (Peace be upon him): "O Messenger of Allâh (Peace be upon him). This is my mother." The Prophet (Peace be upon him) said:

"She is welcome"; and he stopped and waited for her. When she drew near, he consoled her, for her killed son 'Amr bin Mu'adh. But she said: "So long as I see you are safe, my misfortune will certainly go into oblivion." Then the Messenger of Allâh (Peace be upon him) supplicated Allâh for the relatives of those who were killed at Uhud and said: "Cheer up! Umm Sa'd and bear good tidings to their kindred that all their people killed in the battle are comrades in Paradise and they are intercessors for all their kinsfolk." She replied, "O Messenger of Allâh, we are satisfied. Who would cry on them after this cheerful news?" Then she resumed saying: "O Messenger of Allâh, invoke Allâh (for those who stayed behind)" He said: "O Allâh keep sorrow off their hearts! And console them with their misfortunes. Compensate those who stayed behind with goodness and welfare."

In the evening of that day — i.e. Saturday, the seventh of Shawwal, 3rd year A.H. — the Messenger arrived in Madinah. As soon as he reached his house, he handed his sword to his daughter Fatimah and said: "O daughter, wash the blood off this sword. By Allâh it has been helpful to me today." 'Ali bin Abi Talib handed her his sword and said: "And wash the blood of this sword too. By Allâh, it has been helpful to me today." So the Messenger of Allâh (Peace be upon him) said: "Sahl bin Haneef and Abu Dujana have been as courageous as you are in the fight."

Most of the narrations confirmed that seventy Muslims were killed and most of them, sixty-five, Helpers; forty-one of whom were from Khazraj and twenty-four from Aws. This, besides one Jew and four Emigrants.

As for the polytheists, twenty-two of them were killed, but some versions speak of thirty-seven; after all, Allâh knows best.

On Saturday night, the eighth of Shawwal, and after their return from Uhud, the Muslims spent that night in an emergency case — though they were dead-beat, extremely exhausted. They stayed on the alert, and spent that night guarding the outlets and inlets of Madinah. They were specially busy guarding their general leader, the Messenger of Allâh (Peace be upon him) for fear that some suspects could commit an unexpected folly.

HAMRA' AL-ASAD INVASION:

The Messenger of Allâh (Peace be upon him) on his part, spent the night pondering over the situation. He feared that the idolaters might think — while they were still on their way to Makkah — of reversing their way and diverting to Madinah after they had realized that they had availed nothing of that victory. They might regret and decide to invade Madinah as a compensation. Therefore the Messenger of Allâh (Peace be upon him) was determined to go out in pursuit of the Makkan army.

The Prophet (Peace be upon him) called out unto people and ordered them to march to encounter the enemy of Islam. That was on Sunday morning — next day to Uhud — the eighth of Shawwal. He said: "Nobody will march to the fight except those who have already participated in Uhud fight." 'Abdullah bin Ubai said: "I will march out with you." "No," said the Prophet (Peace be upon him).

Whilst the Muslims were suffering a lot from painful pains and deep anxiety, they responded to his call positively. Jabir bin 'Abdullah implored the Prophet (Peace be upon him) to allow him join them in that fresh invasion on account that he always had a liking to witness all the battles that the Prophet (Peace be upon him) was involved in. He had not participated in Uhud because his father asked him to stay in Madinah with his sisters . And he was granted his wish.

The Muslims marched out until they reached a place called Hamra' Al-Asad — about eight miles from Madinah. He encamped there. In that place Ma'bad bin Abi Ma'bad came to the Messenger of Allâh (Peace be upon him) and professed Islam. Some people said that he remained an idolater; he simply desired to give the Messenger some advice out of abidance by a covenant between Khuza'ah (his tribe) and Bani Hashim. He said "O Muhammad (Peace be upon him)! By Allâh, we feel great sorrow for what had happened to you and to your Companions. We really hope you will not suffer again." So, the Messenger of Allâh (Peace be upon him) suggested that he overtake Abu Sufyan and discourage him from pursuing his evil intentions.

The Messenger's fears of a possible return of the idolaters proved to be absolutely true. For no sooner had the idolaters dismounted and encamped at Ar-Rawhâ' — a place thirty-six miles from Madinah, than they started reproaching one another. A group of them said to another one: "You did nothing. You broke down their force but you left them. There are still some distinguished men among them who will probably gather people up to fight you again. So let us go back and annihilate them and crush down their forces."

It was in fact a hasty decision taken by shallow-minded people who misjudged the potential power and morale on both parties, that is why an eminent leader of Quraish, Safwan bin Omaiyah, tried to dissuade his people from pursuing that venture, saying: "O people. Do not do such a thing! For I fear that he will gather up those who had stayed behind and did not share in Uhud. Go back home as winners. For I am not sure of what turn will the consequences take if you get involved in such a fight. It might be to your prejudice in the final place." Notwithstanding that weighty argument, the majority of the polytheists were determined to embark on that risky undertaking.

Ma'bad bin Abu Ma'bad meanwhile arrived on the scene and tried to exaggerate the danger awaiting them in order to thwart their plan, he said: "Muhammad (Peace be upon him) has marched to meet you with a large host of fighters, I have never seen something similar to it before. He has mustered all the troops whohave tarried and did not share in Uhud. They surely regret what they have missed and want to compensate for it now. Their hearts are filled with hate and resentment." Abu Sufyan said: "Woe to you! What do you suggest?" He said: "By Allâh, I see that you would not leave till he comes and you see the heads of their horses; or till the vanguard of his army turns up to you from behind that hill."

Abu Sufyan said: "By Allâh, we have reached a common consent to crush down the Muslims and their power." The man, once more with an implied warning, advised him to stop it.

In the light of this news, the resolution and determination of the Makkan army failed and panic and terror took firm hold of them. They consequently deemed it safest to complete there withdrawal back to Makkah. They, however, as an alternative, started a hostile nerve propaganda aiming at dissuading the Muslims army from pursuing them. A caravan belonging to 'Abd Qais happened to pass by towards Madinah. Abu Sufyan, in the context of his propaganda, asked them to communicate a message to Muhammad (Peace be upon him) to the effect that the Makkans had rallied their ranks to annihilate the Messenger and his Companions, in return Abu Sufyan promised to give the people of the caravan loads of raisins at the forum of 'Ukaz the following year.

The people of the caravan conveyed the message to the Messenger of Allâh (Peace be upon him) at Hamrâ' Al-Asad, but to no effect, on the contrary, Abu Sufyan's words augmented them in Faith. Allâh says:

- "… And they said: 'Allâh (Alone) is Sufficient for us, and He is the Best Disposer of affairs (for us). So they turned with Grace and Bounty from Allâh. No harm touched them; and they followed the good Pleasure of Allâh. And Allâh is the Owner of Great Bounty." [3:173,174]

After the arrival of the caravan on Sunday, the Messenger of Allâh (Peace be upon him) stayed at Hamrâ' Al-Asad for three days — Monday, Tuesday and Wednesday — 9-11 Shawwal, 3 A.H. and then returned to Madinah. Before his return, he took Abu 'Azza Al-Jumahi as a prisoner of war. Incidentally, this man had also been captured at Badr but on account of his poverty, and the large family he supported, the Prophet (Peace be upon him) had been gracious enough to release him on condition that he would not involve himself in war against the Muslims again. Abu 'Azza did not keep his promise and took part in Uhud hostilities on the side of the polytheists. Here again he implored Muhammad (Peace be upon him) for pardon but the latter told him that a believer wouldn't be taken twice in the same snare. He then deservedly merited the sentence of death which was executed by Az-Zubair or, in another version, by 'Asim bin Thabit.

A Makkan spy, called Mu'awiyah bin Al-Mugheerah bin Abi Al-'As, was sentenced to death too. This spy was the grandfather of 'Abdul Malik bin Marwan on his mother side. When the idolaters went back after Uhud, Mu'awiyah came to his paternal cousin 'Uthman bin 'Affan (May Allah be pleased with him) 'Uthman gave him shelter — after securing the Prophet 's permission — on condition that if he was caught there after three days, he would be killed. But he did not comply with it, so when the Muslim army left Madinah, he stayed there for more than three days during which he was spying for Quraish. So when the army returned, Mu'awiyah fled out of Madinah. The Messenger of Allâh (Peace be upon him), on this account, ordered Zaid bin Harithah and 'Ammar bin Yasir to pursue him and kill him. So he was killed.

Undoubtedly, the invasion of Hamrâ' Al-Asad is not a separate invasion, but rather a part, or more specifically, a sequel to Uhud.

That was Uhud Invasion with all its stages and details. It has for long been discussed by scholars and men of research. Was it a defeat or not? Doubtlessly, the military superiority in the second phase of the battle was in favour of the polytheists who could successfully direct the steering mechanism of hostilities and inflict heavy losses in lives on the Muslims. Admittedly, a part of the believers were clearly defeated, but this could never be considered a Makkan victory.

The Makkan army failed to occupy the camp of the Muslims. The greater bulk of the Madinese army, chaos and confusion notwithstanding, did not take to escape, on the contrary they showed matchless and heroic resistance and managed to gather themselves again around their headquarters fighting bravely and courageously. They, moreover, did not allow the Makkans to run after them in pursuit. Neither Muslim captives were taken nor spoils were gained by the Makkans. The enemies of Islam were also too cowardly to conduct the third phase of war, and impress their superiority on the battlefield, on the contrary, they were in hot haste to evacuate the field even before the Muslims did. Madinah itself, the capital of the Muslims, was only a stone's throw from the lines of the enemy, and vulnerably exposed, yet the polytheists were not bold enough to storm it to plunder its wealth or capture the Muslim women therein.

These suggestive details in fact support our argument that the event of Uhud was just a precious occasion on which the Makkans managed only to inflict heavy losses on the Muslims but failed to achieve their ultimate goals of annihilating the Muslim army in the process of their encompassment operation. After all, it is not unusual for conquerors to sustain such casualties and losses, but these could under no circumstances be regarded as victory for the hostile party.

The incident of Hamrâ' Al-Asad is interesting in this regard. It is a curious sight indeed of a victorious army in retreat for fear of disgrace and defeat, and the crestfallen and crippled group of Muslims in pursuit.

Uhud Battle in the final judgement was just one phase of military activities in the whole process of war between two hostile parties each of whom earned their legitimate portion of both success and failure and then desisted further engagement but without cowardly escape or resigned surrender. In this sense, this battle could be rightly regarded as an inseparable war.

In this context, Allâh says:

- "And don't be weak in the pursuit of the enemy; if you are suffering (hardships) then surely, they (too) are suffering (hardships) as you are suffering, but you have a hope from Allâh (for the reward, i.e. Paradise) that for which they hope not." [4:104]

The verse explicitly identifies both attitudes as regards losses and hardships as identical. Both parties concluded the war operations and went back neither victorious nor vanquished.

THE OBSERVATIONS OF THE NOBLE QUR'AN ON THE BATTLE OF UHUD:

Some Qur'ânic verses were revealed to shed light on the most decisive phases of the battle successively, adduce quite clearly the cause that led to that heavy loss, and illustrate the vulnerable areas that were still persisting in the souls of some believers as regards their duties in forging a decisive attitude with respect to the noble objectives for which the Muslim Community, was created and was supposed to accomplish.

The Noble Qur'ân also spoke about the attitude of the pretenders to Faith and made clear the hostility and hatred that they harboured against Allâh and His Messenger. The Words of Allâh managed as well to erase all traces of ambiguities and insinuations, raised by the hypocrites and their allies, the Jews — the authors of conspiracy and intrigue hatching — and which were still in active operation in the hearts of some weak-of-heart Muslims.

The laudable judgement and long-sought objectives that were attributable to the battle of Uhud, were also another topic for the Noble Qur'ân to dwell on at length. Sixty verses relevant to the battle were revealed giving full account of the first phase of the battle:

- "And (remember) when you [Muhammad Peace be upon him)] left your household in the morning to post the believers at their stations for the battle (of Uhud)." [3:121]

And to end in a comprehensive commentary on its results and moralities:

- "Allâh will not leave the believers in the state in which you are now, until He distinguishes the wicked from the good. Nor will Allâh disclose to you the of the *Ghaib* (unseen), but Allâh chooses of His Messengers whom He pleases. So believe in Allâh and His Messengers. And if you believe and fear Allâh, then for you there is a great reward." [3:179]

LESSON AND MORALITIES:

Ibn Al-Qaiyim has made a pointed reference to the battle of Uhud and given full elucidation of the Divine benefits and moralities that resulted from it. Some Muslim scholars, on the authority of Ibn Hajar, said: The reverse in Uhud resulted from the neglect on the part of the archers of the explicit command of the Prophet (Peace be upon him), and leaving the spot which they were ordered to safeguard to the end. In other words, the success of the Muslims depends upon their obedience to the Prophet (Peace be upon him). As long as they carry out his behests, Allâh will help them in facing all kinds of odds. But when they will set aside his commands in their pursuit of worldly riches, they are bound to come to grief. Another relevant issue of great significance says that it is customary for Prophets to be tried with different adversities; nevertheless, the final outcome is positively in their favour. Should the Muslims be victorious all the time, great many pretenders to Faith will enter the fold of Islam, and consequently the clear line of demarcation between true believers and hypocrites will become blurred. Contrarily, if the Muslims were to be defeated all the time, the final objective of the ministry of Prophets will not be effected. It is wise then to combine both success and failure so that sifting between true Muslims and hypocrites could be realized.

In the aftermath of the battle of Uhud, the hypocrites disclosed their real intentions in words and in deeds, consequently, the Muslims got to realize the existence of those wicked elements working secretly in their own homeland; and of course there would be appropriate measures to be taken in due course of time.

A third point in this context refers to purposeful deferment of victory in some areas in order to check the pride of the soul and teach the believers how to observe full patience in times of adversity. Trials and tests are provided by Allâh in order that the true believers could deservedly occupy their abode in the blessed Hereafter. Martyrdom, the highest ranks that the true friends of Allâh could occupy, is provided by Allâh to function as a passport, granted by the Lord, leading to Paradise. In brief, fight in the cause of Allâh is a golden opportunity for the true believers to have their sins effaced, and a Divinely-devised event for the disbelievers and enemies of Allâh to face destruction and annihilation in recompense for their disbelief, tyranny and transgression.

AL-AHZAB (the Confederates) INVASION

Once again, peace and security enveloped the Arabian Peninsula and this turbulent area began to experience a period of lull after a whole year warJews, however, whose treachery, intrigues and . The disloyalty made them taste all types of humiliation and disgrace, were not admonished. After they had been exiled to Khaibar, they remained waiting anxiously for the results of the skirmishes going on between the Muslims and the idolatersthe hopes, the events of the war were in favour of the Muslims, . Contrary to therefore they started a new stage of conspiracy and prepared themselves to deal a deadly blow against the Muslims, but were too cowardly to manoeuvre directly against them, so they laid a dreadful plan in order to achieve their objectivesof the Jews with some celebrities of Bani Nadir went to Makkah to . Twenty chiefs negotiate an unholy alliance with Quraishgoad the people there to attack the Messenger of . They began to Allupon him) promising them full support and backing. People of Quraish, who had been âh (Peace be languid and proved too weak to challenge the Muslims at Badr, seized this opportunity to redeem their stained honour and blemished reputationdelegation set out for Ghatfan, called them to do the . The same same, and they responded positively. The Jewish delegation then started a fresh effort and toured some parts of Arabia and managed to incite the confederates of disbelief against the Prophet (Peace be upon him), his Message and the believers in AllKinanah and other allies from Tihama, in the south; rallied, âh. Quraish, ranked and recruited four thousand men under the leadership of Abu Sufyan. From the east there came tribes of Banu Saleem, Ghatfan, Bani Murrah, etc. They all headed for Madinah and gathered in its vicinity at a time already agreed upongreat army of ten thousand fighters. They in fact outnumbered all the Muslims in . It was a Madinah, women, lads and elders includedtell the truth, if they had launched a surprise attack against . To Madinah, they could have exterminated all the Muslimsthe leadership inside the city was on the . However, alert and the intelligence personnel managed to reconnoitre the area of the enemies, and reported their movement to the people in charge in Madinah. The Messenger of Allâh (Peace be upon him) summoned a high advisory board and conducted a careful discussion of a plan to defend Madinah. After a lengthy talk between military leaders and people possessed of sound advice, it was agreed, on the proposal of an honourable Companion, Salman Al-Farisi, to dig trenches as defensive lines. The Muslims, with the Prophet (encouraging, helping and reminding them of the reward in the Hereafter, Peace be upon him) at their head, most actively and diligently started to build a trench around Madinah. Severe hunger, bordering on starvation, could not dissuade or discourage them from achieving their desperately sought objective. Salman said: O Messenger of Allâh! When siege was to laid to us in Persia, we used to dig trenches to defend ourselves. It was really an unprecedented wise plan. The Messenger of Allâh (Peace be upon him) hurriedly gave orders to implement the planeach group of ten to dig. Sahl bin Sa'd said: We were in . Forty yards was allocated to the company of the Messenger of Allâh (Peace be upon him), the men used to dig and we evacuate the earth on our backs.

Some preternatural Prophetic signs appeared in the process of trenching. Jabir bin 'Abdullah, seeing the Prophet (Peace be upon him) starving, slaughtered a sheep, cooked some barley and requested the Prophet (Peace be upon him) and some Companions to accept his invitation, but the Prophet (Peace be upon him) gathered all the thousand people engaged in digging the trench and they started to eat until they were all completely full and yet the shoulder of mutton and dough that was being baked remained as they were undiminished. A certain woman brought a handful of dates and passed by the Prophet (Peace be upon him), who took the dates, threw them over his cloak and invited his followers to eat. The dates began to increase in number until they dropped over the trim of his robe. Another illustrious preternatural example went to the effect that an obstinate rock stood out as an immune obstacle in the ditch. The Prophet (Peace be upon him) took the spade and struck, and the rock immediately turned into a loose sand dune. In another version, Al-Bara' said: On *Al-Khandaq* (the trench) Day there stood out a rock too immune for our spades to break up. We therefore went to see the Messenger of Allâh (Peace be upon him) for advice. He took the spade, and struck the rock uttering "in the Name of Allâh, Allâh is Great, the keys of Ash-Shâm (Geographical Syria) are mine, I swear by Allâh, I can see its palaces at the moment;" on the second strike he said: "Allâh is Great, Persia is mine, I swear by Allâh, I can now see the white palace of Madain;" and for the third time he struck the rock, which turned into very small pieces, he said: "Allâh is Great, I have been given the keys of Yemen, I swear by Allâh, I can see the gates of San'a while I am in my place." The same version was narrated by Ishaq. The northern part of Madinah was the most vulnerable, all the other sides being surrounded by mountains and palm tree orchards, the Prophet (Peace be upon him) as a skillful military expert, understood that the

Confederates would march in that direction, so the trench was ordered to be on that side. The Muslims went on digging the trench for several days; they used to work on it during the day, and go back home in the evening until it had assumed its full dimensions militarily before the huge army of the idolaters; which numbered, as many as ten thousand fighters, arrived and settled in the vicinity of Madinah in places called Al-Asyal and Uhud.

- "And when the believers saw 'Al-Ahzab' (the confederates), they said: 'This is what Allâh and His Messenger [Muhammad (Peace be upon him)] had promised us, and Allâh and His Messenger [Muhammad (Peace be upon him)] had spoken the truth, and it only added to their Faith and to their submissiveness (to Allâh)." [33:22]

Three thousand Muslims, with Muhammad (Peace be upon him) at their head, came out to encounter the idolaters, with Allâh's Promise of victory deeply established in their minds. They entrenched themselves in Sila' Mountain with the trench standing as a barrier between them and the disbelievers.

On attempting to attack the Muslims and break into Madinah, the idolaters were surprised to see a wide trench, a new stratagem unknown in Arabia before, standing as an obstinate obstruction. Consequently they decided to lay siege to Madinah and began to manoeuvre around the trench trying hard to find a vulnerable spot through which they could infiltrate into Madinah. To deter their enemies from approaching or bridging any gap in their defences, the Muslims hurled arrows, and engaged in skirmishes with them. The veteran fighters of Quraish were averse to this situation waiting in vain in anticipation of what the siege might reveal. Therefore they decided that a group of fighters led by 'Amr bin 'Abd-e-Wudd, 'Ikrima bin Abi Jahl and Dirar bin Al-Khattab, should work its way through the trench. They, in fact, managed to do that and their horsemen captured a marshy area between the trench and Sila' Mountain. 'Amr challenged the Muslims to a duel, and 'Ali bin Abi Talib was deputed. After a short but fierce engagement, 'Ali killed 'Amr and obliged the others to evacuate in a state of panic and confusion. However, some days later, the polytheists conducted fresh desperate attempts but all of them failed due to Muslims' steadfastness and heroic confrontation.

In the context of the events of the Trench Battle, the Messenger of Allâh (Peace be upon him) failed to observe some prayers in their right time. Jabir (May Allah be pleased with him) narrated: On the Day of Trench 'Umar bin Al-Khattab (May Allah be pleased with him) came, cursing the disbelievers of Quraish and said: "O Allâh's Messenger! I have not offered the afternoon prayer and the sun has set." The Prophet (Peace be upon him) replied: "By Allâh! I, , have not offered the prayer yet." The Prophet (Peace be upon him) then went to Buthan, performed ablution and observed the afternoon prayer after the sun had set and then offered the sunset prayer after it." He was so indignant for this failure that he invoked Allâh's wrath on his enemies and besought Allâh to fill their houses and graves with fire because they distracted him from observing the afternoon prayer. It was narrated by Ahmed and Shafa'i that the events of that battle detained him from the noon, afternoon, evening and night prayers, but he observed them combined. The different narrations point to the fact that the situation lasted for a few days.

It is clear that, and because of the trench standing between the two parties, no direct engagement took place, but rather there were military activities confined to arrow hurling, consequently the fight claimed the lives of a small number of fighters, six Muslims and ten polytheists, one or two killed by sword.

During the process of fighting, Sa'd bin Mu'adh was shot by an arrow that pierced his artery. Perceiving his end approaching, he invoked Allâh saying: "Oh, Allâh, you know nothing is closer to my heart than striving in Your way against those people (disbelievers) who belied Your Messenger and banished him from his town. Oh, Allâh, I deeply believe that You have decreed that we should fight them, so if there is still more fighting to go with them, let me stay alive in order to strive more against them. If it has settled down, I beseech you to ignite it again so that I breathe my last in its context."He concluded his supplication beseeching Allâh not to let him die until he had had full revenge on Banu Quraiza. In the midst of these difficult circumstances, plottery and intrigues were in fervent action against the Muslims. The chief criminal of Bani Nadir, Huyai, headed for the habitations of Banu Quraiza to incite their chief Ka'b bin Asad Al-Qurazi, who had drawn a pact with the Messenger of Allâh (Peace be upon him) to run to his aid in times of war. Ka'b, in the beginning resisted all Huyai's temptation, but Huyai was clever enough to manipulate him, speaking of Quraish and their notables in Al-Asyal, as well as Ghatfan and their chieftains entrenched in Uhud, all in one mind, determined to exterminate Muhammad (Peace be upon him) and his followers. He, moreover, promised to stay in Ka'b's fort exposing himself to any potential danger in case Quraish and Ghatfan recanted. The wicked man went on in this manner until he later managed to win Ka'b to his side and persuade him to break his covenant with the Muslims. Banu Quraiza then started to launch war operations against the Muslims especially the secluded garrisons that housed the women and children of the Muslims. On the authority of Ibn Ishaq, Safiyah (May Allah be pleased with her) daughter of 'Abdul Muttalib happened to be in a garrison with Hassan bin Thabit as well as some women and children. Safiyah said: "A Jew was spotted lurking around our site, which was vulnerable to any enemy attacks because there were no men to defend it. I informed Hassan that I was suspicious of that man's presence near us. He might take us by surprise now that the Messenger of Allâh (Peace be upon him) and the Muslims are too busy to come to our aid, why don't you get down and kill him? Hassan answered that he would not do it, so I took a bar of wood, went down and struck the Jew to death. I returned and asked Hassan to loot him but again Hassan refused to do that. This event had a far reaching effect and discouraged the Jews from conducting further attacks thinking that those sites were fortified and protected by Muslim fighters. They, however, went on providing the idolaters with supplies in token of their support against the Muslims.

On hearing this bad news, the Messenger (Peace be upon him) despatched four Muslim prominent leaders Sa'd bin Mu'adh, Sa'd bin 'Ubada, 'Abdullah bin Rawaha and Khawat bin Jubair for investigation but warning against any sort of spreading panic amongst the Muslims and advising that they should declare in public that the rumours are groundless if they happen to be so. Unfortunately the four men discovered that the news was true and that the Jews announced openly that no pact of alliance existed any longer with Muhammad (Peace be upon him). The Messenger of Allâh (Peace be upon him) was briefed on this situation, and the Muslims understood their critical position with the horrible danger implied therein. Their back was vulnerable to the attacks of Banu Quraiza, and a huge army with no way to connive at in front, while their women and children unprotected standing in between. In this regard, Allâh says:

- "And when the eyes grew wild and the hearts reached to the throats, and you were harbouring doubts about Allâh. There, the believers were tried and shaken with a mighty shaking." [33:10, 11]

Now that the Muslims were shut in within the Trench on the defensive, the hypocrites taunted them with having indulged in delusive hopes of defeating Kisra, emperor of Persia, and Caesar, emperor of the Romans. They began to sow the seeds of defeatism, and pretended to withdraw for the defence of their homes, though these were in no way exposed to danger. Here, Allâh says:

- "And when the hypocrites and those in whose hearts is a disease (of doubts) said, 'Allâh and His Messenger (Peace be upon him) promised us nothing but delusions!' And when a party of them said: 'O people of Yathrib (Al-Madinah), there is no stand (possible) for you (against the enemy attack!) therefore go back!' And a band of them asked for permission of the Prophet (Peace be upon him) saying: 'Truly, our homes lie open (to the enemy).' And they lay not open. They but wished to flee." [33:12, 13]

The Messenger of Allâh, (Peace be upon him) wrapped himself in his robe and began to meditate on the perfidy of Banu Quraiza. The spirit of hopefulness prevailed over him and he rose to his feet saying:

- "Allâh is Great. Hearken you Muslims, to Allâh's good tidings of victory and support."

He then started to lay decisive plans aiming at protecting the women and children, and sent some fighters back to Madinah to guard them against any surprise assault by the enemy. The second step was to take action that could lead to undermining the ranks of the disbelieving confederates. There, he had in mind to conclude a sort of reconciliation with the chiefs of Ghatfan on the basis of donating them a third of Madinah's fruit crops. He sought the advice of his chief Companions, namely, Sa'd bin Mu'adh and Sa'd bin 'Ubadah, whose reply went as follows:

"O Messenger of Allâh! If it is Allâh's injunction, then we have to obey, but if it is a new course you want to follow just to provide security for us then we don't need it. We experienced those people in polytheism and idolatry and we can safely say that they don't need the fruit of our orchards, they rather need to exterminate us completely. Now that Allâh has honoured us with Islam, I believe the best recourse in this situation is to put them to the sword." Thereupon the Prophet (Peace be upon him) corrected their Belief saying: "My new policy is being forged to provide your security after all the Arabs have united to annihilate you (Muslims)."

Allâh, the Glorious, the Exalted, praise is to him, created something that led to the dissension of the enemies of Islam and later on to their full defeat. A man from the tribe of Ghatfan called Na'im bin Mas'ud asked to be admitted in the audience of the Prophet (Peace be upon him). He declared that he had embraced Islam secretly and asked the Prophet (Peace be upon him) to order him do anything that might benefit the Muslims. The Prophet (Peace be upon him) asked him to do anything that could help the Muslims in the present distress and use any strategem of avail. The man, in a shuttle movement, between the Jews, Quraish and Ghatfan managed to incite each party to let down the other. He went to see the chiefs of Banu Quraiza and whispered in their ears not to trust Quraish nor fight with them unless the latter pledged some hostages. He tried to lend support to his counsel by claimingthat Quraish would forsake them if they perceived that victory over Muhammad (Peace be upon him) was far fetched, and the Muslims then would have terrible revenge on them. Na'im, then headed for the camp of Quraish and managed to practise a similar strategem in its final result but different in content. He claimed that he felt that the Jews regretted breaching their covenant with Muhammad (Peace be upon him) and his followers. He told them that the Jews maintained regular correspondence with the Muslims to the effect that Quraishite hostages be sent to the camp of the Muslims with full Jewish allegiance paid to them as already agreed upon. Na'im then exhorted Quraish not to send hostages to the Jews. On a third errand, he did the same with the people of Ghatfan.

On Saturday night, Shawwal 5 A.H., both Quraish and Ghatfan despatched envoys to the Jews exhorting them to go into war against Muhammad (Peace be upon him). The Jews sent back messages that they would not fight on Saturday. They added that they needed hostages from them to guarantee their consistency. On receiving the replies, Quraish and Ghatfan came to believe Na'im's words fully. Therefore, they sent a message to the Jews again inviting them to war and asking them to preclude that condition of hostages. Na'im's scheme proved successful, and a state of distrust and suspicion among the disbelieving allies prevailed and reduced their morale to deplorable degree.

Meanwhile, the Muslims were preoccupied supplicating their Lord to protect their homes and provide security for their families. The Messenger of Allâh (Peace be upon him) on his part invoked Allâh's wrath on the Confederates supplicating:

- "Oh, Allâh! You are quick in account, You are the sender of the Book, we beseech You to defeat the confederates."

Allâh the Glorious, the Exalted, responded to the call of the Muslims on the spot. Coupled with the dissension and variance that found their way into the hearts of the disbelievers, forces of nature — wind, rain and cold wearied them, tents were blown down, cooking vessels and other equipage overthrown.

That very cold night the Messenger of Allâh (Peace be upon him) despatched Hudhaifa bin Al-Yaman to hunt around for news about the enemy. He found out that they were preparing to leave frustrated for their inability to achieve their target. Allâh did really fulfill His Promise, spared the Muslims fighting a formidable army, supported His slave [Muhammad (Peace be upon him)] and inflicted a heavy blow on the Confederates.

The battle of the Trench took place in the fifth year Hijri. The siege of Madinah started in Shawwal and ended in Dhul Qa'dah, i.e. it lasted for over a month. It was in fact a battle of nerves rather than of losses. No bitter fighting was recorded; nevertheless, it was one of the most decisive battles in the early history of Islam and proved beyond a shadow of doubt that no forces, however huge, could ever exterminate the nascent Islamic power growing steadily in Madinah. When Allâh obliged the Confederates to evacuate, His Messenger was in a position to confidently declare that thenceforth he would take the initiative in war and would not wait for the land of Islam to be invaded.

INVADING BANU QURAIZA:

Archangel Gabriel (Peace be upon him) on the very day the Messenger of Allâh (Peace be upon him) came back to Madinah after the previous battle, and while he was washing in Umm Salama's house, visited him asking that he should unsheathe his sword and head for the habitation of the seditious Banu Quraiza and fight them. Gabriel noted that he with a procession of angels would go ahead to shake their forts and cast fear in their hearts.

The Messenger of Allâh (Peace be upon him), immediately summoned the prayer caller and ordered him to announce fresh hostilities against Banu Quraiza, instituted Ibn Umm Maktum as a ruler of Madinah, and entrusted the banner of war to 'Ali bin Abi Talib who marched towards the appointed target and came close enough to hear the Jews abusing the Messenger of Allâh (Peace be upon him), who on his part set out at the head of three thousand infantry men and thirty horsemen of *Ansar* (Helpers) and *Muhajireen* (Emigrants). On way to encounter the enemy, the afternoon prayer was due. Some Muslims refused to observe it until they had defeated the enemy, while others offered it in its proper time, as usual. The Prophet (Peace be upon him) objected to neither. When they reached the habitations of Banu Quraiza, they laid tight siege to their forts. Seeing this terrible situation they were in, the chief of the Jews Ka'b bin Asad offered them three alternatives: to embrace Islam, and consequently their life, wealth, women and children would be in full security, and reminded them that such behaviour would not be incongruous with what they had read in their books about the veracity of Muhammad's Prophethood; to kill their children and women and then challenge the Prophet (Peace be upon him) and his followers to the sword to either exterminate the Muslims or be exterminated, or as a third possibility to take Muhammad (Peace be upon him) and his people by surprise on Saturday — a day mutually understood to witness no fighting.

None of those alternatives appealed them, so their chief, angrily and indignantly, turned to them saying: "You have never been decisive in decision-making since you were born" The gloomy future already visible, they made contacts with some Muslims, who had maintained good relation with them, in order to learn about their fate in the light of the current circumstances. They requested that Abu Lubaba be despatched to them for advice. On his arrival, the men began to implore, women and children to cry desperately. In answer to their demand for advice he pointed to his throat saying it was homicide awaiting them. He then immediately realized that he had betrayed the Prophet's trust, so he headed directly for the mosque in Madinah and tied himself to a wooden tall pole swearing that no one would untie him save the Messenger of Allâh (Peace be upon him), and added that he would never enter the habitation of Banu Quraiza in recompense for the deadly mistake he made. When the Messenger (Peace be upon him) was informed of this incident, he said, " I would have begged Allâh to forgive him if he had asked me, but since he had tied himself out of his own free will, then it was Allâh Who would turn to him in forgiveness."

The Jews of Banu Quraiza could have endured the siege much longer because food and water were plentifully available and their strongholds were greatly fortified, whereas the Muslims were in the wild bare land suffering a lot from cold and hunger, let alone too much fatigue consequent on endless warfare operations that had started even before the battle of Confederates. Nevertheless, this was a battle of nerves, for Allâh had cast fear in the the Jews' hearts, and their morale had almost collapsed especially when two Muslim heroes, 'Ali bin Abi Talib and Az-Zubair bin 'Awwam (May Allah be pleased with him) proceeded with 'Ali swearing that he would never stop until he had either stormed their garrisons or been martyred like Hamza (a former Muslim martyr).

In the light of this reluctance, they had nothing except to comply with the Messenger's judgement. The Messenger of Allâh (Peace be upon him) ordered that the men should handcuffed, and this was done under the supervision of Muhammad bin Salamah Al-Ansari while the women and children were isolated in confinement. Thereupon Al-Aws tribe interceded begging the Prophet (Peace be upon him) to be lenient towards them. He suggested that Sa'd bin Mu'adh, a former ally, be deputed to give verdict about them, and they agreed.

Sa'd meanwhile stayed behind in Madinah due to a serious wound he sustained in the Confederates Battle. He was summoned and brought on a donkey. On his way to the Prophet (Peace be upon him) , the Jews used to exhort him to be lenient in his judgement on account of former friendship. Sa'd remained silent but when they persisted he uttered: "It is time for Sa'd not to be afraid of the blame of the blamers." On hearing this decisive attitude, some of them returned to Madinah waiting fa desperate doom.

On arrival, he alighted with the help of some men. He was informed that the Jews had agreed to accept his verdict about them. He immediately wondered if his judgement would pass on all the people present, the Prophet (Peace be upon him) included, turning his face away in honour of him. The reply was positive.

He decided that all the able-bodied male persons belonging to the tribe should be killed, women and children taken prisoners and their wealth divided among the Muslim fighters. The Prophet (Peace be upon him) accepted his judgement saying that Sa'd had adjudged by the Command of Allâh. In fact, the Jews deserved that severe punitive action for the ugly treachery they had harboured against Islam, and the large arsenal they have amassed and which consisted of one thousand and five hundred swords, two thousand spears, three hundred armours and five hundred shields, all of which went into the hands of the Muslims. Trenches were dug in the bazaar of Madinah and a number of Jews between six and seven hundred were beheaded therein. Hot beds of intrigue and treachery were thus exterminated once and for all.

Huyai, a chief criminal of war, a devil of Bani Nadir and Safiyah's father, had joined the ranks of Banu Quraiza when Quraish and Ghatfan defected, was admitted into the audience of the Prophet (Peace be upon him) with his hands tied to his neck with a rope. In audacious defiance, he declared obstinate enmity to the Prophet (Peace be upon him) but admitted that Allâh's Will was to be fulfilled and added that he was resigned to his fate. He was ordered to sit down, and was beheaded on the spot.

Only one woman of the Jews was killed because she had killed a Muslim warrior by flinging a grinding stone upon him. A few elements of the enemy embraced Islam and their lives, wealth and children were spared. As for the spoils of the war, the Prophet (Peace be upon him) divided them, after putting a fifth aside, in accordance with Allâh's injunctions. Three shares went to the horseman and one to the infantry fighter. Women captives were sent to Najd to be bartered with horses and weaponry. For himself, the Prophet (Peace be upon him) selected Rehana bint 'Amr bin Khanaqah, manumitted and married her in the year 6 Hijri. She died shortly after the farewell pilgrimage and was buried in Al-Baqi'..

After the war with Banu Quraiza had been settled and they had been defeated, Sa'd bin Mu'adh's wish was gratified and he gave his last breath. In response to his supplication 'Aishah (May Allah be pleased with her) narrated, Sa'd's wounds began to bleed from the front part of his neck while he was in his tent which the Prophet (Peace be upon him) had pitched for him in the mosque so that he would be in close proximity in order to inquire about and watch his well-being closely. The people were not scared except when the blood flowed towards them, and in the Mosque along with Sa'd's tent, there was the tent of Banu Ghifar. They said: O people of the tent, what is it that is coming to us from you? Lo! it was Sa'd's wound that was bleeding and he died thereon.

Jabir narrated that the Messenger of Allâh (Peace be upon him) had said: "The Throne of the Compassionate shook for the death of Sa'd bin Mu'adh. " When his bier was carried, At-Tirmidhi said: The hypocrites alleged it was too light. The Messenger of Allâh (Peace be upon him) retorted:

- "The angels are carrying him."

In the process of the sieze laid to Banu Quraiza, one man of the Muslims, Khallad bin Suwaid was killed when a women of the Jews dropped the grinding stone on him, and another, Abu Sinan bin Mihsan, the brother of 'Ukasha, died.

Abu Lubaba stayed tied for six nights. His wife used to untie him at prayer times and then he tied himself again to the pole. One early morning, Allâh the All-Forgiving revealed a verse to the Messenger of Allâh (Peace be upon him) to the effect that Allâh had turned to Abu Lubaba with forgiveness. The Muslims rushed to release him but he insisted that the Messenger of Allâh (Peace be upon him) himself do it. And this was done shortly before the morning prayer.

This *Ghazwah* took place in the month of Dhul Qa'dah in the year five Hijri, and the siege of Banu Quraiza's forts lasted for 25 days. The Chapter of Confederates was revealed containing Allâh's Words concerning the basic issues relating to the believers and hypocrites during the battle of the Confederates, and the consequences of the treachery and breaching of covenants by the Jews.

MILITARY ACTIVITIES CONTINUED:

Salam bin Abi Al-Huqaiq (Abu Rafi') was a terrible Jew criminal, who had mustered the troops of the Confederates and provided them with a lot of wealth and supplies, on the one hand, and used to malign the Prophet (Peace be upon him), on the other. When the Muslims had settled their affair with Banu Quraiza; Al-Khazraj tribe, a rival of Al-Aws, asked for the Prophet's permission to kill that criminal in order to merit a virtue equal to that of Al-Aws who had killed another criminal of the Jews, Ka'b bin Al-Ashraf. The Prophet (Peace be upon him) gave them his permission provided that no women or children be killed.

A group of five people with 'Abdullah bin 'Ateeq at their head, headed for Khaibar where 'Abu Rafi''s fort was situated. When they approached the place, 'Abdullah advised his men to stay a little behind, while he went ahead disguised himself in his cloak as if he had been relieving himself. When the people of the fort went in, the gate-keeper called him to enter thinking he was one of them. 'Abdullah went in and lurked inside. He then began to unbolt the doors leading to Salam's room. There it was absolutely dark but he managed to put him to the sword, and then leave in safety. On his way back, his leg broke so he wrapped it up in a band, and hid in a secret place until morning when someone stood on the wall and announced the death of Salam bin Abi Al-Huqaiq officially. On hearing the glad news he left and went to see the Prophet (Peace be upon him), who listened to the whole story, and then asked 'Abdullah to stretch his leg, which he wiped and the fracture healed on the spot.

In another version, all the group of five participated in killing that enemy of Islam. This incident took place in Dhul Qa'dah or Dhul Hijjah in the year five Hijri.

Shortly after the conclusion of the battle with the Confederates and Quraiza, the Prophet (Peace be upon him) began to despatch punitive expeditions to force the aggressive tribes and rebellious Arabians to come to peaceful terms with the rising state of Islam.

A platoon of thirty believers under the leadership of Muhammad bin Maslamah was despatched on a military mission in Muharram, the sixth year Hijri, following the two previous battles. It headed for the habitation of Bani Bakr sept. The Muslims attacked that sept and dispersed them in all directions. Plenty of spoils fell to the lot of the Muslims who returned home with a terrible disbeliever, Thumamah bin Uthal Al-Hanafi, chief of Bani Hanifa, who had gone out by order of Musailama, the Liar, to assassinate the Prophet (Peace be upon him). The Prophet's Companions tied him to a pole of the Prophetic Mosque. To a question posed by the Prophet (Peace be upon him), Thumamah used to say: "If you were to kill someone, then you would have to choose one of noble descent, if you were to be gracious, then let it be to a grateful man and if you were to ask for money, you would have to ask for it from a generous man." He repeated that three times on three different occasions. On the third time, the Prophet (Peace be upon him) ordered that he should be released. He soon went nearby, washed and then came back to profess the new faith addressing the Prophet (Peace be upon him) : "No face had been more awful to me than yours but now it is the closest to my heart, no religion had ever been more repugnant to me than yours, now it is the dearest in my heart. Now I want to perform the *'Umrah* (lesser pilgrimage)." The Prophet (Peace be upon him) gave him good tidings and asked him to do that. On his arrival in Makkah, the Quraishites accused him of apostasy. He denied it and affirmed that he had embraced Islam, then swore that they would never get a grain from Yamama, a suburban area around Makkah, unless the Prophet (Peace be upon him) would allow it. In fact, he did it and refused to send food supplies to Makkah until the Prophet (Peace be upon him) interceded at the Makkans' earnest plea.

BANI LIHYAN INVASION:

Bani Lihyan had acted treacherously towards ten of the Prophet's Companions and had them hanged. Their habitation being situated deep in the heart of Hijaz on the borders of Makkah, and due to deep-seated blood-revenge between the Muslims on the one hand, and Quraish and the Arabians on the other, the Prophet (Peace be upon him) deemed it unwise to penetrate deep and come close to the greatest enemy, Quraish. However, when the power of the allied Confederates collapsed and they began to slacken and resign to the current unfavourable balance of power, the Messenger of Allâh (Peace be upon him) seized this rare opportunity and decided that it was time to take revenge on Bani Lihyan. He set out in Rabi' Al-Awwal or Jumada Al-Ula in the year six Hijri at the head of two hundred Muslim fighters and made a feint of heading for Syria, then soon changed route towards Batn Gharran, the scene of his Companions' tragedy, and invoked Allâh's mercy on them. News of his march reached Bani Lihyan, who immediately fled to the mountain tops nearby and thus remained out of his reach. On his way back, the Prophet (Peace be upon him) despatched a group of ten horsemen to a place called Kura' Al-Ghamim, in the vicinity of the habitation of Quraish in order to indirectly confirm his growing military power. All these skirmishes took fourteen days, after which he left back for home.

EXPEDITIONS AND DELAGATIONS CONTINUED:

1. A platoon led by 'Ukasha bin Al-Mihsan was despatched to a place called Al-Ghamir inhabited by Bani Asad in the year six Hijri. The enemy immediately fled leaving behind them two hundred camels which were taken to Madinah.
1. A platoon led by Muhammad bin Maslamah set out towards the habitation of Bani Tha'labah in Dhil Qassa. But a hundred men of the enemies ambushed and killed all of them except Muhammad bin Maslamah who managed to escape but badly wounded.
2. In retaliation against Bani Tha'labah, Abu 'Ubaidah bin Al-Jarrah, at the head of forty men, was despatched to Dhil Qassa. They walked that night and took the enemy by surprise in the morning. Again, they fled to the mountains except one who was injured, and later embraced Islam. A lot of booty fell to their lot in that particular incident.
3. A platoon, under the leadership of Zaid bin Haritha, was sent to Al-Jumum, the habitation of Bani Saleem, in the same year. A woman from Bani Muzaina showed them the way to the enemy's camp. There the Muslims took some captives and gained a lot of booty. Later on, the Messenger of Allâh (Peace be upon him) granted the woman her freedom and married her to one of his followers.
4. Zaid bin Haritha, in Jumada Al-Ula 6 Hijri, at the head of a hundred and seventy horsemen, set out to a place called Al-'Ais, intercepted a caravan of Quraish led by Abul-'As, the Prophet's relative and looted their camels. Abul-'As escaped and took refuge in Zainab's (his wife and the Prophet's daughter) house. He begged her to ask the Prophet (Peace be upon him) for the restitution of his wealth. The Prophet (Peace be upon him) recommended, but without coercion, that the people do that. They immediately gave the man back all his wealth. He went back to Makkah, gave over the trusts to those entitled to them, embraced Islam and emigrated to Madinah where the Prophet (Peace be upon him) reunited him with his wife, Zainab, after three and a half years of their first marriage contract. The verse relating to prohibition of marriage between women Muslims and disbelievers had not been revealed then.
5. In Jumada Ath-Thania, the same year, Zaid at the head of fifteen men raided Bani Tha'labah and captured twenty of their camels but the people had fled.
6. In Rajab of the same year, Zaid, at the head of twelve men, set out to a place called Wadi Al-Qura in a reconnaissance mission to explore the movements of the enemy. The people there attacked the Muslims, killed nine of them, while the rest including Zaid bin Haritha managed to escape.
7. The invasion of *Al-Khabt* (diluted yoghurt) took place in the year eight Hijri i.e. before Al-Hudaibiyah Treaty. Abu 'Ubaidah bin Al-Jarrah led three hundred horsemen to observe a caravan

belonging to Quraish. Because of the inadequacy of food supplies, they began to starve so much that they had *Khabt* (diluted yoghurt), hence the appellation "*The Army of Al-Khabt*". One of the men slaughtered nine camels at three times, three each time at different stages of the mission. Abu 'Ubaidah, the leader of the campaign prohibited him from doing so. The sea was generous and presented them with an animal called *Al-'Anbar* (sperm-whale) so rich in fat that they subsisted on it for half a month. When they came back home, they narrated the story to the Prophet (Peace be upon him), who commented that it was provision granted by Allâh, and asked them to share him some of its meat.

- This campaign came chronologically prior to Al-Hudaibiyah Treaty because of and after which the Muslims stopped intercepting Quraishi caravans.

BANI AL-MUSTALIQ (Muraisi') GHAZWAH, SHA'BAN 6 HIJRI:

Though militarily it did not assume its full dimension, this Ghazwah had certain implications that brought about a state of turbulence within the Islamic State, and resulted in disgracefulness to clothe in the hypocrites. Moreover, it entailed enactment of consolidating legislations that attached an impression of nobility, dignity and purity of souls to the Islamic community.

News reached the Prophet (Peace be upon him) on Sha'ban 2nd. to the effect that the chief of Bani Al-Mustaliq, Al-Harith bin Dirar had mobilised his men, along with some Arabs, to attack Madinah. Buraidah bin Al-Haseeb Al-Aslami was immediately despatched to verify the reports. He had some words with Abi Dirar, who confirmed his intention of war. He later sent a reconnoiterer to explore the positions of the Muslims but he was captured and killed. The Prophet (Peace be upon him) summoned his men and ordered them to prepare for war. Before leaving, Zaid bin Haritha was mandated to see to the affairs of Madinah and dispose them. On hearing the advent of the Muslims, the disbelievers got frightened and the Arabs going with them defected and ran away to their lives. Abu Bakr was entrusted with the banner of the Emigrants, and that of the Helpers went to Sa'd bin 'Ubada. The two armies were stationed at a well called Muraisi. Arrow shooting went on for an hour, and then the Muslims rushed and engaged with the enemy in a battle that ended in full victory for the Muslims. Some men were killed, women and children of the disbelievers taken as captives, and a lot of booty fell to the lot of the Muslims. Only one Muslim was killed by mistake by a Helper. Amongst the captives was Juwairiyah, daughter of Al-Harith, chief of the disbelievers. The Prophet (Peace be upon him) married her and, in compensation, the Muslims had to manumit a hundred others of the enemy prisoners who embraced Islam, and were then called the Prophet's in-laws.

THE TREACHROUS ROLE OF THE HYPOCRITES PRIOR TO THE BANI AL-MUSTALIQ GHAZWAH:

'Abdullah bin Ubai, a terrible hypocrite was full of rancour against Islam and the Muslims because he believed that the Prophet (Peace be upon him) had dispossessed him of his leadership over Al-Aws and Al-Khazraj, two clans already agreed on the Prophethood of Muhammad (Peace be upon him) and his masterhood over them.

'Abdullah's rancour had appeared before he feigned Islam. Following the battle of Badr, he made pretensions of being a Muslim, but deep at heart, he remained that terrible enemy of Allâh, His Messenger; and all the believers, in general. His sole target had always been to sow the seeds of dissension in the Muslim community, and undermine the cause of the new heavenly religion it has. His treacherous behaviour could be witnessed everywhere but was strikingly evident in his wicked attempts at creating a state of confusion and diamongst the Muslims at Uhud Battle. His hypocrisy and deceit assumed serious and ugly dimensions when he used to stand up among the Muslims shortly before the Prophet's Friday speech, and mockingly say to them: "This is the Messenger of Allâh, who has honoured you with Allâh, so you have got to support, obey and listen to him," and then he would sit down.

He did the same following Uhud Battle on Friday. He was so rude and presumptuous that his words smacked unmistakingly of deeply-rooted rancour, so that some of the Muslims took him by his cloak reproachingly and silenced him. He immediately left, uttering rude and mocking words. A Helper met him at the Mosque gate and ordered him to return and beg the Messenger for Allâh's forgiveness, but he retorted that he had never wanted him to ask for that. He, moreover, conducted clandestine contacts with Bani Nadir, another tribe of Jews, encouraging them to make alliance with him and promising support for them; all of this in his ceaseless efforts in a long process of conspiracy and intrigue hatched against the Muslims. Allâh's Words as regards his treacherous acts and awe-inspiring attempts during the Trench Battle came to testify quite clearly to this mode of hypocrisy:

- "And when the hypocrites and those in whose hearts is a disease (of doubts) said: 'Allâh and His Messenger (Peace be upon him)promised us nothing but delusions!" [33:12]

The verses go on in the same context to describe the hypocrite as a coward and a defeatist. He is a liar and has no regard for pledges solemnly made. He is treacherous, disloyal and perfidious. He is niggardly and greedy. In short, he is the complete antithesis of a true believer:

- "They think that *Al-Ahzab* (the Confederates) have not yet withdrawn, and if *Al-Ahzab* (the Confederates) should come (again), they would wish they were in the deserts (wandering) among the bedouins, seeking news about you (from a far place); and if they (happen) to be among you, they would not fight but little." [33:20]

All enemies of Islam from the Jews, hypocrites and polytheists did acknowledge that Islam had the upper hand not because of material superiority, multitudes of troops or much equipment; but it was rather due to the noble values, refined ethics and high attributes that imbued the Muslim community and whoever was attached to it. The enemies of Islam were already aware of that flood of light derived wholly from the person of the Prophet (Peace be upon him) , who always stood as an excellent exemplar for men to copy and follow.

The enemies of Islam, after steering the course of futile warfare against the new religion for five years, came to realize fully that exterminating Islam is not accessible in the battlefields, so they resorted to other tactics. They, being reputed gossip-mongers, decided to launch a widespread propaganda campaign aiming at slandering the person of the Prophet (Peace be upon him) in a most sensitive area of the Arabian life, namely ethics and traditions. Following the battle of the Confederates, the Prophet (Peace be upon him) married Zainab bint Jahsh after her marriage with Zaid bin Haritha, his adopted son, had broken up. They seized this opportunity and began to circulate idle talk against the Prophet (Peace be upon him) in Arabia depending on a tradition among the desert Arabs that prohibits contracting a marriage with an adopted son's divorcee. They alleged that his marriage would be considered a heinous sin. They also based their malicious propaganda on the fact that Zainab was his fifth wife whereas the number was strictly limited to a maximum of four in the Noble Qur'ân, hence the validity of this marriage was in doubt, according to them.

These rumours and gossips had a negative impact on the morale of some weak-hearted Muslims until the decisive verses were revealed acquitting the Prophet (Peace be upon him) and invalidating all those ill designs and obnoxious schemes:

- "O Prophet [Muhammad (Peace be upon him)]! Keep your duty to Allâh, and obey not the disbelievers and the hypocrites (i.e. do not follow their advices). Verily! Allâh is Ever All-Knower, All-Wise." [33:1]

THE WICKED ROLE THEY PLAYED IN THE COURSE OF THE GHAZWAH OF BANI AL-MUSTALIQ:

During this *Ghazwah*, the hypocrites almost managed to create a sort of discord among the Muslims themselves, coupled with a serious and ugly slander against the Prophet (Peace be upon him) himself. In short, their behaviour was an authentic translation of Allâh's Words:

- "Had they marched out with you, they would have added to you nothing except disorder, and they would have hurried about in your midst (spreading corruption) and sowing sedition among you ..." [9:47]

A quarrel was about to break out between the Emigrants and the Helpers on account of plots and evil intentions designed by the hypocrites. The Prophet (Peace be upon him) told them off describing their misbehaviour as something smacking of pre-Islamic practices. They, hypocrites with 'Abdullah bin 'Ubai at their head, were furious for the challenge which the Muslims showed towards the hostile plans and vicious intrigues woven behind closed doors, and swore "the most honourable will expel the meanest out of Madinah," and added: "They (the Muslims) have outnumbered and shared us our land. If you fatten your dog, it will eat you." When that talk was reported to the Prophet (Peace be upon him), 'Umar, a venerable Companion, asked for permission to have Ibn 'Ubai killed. The Prophet (Peace be upon him) naturally turned down his proposal on the grounds that it did not become of a Prophet

(Peace be upon him) to be accused of killing his people. He, on the contrary in an unexpected move, asked 'Umar to announce departure. He marched with his men for two days until the sun grew too hot. They stopped and fell asleep, a clever attempt at diverting his people's attention from the previous event. 'Abdullah's son heard of that vile of his father and as the party reached Madinah, he drew his sword and barred his father's entry into the town until he had confessed and declared that he himself was the meanest of the citizens of Madinah and the Prophet (Peace be upon him) the most honourable of them. Thus the boast recoiled on his head. It was also reported that the son was ready to kill his father if the Prophet (Peace be upon him) had wanted him to.

THE SLANDER AFFAIR:

This extremely painful incident took place on the Prophet's return from the expedition against Bani Mustaliq. The Muslim army had to halt for a night at a place, a short distance from Madinah. In this expedition, the Prophet (Peace be upon him) was accompanied by his noble and talented wife, 'Aishah (May Allah be pleased with her) As it so happened, 'Aishah (May Allah be pleased her) went out some distance from the camp to attend to the call of nature. When she returned, she discovered that she had dropped her necklace somewhere. The necklace itself was of no great value, but as it was a loan from a friend, 'Aishah (May Allah be pleased her) went out again to search for it. On her return, to her great grief and mortification, the army had already marched away with the camel she was riding, her attendants thinking that she was in the litter as she was then thin, very young and light of weight. In her helplessness she sat down and cried till sleep overpowered her. Safwan bin Mu'attal, an Emigrant, who was coming in the rear recognized her as he had seen her before the verse enjoining the veil was revealed, and brought her on his camel to Madinah without saying a single word to her, himself walking behind the animal. The hypocrites of Madinah led by 'Abdullah bin 'Ubai bin Salul, sought to make capital out of this incident and spread a malicious scandal against 'Aishah (May Allah be pleased her) and unfortunately some of the Muslims also became involved in it. On arrival in Madinah, the Prophet (Peace be upon him) held counsel with his Companions, who pronounced different opinions ranging from divorce to retention. The incident almost roused a fight between two rival factions, Al-Aws and Al-Khazraj, but the Prophet's intervention silenced both parties on the sport. 'Aishah (May Allah be pleased with her) unaware of the rumours being circulated, fell ill and was confined to bed for a month. On recovering, she heard of the slander and took permission to go and see her parents seeking authentic news. She then burst into tears and stayed for two days and one sleepless night ceaselessly weeping to such an extent that she felt her liver was about to rip open. The Prophet (Peace be upon him) visited her in that situation, and after testifying to the Oneness of Allâh he told her, "If you are innocent, Allâh will acquit you, otherwise, you have to beg for His forgiveness and pardon." She stopped weeping and asked her parents to speak for her, but they had nothing to say, so she herself took the initiative and said "Should I tell you I am innocent, and Allâh knows that I am surely innocent, you will not believe me; and if I were to admit something of which, Allâh knows, I am innocent, you will believe me, then I will have nothing to make recourse to except the words of the father of Prophet Yusuf (Joseph):

- "So (for me) patience is most fitting. And it is Allâh (Alone) Whose Help can be sought against that which you assert." [12:18]

She then turned away and lay down for some rest. At that decisive moment the Revelation came acquitting 'Aishah (May Allah be pleased with her) of all the slanderous talk fabricated in this concern. 'Aishah (May Allah be pleased with her) of course, was wholeheartedly joyful and praised Allâh thankfully. Allâh's Words in this regard went as follows:

- "Verily! Those who brought forth the slander (against 'Aishah (May Allah be pleased with her) — the wife of the Prophet (Peace be upon him) are a group among you." [24:11]

The principal elements involved in the slander affair, Mistah bin Athatha, Hassan bin Thabit and Hamnah bint Jahsh, were flogged with eighty stripes.

As for the man who took the principal part, 'Abdullah bin Ubai, he was not flogged, either because the corporal punishment commutes the chastisement in store for him in the Hereafter, and he does not deserve this merit, or for the same public interest for which he was not killed previously. He, moreover, became the butt of reproach and humiliation amongst his people after his real intentions had been unequivocally exposed to all the public.

Almost a month later, the Messenger of Allâh (Peace be upon him) and 'Umar bin Al-Khattab were engaged in the following talk: "Don't you see 'Umar if I had had him (Abdullah bin Ubai) killed, a large number of dignitaries would have furiously hastened to fight for him. Now, on the contrary, if I ask them to kill him, they will do so out of their own free will." 'Umar replied "I swear by Allâh that the Prophet's judgement is much more sound than mine."

Delegations and Expeditions following Al-Muraisi' Ghazwah

1. A military expedition led by 'Abdur Rahman bin 'Auf was despatched to the habitation of Bani Kalb in Doumat Al-Jandal in Sha'ban 6 Hijri. Before setting out, the Prophet (Peace be upon him) summoned 'Abdur Rahman, and placed his hand on the latter's hand invoking Allâh's blessings and giving him commandments to act magnanimously during the war. He told him to marry the king's daughter if they obeyed him. 'Abdur Rahman stayed among those people for three days, invited them to Islam and they responded positively. He then did marry the king's daughter Tamadur bint Al-Asbagh.
2. In the same month and year, 'Ali bin Abi Talib was despatched at the head of a platoon to the habitation of Bani Sa'd bin Bakr in a place called Fadk. Prophet Muhammad (Peace be upon him) had been reported that those had rallied ranks to support the Jews. The Muslim fighters used to march in the day and lurk at night. On their way, they captured an enemy scout who admitted being sent to Khaibar tribe, to offer them support in return for their dates. 'Ali and his companions raided their encampment, captured five hundred camels and two thousand goats, but Banu Sa'd, with their chieftain Wabr bin 'Aleem had fled away.
3. An expedition led by Abu Bakr As-Siddiq or Zaid bin Haritha was despatched to Wadi Al-Qura in Ramadan 6 Hijri after Fazara sept had made an attempt at the Prophet's life. Following the morning prayer, the detachment was given orders to raid the enemy. Some of them were killed and others captured. Amongst the captives, were Umm Qirfa and her beautiful daughter, who was sent to Makkah as a ransom for the release of some Muslim prisoners there. Umm Qirfa's attempts at the Prophet's life recoiled on her, and the thirty horsemen she had gathered and sustained to implement her evil scheme were all killed.
4. Anas bin Malik reported that some people belonging to tribe of 'Uraina came to Allâh's Messenger (Peace be upon him) and made pretensions to Islam. They stayed in Madinah but found its climate uncongenial, so they were asked to pitch their tents in the pastures nearby. They did so and were all right. They then fell on the Prophet's shepherd and killed him, turned apostates from Islam and drove off the camels. This news reached the Prophet (Peace be upon him), who sent a group of twenty Muslims led by Karz bin Jabir Al-Fihri on their track. They were brought and handed over to him. He had their hands and feet cut off, their eyes gouged out in recompense for their behaviour, and then they were thrown on the stony ground until they died.

- Biographers also reported 'Amr bin Omaiya Ad-Damari and Salamah bin Abi Salamah to have been sent on an errand to kill Abu Sufyan, the chief of Quraish, who had already sent a bedouin to kill the Prophet (Peace be upon him). The two-men mission failed except for three polytheists killed on the way. It is noteworthy that all the foregone invasions did not imply real bitter fighting, they were rather skirmishes or punitive military manoeuvres carried out to deter some enemies still unsubdued. Deep meditation on the development of war circumstances reveal the continuous collapse of the morale among the enemies of Islam, who had come to understand that they were no longer in a position to contain the Islamic call or weaken its active drive. This state of affairs reached its climax in Al-Hudaibiyah Treaty when the two belligerent parties, believers and disbelievers, entered into a truce agreement that pointed markedly to the ever-growing power of Islam, and recorded unequivocally the perpetuity of this heavenly religion in pan-Arabia.

Al-HUDAIBIYAH TREATY (Dhul Qa'dah 6 A.H.):

When Arabia began to witness the large impressive sweep in favour of the Muslims, the forerunners of the great conquest and success of the Islamic Call started gradually to loom on the demographic horizon, and the true believers restored their undisputed right to observe worship in the sacred sanctuary.

It was about the sixth year Hijri when the Prophet (Peace be upon him) saw in a dream, while he was still in Madinah, that he had entered the sacred sanctuary in Makkah in security with his followers, and was performing the ceremonies of *Umrah* (lesser pilgrimage). Their heads were being shaved and hair cut off. As soon as he informed some of his Companions the contents of his dream, their hearts leapt up with joy since they found in it the actualization of their deep longing to take part in pilgrimage and its hallowed rites after an exile of six years.

The Prophet (Peace be upon him) had his clothes washed, mounted his camel and marched out towards Makkah at the head of fifteen hundred Muslims including his wife Umm Salamah. Some desert bedouins whose Faith was lukewarm hung back and made excuses. They carried no weapons with them except sheathed swords because they had no intention of fighting. Ibn Umm Maktum was mandated to dispose the affairs of Madinah during the Prophet's absence. As they approached Makkah, and in a place called Dhi Hulaifa, he ordered that the sacrificial animals be garlanded, and all believers donned *Al-Ihrâm*, the pilgrim's garb. He despatched a reconnoiterer to hunt around for news of the enemy. The man came back to tell the Prophet (Peace be upon him) that a large number of slaves, as well as a huge army, were gathered to oppose him, and that the road to Makkah was completely blocked. The Prophet (Peace be upon him) consulted his Companions, who were of the opinion that they would fight none unless they were debarredfrom performing their pilgrimage.

The Quraishites, on their part, held a meeting during which they considered the whole situation and decided to resist the Prophet's mission at all costs. Two hundred horsemen led by Khalid bin Al-Waleed were despatched to take the Muslims by surprise during *Zuhr* (the afternoon) prayer. However, the rules of prayer of fear were revealed meanwhile and thus Khalid and his men missed the chance. The Muslims avoided marching on that way and decided to follow a rugged rocky one. Here, Khalid ran back to Quraish to brief them on the latest situation.

When the Muslims reached a spot called Thaniyat Al-Marar, the Prophet's camel stumbled and knelt down and was too stubborn to move. Muhammad (Peace be upon him) swore he would willingly accede to any plan they put forward that would glorify Allâh's sanctities. He then reprovingly spurred his camel and it leapt up. They resumed their march and came to pitch their tents at the furthest part of Al-Hudaibiyah beside a well of scanty water. The Muslims reported thirst to the Prophet (Peace be upon him), who took an arrow out of his quiver, and placed it in the ditch. Water immediately gushed forth, and his followers drank to their fill. When the Prophet (Peace be upon him) had rested, Budail bin Warqa' Al-Khuza'i with some celebrities of Khuza'ah tribe, the Prophet's confidants, came and asked him what he had come for. The Prophet (Peace be upon him) replied that it was not for war that he had come forth: "I have no other design," he said, "but to perform *'Umrah* (the lesser pilgrimage) in the Holy Sanctuary. Should Quraish embrace the new religion, as some people have done, they are most welcome, but if they stand in my way or debar the Muslims from pilgrimage, I will surely fight them to the last man, and Allâh's Order must be fulfilled." The envoy carried the message back to Quraish, who sent another one called Mikraz bin Hafs. On seeing him, the Prophet (Peace be upon him) said that that was a treacherous man. He was given the same message to communicate to his people. He was followed by another ambassador known as Al-Hulais bin 'Alqamah. He was very much impressed by the spirit of devotion that the Muslims had for the Sacred Ka'bah. He went back to his men and warned them against debarring Muhammad (Peace be upon him) and his Companions from doing honour to Allâh's house on the peril of breaking his alliance with them. Hulais was succeeded by 'Urwa bin Mas'ud Ath-Thaqafi to negotiate with Muhammad (Peace be upon him). In the course of discussion he said to the Prophet (Peace be upon him): "Muhammad! Have you gathered around yourself mixed people and then brought them against your kith and kin in order to destroy them. By Allâh I think I see you deserted by these people tomorrow." At this point Abu Bakr stood up and expressed his resentment at this imputation. Al-Mugheerah bin Shu'bah expressed the same attitude and reprovingly forbade him from touching the Prophet's beard. Here, Quraish's envoy remarked indignantly and alluded to the latter's treacherous act of killing his companions and looting them before he embraced Islam. Meanwhile, 'Urwah, during his stay in the Muslim camp, had been closely watching the unfathomable love and profound respect that the followers of Muhammad (Peace be upon him) showed him. He returned and conveyed to Quraish his impression that those people could not forsake the Prophet (Peace be upon him) under any circumstances. He expressed his feelings in the following words: "I have been to Chosroes, Caesar and Negus in their kingdoms, but never have I seen a king among a people like Muhammad (Peace be upon him) among his Companions. If he performs his ablution, they would not let the water thereof fall on the ground; if he expectorates, they would have the mucus to rub their faces with; if he speaks, they would lower their voices. They will not abandon him for anything in any case. He, now, offers you a reasonable plan, so do what you please."

Seeing an overwhelming tendency towards reconciliation among their chiefs, some reckless, fight-prone youngsters of Quraish devised a wicked plan that could hinder the peace treaty. They decided to infiltrate into the camp of the Muslims and produce intentional skirmishes that might trigger the fuse of war. Muhammad bin Maslamah, chief of the Muslim guards, took them captives, but in view of the far-reaching imminent results about to be achieved, the Prophet (Peace be upon him) set them free. In this context Allâh says:

- "And He it is Who has withheld their hands from you and your hands from them in the midst of Makkah, after He had made you victors over them." [48:24]

Time passed. Negotiations went on but with no results. Then the Prophet (Peace be upon him) desired 'Umar to see the nobles of Quraish on his behalf. 'Umar excused himself on account of the personal enmity of Quraish; he had, moreover, no influential relatives in the city who could shield him from danger; and he pointed to 'Uthman bin 'Affan, who belonged to one of the most powerful families in Makkah, as the suitable envoy. 'Uthman went to Abu Sufyan and other chiefs and told them that the Muslims had come only to visit and pay their homage to the Sacred House, to do worship there, and that they had no intention to fight. He was also asked to call them to Islam, and give glad tidings to the believers in Makkah, women and men, that the conquest was approaching and Islam was surely to prevail because Allâh would verily establish His religion in Makkah. 'Uthman also assured them that after the performance of ceremonies they would soon depart peacefully, but the Quraishites were adamant and not prepared to grant them the permission to visit Al-Ka'bah. They, however, offered 'Uthman the permission to perform the pilgrimage, if he so desired in his individual capacity, but

'Uthman declined the offer saying: "How is it possible that I avail myself of this opportunity, when the Prophet (Peace be upon him) is denied of it?" The Muslims anxiously waited for the arrival of 'Uthman with mingled feelings of fear and anxiety. But his arrival was considerably delayed and a foul play was suspected on the part of Quraish. The Muslims were greatly worried and took a solemn pledge at the hand of the Prophet (Peace be upon him) that they would sacrifice their lives to avenge the death of their Companion and stand firmly by their master, Muhammad (Peace be upon him), under all conditions. This pledge goes by the name of *Bay'at Ar-Ridwan* (a covenant of fealty). The first men to take a pledge were Abu Sinan Al-Asadi and Salamah bin Al-Akwa', who gave a solemn promise to die in the cause of Truth three times, at the front of the army, in the middle and in the rear. The Prophet (Peace be upon him) caught his left hand on behalf of 'Uthman. This fealty was sworn under a tree, with 'Umar holding the Prophet's hand and Ma'qil bin Yasar holding a branch of the tree up. The Noble Qur'ân has referred to this pledge in the following words:

- "Indeed, Allâh was pleased with the believers when they gave their *Bai'a* (pledge) to you [O Muhammad (Peace be upon him)] under the tree." [48:18]

When Quraish saw the firm determination of the Muslims to shed the last drop of blood for the defence of their Faith, they came to their senses and realized that Muhammad's followers could not be cowed down by these tactics. After some further interchange of messages they agreed to conclude a treaty of reconciliation and peace with the Muslims. The clauses of the said treaty go as follows:

1. The Muslims shall return this time and come back next year, but they shall not stay in Makkah for more than three days.
2. They shall not come back armed but can bring with them swords only sheathed in scabbards and these shall be kept in bags.
3. War activities shall be suspended for ten years, during which both parties will live in full security and neither will raise sword against the other.
4. If anyone from Quraish goes over to Muhammad (Peace be upon him) without his guardian's permission, he should be sent back to Quraish, but should any of Muhammad's followers return to Quraish, he shall not be sent back.
5. Whosoever to join Muhammad (Peace be upon him), or enter into treaty with him, should have the liberty to do so; and likewise whosoever wishes to join Quraish, or enter into treaty with them, should be allowed to do so.

Some dispute arose with regard to the preamble. For example, when the agreement was to be committed to writing, 'Ali bin Abi Talib, who acted as a scribe began with the words: *Bismillâh ir-Rahman ir-Raheem,* i.e., "In the Name of Allâh, the Most Beneficent, the Most Merciful" but the Makkan plenipotentiary, Suhail bin 'Amr declared that he knew nothing about *Ar-Rahman* and insisted upon the customary formula *Bi-ismika Allâhumma,* i.e., "In Your Name, O Allâh!" The Muslims grumbled with uneasiness but the Prophet (Peace be upon him) agreed. He then went on to dictate, "This is what Muhammad, the Messenger of Allâh has agreed to with Suhail bin 'Amr." Upon this Suhail again protested: "Had we acknowledged you as Prophet, we would not have debarred you from the Sacred House, nor fought against you. Write your own name and the name of your father." The Muslims grumbled as before and refused to consent to the change. The Prophet (Peace be upon him), however, in the larger interest of Islam, attached no importance to such an insignificant detail, erased the words himself, and dictated instead: "Muhammad, the son of 'Abdullah." Soon after this treaty, Khuza'a clan, a former ally of Banu Hashim, joined the ranks of Muhammad (Peace be upon him), and Banu Bakr sided with Quraish.

It was during this time while the treaty was being written that Abu Jandal, Suhail's son, appeared on the scene. He was brutally chained and was staggering with privation and fatigue. The Prophet (Peace be upon him) and his Companions were moved to pity and tried to secure his release but Suhail was adamant and said: "To signify that you are faithful to your contract, an opportunity has just arrived." The Prophet (Peace be upon him) said: "But the treaty was not signed when your son entered the camp." Upon this, he burst forth and said, "but the terms of the treaty were agreed upon." It was indeed an anxious moment. On the one hand, Abu Jandal was lamenting at the top of his voice, "Am I to be returned to the polytheists that they might entice me from my religion, O Muslims!" but, on the other hand, the faithful engagement was also considered to be necessary, above all other considerations. The Prophet's heart welled up with sympathy, but he wanted to honour his word at all costs. He consoled Abu Jandal and said, "Be patient, resign yourself to the Will of Allâh. Allâh is going to provide for you and your helpless companions relief and means of escape. We have concluded a treaty of peace with them and we have taken the pledge in the Name of Allâh. We are, therefore, under no circumstances prepared to break it." 'Umar bin Al-Khattab could not help giving vent to the deep-seated agony of his heart. He rose to his feet uttering words implying deep hatred and extreme indignation and requested Abu Jandal to take his sword and kill Suhail, but the son spared his father. However, in silent resignation was therefore, Abu Jandal borne away with his chains.

When the peace treaty had been concluded, the Prophet (Peace be upon him) ordered his Companions to slaughter their sacrificial animals, but they were too depressed to do that. The Prophet (Peace be upon him) gave instructions in this regard three times but with negative response. He told his wife Umm Salamah about this attitude of his Companions. She advised that he himself take the initiative, slaughter his animal and have his head shaved. Seeing that, the Muslims, with rended hearts, started to slaughter their animals and shave their heads. They even almost killed one another because of their distress. The Prophet (Peace be upon him) prayed three times for those who shaved their heads and once for those who cut their hair. A camel was sacrificed on behalf of seven men and a cow on behalf of the same number of people. The Prophet (Peace be upon him) sacrificed a camel which once belonged to Abu Jahl and which the Muslims had seized as booty at Badr, thus enraging the polytheists. During Al-Hudaibiyah campaign, the Prophet (Peace be upon him) permitted Ka'b bin 'Ujrah, who was in a state of *Ihram* (state of ritual consecration of the pilgrim) for *'Umrah* (lesser pilgrimage) to shave his head due to illness, on the condition that he will pay compensation by sacrificing a sheep, fasting for three days or feeding six needy persons. Concerning this, the following verse was revealed:

- "And whosoever of you is ill or has an ailment in his scalp (necessitating shaving), he must pay a *Fidyah* (ransom) of either fasting (three days) or giving *Sadaqa* (feeding six poor persons) or offering sacrifice (one sheep)." [2:196]

Meanwhile some believing women emigrated to Madinah and asked the Prophet (Peace be upon him) for refuge which they were granted. When their families demanded their return, he would not hand them back because the following verse was revealed:

- "O you who believe! When believing women come to you as emigrants, examine them, Allâh knows best as to their Faith, then if you know them for true believers, send them not back to the disbelievers, they are not lawful (wives) for the disbelievers nor are the disbelievers lawful (husbands) for them. But give the disbelievers that (amount of money) which they have spent [as their *Mahr*] to them. And there will be no sin on you to marry them if you have paid their *Mahr* to them. Likewise hold not the disbelieving women as wives ..." [60:10]

The reason why the believing women were not handed back was either because they were not originally included in the terms of the treaty, which mentioned only men, or because the Qur'ân abrogated any terms dealing with women in the verse:

- "O Prophet! When believing women come to you to give you the *Bai'a* (Pledge), that they will not associate anything in worship with Allâh ..." [60:12]

This is the verse which forbade Muslim women from marrying disbelieving men. Likewise, Muslim men were commanded to terminate their marriages to disbelieving women. In compliance with this injunction, 'Umar bin Al-Khattab divorced two wives he had married before he embraced Islam; Mu'awiyah married the first woman, and Safwan bin Omaiyah married the second.

ALHUDAIBIYAH TREATY: SOCIO-POLITICAL IMPACT:

A series of events confirmed the profound wisdom and splendid results of the peace treaty which Allâh called "a manifest victory". How could it be otherwise when Quraish had recognized the legitimate Muslims' existence on the scene of political life in Arabia, and began to deal with the believers on equal terms. Quraish in the light of the articles of the treaty, had indirectly relinquished its claim to religious leadership, and admitted that they were no longer interested in people other than Quraish, and washed their hands of any sort of intervention in the religious future of the Arabian Peninsula. The Muslims did not have in mind to seize people's property or kill them through bloody wars, nor did they ever think of pursuing any coercive approaches in their endeavours to propagate Islam, on the contrary, their sole target was to provide an atmosphere of freedom as regards ideology or religion:

- "Then whosoever wills, let him believe, and whosoever wills, let him disbelieve." [18:29]

The Muslims, on the other hand, had the opportunity to spread Islam over areas not then explored. When there was armistice, war was abolished, and men met and consulted together, none talked about Islam intelligently without entering it; within the two years following the conclusion of the treaty double as many entered Islam as ever before. This is supported by the fact that the Prophet (Peace be upon him) went out to Al-Hudaibiyah with only 1,400 men, but when he set out to liberate Makkah, two years later, he had 10,000 men with him.

The article of the treaty pertaining to cessation of hostilities for ten years points directly to the utter failure of political haughtiness exercised by Quraish and its allies, and functions as evidence of the collapse and impotence of the war instigator.

Qhad been obliged to lose those advantages in return for one seemingly in its favour but does not actually bear any harm against the Muslims, i.e., the article that speaks of handing over believing men who seek refuge with the Muslims without their guardians' consent to Quraish. At first glance, it was a most distressing clause and was considered objectionable in the Muslim camp. However, in the course of events, it proved to be a great blessing. The Muslims sent back to Makkah were not likely to renounce the blessings of Islam; contrariwise, those very Muslims turned out to be centres of influence for Islam. It was impossible to think that they would become apostates or renegades. The wisdom behind this truce assumed its full dimensions in some subsequent events. After the Prophet (Peace be upon him) had reached Madinah, Abu Baseer, who had escaped from Quraish, came to him as a Muslim; Quraish sent two men demanding his return, so the Prophet (Peace be upon him) handed him over to them. On the way to Makkah, Abu Baseer managed to kill one of them, and the other one fled to Madinah with Abu Baseer in pursuit. When he reached the Prophet (Peace be upon him), he said, "Your obligation is over and Allâh has freed you from it. You duly handed me over to the men, and Allâh has rescued me from them." The Prophet (Peace be upon him) said, "Woe is his mother, he would have kindled a war if there had been others with him." When he heard that, he knew that he would be handed back to them, so he fled from Madinah and went as far as Saif Al-Bahr. The other Muslims who were oppressed in Makkah began to escape to Abu Baseer. He was joined by Abu Jandal and others until a fair-sized colony was formed and soon sought revenge on Quraish and started to intercept their caravans. The pagans of Makkah finding themselves unable to control those exiled colonists, begged the Prophet (Peace be upon him) to do away with the clause which governed the extradition. They implored him by Allâh and by their ties of kinship to send for the group, saying that whoever joined the Muslims in Madinah would be safe from them. So the Prophet (Peace be upon him) sent for the group and they responded, as expected, positively.

These are the realities of the clauses of the truce treaty and as it seems they all function in favour of the nascent Islamic state. However, two points in the treaty made it distasteful to some Muslims, namely they were not given access to the Holy Sanctuary that year, and the seemingly humiliating attitude as regards reconciliation with the pagans of Quraish. 'Umar, unable to contain himself for the distress taking full grasp of his heart, went to the Prophet (Peace be upon him) and said: "Aren't you the true Messenger of Allâh?" The Prophet (Peace be upon him) replied calmly, "Why not?" 'Umar again spoke and asked: "Aren't we on the path of righteousness and our enemies in the wrong?" Without showing any resentment, the Prophet (Peace be upon him) replied that it was so. On getting this reply he further urged: "Then we should not suffer any humiliation in the matter of Faith." The Prophet (Peace be upon him) was unruffled and with perfect confidence said: "I am the true Messenger of Allâh, I never disobey Him, He shall help me." "Did you not tell us," rejoined 'Umar, "that we shall perform pilgrimage?" "But I have never told you," replied the Prophet (Peace be upon him), "that we shall do so this very year." 'Umar was silenced. But his mind was disturbed. He went to Abu Bakr and expressed his feelings before him. Abu Bakr who had never been in doubt as regards the Prophet's truthfulness and veracity confirmed what the Prophet (Peace be upon him) had told him. In due course the Chapter of Victory (48th) was revealed saying:

- "Verily, We have given you [O Muhammad (Peace be upon him)] a manifest victory." [48:1]

The Messenger of Allâh(Peace be upon him) summoned 'Umar and imported to him the happy tidings. 'Umar was overjoyed, and greatly regretted his former attitude. He used to spend in charity, observe fasting and prayer and free as many slaves as possible in expiation for that reckless attitude he had assumed.

The early part of the year 7 A.H. witnessed the Islamization of three prominent men of Makkah, 'Amr bin Al-'As, Khalid bin Al-Waleed and 'Uthman bin Talhah. On their arrival and entrance into the fold of Islam, the Prophet (Peace be upon him) said, "Quraish has given us its own blood."

THE SECOND STAGE

A NEW PHASE OF ISLAMIC ACTION

Al-Hudaibiyah Truce marked a new phase in the process of Islamic action and life of the Muslims. Quraish, a bitter enemy of Islam, now withdraws from the war arena and embraces a peaceful settlement with the Muslims, thus the third support of a tripartite enemy (Quraish, Ghatfan and the Jews) is broken, and being the holder of the banner of paganism in Arabia, the other pagans' aggressive feelings towards Islam considerably subsided. Ghatfan Tribe no longer constituted any remarkable threat, and their provocative deeds were mainly Jewish-instigated actions. The Jews, after being banished from Madinah, resorted to Khaibar to change it into a hot bed of intrigues against the Prophet (Peace be upon him). There, they used to hatch their plots, ignite the fire of dissension and allure the Arabs living in the vicinity of Madinah to join them with the aim of exterminating the new Islamic state, or at least inflict heavy losses on the Muslims. The Prophet (Peace be upon him), not heedless of their devilish schemes, placed a decisive war with them as a first priority on his agenda shortly after the endorsement of the above-mentioned treaty. The treaty of Hudaibiyah allowed the Muslims to intensify their Islamic career and double up their ceaseless efforts in propagating their *Da'wah*, and consequently give this sort of action preponderance over the military activities. Hence, we deem it imperative to divide this post-treaty stage into two sections:

1. Ceaseless peaceful efforts in propagating the Islamic *Da'wah* (Call) and initiating a sort of correspondence with kings and princes of the neighbouring political entities.
2. Military activities.

THE PROPHET'S PLANS TO SPREAD THE MESSAGE OF ISLAM BEYOND ARABIA

Late in the six year A.H., on his return from Hudaibiyah, the Prophet (Peace be upon him) decided to send messages to the kings beyond Arabia calling them to Islam. In order to authenticate the credentials of his envoys, a silver seal was made in which were graven the words: *"Muhammad the Messenger of Allâh"* in the following formation:

محمد

رسول

الله

Envoys were chosen on the basis of their experience and knowledge, and sent on their errands in Muharram in the year 7 A.H., a few days before heading for Khaibar.

1. A Deputation to Abyssinia (Ethiopia):

Negus, king of Abyssinia (Ethiopia), his name was Ashama bin Al-Abjar, received the Prophet's message, despatched by Amr bin Omaiyah Ad-Damari, which At-Tabari referred to, either late in the sixth year or early in the seventh year A.H. Deep scrutiny into the letter shows that it was not the one sent after Al-Hudaibiyah event. Wording of the letter rather indicates that it was sent to that king when Ja'far and his companions emigrated to Abyssinia (Ethiopia) during the Makkan period. One of its sentences read "I have despatched my cousin, Ja'far with a group of Muslims, to you. Do be generous towards them and give up haughtiness."

Al-Baihaqi, on the authority of Ibn Ishaq, gave the following narration of the Prophet's letter sent to Negus:

"This letter is sent from Muhammad, the Prophet to Negus Al-Ashama, the king of Abyssinia (Ethiopia).

Peace be upon him who follows true guidance and believes in Allâh and His Messenger. I bear witness that there is no god but Allâh Alone with no associate, He has taken neither a wife nor a son, and that Muhammad is His slave and Messenger. I call you unto the fold of Islam; if you embrace Islam, you will find safety,

- "Say [O Muhammad (Peace be upon him)]: 'O people of the Scripture (Jews and Christians), come to a word that is just between us and you, that we worship none but Allâh, and that we associate no partners with Him, and that none of us shall take others as lords besides Allâh.' Then, if they turn away, say: 'Bear witness that we are Muslims.' " [3:64]

Should you reject this invitation, then you will be held responsible for all the evils of the Christians of your people."

Dr. Hameedullah (Paris), a reliable verifier, has adduced a version of the above letter disclosed only a short time ago and identical to Ibn Al-Qaiyim's narration. Dr. Hameedullah exerted painstaking effort and used all means of modern technology to verify the text of the letter, which reads as follows:

"In the Name of Allâh, the Most Beneficent, the Most Merciful.

From Muhammad the Messenger of Allâh to Negus, king of Abyssinia (Ethiopia).
Peace be upon him who follows true guidance. Salutations, I entertain Allâh's praise, there is no god but He, the Sovereign, the Holy, the Source of peace, the Giver of peace, the Guardian of faith, the Preserver of safety. I bear witness that Jesus, the son of Mary, is the spirit of Allâh and His Word which He cast into Mary, the virgin, the good, the pure, so that she conceived Jesus. Allâh created him from His spirit and His breathing as He created Adam by His Hand. I call you to Allâh Alone with no associate and to His obedience and to follow me and to believe in that which came to me, for I am the Messenger of Allâh. I invite you and your men to Allâh, the Glorious, the All-Mighty. I hereby bear witness that I have communicated my message and advice. I invite you to listen and accept my advice. Peace be upon him who follows true guidance."

The text of this letter is doubtlessly authentic, but to maintain that it was written after Al-Hudaibiyah event is still a question lacking in definite evidence.

When 'Amr bin Omaiyah Ad-Damari communicated the Apostolic letter to Negus, the latter took the parchment and placed it on his eye, descended to the floor, confessed his faith in Islam and wrote the following reply to the Prophet (Peace be upon him).

"In the Name of Allâh, the Most Beneficent, the Most Merciful.

From Negus Ashama to Muhammad, the Messenger of Allâh. Peace be upon you, O Messenger of Allâh! and mercy and blessing from Allâh beside Whom there is no god. I have received your letter in which you have mentioned about Jesus and by the Lord of heaven and earth, Jesus is not more than what you say. We fully acknowledge that with which you have been sent to us and we have entertained your cousin and his companions. I bear witness that you are the Messenger of Allâh, true and confirming (those who have gone before you), I pledge to you through your cousin and surrender myself through him to the Lord of the worlds."

The Prophet (Peace be upon him) had asked Negus to send Ja'far and his companions, the emigrants to Abyssinia (Ethiopia), back home. They came back to see the Prophet (Peace be upon him) in Khaibar. Negus later died in Rajab 9 A.H. shortly after Tabuk *Ghazwa*. The Prophet (Peace be upon him) announced his death and observed prayer in absentia for him. Another king succeeded Negus to the throne and another letter was sent to him by the Prophet (Peace be upon him) but whether or not he embraced Islam is still a question not answered yet.

2. Letter to the Vicegerent of Egypt, called Muqawqas:

The Prophet (Peace be upon him) wrote to Juraij bin Matta, called Muqawqas, vicegerent of Egypt and Alexandria saying:

"In the Name of Allâh, the Most Beneficent, the Most Merciful.

From Muhammad slave of Allâh and His Messenger to Muqawqas, vicegerent of Egypt.
Peace be upon him who follows true guidance. Thereafter, I invite you to accept Islam. Therefore, if you want security, accept Islam. If you accept Islam, Allâh, the Sublime, shall reward you doubly. But if you refuse to do so, you will bear the burden of the transgression of all the Copts.

- "Say [O Muhammad (Peace be upon him)]: 'O people of the Scripture (Jews and Christians), come to a word that is just between us and you, that we worship none but Allâh, and that we associate no partners with Him, and that none of us shall take others as lords besides Allâh.' Then, if they turn away, say: 'Bear witness that we are Muslims.' " [3:64]

Hatib bin Abi Balta'a, who was chosen to communicate the message, requested an audience with Muqawqas before imparting the contents of the letter. He addressed Egypt's vicegerent saying: "There used to be someone before you who had arrogated the status of the Supreme Lord, so Allâh puhim and made an example of him in the Hereafter, and in this life; therefore, take warning and never set a bad example to others." Muqawqas answered: "We are in no position to relinquish our religion except for a better one." Hatib resumed: "We invite you to embrace Islam, which will suffice you all what you may lose. Our Prophet has called people to profess this Faith, Quraish and the Jews stood against him as bitter enemies, whereas Christians stood closest to his Call. Upon my life, Moses's news about Christ is identical to the latter's good tidings about the advent of Muhammad; likewise, this invitation of ours to you to embrace Islam is similar to your invitation to the people of Torah to accept the New Testament. Once a Prophet rises in a nation, he is eligible for positive response, hence you are subject to the same Divine Law. Bear in mind that we have not come to dissuade you from religion of Christ but rather bidding you to adhere to its tenets." Muqawqas meditated over the contents of the letter deeply and said: "I have come to the conviction that this Prophet bids nothing abominable; he is neither a straying magician nor a lying soothsayer. He bears the true manifest seeds of Prophethood, and so I will consider the affair deeply." He took the parchment and ordered that it be kept in an ivory casket. He called a scribe to write the following reply in Arabic:

"In the Name of Allâh, the Most Beneficent, the Most Merciful.

From Muqawqas to Muhammad bin 'Abdullah:
Peace be upon you. I have read your letter and understood its contents, and what you are calling for. I already know that the coming of a Prophet is still due, but I used to believe he would be born in Syria. I am sending you as presents two maids, who come from noble Coptic families; clothing and a steed for riding on. Peace be upon you."

It is noteworthy that Muqawqas did not avail himself of this priceless opportunity and he did not embrace Islam. The presents were accepted; Maria, the first maid, stayed with the Prophet (Peace be upon him), and gave birth to his son Ibrahîm; the other Sirin, was given to Hassan bin Thabit Al-Ansari.

3. A Letter to Chosroes, Emperor of Persia:

"In the Name of Allâh, the Most Beneficent, the Most Merciful.

From Muhammad, the Messenger of Allâh to Chosroes, king of Persia.
Peace be upon him who follows true guidance, believes in Allâh and His Messenger and testifies that there is no god but Allâh Alone with no associate, and that Muhammad is His slave and Messenger. I invite you to accept the religion of Allâh. I am the Messenger of Allâh sent to all people in order that I

may infuse fear of Allâh in every living person, and that the charge may be proved against those who reject the Truth. Accept Islam as your religion so that you may live in security, otherwise, you will be responsible for all the sins of the Magians."

'Abdullah bin Hudhafa As-Sahmi was chosen to carry the letter. This envoy carried it to the king of Bahrain but we do not know as yet if the latter despatched to Chosroes by one of his men or chose 'Abdullah himself.

The proud monarch was enraged by the style of the letter as the name of the Prophet (Peace be upon him) had been put above his own name. He tore the letter into shreds and forthwith dictated a command to his viceroy in Yemen to send a couple of troopers to arrest the Prophet and bring him to his presence. The governor, Bazan by name, immediately sent two men to Madinah for the purpose. As soon as the men reached Madinah, the Prophet (Peace be upon him) was informed by a Divine Revelation that Pervez, the emperor of Persia, had been murdered by his son. The Prophet (Peace be upon him) disclosed to them the news and they were stunned. He added asking them to tell their new monarch that Islam would prevail everywhere and outstrip the sovereignty of Chosroes himself. They hurried back to Bazan and communicated to him what they heard. Meanwhile, Sherweh, the new monarch sent a letter to Bazan confirming the news and bidding him to stop any procedures as regards the Prophet till further notice. Bazan, together with the Persians in Yemen, went into the folds of Islam, and gladly signified his adhesion to the Prophet.

4.The Envoy to Caesar, King of Rome:

Al-Bukhari gave a long narration of the contents of the letter sent by the Prophet (Peace be upon him) to Hercules, king of the Byzantines:

"In the Name of Allâh, the Most Beneficent, the Most Merciful.

From Muhammad, the slave of Allâh and His Messenger to Hercules, king of the Byzantines.

Blessed are those who follow true guidance. I invite you to embrace Islam so that you may live in security. If you come within the fold of Islam, Allâh will give you double reward, but in case you turn your back upon it, then the burden of the sins of all your people shall fall on your shoulders.

- "Say [O Muhammad (Peace be upon him)]: 'O people of the Scripture (Jews and Christians), come to a word that is just between us and you, that we worship none but Allâh, and that we associate no partners with Him, and that none of us shall take others as lords besides Allâh.' Then, if they turn away, say: 'Bear witness that we are Muslims.' " [3:64]

The Muslim envoy, Dihyah bin Khalifah Al-Kalbi, was ordered to hand the letter over to king of Busra, who would in turn, send it to Caesar.

Incidentally, Abu Sufyan bin Harb, who by that time had not embraced Islam, was summoned to the court and Hercules asked him many questions about Muhammad (Peace be upon him) and the religion which he preached. The testimony which this avowed enemy of the Prophet gave regarding the personal excellence of the Prophet's character and the good that Islam was doing the human race, left Hercules wonder-struck.

Al-Bukhâri, on the authority of Ibn Abbas, narrated that Hercules sent for Abu Sufyan and his companions, who happened to be trading in Ash-Sham, Jerusalem. That was during the truce that had been concluded between the polytheists of Quraish and the Messenger of Allâh (Peace be upon him). Hercules, seated amongst his chiefs of staff, asked, "Who amongst you is the nearest relative to the man who claims to be a Prophet?" "I (Abu Sufyan) replied: 'I am the nearest relative to him from amongst the group.' So they made me sit in front of him and made my companions sit behind me. Then he called upon his translator and said (to him). 'Tell them (i.e. Abu Sufyan's companions) that I am going to ask him (i.e. Abu Sufyan) regarding that men who claims to be a Prophet. So if he tells a lie, they should contradict him (instantly)'. By Allâh had I not been afraid that my companions would consider me a liar, I would have told lies", Abu Sufyan later said.

Abu Sufyan's testimony went as follows: "Muhammad descends from a noble family. No one of his family happened to assume kingship. His followers are those deemed weak with numbers ever growing. He neither tells lies nor betrays others, we fight him and he fights us but with alternate victory. He bids people to worship Allâh Alone with no associate, and abandon our fathers' beliefs. He orders us to observe prayer, honesty, abstinence and maintain strong family ties." "Hercules, on hearing this testimony, turned to his translator bidding him to communicate to us his following impression which reveals full conviction in the truthfulness of Muhammad's Prophethood: 'I fully realize that Prophets come from noble families; he does not affect any previous example of Prophethood. Since none of his ancestors was a monarch, we cannot then allege that he is a man trying to reclaim his father's monarchy. So long as he does not tell lies to people, he is for the more reason, immune to telling lies as regards Allâh. Concerning his followers being those deemed weak with numbers ever growing, it is something that goes in agreement with questions of Faith until this latter assumes its full dimensions geographically and demographically. I have understood that no instance of apostasy has as yet appeared among his followers, and this points to the bliss of Faith that finds its abode in the human heart. Betrayal, as I see, is alien to him because real Prophets hold betrayal in . Bidding worship of Allâh with no associates, observance of prayer, honesty and abstinence and prohibition of paganism are traits bound to subject to him all my possessions. I have already known that a Prophet must arise but it has never occurred to me that he will be an Arab from among you. If I was sure I would be faithful to him, I might hope to meet him, and if I were with him, I would wash his feet.' Hercules then requested that the Prophet's letter be read. The observations of the emperor and finally the definite and clear-cut exposition of the Islamic message could not but create a tense atmosphere amongst the clergy present at the court. We were ordered to go out." Abu Sufyan said, "While coming out, I said to my companions, 'The matter of Ibn Abi Kabshah [i.e. Muhammad (Peace be upon him)] has become so prominent that even the king of Banu Al-Asfar (i.e. the Romans) is afraid of him.' So I continued to believe that Allâh's Messenger (Peace be upon him) would be victorious, till Allâh made me embrace Islam." The king did not embrace Islam — for it was differently ordained. However, the Muslim envoy was returned to Madinah with the felicitations of the emperor.

On his way back to Madinah, Dihyah Al-Kalbi was intercepted by people from Judham tribe in Hasmi, who looted the presents sent to the Prophet صلى الله عليه وسلم. Zaid bin Haritha at the head of five hundred men was despatched to that spot, inflicted heavy losses on those people and captured 1000 camels, 5000 of their cattle and a hundred women and boys. The chief of Judham who had embraced Islam filed a complaint with the Prophet, who gave a positive response to the former's protest, and ordered that all the spoils and captives be returned.

5. A Letter to Mundhir bin Sawa, Governor of Bahrain:

The Prophet (Peace be upon him) despatched 'Al-'Ala' bin Al-Hadrami to the governor of Bahrain, carrying a letter inviting him to embrace Islam. In reply, Al-Mundhir bin Sawa wrote the following letter:

"Allâh's Messenger (Peace be upon him)! I received your injunctions. Prior to this, I read your letter, which you wrote to the people of Bahrain extending to them an invitation to Islam. Islam appealed to some of them and they entered the fold of Islam, while others did not find it appealing. In my country, there live Magians and Jews, and therefore you may inform me of the treatment to be extended to them."

The Prophet (Peace be upon him) wrote the following letter in reply to his:

"In the Name of Allâh, the Most Beneficent, the Most Merciful.

From Muhammad, Messenger of Allâh to Mundhir bin Sawa.

Peace be on you! I praise Allâh with no associate, and I bear witness that Muhammad is His slave and Messenger.

Thereafter, I remind you of Allâh, the Mighty, the Glorious. Whoever accepts admonition, does it for his own good. Whoever follows my messengers and acts in accordance with their guidance, he, in fact, accepts my advice.

My messengers have highly praised your behaviour. You shall continue in your present office. Give the new Muslims full chance to preach their religion. I accept your recommendation regarding the people of Bahrain, and I pardon the offences of the offenders; therefore, you may also forgive them.

Of the people of Bahrain whoever wants to go on in their Jewish or Magian faith, should be made to pay *Jizya* (poll-tax)."

6. A Letter to Haudha bin 'Ali, Governor of Yamama:

"In the Name of Allâh, the Most Beneficent, the Most Merciful.

From Muhammad, Messenger of Allâh to Haudha bin 'Ali:
Peace be upon him who follows true guidance. Be informed that my religion shall prevail everywhere. You should accept Islam, and whatever under your command shall remain yours."

The envoy chosen was Sulait bin 'Amr Al-'Amiri, who after communicating his message, carried back the following reply to the Prophet (Peace be upon him):

"The Faith, to which you invite me, is very good. I am a famous orator and poet, the Arabs highly respect me and I am of account among them. If you include me in your government, I am prepared to follow you."

The governor then bestowed a reward on Sulait and presented him with clothes made of Hajr fabric. Of course, he put all those presents in the trust of the Prophet (Peace be upon him):

The Prophet (Peace be upon him) did not accept Haudha's demand. He usually turned down such peremptory tone, and would say that the whole matter was in the Hand of Allâh, Who gave His land to whoever He desired. Gabriel later came with the Revelation that Haudha had died. The Prophet (Peace be upon him), in the context of his comment on this news, said: "Yamama is bound to give rise to a liar who will arrogate Prophethood to himself but he will subsequently be killed." In reply to a question relating to the identity of the killer, the Prophet said "It is one of you, followers of Islam."

7. A Letter to Harith bin Abi Shamir Al-Ghassani, King of Damascus:

"In the Name of Allâh, the Most Beneficent, the Most Merciful.

From Muhammad, Messenger of Allâh to Al-Harith bin Abi Shamir.
Peace be upon him who follows true guidance, believes in it and regards it as true. I invite you to believe in Allâh Alone with no associate, thenceafter your kingdom will remain yours."

Shuja' bin Wahab had the honour of taking the letter to Harith, who upon hearing the letter read in his audience, was madly infuriated and uttered: "Who dares to disposs me of my country, I'll fight him (the Prophet)," and arrogantly rejected the Prophet's invitation to the fold of Islam.

8. A Letter to the King of 'Oman, Jaifer, and his Brother 'Abd Al-Jalandi:

"In the Name of Allâh, the Most Beneficent, the Most Merciful.

From Muhammad bin 'Abdullah to Jaifer and 'Abd Al-Jalandi.
Peace be upon him who follows true guidance; thereafter I invite both of you to the Call of Islam. Embrace Islam. Allâh has sent me as a Prophet to all His creatures in order that I may instil fear of Allâh in the hearts of His disobedient creatures so that there may be left no excuse for those who deny Allâh. If you two accept Islam, you will remain in command of your country; but if you refuse my Call, you've got to remember that all your possessions are perishable. My horsemen will appropriate your land, and my Prophethood will assume preponderance over your kingship."

'Amr bin Al-'As, who was chosen to carry the letter, narrated the following story that happened before he was admitted into the audience of Jaifer.

"When I arrived in 'Oman I contacted 'Abd, who was known to be more mild-tempered than his brother:

- 'Amr: I am the messenger of Allâh's Prophet coming to see both, you and your brother.

    'Abd: You have to see my brother and read to him the letter you are carrying. He is my senior in both age and kingship. Incidentally, what is the purport of your mission?

    'Amr: The Prophet calls upon you to believe in Allâh Alone with no associate, discard any other deities and testify to the slavehood and Messengership of Muhammad.

    'Abd: O 'Amr! You come from a noble family, but first of all, tell me what was your father's attitude concerning this Faith? You know, we used to follow his steps.

    'Amr: Death overtook him before believing in Muhammad's mission; I wish now he had embraced Islam and been truthful to it before his death. I myself had adopted the same attitude until Allâh guided me towards Islam.

    'Abd: When did you embrace Islam?

    'Amr: When I was at Negus's court. By the way, the latter did also enter into the fold of Islam.

    'Abd: What was his people's reaction?

    'Amr: They approved of him and followed his steps.

    'Abd: The bishops and monks?

    'Amr: They did the same.

    'Abd: Beware 'Amr of lying for this soon betrays man.

    'Amr: I never tell lies; moreover, our religion never allows it.

    'Abd: Has Hercules been informed of the Islamization of Negus?

'Amr: Yes, of course.

'Abd: How did you happen to know that?

'Amr: Negus used to pay land tax to Hercules, but when the former embraced Islam, he swore he would discontinue that tax. When this news reached Hercules, his courtiers urged him to take action against Negus but he refused and added that he himself would do the same if he were not sparing of his kingship.

'Abd: What does your Pexhort you to do?

'Amr: He exhorts us to obey Allâh, the All-Mighty, the All-Glorious, be pious and maintain good ties with family kin; he forbids disobedience, aggression, adultery, wine, idolatry and devotion to the cross.

'Abd: Fair words and fair beliefs are those you are calling for. I wish my brother would follow me to believe in Muhammad صلى الله عليه وسلم and profess his religion, but my brother is too sparing of his kingship to become a subordinate.

'Amr: Should your brother surrender himself to Islam, the Prophet would give him authority over his people and take alms tax from the wealthy people to be given to the needy.

'Abd: That is fair behaviour. But what is this alms tax you have mentioned?

'Amr: It is a Divine injunction that alms tax be taken from the well-to-do people who have surplus wealth and be distributed to the poor.

'Abd: I doubt if this can work among our people.

'Amr stayed for some days to be admitted into Jaifer's court until he was finally granted this permit.

"He asked me to hand him the letter to read it. After that he asked me how Quraish reacted and I answered that they had followed him, some out of their own freewill and others overpowered by military fighting. Now, people have chosen Islam in preference to other creeds, and have realized through their mental insight that they had been straying in darkness. None, except you, is now out of the domain of Islam, so I advise you to embrace Islam so that you can provide security to yourself and your country."

Here, he asked me to call on him the following day. The following day he showed some reluctance in receiving me but his brother, 'Abd, interceded and I was given the chance to see him again but this time to address me in a threatening arrogant tone. However, after a private talk with his brother and reconsidering the whole situation, both brothers embraced Islam and proved to be true to Islam that had begun to make its way into this new area.

The context of this story reveals that this letter was sent at a much later date than the others, most likely after the conquest of Makkah.

Through these letters, the Prophet managed to communicate his Message to most monarchs at that time; some believed, while others remained obdurate and persisted in their disbelief. However, the idea of embracing Islam, and the advent of a new Prophet preoccupied all of them.

POST-HUDAIBIYAH HOSTILITIES DHU QARAD INVASION:

It was in fact not a battle but rather a skirmish carried out against a platoon of Bani Fazarah. The place by which it was fought is known as Dhu Qarad, a reservoir of water at a day's journey from Madinah. According to the majority of scholars, this incident took place three days before the battle of Khaibar.

It has been narrated on the authority of Salamah bin Al-Akwa', the hero of this battle, that the Messenger of Allâh (Peace be upon him) sent his hireling Rabah, with his camels to a nearby pasture. I, taking Talhah's horse, went there for the same purpose. When the day dawned, 'Abdur Rahman Al-Fazari made a raid, drove away all the camels, and killed the man who looked after them. I told Rabah to ride the horse, take it to Talhah and inform the Messenger of Allâh (Peace be upon him) that the polytheists had made away with his camels. Then I stood upon a hillock and turning my face to Madinah, shouted thrice: "Come to our help!" After that I set out in pursuit of the raiders, shooting at them with arrows and chanting (self-eulogatory) verse:

I am the son of Al-Akwa' Today is the day of defeat for the mean.

By Allâh, I continued shooting at them and hamstringing their animals. Whenever a horseman turned upon me, I would come to a tree (hid myself) sitting at its base, shoot at him and hamstring his horse. At last they entered a narrow mountain gorge. I ascended that mountain and held them at bay throwing stones at them. I continued to chase them in this way until I got all the camels released with no one left with them. They fled in all directions and I following and shooting at them continually until they dropped more than thirty mantles and thirty lances, lightening their burden. On everything they dropped, I put a mark with a stone so that the Messenger of Allâh (Peace be upon him) and his Companions might recognize them (that it was booty left by the enemy). They went on until they came to a narrow valley. They sat down to eat something, and I sat on the top of a tapering rock. Four of them ascended the mountain coming towards me. When they were near enough to hear me, I shouted: "Do you recognize me?" They said: "No. Who are you?" I said: "I am Salamah son of Al-Akwa'. I can kill anyone of you I like but none of you can kill me." So they returned. I did not move from my place until I saw the horsemen of the Messenger of Allâh (Peace be upon him), who came riding through the trees. The foremost among them was Akhram, behind him was Abu Qatadah Al-Ansari followed by Al-Miqdad bin Al-Aswad. Akhram and 'Abdur Rahman Al-Fazari met in combat. Akhram hamstrung 'Abdur Rahman's horse but the latter managed to strike him with his lance and kill him. 'Abdur Rahman turned around riding Akhram's horse. Abu Qatadah, seeing this, got engaged in fierce combat with 'Abdur Rahman, smote him with his lance and it was fatal. The polytheists consequently fled away and I was in their pursuit until before sunset they reached a valley with a spring of water called Dhu Qarad. They rested there to have a drink. I however, running in hot pursuit, turned them out of the valley before they could drink a drop of water. Later on, the Prophet (Peace be upon him), along with his Companions, overtook me. I addressed him saying: Messenger of Allâh, let me select from our people one hundred men and I will follow the marauders and finish them. In reply, the Prophet (Peace be upon him) said: "Ibn Al-Akwa', you have taken enough and so now you have to show magnanimity; now they have reached the habitation of Ghatfan where they are being feted." He added saying: "Our best horseman today is Abu Qatadah, and our best footman today is Salamah." He allotted me two shares of the booty - the share meant for the horseman and the other meant for the footman, and combined both of them for me. Intending to return to Madinah, he made me mount behind him on his she-camel called Al-'Adba'.

THE CONQUEST OF KHAIBAR (In Moharram, 7A.H.)

Khaibar was a spacious strongly fortified territory, studded with castles and farms, lying at a distance of 60-80 miles north of Madinah, now a village known for its uncongenial climate. After Al-Hudaibiyah Treaty, the major party of the anti-Islam tripartite coalition — Quraish, the bedouin horde of Najd tribes and the Jews — was neutralized, therefore, the Prophet (Peace be upon him) deemed it an appropriate time to settle his affairs with the other two wings — the Jews and the Najd tribes — in order that peace and security could prevail and the Muslims may devote their time and effort in propagating the Message of Allâh and calling people to embrace it. Khaibar itself had always remained a hotbed of intrigue and conspiracy, and the Jews had always constituted it a source of military provocations and war instigation centre, so it was given a top priority on the agenda of the Prophet's compelling exigencies. The Jews of Khaibar had united by an ancient alliance with the Confederates, triggered Bani Quraiza to practise treachery, maintained contacts with Ghatfan and the Arabians and they even devised an attempt at the Prophet's life. In fact, the continual afflictions that the Muslims had sustained were primarily attributable to the Jews. Envoys were repeatedly sent to them for peaceful settlement, but all in vain. Consequently the Prophet (Peace be upon him) came to the conclusion that a military campaign was a must in order to forestall their hostilities.

Interpreters of the Noble Qur'ân suggest that capturing Khaibar had been a Divine promise implied in Allâh's Words:

- "Allâh has promised you abundant spoils that you will capture, and He has hastened for you this." [48:20]

i.e., Al-Hudaibiyah Peace Treaty and the surrender of Khaibar.

The hypocrites and people weak oheart had hung back from joining the true Muslims in Al-Hudaibiyah campaigns, so now Allâh, the All-Mighty inculcated the following words in His Prophet's ears:

- 'Those who lagged behind will say, when you set forth to take the spoils, 'Allow us to follow you.' They want to change Allâh's Words. Say: 'You shall not follow us; thus Allâh has said beforehand.' Then they will say: 'Nay, you envy us.' Nay, but they understand not except a little." [48:15]

For this reason, the Prophet (Peace be upon him) invited only those who were willing to fight in the cause of Allâh to accompany him in his march against Khaibar. 1400 men only, who had sworn allegiance in response to his call.

Meanwhile, Siba' bin 'Arfatah Al-Ghifari was chosen to run the affairs of Madinah. Another incident of high significance is noteworthy, namely the Islamization of Abu Huraira, a venerable Muslim scholar and an authentic narrator of the Prophetic traditions.

The hypocrites of Arabia took notice of the fresh Islamic intentions so they began to alert the Jews to the imminent military activities. Their chief, 'Abdullah bin Ubai delegated an envoy to the Jews of Khaibar warning them against the dangers approaching, and nerving them to resist the Muslims as they outnumbered the latter and were better equipped. On hearing the news the Jews despatched Kinanah bin Abi Al-Huqaiq and Haudha bin Qais to their former allies, the tribe of Ghatfan requesting military assistance, promising to grant them half the yield of the fruit that their farms could yield if they managed to beat the Muslims.

The Prophet marched by way of Isra Mountain and then went forward with the army till he halted in a valley called Ar-Raji', encamping between Khaibar and Ghatfan so as to prevent the latter from reinforcing the Jews. The guides accompanying him led him to an intersection from which branched out three roads with different designations; all leading to his destination. He abstained from following the first two roads on grounds of their ominous designation and chose the third for its propitious indications.

It is noteworthy that some interesting incidents featured the Muslims' march towards Khaibar; of which we mention the following:

1. It has been narrated on the authority of Salamah bin Al-Akwa', who said: We marched upon Khaibar with the Messenger of Allâh (Peace be upon him). We journeyed during the night. One of the men said to my brother 'Amir: Won't you recite to us some of your verses, 'Amir? So he began to chant his verses to urge the camels, reciting:

- O Allâh, if You had not guided us,
  We would have neither been guided rightly nor practised charity, nor offered prayers.
  We wish to lay down our lives for You; so forgive You our lapses,
  And keep us steadfast when we encounter (our enemies).
  Bestow upon us peace and tranquility,
  Behold, when with a cry they called upon us to help.

The Messenger of Allâh (Peace be upon him) said: "Who is this driver (of the camels)?" They said: "It is 'Amir." He said: "Allâh will show mercy to him." A man said: "Martyrdom is reserved for him; O Messenger of Allâh, would that you had allowed us to benefit ourselves from his life." The Prophet's Companions had already known that he would never invoke Allâh's mercy upon a close Companion but to single him out for martyrdom.

2. On their way down a valley, the Muslims began to entertain Allâh's Greatness: shouting at the top of their voices: "Allâh is Great, Allâh is Great, there is no god but Allâh." The Prophet (Peace be upon him) asked them to lower down their voices saying: "The One you are invoking is neither absent nor deaf; He is close to you, All-hearing."
3. In a spot called As-Sahba', not far from Khaibar, the Prophet (Peace be upon him) observed the afternoon prayer, then he called his Companions to have whatever food provisions they had. What they brought was too scanty to satisfy them all. The Prophet took it by his hand and it immediately grew in quantity, so they all ate to their fill. Shortly afterward, he and the others, rinsed their mouths and performed the evening prayer without ablution; he did the same for the night prayer.

The following morning, at sunrise, the Muslims encountered the Jews when they had come out about their jobs with their axes, spades and strings driving their cattle along. They began to shout in surprise: "Muhammad has come along with his force!" The Messenger of Allâh صلى الله عليه وسلم said: "Allâh is Great, Khaibar shall face destruction. Behold! When we descend in the city centre, it will be a bad day for those who have been warned (but have not taken heed)."

For encampment, the Prophet (Peace be upon him) had chosen a certain plot of land he deemed suitable to serve as the headquarters of his army. However, a veteran fighter of his called Hubab bin Al-Mundhir suggested that they, under the exigencies of war requirements and for the sake of providing maximum logistic facilities, shift to another place. On approaching the vicinity of Khaibar, the Prophet ordered his troops to halt, and began to invoke his Lord saying: "O Allâh! Lord of the seven heavens and what they harbour beneath, Lord of the seven earths and what lies in their wombs, Lord of devils and whomsoever they have led astray; we beseech You to grant us the good of this village (Khaibar), the good of its inhabitants and the good that lies in it. We seek refuge with You from the evil of this village, the evil of its inhabitants, and the evil that lies in it." Then he ordered, "Now march (towards the village) in the Name of Allâh."

"The banner", the Prophet (Peace be upon him) declared "would be entrusted to a man who loves Allâh and His Messenger and they (Allâh and His Messenger) love him." All the Muslims came forward in the following morning hoping to be granted the honour of carrying the banner. The Prophet (Peace be upon him) called for 'Ali bin Abi Talib whose eyes used to hurt, and handed it to him. 'Ali, on his part, pledged he would fight the enemies until they embraced Islam. The Prophet (Peace be upon him) answered him saying: "Take things easy and invite them to accept Islam and brief them on their duties towards Allâh. I swear by Allâh that if only one should be guided through your example, that would surely outweigh the best of our camels."

Khaibar, it seems, was split into two parts with five forts in the first: Na'im, As-Sa'b bin Mu'adh, the castle of Az-Zubair, 'Abi Castle, and An-Nizar in Ash-Shiqq; three others were in part two: Al-Qamus, Al-Wateeh and As-Salalim.

The Actual Operation begins:

The Prophet (Peace be upon him) began the campaign by reducing the minor strongholds one after the other. The first fort he was to attack was Na'im, the first defence line with a formidable strategic position. Marhab, the leader of the fort, invited 'Amr bin Al-Akwa' to meet him in combat and the latter responded; when 'Amr struck the Jew, his sword recoiled and wounded his knee, and he died of that wound. The Prophet (Peace be upon him) later said: "For him ('Amir) there is a double reward in the Hereafter." He indicated this by putting two of his fingers together. 'Ali bin Abi Talib then undertook to meet Marhab in combat, and managed to kill him. Yasir, Marhab's brother, then turned up challenging the Muslims to a fight. Az-Zubair was equal to it and killed him on the spot. Real fighting then broke out and lasted for a few days. The Jews showed courage and proved to be too formidable even to the repeated rushes of the veteran soldiers of Islam. However, they later realized the futility of resistance and began to abandon their positions in An-Na'im and infiltrate into the fortress of As-Sa'b.

Al-Hubab bin Al-Mundhir Al-Ansari led the attack on As-Sa'b fortress and laid siege to it for three days after which the Muslims stormed it with a lot of booty, provisions and food to fall to their lot therein. This victory came in the wake of the Prophet's (Peace be upon him) invocation to Allâh to help Banu Aslam in their relentless and daring attempts to capture that fort.

During the process of the war operations, extreme hunger struck the Muslims. They lit fires, slaughtered domestic asses and beto cook them. When the Prophet (Peace be upon him) inquired about the fires and cooking, he ordered that they throw away the meat and wash the cooking pots, forbidding the practice of eating such meat.

The Jews, meanwhile, evacuated An-Natat and barricaded themselves in Az-Zubair fort, a formidable defensive position inaccessible to both cavalry and infantry. The Muslims besieged it for three days, but in vain. A Jew spy told the Prophet about a subterranean water source that provided them with water, and advised that it be cut off in order to undermine their resistance. The Prophet (Peace be upon him) did that so the Jews got out to engage with the Muslims in fierce fighting during which some Muslims and ten Jews were killed, but the fort was eventually conquered.

Shortly after this battle, the Jews moved to 'Abi Castle and barricaded themselves inside. The same events recurred; the Muslims besieged the new site for three days and then the great Muslim hero Abu Dujanah Sammak bin Kharshah Al-Ansari — of the red ribbon — led the Muslim army and broke into the castle, conducted fierce military operations within and forced the remaining Jews to flee for their lives into another fort, An-Nizar.

An-Nizar was the most powerful fort, and the Jews came to the established conviction that it was too immune to be stormed, so they deemed it a safe place for their children and women. The Muslims, however, were not dismayed but dragged on the siege, but because standing at a commanding top, the fort was impregnable. The Jews inside were too cowardly to meet the Muslims in open fight but rather hurled a shower of arrows and stones on the attackers. Considering this situation, the Prophet (Peace be upon him) ordered that rams be used and these proved effective and caused cracks in the ramparts providing an easy access into the heart of the fort, where the Jews were put to rout and fled in all directions leaving behind their women and children.

With these series of military victories, the first division of Khaibar was totally reduced, and the Jews in the other minor fortresses evacuated them and fled to the second division.

THE SECOND PART OF OF KHAIBAR CONQURED:

When the Prophet (Peace be upon him), along with his army, moved to this part of Khaibar, Al-Katiba, he laid a heavy siege to it for fourteen days with the Jews barricading themselves inside their forts. When he was about to use the rams, the Jews realized that they would perish, therefore, they asked for a negotiable peace treaty.

There is one controversial point in this context. Was this part of Khaibar (with its three forts) conquered by force? Ibn Ishaq clearly stated that Al-Qamus fort was conquered by force. Al-Waqidi, on the other hand, maintained that the three forts were taken through peace negotiations, and force, if any, was resorted to only to hand the fort over to the Muslims; the two other forts surrendered without fighting.

NEGOTIATIONS:

Ibn Abi Al-Huqaiq was despatched to the Messenger of Allâh (Peace be upon him) to negotiate the surrender treaty. The Prophet (Peace be upon him) agreed to spare their lives on condition they evacuate Khaibar and the adjacent land, leaving whatever gold and silver they had in their possession. However, he stipulated that he would disavow any commitment if they concealed anything. Shortly afterwards, the forts were handed over to the Muslims and all Khaibar was reduced and brought under the sway of Islam.

This treaty notwithstanding, Abi Al-Huqaiq's two sons concealed a leather bag full of jewels, and money belonging to Huyai bin Al-Akhtab, who carried it with him when Banu Nadir had been banished. Kinanah bin Ar-Rabi', who had hidden the musk somewhere, was obdurate in his denial and so he was killed when the musk was discovered and his dishonesty was proven. Abi Al-Huqaiq's two sons were killed in recompense for breaching the covenant, and Safiyah, Huyai's daughter was taken as a captive.

DISTRIBUTION OF SPOILS:

In accordance with the agreement already concluded, the Jews would be obliged to evacuate Khaibar, but they were anxious to keep on cultivating the rich soil and fine orchard for which Khaibar was famous. They, therefore, approached the Prophet (Peace be upon him) with the request that they be allowed to cultivate their lands and they would give half of the produce to the Muslims. Muhammad (Peace be upon him) was kind enough to accede to their request.

The Messenger (Peace be upon him) divided the land of Khaibar into two: one half to provide the food to be stored in case of any accidental calamity that might befall the Muslims, and for entertaining the foreign delegates who started to frequent Madinah a lot; the other half would go to the Muslims who had witnessed Al-Hudaibiyah event whether present or absent. The total number of shares came to 36, of which 18 were given to the people above-mentioned. The army consisted of 1400 men of whom were 200 horsemen. The horseman was allotted 3 shares and the footman one.

The spoils taken at Khaibar were so great that Ibn 'Umar said: "We never ate our fill until we had conquered Khaibar." 'Aishah (May Allah be pleased with her) is narrated to have said: "Now we can eat our fill of dates."

On their return to Madinah, the Emigrants were able to return to the Helpers of Madinah all the gifts they had received. All of this affluence came after the conquest of Khaibar and the great economic benefits that the Muslims began to reap.

The conquest of Khaibar coincided with the arrival of the Prophet's cousin Ja'far bin Abi Talib and his companions along with Abi Musa Al-Ash'ari and some Muslims from Abyssinia (Ethiopia).

Abu Musa Al-Ash'ari narrated that he and over fifty companions, while in Yemen, took a ship which landed them in Abyssinia (Ethiopia) and they happened to meet there Ja'far and his companions. He said, "We stayed together until the Prophet (Peace be upon him) sent an envoy asking us to come back. When we returned, we found out that he had already conquered Khaibar, yet he gave us our due shares of the spoils." The advent of those men came at the request made by the Messenger of Allâh (Peace be upon him) to Negus, king of Abyssinia (Ethiopia), through a Prophetic deputy, 'Amr bin Omaiya Ad-Damari. Negus sent them back, 16 men altogether with their wives and children on two boats. The rest of emigrants had arrived in Madinah earlier.

In the same context, Safiyah, whose husband Kinanah bin Abi Al-Huqaiq was killed for treachery, was taken as a captive and brought along with other prisoners of war. After the permission of the Prophet (Peace be upon him) was sought, Dihyah Al-Kalbi chose one of them and she happened to be Safiyah. The other Muslims, however, advised that Safiyah, being the daughter of the chief of Bani Quraiza and Bani Nadir, should be married to the Prophet (Peace be upon him), who agreed to their opinion, invited her to Islam, freed and took her as wife on her embracing Islam. The wedding feast consisted of dates and fat, and was held on his way back to Madinah at a spot called Sadd As-Sahba'.

After the conquest of Khaibar, a Jewish woman called Zainab bint Al-Harith offered the Prophet (Peace be upon him) a roasted sheep she had poisoned. He took a mouthful, but it was not to his liking so he spat it out. After investigation, the woman confessed that she had stuffed the food with poison alleging that if the eater were a king, she would then rid herself of him, but should he be a Prophet, then he would be bound to learn about it. The Prophet (Peace be upon him), however, connived at her treacherous attempt, but ordered that she be killed when Bishr bin Al-Bara' died of that poison.

The number of Muslims who were martyred was controversial, but it ranged between 16 and 18, while the number of Jews killed came to 93.

The rest of Khaibar also fell to the Muslims. Allâh cast fear into the hearts of the people of Fadak, a village standing to the north of Khaibar, and they hastened to ask for peace, and be allowed to leave in safety, and give up their wealth in return for that. The Prophet (Peace be upon him) entered into an agreement with them similar to the previous one with the people of Khaib. Fadak was exclusively the Prophet's because neither Muslim cavalry nor camelry were involved in fight thereby.

No sooner had the Prophet (Peace be upon him) discharged the affair of Khaibar than he started a fresh move towards Wadi Al-Qura, another Jewish colony in Arabia. He mobilized his forces and divided them into three regiments with four banners entrusted to Sa'd bin 'Ubada, Al-Hubab bin Mundhir, 'Abbad bin Bishr and Sahl bin Haneef. Prior to fighting, he invited the Jews to embrace Islam but all his words and exhortations fell on deaf ears. Eleven of the Jews were killed one after another and with each one newly killed, a fresh call was extended inviting those people to profess the new faith. Fighting went on ceaselessly for approximately two days and resulted in full surrender of the Jews. Their land was conquered, and a lot of booty fell in the hands of the Muslims.

The Prophet (Peace be upon him) stayed in Wadi Al-Qura for four days, distributed the booty among the Muslim fighters and reached an agreement with the Jews similar to that of Khaibar.

The Jews of Taima', hearing beforehand about the successive victories of the Muslim army and the defeats that their brethren, the Jews, had sustained, showed no resistance when the Prophet (Peace be upon him) reached their habitation. On the contrary, they took the initiative and offered to sign a reconciliation treaty to the effect that they receive protection but pay tribute in return. Having achieved his objective and subdued the Jews completely, the Prophet (Peace be upon him) made his way back home and arrived in Madinah in late Safar or early Rabi' Al-Awwal 7 A.H.

It is noteworthy that the Prophet (Peace be upon him), being the best amongst war experts, realized quite readily that evacuating Madinah after the lapse of the prohibited months (Muharram, Dhul Qa'da and Dhul Hijja) would not be wise at all with the presence of the desert bedouins roaming in its vicinity. Such a careless attitude, the Prophet (Peace be upon him) believed, would tempt the undisciplined mob to practise their favourite hobby of plundering, looting and all acts of piracy. This premonition always in mind, the Prophet (Peace be upon him) despatched Aban bin Sa'id at the head of a platoon to deter those bedouins and forestall any attempt at raiding the headquarters of the nascent Islamic state during his absence in Khaibar. Aban achieved his task successfully and joined the Prophet صلى الله عليه وسلم

in Khaibar after it had been conquered.

Sporadic Invasions

The Expedition called Dhat-ur-Riqa' (in the year 7 A.H.):

Having subdued two powerful sides of the Confederates coalition, the Prophet peace be upon him started preparations to discipline the third party, i.e. the desert bedouins, who took Najd for habitation, and continued in their usual practices of looting and plundering. Unlike the Jews of Khaibar and people of Makkah, they had a liking for living in the wilderness dispersed in scattered spots, hence the difficulty of bringing them under control, and the futility of carrying out deterrent campaigns against them. However, the Prophet peace be upon him was determined to put an end to this unacceptable situation and called the Muslims around him to get ready to launch a decisive campaign against those harassing rebels. Meanwhile it was reported to him that Bani Muharib and Banu Tha'lbah of the Ghatfan tribe were gathering army in order to encounter the Muslims. The Prophet peace be upon him proceeded towards Najd at the head of 400 or 700 men, after he had mandated Abu Dhar - in another version, 'Uthman bin 'Affan - to dispose the affairs of Madinah during his absence. The Muslim fighters penetrated deep into their land until they reached a spot called Nakhlah where they came across some bedouins of Ghatfan, but no fighting took place because the latter had agreed to go into reconciliation with the Muslims. The Prophet peace be upon him led his followers that day in a prayer of fear.

Al-Bukhari, on the authority of Abu Musa Al-Ash'ari, narrated that they set out on an expedition with the Messenger of Allâh peace be upon him. "We were six in number and had (with us) only one camel which we rode turn by turn. Our feet were injured. My feet were so badly injured that my nails came off. We, therefore, bandaged our feet with rags, so this expedition was called Dhat-ur-Riqa' (i.e. the expedition of rags.)"

Jabir narrated: In the course of Dhat-ur-Riqa' expedition, we came to a leafy tree where the Prophet peace be upon him sat shading himself off the burning sun. The others dispersed here and there seeking shelter from heat. The Prophet peace be upon him had a short nap after he had hung his sword on the tree. A polytheist, meanwhile came, seized the sword and unsheathed it.

The Prophet peace be upon him woke up to find his sword drawn in the man's hand. The bedouin here asked the Prophet (unarmed then): "Who would hold me back from killing you now?" The Prophet peace be upon him then answered: "It is Allâh." In another version, it was reported that the Prophet peace be upon him took the sword when it had fallen down and the man said: "You (the Prophet) are the best one to hold a sword." The Prophet peace be upon him asked the man if he would testify to the Oneness of Allâh and the Messengership of Muhammad. The Arabian answered that he would never engage in a fight against him, nor would he ally people fighting the Muslims. The Prophet peace be upon him set the man free and let him go to his people to say to them that he had seen the best one among all people.

A woman from the Arabians was taken prisoner in the context of this battle. Her husband, on hearing the news, swore he would never stop until he had shed the blood of a Muslim. Secretly at night, he approached the camp of the Muslims when he saw two sentries stationed there to alert the Muslims against any emergency. He shot the first one, Abbad bin Bishr, who was observing prayer, with an arrow but he did not stop prayer, he simply pulled it out. Then he was shot by three other arrows but would not interrupt his prayer. After he had done the closing salutations, he awakened his companion 'Ammar bin Yasir, who remonstrated that he should have alerted him to which the latter replied that he was half way through a Chapter and did not like to interrupt it.

The victory at the expedition of Dhat-ur-Riqa' had a tremendous impact on all the Arabians. It cast fear into their hearts and rendered them too powerless to antagonize the Muslim society in Madinah. They began to acquiesce in the prevailing situation and resigned themselves to new geo-political conditions working in favour of the new religion. Some of them even embraced Islam and took an active part in the conquest of Makkah and the battle of Hunain, and received their due shares of the war booty.

From that time onward, the anti-Islam tripartite coalition had been subdued, and peace and security prevailed. The Muslims, then started to redress any political imbalance and fill in the small gaps that still triggered unrest here and there in the face of the great drive of Islamization that enveloped the whole area. We could in this context mention some of these incidental skirmishes which pointed markedly to the ever-growing power of the Muslim society.

- 1. A platoon headed by Ghalib bin 'Abdullah Al-Laithi in Safar or in Rabi' Al-Awwal 7 A.H. was despatched to muffle the provocative behaviour of Bani Al-Muluh. The Muslims managed to kill a large number of the enemy soldiers and captured a great deal of booty. A large army of polytheists rushed in their heel but floods hindered the pursuit, and the Muslims managed to withdraw in safety.
- 2. 'Umar bin Al-Khattab, at the head of a 30-soldier group, set out to a spot called Turbah in Sha'ban 7 A.H. to discipline the people of Hawazin. He no longer arrived at their habitation that they fled for their lives.
- 3. Thirty men with Basheer bin Sa'd Al-Ansari headed for Bani Murrah in Sha'ban 7 A.H. in Fadak area. He killed a large number of the enemy and seized a lot of their camels and cattle. On his way back, the enemy gathered up forces and overtook the Muslims at night. They showered Basheer and his men with arrows, and killed all the Muslims except Basheer, who took refuge in Fadak and stayed with the Jews there until his wounds healed.
- 4. Ghalib bin 'Abdullah Al-Laithi at the head of a platoon of 130 men launched an attack against Bani 'Awâl and Bani 'Abd bin Tha'lbah in Ramadan 7 A.H. They killed some of the enemy's men and captured their cattle and camels. 'Usama bin Zaid killed Mardas bin Nahik, a polytheist, but after he had pronounced the testimony of Allâh's Oneness to which incident the Prophet peace be upon him commented addressing his Companions: "Would you rip open his heart to discern whether he is truthful or a liar?"
- 5. A thirty-horseman group headed by 'Abdullah bin Rawaha marched towards Khaibar on reports that Aseer (or Basheer bin Razam) was rallying the ranks of Bani Ghatfan to attack the Muslims: They managed to persuade that Jew to follow them to Madinah encouraging him that the Prophet peace be upon him would institute him as a ruler of Khaibar. On their way back there occurred a sort of misunderstanding that gave rise to fierce fighting between the two parties resulting in the death of Aseer and the thirty men with him.
- 6. In Shawwal 7 A.H., Basheer bin Sa'd Al-Ansari marched towards Yemen and Jabar at the head of 300 Muslim fighters to subdue a large mob of polytheists who gathered to raid the outskirts of Madinah. Basheer and his men used to march at night and lurk during the day until they reached their destination. Having heard about the advent of the Muslims, the polytheists fled away leaving behind them a large booty and two men who later embraced Islam on arrival in Madinah.
- 7. In the year 7 A.H., shortly before the Compensatory 'Umrah (lesser pilgrimage), a man called Jashm bin Mu'awiyah came to a spot called Ghabah where he wanted to gather the people of Qais and entice them into fighting the Muslims. The Prophet peace be upon him, on hearing these reports, despatched Abu Hadrad with two men to see to the situation. Abu Hadrad, through a clever strategy, managed to rout the enemy and capture a lot of their cattle.

The Compensatory 'Umrah (Lesser Pilgrimage)

When Dhul Qa'da month approached towards the close of the seventh year A.H., the Prophet peace be upon him ordered his people, and the men who witnessed Al-Hudaibiyah Truce Treaty in particular, to make preparations to perform 'Umrah (lesser pilgrimage). He proceeded with 2000 men besides some women and children, and 60 camels for sacrifice, to visit the Holy Sanctuary in Makkah. The Muslims took their weapons with them fearing the treachery of the Quraishites, but left them with a party of two hundred men at a place some eight miles from Makkah. They entered the city with the swords in their scabbards, with the Prophet peace be upon him at their head on his she-camel, Al-Qaswa', while the surrounding Companions attentively focusing their look on him, all saying: "Here I am! at Your service O Allâh!" The Quraishites had left the place and retired to their tents on the adjoining hills. The Muslims performed the usual circumambulation vigorously and briskly; and on recommendation by the Prophet peace be upon him they did their best to appear strong and steadfast in their circumambulation as the polytheists had spread rumours that they were weak because the fever of Yathrib (Madinah) had sapped their strength. They were ordered to run in the first three rounds and then walk in the remaining ones. The Makkans meanwhile aligned on the top of Qu'aiqa'an Mount watching the Muslims, tongue-tied at witnessing their strength and devotion. When they entered the Holy Sanctuary, 'Abdullah bin Rawaha walked before the Prophet peace be upon him reciting:

"Get out of his way, you disbelievers, make way, we will fight you about its revelation with strokes that will remove heads from shoulders and make friend unmindful of friend." After ritual walking and running between the two hills of Makkah, Safa and Marwah, the Prophet peace be upon him with the Muslims halted at the latter spot to slaughter the sacrificial animals and shave their heads.

The main body of the pilgrims had now performed the basic rites of the lesser pilgrimage, but there remained those who were entrusted the charge of the weapons. The Prophet had these relieved, and they went through the same devotions as the others did.

On the morning of the fourth day of the pilgrimage, the notables of Quraish asked 'Ali bin Abi Talib to tell the Prophet peace be upon him to leave Makkah along with his Companions. He, of course, could not conceive of violating the terms of Al-Hudaibiyah Treaty, therefore he ordered his men to depart for a village called Sarif where he stayed for some time.

It was during this visit of the Prophet peace be upon him to Makkah for pilgrimage that his uncle 'Abbas offered the hand of his sister-in-law, Maimuna - the daughter of Harith, to him. The Prophet peace be upon him was kind enough to accept this offer since it was an effective step towards cementing the ties of relationship between the Prophet peace be upon him and the influential men of Makkah. The wedding took place in Sarif.

Narrators attached different designations to this lesser pilgrimage. Some called it the compensatory lesser pilgrimage, performed instead of that uncompleted of Hudaibiyah; and the other one, given preponderance by jurists, is the lesser pilgrimage consequent on certain terms of a treaty already agreed upon. On the whole, compensatory, judicial consent, retribution and reconciliation are all terms applicable to that visit.

Some military operations, directed against some still obdurate desert Arabians, took place at the conclusion of the lesser pilgrimage, of which we could mention:

- 1. A platoon of 50 men led by Ibn Abi Al-'Awja' was despatched by the Prophet peace be upon him to the habitations of Bani Saleem inviting them to embrace Islam, but all the words fell on deaf ears. Fierce fighting erupted between both parties during which the Muslim leader was wounded, and two of the enemy were captured.
- 2. Ghalib bin 'Abdullah at the head of 200 men was despatched to Fadak where they killed some rebels and a lot of booty fell to their lot.
- 3. Banu Quda'a had gathered a large number of men to raid the Muslim positions. On hearing the news, the Prophet peace be upon him despatched Ka'b bin 'Umair Al-Ansari at the head of 15 men to deal with this situation. They encountered the army, and called them to enter into the fold of Islam but the rebels gave a negative response and showered the Muslims with arrows killing all of them except one who was carried back home later seriously wounded.

There was also an insignificant skirmish that occurred in Rabi' Al-Awwal 8 A.H. Shuja' bin Wahab Al-Asadi, along with 25 men, marched towards Bani Hawazin tribe where they encountered no resistance but managed to gain some booty.

The Battle of Mu'tah

It was the most significant and the fiercest battle during the lifetime of the Messenger of Allâh peace be upon him, a preliminary and a prelude to the great conquests of the land of the Christians. It took place in Jumada Al-Ula 8 A.H. / September 629 A.D. Mu'tah is a village that lies on the borders of geographical Syria.

The Prophet peace be upon him had sent Al-Harith bin 'Umair Al-Azdi on an errand to carry a letter to the ruler of Busra. On his way, he was intercepted by Sharhabeel bin 'Amr Al-Ghassani, the governor of

Al-Balqa' and a close ally to Caesar, the Byzantine Emperor. Al-Harith was tied and beheaded by Al-Ghassani.

Killing envoys and messengers used to be regarded as the most awful crime, and amounted to the degree of war declaration. The Prophet peace be upon him was shocked on hearing the news and ordered that a large army of 3000 men be mobilized and despatched to the north to discipline the transgressors. It was the largest Muslim army never mobilized on this scale except in the process of the Confederates Battle.

Zaid bin Haritha was appointed to lead the army. Ja'far bin Abi Talib would replace him if he was killed, and 'Abdullah bin Rawaha would succeed Ja'far in case the latter fell. A white banner was raised and handed over to Zaid.

The Prophet peace be upon him recommended that they reach the scene of Al-Harith's murder and invite the people to profess Islam. Should the latter respond positively, then no war would ensue, otherwise fighting them would be the only alternative left. He ordered them:

"Fight the disbelievers in the Name of Allâh, neither breach a covenant nor entertain treachery, and under no circumstances a new-born, woman, an ageing man or a hermit should be killed; moreover neither trees should be cut down nor homes demolished." At the conclusion of the military preparations, the people of Madinah gathered and bade the army farewell. 'Abdullah bin Rawaha began to weep at that moment, and when asked why he was weeping, he swore that it was not love for this world nor under a motive of infatuation with the glamour of life but rather the Words of Allâh speaking of Fire that he heard the Prophet peace be upon him reciting:

"There is not one of you but will pass over it (Hell); this is with your Lord, a Decree which must be accomplished." [19:71]

The Muslim army then marched northward to Ma'ân, a town bordering on geographical Syria. There news came to the effect that Heraclius had mobilized a hundred thousand troops together with another hundred thousand men of Lakham, Judham and Balqain - Arabian tribes allied to the Byzantines. The Muslims, on their part had never thought of encountering such a huge army. They were at a loss about what course to follow, and spent two nights debating these unfavourable conditions. Some suggested that they should write a letter to the Prophet peace be upon him seeking his advice. 'Abdullah bin Rawaha was opposed to them being reluctant and addressed the Muslims saying: "I swear by Allâh that this very object which you hold in abhorrence is the very one you have set out seeking, martyrdom. In our fight we don't count on number of soldiers or equipment but rather on the Faith that Allâh has honoured us with. Dart to win either of the two, victory or martyrdom." In the light of these words, they moved to engage with the enemy in Masharif, a town of Al-Balqa', and then changed direction towards Mu'tah where they encamped. The right flank was led by Qutba bin Qatadah Al-'Udhari, and the left by 'Ubadah bin Malik Al-Ansari. Bitter fighting started between the two parties, three thousand Muslims against an enemy fiftyfold as large.

Zaid bin Haritha, the closest to the Messenger's heart, assumed leadership and began to fight tenaciously and in matchless spirit of bravery until he fell, fatally stabbed. Ja'far bin Abi Talib then took the banner and did a miraculous job. In the thick of the battle, he dismounted, hamstrung his horse and resumed fighting until his right hand was cut off. He seized the banner with his left hand until this too was gone. He then clasped the banner with both arms until a Byzantine soldier struck and cut him into two parts. he was posthumously called "the flying Ja'far" or "Ja'far with two wings" because Allâh has awarded him two wings to fly wherever he desired there in the eternal Garden. Al-Bukhari reported fifty stabs in his body, none of them in the back.

'Abdullah bin Rawaha then proceeded to hold up the banner and fight bravely on his horseback while reciting enthusiastic verses until he too was killed. Thereupon a man, from Bani 'Ajlan, called Thabit bin Al-Arqam took the banner and called upon the Muslims to choose a leader. The honour was unanimously granted to Khalid bin Al-Waleed, a skilled brave fighter and an outstanding strategist. It was reported by Al-Bukhari that he used nine swords that broke while he was relentlessly and courageously fighting the enemies of Islam. He, however, realizing the grave situation the Muslims were in, began to follow a different course of encounter, revealing the super strategy-maker, that Khalid was rightly called. He reshuffled the right and left flanks of the Muslim army and introduced forward a division from the rear in order to cast fear into the hearts of the Byzantine by deluding them that fresh reinforcements had arrived. The Muslims engaged with the enemies in sporadic skirmishes but gradually and judiciously retreating in a fully organized and well-planned withdrawal.

The Byzantines, seeing this new strategy, believed that they were being entrapped and drawn in the heart of the desert. They stopped the pursuit, and consequently the Muslims managed to retreat back to Madinah with the slightest losses. The Muslims sustained twelve martyrs, whereas the number of casualties among the Byzantines was unknown although the details of the battle point clearly to a large number. Even though the battle did not satisfy the Muslims' objective, namely avenging Al-Harith's murder, it resulted in a far-ranging impact and attached to the Muslims a great reputation in the battlefields.

The Byzantine Empire, at that time, was a power to be reckoned with, and mere thinking of antagonizing it used to mean self-annihilation, let alone a three-thousand-soldier army going into fight against 200,000 soldiers far better equipped and lavishly furnished with all luxurious conveniences. The battle was a real miracle proving that the Muslims were something exceptional not then familiar. Moreover, it gave evidence that Allâh backed them and their Prophet, Muhammad, was really Allâh's Messenger. In the light of these new strategic changes, the archenemies among the desert bedouins began to reconcile themselves with the new uprising faith and several recalcitrant tribes like Banu Saleem, Ashja', Ghatfan, Dhubyan, Fazarah and others came to profess Islam out of their own sweet free will.

Mu'tah Battle, after all, constituted the forerunner of the blood encounter to take place with the Byzantines subsequently. It pointed markedly to a new epoch of the Islamic conquest of the Byzantine empire and other remote countries, to follow at a later stage.

Dhat As-Salasil Campaign:

Dhat As-Salasil is a spot situated ten days' walk north of Madinah. The Muslims are said to have encamped in a place with a well of water called Salsal, hence the terminology Dhat As-Salasil. In view of the alliance between the Arabian tribes on the borders of Syria and the Byzantines, the Prophet peace be upon him deemed it of top urgency to carry out a wisely-planned manoeuvre that might bring about a state of rapport with those bedouins, and would at the same time detach them from the Byzantines. For the implementation of this plan, he chose 'Amr bin Al-'As, whose paternal grandmother came from Bali, a tribe dwelling in that area. This motive in mind, combined with provocative military movements, by Bani Quda'a, precipitated this preemptive strike which started in Jumada Ath-Thaniya, 8 A.H.

'Amr bin Al-'As was awarded a white flag with a black banner to go with it. He set out at the head of 300 Emigrants and Helpers assisted by a cavalry of 30 men, and was recommended to seek help from Bali, 'Udhra and Balqain tribes. He used to march at night and lurk during the day. On approaching the enemy lines and realizing the large build up of men, he sent for reinforcements from Madinah, and these arrived on the spot headed by Abu 'Ubaidah bin Al-Jarrah leading further 200 men as well as other platoons including Abu Bakr and 'Umar bin Al-Khattab. All of them were given strict orders to cooperate, work in harmony and never leave any area for disagreement. At noon, Abu 'Ubaidah wanted to lead the Muslims in prayer, but 'Amr objected on grounds that the former came only to assist, and leadership in prayer was given to 'Amr.

The Muslim army reached the habitations of Quda'a and penetrated deep in their land, destroyed the enemies and obliged the others to flee for their lives in different directions. At the conclusion of the military operations, a courier was despatched to the Messenger of Allâh peace be upon him to brief him on the developments of events and the ultimate victory achieved.

Khadrah Campaign:

In Sha'ban month 8 A.H., news reached the Prophet peace be upon him of amassing troops by Bani Ghatfan, still outside the domain of Islam. He urgently summoned Abu Qatadah and sent him at the head of fifteen men to discipline those outlaws. It took fifteen days to teach them an unforgettable lesson. Some were killed, others captured and all their property confiscated.

The Conquest of Makkah

Ibn Al-Qaiyim described the conquest of Makkah as the greatest one by which Allâh honoured His religion, Messenger, soldiers and honest party. He thereby rescued the Sacred House, whose guidance all people seek. It was the greatest propitious event in heaven and on earth. It was the most significant prelude to a new era that was to witness the great march of Islamization and the entry of people into the fold of Islam in huge hosts. It provided an ever shining face and a most glowing source of inspiration to the whole earth.

Pre-Conquest Events:

According to the terms of the treaty of Hudaibiyah, the Arab tribes were given the option to join either of the parties, the Muslims or Quraish, with which they desired to enter into treaty alliance. Should any of these tribes suffer aggression, then the party to which it was allied would have the right to retaliate. As a consequence, Banu Bakr joined Quraish, and Khuza'ah joined the Prophet peace be upon him. They thus lived in peace for sometime but ulterior motives stretching back to pre-Islamic period ignited by unabated fire of revenge triggered fresh hostilities. Banu Bakr, without caring a bit for the provisions of the treaty, attacked Banu Khuza'ah in a place called Al-Wateer in Sha'ban, 8 A.H. Quraish helped Banu Bakr with men and arms taking advantage of the dark night. Pressed by their enemies, the tribesmen of Khuza'ah sought the Holy Sanctuary, but here too, their lives were not spared, and, contrary to all accepted traditions, Nawfal, the chief of Banu Bakr, chasing them in the sanctified area - where no blood should be shed - massacred his adversaries.

When the aggrieved party sought justice from their Muslim allies, the Prophet peace be upon him, as their leader, demanded an immediate redress for not only violating the treaty but also slaying men allied to him in the sanctified area. Three demands were made, the acceptance of any one of them was imperative:

- a) to pay blood money for the victims of Khuza'ah,
- b) to terminate their alliance with Banu Bakr; or
- c) to consider the truce to have been nullified.

This behaviour on the part of Quraish was clearly a breach of the treaty of Al-Hudaibiyah and was obviously an act of hostility against the allies of the Muslims, i.e. Banu Khuza'ah. Quraish immediately realized the grave situation and feared the horrible consequences looming on the horizon. They immediately called for an emergency meeting and decided to delegate their chief Abu Sufyan to Madinah for a renewal of the truce. He directly headed for the house of his daughter Umm Habiba (the Prophet's wife). But as he went to sit on the Messenger's carpet, she folded it up. "My daughter," said he, "I hardly knew if you think the carpet is too good for me or that I am too good for the carpet." She replied, "It is the Messenger of Allâh's carpet, and you are an unclean polytheist."

Being disgusted at the curt reply of his daughter, Abu Sufyan stepped out of her room and went to see the Prophet peace be upon him, but the latter was well aware of his tricks and did not hold him any assurance. He then approached Abu Bakr, but the latter too declined to interfere. He contacted 'Umar to intercede but this great Companion made a point-blank refusal. At last he saw 'Ali bin Abi Talib and began begging him in the most humble words, cunningly alluding to the prospects of mastery over all the Arabs if he were to intercede for the renewal of the treaty. 'Ali also briefly regretted his inability to do anything for him. Abu Sufyan turned his steps back to Makkah in a state of bitter disappointment and utter horror. There he submitted a report of his meeting with his daughter, Abu Bakr, 'Umar and 'Ali's reaction and the meaningful silence of the Prophet. The Makkans were dismayed, but did not expect imminent danger.

Preparations for the Attack on Makkah, and the Prophet's Attempt at imposing a News Black-out:

On the authority of At-Tabari, the Messenger of Allâh peace be upon him asked 'Aishah رضى‌الله عنها, his spouse three days prior to receiving news relating to breaching of covenant, to make preparations peculiar to marching out for war. Abu Bakr, meanwhile, came in and asked 'Aishah رضى‌الله عنها what the matter was, showing surprise at the preparations being made as it was not, as he said, the usual time for war. She replied that she had no idea. On the morning of the third day 'Amr bin Sâlim Al-Khuza'i arrived in the company of forty horsemen to brief the Prophet peace be upon him on the plight of his people and seeking the Muslims' help for retaliation. People of Madinah then got to know that Quraish had breached the covenant. Budail followed 'Amr, and then Abu Sufyan and the news was unequivocally confirmed.

With view of securing a complete news black-out concerning his military intentions, the Prophet peace be upon him despatched an eight-men platoon under the leadership of Qatadah bin Rab'i in the direction of Edam, a short distance from Madinah, in Ramadan 8 A.H., in order to divert the attention of people and screen off the main target with which he was preoccupied.

There was so much dread and fear everywhere that Hatib, one of the most trusted followers of the Prophet peace be upon him secretly despatched a female messenger with a letter to Makkah containing intimation of the intended attack. The Prophet peace be upon him received news from the heaven of Hatib's action and sent 'Ali and Al-Miqdad with instructions to go after her. They overtook the messenger, and after a long search discovered the letter carefully hidden in her locks. The Prophet peace be upon him summoned Hatib and asked him what had induced him to this act. He replied, "O Messenger of Allâh peace be upon him! I have no affinity of blood with Quraish; there is only a kind of friendly relationship between them and myself. My family is at Makkah and there is no one to look after it or to offer protection to it. My position stands in striking contrast to that of the refugees whose families are secure due to their blood ties with Quraish. I felt that since I am not related to them, I should, for the safety of my children, earn their gratitude by doing good to them. I swear by Allâh that I have not done this act as an apostate, forsaking Islam. I was prompted only by the considerations I have just explained."

'Umar wanted to cut his head off as a hypocrite, but the Prophet peace be upon him accepted his excuse and granted him pardon, then addressed 'Umar saying: "Hatib is one of those who fought in the battle of Badr. How do you know that he is a hypocrite? Allâh is likely to look favourably on those who participated in that battle. Turning then, to Hatib, he said: "Do as you please, for I have forgiven you."

After making full preparation, the Prophet peace be upon him proceeded to Makkah at the head of ten thousand soldiers on the 10th of Ramadan, 8 A.H. He mandated Abu Ruhm Al-Ghifari to dispose the affairs of Madinah during his absence. When they reached Al-Juhfa, Al-'Abbas bin 'Abdul Muttalib and his family came to join the Prophet peace be upon him. At Al-Abwa', the Muslims came across Abu Sufyan bin Al-Harith and 'Abdullah bin Omaiyah, the Prophet's cousins, but, on account of the harm they had inflicted, and their satiric language, on the believers, they were not welcomed. 'Ali addressed Abu Sufyan to go and beseech the Prophet peace be upon him for pardon and confess his ill-behaviour in a manner similar to that of Yusuf's (the Prophet Joseph) brothers:

"They said: 'By Allâh! Indeed Allâh has preferred you above us, and we certainly have been sinners.'" [12:91] Abu Sufyan observed 'Ali's counsel, to which the Prophet quoted Allâh's Words:

"He said: 'No reproach on you this day, may Allâh forgive you, and He is the Most Merciful of those who show mercy!'" [12:92]

Abu Sufyan recited some verses paying a generous tribute to the Prophet peace be upon him and professing Islam as his only religion.

The Muslims then marched on in a state of fasting until they reached a place called Al-Qadeed where water was available. There they broke fast and resumed their movement towards Mar Az-Zahran. The Quraishites were quite unaware of the development of affairs, but the Prophet peace be upon him did not like to take them by surprise. He, therefore, ordered his men to kindle fire on all sides for cooking purposes. The idea behind this was that Quraish should be afforded full opportunity to assess the situation in which they were pitchforked correctly, and should not endanger their lives by leaping blindly in the battlefield. 'Umar bin Al-Khattab was entrusted with the guard duty. In the meanwhile, Abu Sufyan along with Hakim bin Hizam and Budail bin Warqua', two terrible polytheists, went out to reconnoiter. Before they got near the camp, they met 'Abbas, the Prophet's uncle. He apprised Abu Sufyan of the situation and advised him to accept Islam and persuade his people to surrender before Muhammad peace be upon him; otherwise, his head would be struck off.

Under the prevailing compelling circumstances, Abu Sufyan went in the company of 'Abbas seeking the Prophet's peace be upon him audience. The Muslims were furious to see Abu Sufyan and wanted to kill him on the spot. But the two men managed, not without difficulties, to see the Messenger of Allâh peace be upon him who advised that they see him the following day. The Prophet peace be upon him addressed Abu Sufyan saying: "Woe to you! Isn't it time for you to bear witness to the Oneness of Allâh and Prophethood of Muhammad?" Here, the archenemy of Islam began to beseech the Prophet peace be upon him in the most earnest words that testify to the Prophet's generosity and mild temper begging for pardon and forgiveness, and professing wholeheartedly the new faith. On request by 'Abbas, the Prophet peace be upon him, in the context of the general amnesty he proclaimed, gave Abu Sufyan, who had a liking for bragging, a special privilege, saying: "He who takes refuge in Abu Sufyan's house is safe; whosoever confines himself to his house, the inmates thereof shall be in safety, and he who enters the Sacred Mosque is safe."

On the morning of Tuesday, 17th. Ramadan, 8 A.H., the Prophet peace be upon him left Mar Az-Zahran. He ordered Al-'Abbas to detain Abu Sufyan at a commanding gorge that could afford a full view of the Muslim army parading on its way towards Makkah, and hence give him the chance to see the great and powerful soldiers of Allâh. The different tribes successively passed with their banners flown up, until at last the battalion of the Emigrants and Helpers with the Prophet peace be upon him at their head heavily armed marched by. Abu Sufyan began to wonder who those people were, to which Al-'Abbas told him that they were Muhammad peace be upon him and his Companions. Abu Sufyan said that no army however powerful could resist those people and addressing Al-'Abbas, he said: "I swear by Allâh that the sovereignty of your brother's son has become too powerful to withstand." Al-'Abbas answered, "It is rather the power of Prophethood," to which the former agreed.

Sa'd bin 'Ubadah carried the flag of the Helpers. When he passed by Abu Sufyan, he said "Today will witness the great fight, you cannot seek sanctuary at Al-Ka'bah. Today will witness the humiliation of Quraish." Abu Sufyan complained about this to the Prophet peace be upon him who got angry and said "Nay, today Al-Ka'bah will be sanctified, and Quraish honoured," and quickly ordered that Sa'd should be stripped off the flag, and that it should be entrusted to his son Qais, in another version, to Az-Zubair.

Al-'Abbas urged Abu Sufyan to hasten into Makkah and warn the Quraishites against any aggressive behaviour towards the Muslims. There in Makkah, he shouted at the top of his voice and warned against any hostilities advising them to seek safety in his house. His wife got indignant and tugged at his moustache cursing him and abusing his cowardly stance. The people within Makkah mocked Abu Sufyan and dispersed in different directions, some into their houses, others into the Holy Sanctuary while some undisciplined reckless ruffians led by 'Ikrimah bin Abi Jahl, Safwan bin Omaiyah and Suhail bin 'Amr encamped themselves in a place called Khandamah, with a murderous intent in their minds.

The Prophet peace be upon him, on his part, was quite modestly and calmly drawing the final touches for the military breakthrough awaiting the Muslims, by Allâh's Will. He appointed Khalid bin Al-Waleed as a leader of the right flank of the army with Aslam, Sulaim, Ghifar, Muzainah and Juhainah tribes under his command to enter Makkah through its lower avenues. Az-Zubair bin 'Awwam was to lead the left flank and would storm Makkah from the upper side holding up the Messenger's banner. Abu 'Ubaidah took command of the infantry and was to penetrate into the city via a side valley. They were given full and decisive orders not to kill unless in self defence and in that case they would exterminate any aggressive elements and quell any opposition.

The Muslim battalions marched out each in its already drawn route to fulfill the missions they were supposed to carry out. Khalid bin Al-Waleed worked his way into the heart of the town quite successively killing twelve of the ruffians and sustaining two martyrs. Az-Zubair set out and reached the fixed destination where he planted the banner at Al-Fath (conquest) Mosque and waited there for the arrival of the Prophet peace be upon him. A tent was pitched for him where he offered prayers of thanks to the All-Mighty Allâh, Who, out of His immense grace, had granted him a splendid victory. But he did not repose long. He, in the company of the Helpers and Emigrants, got up and proceeded towards Al-Ka'bah, the Sacred House, which is an emblem of the Oneness and Supremacy of Allâh. It was unfortunately infested with idols that numbered 360. He knocked them down with his bow while reciting the verse of the Noble Qur'ân:

"And Say: 'Truth (i.e. Islamic Monotheism or this Qur'ân or Jihâd against polytheists) has come and Batil (falsehood, i.e. Satan or polytheism, etc.) has vanished. Surely! Batil is ever bound to vanish.'" [17:81] And Allâh further said:

"Say (O Muhammad peace be upon him): "The Truth (the Qur'ân and Allah's Inspiration) has come, and Al-Batil (falsehood - Iblis) can neither create anything nor resurrect (any thing)." [34:49] He then started the usual circumambulation on his ride. He was not in a state of Ihram (ritual consecration) then. On completion, he called for 'Uthman bin Talhah, the janitor of Al-Ka'bah, from whom he took the key. He went in and saw images of Prophets Ibrahim and Ishmael, عليهما السلام, throwing divination arrows. He denounced these acts of Quraish and ordered that all idols be dismantled, images and effigies deleted. He then entered the sacred hall to face the wall opposite the door and there again performed devout prostrations, and went around acclaiming Allâh's Greatness and Oneness. Shortly afterwards, he returned to the door-way and standing upon its elevated step, gazed in thankfulness on the thronging multitude below and delivered the following celebrated address:

"There is no god but Allâh Alone. He has no associates. He made good His Promise that He held to His slave and helped him and defeated all the Confederates along. Bear in mind that every claim of privilege, whether that of blood, or property, is under my heel, except that of the custody of Al-Ka'bah and supplying of water to the pilgrims. Bear in mind that for anyone who is slain, even though semi-deliberately, with club or whip, for him the blood-money is very severe: a hundred camels, forty of them to be pregnant.

"O people of Quraish! surely Allâh has abolished from you all pride of the pre-Islamic era and all conceit in your ancestry, (because) all men are descended from Adam, and Adam was made out of clay." He then recited to them the verse:

"O mankind! We have created you from a male and a female, and made you into nations and tribes, that you may know one another. Verily, the most honourable of you near Allâh is that (believer) who has At-Taqwa [i.e. one of the Muttaqûn: i.e. pious and righteous persons who fear Allâh much (abstain from all kinds of sins and evil deeds which He has forbidden), and love Allâh much (perform all kinds of good deeds which He has ordained)]. Verily, Allâh is All-Knowing, All-Aware." [49:13] He further added:

"O you people of Quraish! What do you think of the treatment that I am about to accord to you?" They replied:

"O noble brother and son of noble brother! We expect nothing but goodness from you." Upon this he said:

"I speak to you in the same words as Yusuf (the Prophet Joseph) spoke unto his brothers: He said: "No reproach on you this day," [12:92] go your way, for you are freed ones." As for the door-keeping of Al-Ka'bah and supplying of water to pilgrims, the Prophet peace be upon him ordered that these jobs remain in the hand of 'Uthman bin Talhah and that the key will stay with him and his descendants for ever.

When time for prayer approached, Bilal ascended Al-Ka'bah and called for prayer. Abu Sufyan bin Harb, 'Itab bin Usaid and Al-Harith bin Hisham were meanwhile sitting in the yard. 'Itab bin Usaid commented on the new situation (Bilal ascending Al-Ka'bah and calling for prayer) saying that Allâh honoured Usaid (his father) having not heard such words. The Prophet peace be upon him approached and assisted by Divine Revelation told them that he had learnt about what they had spoken of. Al-Harith and 'Itab, taken by incredible surprise, immediately professed Islam and bore witness to the Messengership of Muhammad peace be upon him adding that "We swear by Allâh that none had been with us to inform you."

On that very day, the Prophet peace be upon him entered 'Umm Hani's house where he washed and offered prayers of victory. 'Umm Hani had sheltered two Makkan relatives of hers in her house in which act she was granted support by the Prophet peace be upon him.

Shedding blood of nine arch-criminals was declared lawful even under the curtains of Al-Ka'bah. Nevertheless, only four of them were killed while the others were pardoned for different reasons. As for those who were killed, mention could be made of 'Abdul 'Uzza bin Khatal who had become a Muslim and then deputed to collect alms-tax in the company of a Helper. They had also a slave with them. 'Abdullah, in a fit of rage, killed the Helper's slave on account of a mere trifling dispute, and joined the pagan Arabs as an apostate. He was never repentant at this heinous crime but rather employed two women singers and incited them to sing satirically about the Prophet peace be upon him.

The other man who was put to death was Miqyas bin Sababa. He was a Muslim. A Helper accidently killed his brother Hisham. The Prophet peace be upon him had arranged the payment of blood money to him, which he had accepted. His revengeful nature, however, was never appeased, so he killed the Helper and went to Makkah as an apostate.

Similarly, Huwairith and one woman singer went to death.

On the other hand, every attempt was made to grant pardon to the people. 'Ikrimah bin Abu Jahl, who had attacked Khalid's detachment at the time of the entry into Makkah, was forgiven. To Wahshi, the murderer of Hamzah, the Prophet's uncle, and to Hind, who had chewed his liver, was also extended his generous clemency. The same generous treatment was accorded to Habar who had attacked the Prophet's daughter with a spear, while on her way from Makkah to Madinah, so grievously that she ultimately died of the fatal injuries.

In the same context of magnanimity peculiar to Muhammad peace be upon him, two chiefs of Quraish were pardoned once they had embraced Islam. They were Safwan bin Omaiyah and Fudalah bin 'Umair. The latter had attempted to assassinate the Prophet peace be upon him while circumambulating in the Holy Sanctuary. The Prophet's matchless tolerance and broad-mindedness instigated by his mission as 'A mercy to all people', converted a terrible hypocrite into a faithful devout believer.

On the second day of the great conquest, the Prophet peace be upon him stood up and addressed the people in matters relating to the holy status of Makkah. After entertaining Allâh's praise, he proclaimed that Makkah was a holy land and would remain so till the Day of Judgement. No bloodshed was allowed therein. Should anyone take the liberty of fighting within Makkah on grounds derived from the events that characterized the conquest, he should remember that it had been a licence granted temporarily to the Prophet, and virtually does not go for others. Ibn 'Abbas رضى الله عنهما narrated: The Prophet صلى الله عليه و سلم said: "Allâh has made Makkah, a sanctuary, so it was a sanctuary before me and will continue to be a sanctuary after me. It was made legal for me (i.e. I was allowed to fight in it) for a few hours of a day. It is not allowed to uproot its shrubs or to cut its trees, or to chase (or disturb) its game, or to pick up its fallen things except by a person who would announce that (what has found) publicly." Al-'Abbas said: "O Allâh's Messenger! Except the lemon grass (for it is used) by our goldsmiths and for our homes." The Prophet peace be upon him then said: "Except the lemon grass." In this context, out of the spirit of revenge, the tribesmen of Khuza'ah killed a man from Laith Tribe. Here the Prophet was indignant and ordered Khuza'ah to stop those pre-Islamic practices. He, moreover, gave the family of anyone killed the right to consider either of two options, blood-money or just retribution (the killer is killed).

After having delivered his address, the Prophet peace be upon him rode to a small hill, Safa, not far from Al-Ka'bah. Turning his face towards the Sacred House, amidst a vast admiring and devotional multitude, he raised his hand in fervent prayer to Allâh. The citizens of Madinah who had gathered round him entertained fear, as Allâh had given him victory over his native city, he might choose to stay here. He insisted on explanation of their fear and so they spoke openly. He immediately dispelled their fears and assured them that he had lived with them and would die with them.

Immediately after the great conquest, the Makkans came to realize that the only way to success lay in the avenue of Islam. They complied with the new realities and gathered to pledge fealty to the Prophet peace be upon him. The men came first pledging full obedience in all areas they can afford. Then came the women to follow the men's example. The Prophet peace be upon him with 'Umar bin Al-Khattab receiving the pledge of fealty and communicating to them for him. Hind bint 'Utbah, Abu Sufyan's wife, came in the trail of women disguised lest the Prophet peace be upon him should recognize and account for her, having chewed the liver of Hamzah, his uncle. The Prophet peace be upon him accepted their allegiance on condition that they associate none with Allâh, to which they immediately agreed. He added that they should not practise theft. Here Hind complained that her husband, Abu Sufyan, was tight-fisted. Her husband interrupted granting all his worldly possessions to her. The Prophet peace be upon him laughed and recognized the woman. She implored him to extend his pardon to her and efface all her previous sins. Some other conditions were appended including the prohibition of adultery, infanticide or forging falsehood. To all these orders, Hind replied positively swearing that she would not have come to take an oath of allegiance if she had had the least seed of disobedience to him. On returning home, she broke her idol admitting her delusion as regards stone-gods.

The Messenger of Allâh peace be upon him stayed in Makkah for 19 days. During that period he used to define the way to Islam, guide people to the orthodox path. He ordered Abu Usaid Al-Khuza'i to restore the pillars of the Holy Sanctuary, sent missions to all quarters inviting them to adopt Islam and break down the graven images still lying in the vicinity of Makkah, and he did have all of them scrapped, inculcating in the believers' ears his words:

"Whoever believes in Allâh and the Hereafter is supposed to scrap out the idols that should happen to be in his house."

Shortly after the great conquest, the Prophet peace be upon him began to despatch platoons and errands aiming at eliminating the last symbols reminiscent of pre-Islamic practices. He sent Khalid bin Al-Waleed in Ramadan 8 A.H. to a spot called Nakhlah where there was a goddess called Al-'Uzza venerated by Quraish and Kinanah tribes. It had custodians from Bani Shaiban. Khalid, at the head of thirty horsemen arrived at the spot and exterminated it. On his return, the Prophet peace be upon him asked him if he had seen anything there, to which Khalid gave a negative answer. Here, he was told that it had not been destroyed and he had to go there again and fulfill the task. He went back again and there he saw a black woman, naked with torn hair. Khalid struck her with his sword into two parts. He returned and narrated the story to the Prophet peace be upon him, who then confirmed the fulfillment of the task.

Later, in the same month, 'Amr bin Al-'As was sent on an errand to destroy another idol, venerated by Hudhail, called Suwa'. It used to stand at a distance of three kilometres from Makkah. On a question posed by the door-keeper, 'Amr said he had been ordered by the Prophet peace be upon him to knock down the idol. The man warned 'Amr that he would not be able to do it. 'Amr was surprised to see someone still in the wrong, approached the idol and destroyed it, then he broke the casket beside it but found nothing. The man immediately embraced Islam. Sa'd bin Zaid Al-Ashhali was also sent in the same month and on the same mission to Al-Mashallal to destroy an idol, Manat, venerated by both Al-Aws and Al-Khazraj tribes. Here also a black woman, naked with messy hair appeared wailing and beating on her chest. Sa'd immediately killed her, destroyed the idol and broke the casket and returned at the conclusion of his errand. Khalid bin Al-Waleed at the head of 350 horsemen of Helpers, Emigrants and Bani Saleem was despatched once again in the same year 8 A.H. to the habitation of Bani Khuzaimah bedouins to invite them to the fold of Islam. He was instructed to carry out his mission with peace and goodwill. There, the people were not articulate enough to communicate their intentions, so Khalid ordered his men to kill them and take the others as captives. He even had in mind to kill the captives but some of the Companions were opposed to his plan. News of bloodshed reached the Prophet peace be upon him. He was deeply grieved and raised his hands towards the heaven, uttering these words: "O Allâh! I am innocent of what Khalid has done," twice. He immediately sent 'Ali to make every possible reparation to the tribes who had been wronged. After a careful inquiry, 'Ali paid the blood-money to all those who suffered loss. The remaining portion was also distributed amongst the members of the tribe in order to alleviate their suffering. Khalid, due to his irrational behaviour, had a row with 'Abdur Rahman bin 'Awf. Hearing this, the Prophet peace be upon him got angry, and ordered Khalid to stop that altercation adding that his Companions (meaning 'Abdur Rahman bin 'Awf) were too high in rank to be involved in such arguments.

That is the story of the conquest of Makkah and the decisive battle that exterminated paganism once and for all. The other tribes in the Arabian Peninsula were waiting and closely watching the final outcome of the bitter struggle between the Muslims and idolaters, already convinced that the Holy Sanctuary would not fall but in the hands of the righteous party. It had been a conviction deeply established in their minds ever since the elephant army of Abraha Al-Ashram advanced from Yemen intending to destroy the Sacred House 50 years before.

Al-Hudaibiyah Peace Treaty was the natural prelude to this great victory in which people believed deeply and over which people talked a lot. The Muslims in Makkah, who had feared to declare their Faith in public, began to appear and work ardently for this new approach of life. People began to convert into Islam in hosts, and the Muslim army that numbered 3000 only in the previous Ghazwah, now came to reach 10,000 in number. In fact, this decisive change provided people with the keen insight to perceive things and the world around them as a whole in a different perceptive. The Muslims were then to steer the whole political and religious affairs of all Arabia. They had monopolised both the religious supremacy and temporal power.

The whole post-Hudaibiyah phase had been well-fledged in favour of the new Islamic movement. Streams of the desert Arabians began to pour in paying full homage to the Messenger of Allâh peace be upon him, embracing the new faith and then carrying it to different quarters for propagation.

THE THIRD STAGE

The third and last stage of the life of the Messenger (peace be upon him) embodies the fruitful results of his call to Islam, which were the consequences of long-timed holy fights in the way of Allâh (Jihad), troubles, toil, disturbances, trials and a lot of bloody conflicts and battles, which lasted for over twenty years.

The conquest of Makkah was considered the most serious profit achieved by Muslims during those years. For it affected the course of events and consequently altered the Arabs' whole life. It was a decisive distinction between preconquest and post-conquest periods. For Quraish, at that time, was in the eyes of Arabs the defenders and helpers of Arabs. Other Arabs are only their ancillaries. The submission of Quraish is, therefore, estimated to be a final elimination of paganism in the Arabian Peninsula.

THIS STAGE CANE BE DIVIDED INTO TWO MAIN PHASE:

The phase of:
(1) holy wars and fighting.
(2) the tribes and people's race to embrace Islam.

Being so close and rather inseparable, the two phases of this stage intervene in such a way that a happening of one phase occurs during the progress of the other. However, we have preferred — for expository purposes — to deal with these two phases distinctively. The fighting phase was given the priority in order, due to the fact that it is more intimate and fit than the other.

HUNAIN GHAZWAH

The conquest of Makkah which came forth as a consequence of a swift blow astounded both the Arabs and other tribes who realized that they were doomed and had to submit to the new situation as a fait accompli. Some of the fierce, powerful proud tribes did not submit and favoured resistance. Ahead of these were the septs of Hawazin and Thaqif. Nasr, Jashm and Sa'd bin Bakr and people of Bani Hilal — all of whom of Qais 'Ailan. They thought that they were too mighty to admit or surrender to such a victory. So they met Malik bin 'Awf An-Nasri and made up their mind to proceed fighting against the Muslims.

ENEMY'S MARCH AND ENCAMPMENT AT AWTAS:

When Malik bin 'Awf — the general leader — decided to march and fight the Muslims, he made his countrypeople take their wealth, women and children with them to Awtas — which is a valley in Hawazin land and is quite near Hunain. It differs from Hunain in its being adjacent to Dhi-Al-Majaz which is around ten miles from Makkah in 'Arafat's direction.

THE WAR-EPERIENCED MAN WRONGS THE LEADER'S JUDGEMENT:

As soon as they had camped in Awtas, people crowded round Malik. The old sane Duraid bin As-Simmah, who was well-known as a war-experienced man, and who was among those who gathered round Malik, asked: "What valley are we in?" "In Awtas," they said. "What a good course it is for horses! It is neither a sharp pointed height nor a loosed soiled plain. What? Why do I hear camels' growling, the donkeys' braying, the children's cries and the sheep bleating?" asked Duraid. They said: "Malik bin 'Awf had made people bring their women, properties and children with them." So he called Malik and asked him what made him do such a thing. Malik said that his aim was to have everybody's family and properties around them so that they fight fiercely to protect them." "I swear by Allâh that you are nothing but a shepherd," answered Duraid, "Do you believe that there is anything whatsoever, can stand in the way of a defeated one or stop him from fleeing? If you win the battle you avail nothing but a man with a sword and a spear; but if you lose you will bring disgrace on your people and properties," then he resumed his talk and went on wondering about some septs and their leaders. "O Malik, thrusting the distinguished people of Hawazin into the battlefield will avail you nothing. Raise them up to where they can be safe. Then make the young people mount their horses and fight. If you win, those whom you tarried will follow you, but if you were the loser it would be a loss of a battle, but your kinsmen, people and properties would not be lost."

But Malik, the general leader, refused this suggestion. "By Allâh," he said, "I will not do such a thing. You must have grown a senile. Hawazin have to obey me, or else I will lean my body against this sword so that it penetrates through my back." He rejected any sort of contribution of Duraid's in that concern.

"We obey you," said his people, Duraid consequently said: "Today is a day that I have not missed but surely I will not be tempted to witness."

RECONNOITERING THE WEAPONS OF THE WEAPONS OF THE MESSENGER OF ALLAH:

The spies that Malik had already dispatched to spy Muslim forces, returned with their limbs cut off. "Woe unto you! What happened to you?" Said Malik. They said: "We have seen distinguished people on spotted horsebacks. What you see, would not have happened if we had been firmly together."

RECONNOITERING THE ENEMY'S WEAPON:

News about the enemy's marching were conveyed to the Messenger of Allâh (peace be upon him) , so he sent out Al-Aslami with orders to mix with people, stay with them so that he would be able to know their news and to convey it to the Messenger of Allâh (peace be upon him) when he turns back. That was exactly what he managed to do.

THE MESSENGER OF ALLAH (peace be upon him) LEAVES MAKKAH FOR HUNAIN:

On Shawwal, the nineteenth, the captive day, the Messenger of Allâh (peace be upon him) left Makkah accompanied by twelve thousand Muslims. Ten thousand of those had previously shared in Makkah Conquest. A great number of the other two thousand, who were Makkans, had recently embraced Islam. That march was on the nineteenth day of his conquest to Makkah. He borrowed a hundred armours with their equipment from Safwan bin Omaiyah. He appointed 'Itab bin Usaid as a governor over Makkah. When it was evening time, a horseman came to the Messenger of Allâh (peace be upon him) and said: "I have climbed up so and so mountains and came across Hawazin with their riding camels, livestock and sheep. Hawazin wholly were gathered together there." The Messenger of Allâh (peace be upon him) smiled then and said: "They will all be Muslims' spoils tomorrow, if Allâh will." That night Anas bin Abi Murthid Al-Ghanawi volunteered to guard.

On their way to Hunain they saw a great green *Nabk* plant, that was called *Dhat-Anwat* (the one with suspenders). That was because the Arabs used to hang their weapons on it, slay beasts under it and keep to it. So some of army members asked the Messenger of Allâh (peace be upon him) to make them a *Nabk* with suspenders as the one they had. "Allâh is the Greatest of all!" He said, "I swear by the One in Whose Hand is Muhammad's soul, that you have just said what the people of Moses said to him. They said 'Make us a god as the one they have.' Surely you are ignorant people. These are *Sunnah*, but you will follow and comply with the modes of life of those who preceded you."

Seeing how great in number the army was, some of them said: "We shall not be defeated." Their statement sounded hard upon the Messenger of Allâh (peace be upon him):

THE ISLAMIC ARMY STUNNED THE ARCHERS AND THE ATTACKERS:

On Wednesday night the tenth of Shawwal, the Muslim army arrived at Hunain. Malik bin 'Awf, who had previously entered the valley by night, gave orders to his army to hide inside the valley and lurk for the

Muslims on roads, entrances, narrow hiding places. His orders to his men were to hurl stones at Muslims whenever they caught sight of them and then to make a one-man attack against them.

At early dawn the Messenger of Allâh (peace be upon him) started mobilizing his army and distributing posts and flags to people. In the dark and just before dawn the Muslims moved towards Hunain Valley. They started descending into it unaware of the presence of an enemy lurking for them inside the valley. So at the moment they were camping, arrows began showering intensively at them, whereas the enemy's battalions started a fierce attack against the Muslims, who had to retreat in disorder and utter confusion. It was such a shatteringly defeat that Abu Sufyan bin Harb, who had recently embraced Islam, said that their retreat would not stop till they got to the Red Sea. Jablah or Kildah bin Al-Junacommented on that by saying: "Surely magic has grown inactive today."

The Messenger of Allâh (peace be upon him) turned to the right and said: "Come on, people! I am the Messenger of Allâh. I am Muhammad, the son of Abdullah." Those who stoodfast by him were only few Emigrants and some of his kinsmen. The matchless bravery of the Prophet (peace be upon him) was then brought to light. He went on and on in his attempts to make his mule standfast in the face of the disbelievers while saying loudly:

- "Truly saying, I am the Prophet I am the (grand) son of Abdul Muttalib."

However, Abu Sufyan, who was then holding the rein of the Prophet's mule, and Al-'Abbas, who was holding its stirrup; were endeavouring to make it halt. The Messenger of Allâh (peace be upon him) dismounted and asked his Lord to render him help.

- "O, Allâh, send down Your Help!"

MUSLIMS' RETURN TO THE BATTLE FIELD, AND THE FIERCENESS OF THE FIGHT:

The Messenger of Allâh (peace be upon him) ordered his uncle Al-'Abbas — who was a sonorous voiced man — to call out on the followers. As loudly as he could, Al-'Abbas shouted: "Where are the lancers?" "By Allâh," Al-'Abbas said, "Upon hearing my voice calling them back, they turned round to the battlefield as if they had been oryxes (wild cows) tending towards their calves."

"Here we are, at your service. Here we are. " They said. There you see them trying to stop their camels and reverse to the battle. He who was unable to force his camel to turn back, would take his armour, fling it round his neck, and hastily dismount his camel with his weapon in his hand letting his camel move freely and run towards the voice source. Voices would grow louder and louder till a hundred of them gathered round the Prophet and resumed the fight.

Those who were called out upon next were Al-Ansar, the Helpers, "O, folks of Al-Ansar! Folks of Al-Ansar!"

The last group to be called out upon were Bani Al-Harith bin Al-Khazraj. Muslims battalions poured successively into the battlefield in the same manner that they had left it. The stamina of both parties was superb. Both of them stoodfast and fought fiercely. The Messenger of Allâh (peace be upon him) was so eagerly and furiously watching the battle that he said:

- "Now the fight has grown fierce."

Picking up a handful of earth, he hurled it at their faces while saying:

- "May your faces be shameful."

Their eyes were thick with dust and the enemy began to retreat in utter confusion.

REVERSE OF FORTUNES AND THE ENEMY'S UTTER DEFEAT:

Few hours had elapsed since the earth-handful was hurled at the enemy's faces, when they were shatteringly defeated. About seventy men of Thaqif alone were killed, and the Muslims plundered all their riding camels, weapons and cattle.

Allâh, Glory is to Him, alluded to this sudden change in the Qur'ân when He said:

- "...and on the Day of Hunain (battle) when you rejoiced at your great number but it availed you naught and the earth, vast as it is, was straitened for you, then you turned back in flight. Then Allâh did send down His *Sakinah* (calmness, tranquillity, and reassurance, etc.) on the Messenger [Muhammad (peace be upon him)] and on the believers, and sent down forces (angels) which you saw not, and punished the disbelievers. Such is the recompense of disbelievers." [9:25,26]

HOT PURSUIT OF THE ENEMY:

After their defeat, some enemy troops headed for Ta'if, others to Nakhlah and Awtas. A group of Muslims headed by Abu 'Amir Al-Ash' ari, were despatched to chase the enemy, some skirmishes took place during which Abu 'Amir was killed.

A similar battalion of horsemen pursued the idolaters who threaded the track to Nakhlah and caught up with Duraid bin As-Simmah, who was killed by Rabi'a bin Rafi'. After collecting the booty, the Messenger of Allâh (peace be upon him) left for Ta'if to face the greatest number of the defeated idolaters. The booty was six thousand captives, twenty four thousand camels; over forty thousand sheep and four thousand silver ounces. The Messenger of Allâh (peace be upon him) gave orders that booty should be confined at Al-J'iranah and ordained Mas'ud bin 'Amr Al-Ghifari to be in charge of it. It was only when he was entirely free from Ta'if Campaign, that one of the captives As-Shaimâ', the daughter of Al-Harith As-Sa'diya, the Messenger's foster sister was brought to the Messenger of Allâh (peace be upon him) , she introduced herself to him. Upon recognizing her by a certain mark, he honoured her, spread for her his garment and seated her on it. He was graceful and released her and made her turn back to her people.

TA'IF CAMPAIGN:

Ta'if Campaign is in fact an extension of Hunain *Ghazwah;* that is because the majority of the defeated troops of Hawazin and Thaqif went into Ta'if with the general commander — Malik bin 'Awf An-Nasri — and fortified themselves within it. So upon finishing with Hunain Invasion, he gathered the booty at Al-Ji'ranah in the very month (i.e. Shawwal) and in the eighth year A.H.

A vanguard battalion of a thousand men led by Khalid bin Al-Waleed marched towards At-Ta'if. Whereas the Messenger of Allâh (peace be upon him) proceeded passing through Nakhlah Al-Yamaniyah, Qarn Al-Manazil and through Laiyah. At Laiyah there was a castle that belonged to Malik bin 'Awf, so the Messenger of Allâh (peace be upon him) gave orders to have it destroyed. He resumed his march till he got to Ta'if. There he dismounted, camped near its castle and laid siege to the castle inhabitants; but not for long.

How long the siege continued, is still a matter of disagreement. It however stands between 10-20 days.

A lot of arrow-shooting and rock-hurling occurred during the siege. For as soon as the Muslims laid siege round the castle, its people started shooting arrows against them. The arrows were so intense and fierce that they looked as if they had been locusts on the move. A number of Muslims were wounded and twelve were killed.

To be far from the arrow-range, the Muslims had to ascend to a higher location and camped on — i.e. to what is now called At-Ta'if Mosque. The Prophet (peace be upon him) set up a mangonel and shelled the castle. Eventually a gap was made in the castle wall, through which a number of Muslims managed to pass into the castle, sheltered by a wooden tank, with the purpose of setting fire into it. Anyway, the enemy poured down molten hot iron on them. Affected by this the Muslims stepped out of the tank and were again exposed to arrow shooting and consequently some of them were killed.

To force the enemy to surrender, the Prophet (peace be upon him) tended to a war policy of burning and cutting the enemy's crops. His order was to cut their vineyards and burn them. Seeing that the Muslims started rapidly cutting and burning their vines, they implored the Prophet (peace be upon him) to stop and have mercy on them for the sake of Allâh and out of kinship motives. So the Prophet agreed. When the caller of the Messenger of Allâh (peace be upon him) called out unto people saying "He whosoever descends and steps out of the castle is free." Twenty-three men came out. One of them was Abu Bakrah who tied himself to a wall and let himself down by means of a small wheel, that would normally be used for drawing up water from a well. The way he let himself down made the Prophet nickname him "Abu Bakrah", i.e. the man with the wheel. The Messenger of Allâh (peace be upon him) set them all free and entrusted each one of them to a Muslim to care about their living affairs, which was too hard for the castle folkspeople to bear.

Seeing that the siege lasted too long and that the castle was immune and could stand any siege (for they had already stored a supply that suffices for over a year) and that the Muslims were suffering — day by day — from arrow-shots and heated iron hooks, the Messenger of Allâh (peace be upon him) consulted Nawfal bin Mu'âwiyah Ad-Daili about that. He said: "They are like a fox hiding inside its burrow. If you stoodfast at it you would catch it, but if you parted with it, no harm would afflict you." The Messenger of Allâh (peace be upon him) decided to lift the siege and depart. 'Umar bin Al-Khattab, who was orderedby the Prophet to notify people, said to them "If Allâh will, we are leaving the castle and going back tomorrow." As it was too hard for the Muslims to go back and leave the castle unconquered they complained saying, "Should we go away while the castle is still unopened?" His reply was: "Then, start fighting in the morning." In the morning they fought and were wounded. So when he repeated this statement: "If Allâh will, we are leaving the castle and going back tomorrow", they were pleased and carried out the order submissively and started moving, which made the Messenger of Allâh (peace be upon him) laugh.

As soon as they mounted and started moving the Messenger (peace be upon him) said:

- "Say! Here we are returning, repenting, worshipping (Allâh) and to our Lord we offer praise."

When the Messenger of Allâh was asked to invoke Allâh against Thaqif, he said:

- "O Allâh, guide Thaqif and bring them to us as Muslims."

THE DISTRIBUTION OF THE BOOTY AT AL-JI'RANAH:

Upon returning and lifting the siege in Ta'if, the Messenger of Allâh (peace be upon him) had stayed over ten nights at Al-Ji'ranah before starting to distribute the booty. Distribution delay was due to the Prophet's hope that Hawazin's delegation might arrive and announce their repentance and consequently reclaim their loss. Seeing that none of them arrived, he started dividing the booty so as to calm down the tribes' chiefs and the celebrities of Makkah. The first to receive booty and the ones who obtained the greatest number of shares were the people who had recently embraced Islam.

Abu Sufyan bin Harb was given a hundred camels and forty (gold) ounces and yet he said, "What about my son, Yazeed's Share?" So he was given the same quantity for his son as well. But yet he exclaimed: "And what about the share of Mu'âwiyah, my second son?" So the Prophet (peace be upon him) gave Mu'âwiyah as much as he gave his father and brother. Hakeem bin Hizam was given a hundred camels, but he was given a hundred more when he demanded. Safwan bin Omaiyah was given three hundred camels - a hundred camels at each time. It is thus mentioned in Shifâ, Book by Qadi Iyadh. The Prophet (peace be upon him) gave Al-Harith bin Harith bin Kilda a hundred camels. He also gave some chiefs of Quraish and other clans a hundred camels; he gave others fifty and some others had forty.

Eventually it was spread among people that "Muhammad grants generously and fears not to grow poor." This made bedouins gather around him expecting to be given some wealth. They were so many that they forced the Prophet (peace be upon him) to seek refuge against a tree and they even took away his garment, "O people!" He said, "Give me back my garment! For I swear by the One in Whose Hand is Muhammad's soul, that if I had as many numerous camels as the number of Tihama trees, I would distribute them among you. You know quite well that I am neither mean nor coward or a liar." Standing by his camel he plucked out a hair of his camel's hump and held it between his two fingers, lifted it up and said: "O people, I swear by Allâh that I get nothing but one-fifth of your booty, and this very fifth goes back to you."

As soon as he had given the new converts, the Messenger of Allâh (peace be upon him) ordered Zaid bin Thabit to fetch the booty and summon people. Then he ordained shares to people. A footman's share was four camels and forty sheep, and a horseman would take twelve camels and a hundred and twenty sheep. This distribution of booty was based on a wise policy. In this world there are lots of people who know the truth only when it comes through their stomachs and they do not recognize it if it comes through their brains. The similitude of such people is as the guidance of an animal to its herd by means of a bunch of clover held at a constant distance off its mouth. The animal would try all the time to catch it, so it would eventually go into the herd safely. In the same way you have to do various kinds of temptations to make certain kind of people familiarize Islam and be pleased with.

THE HELPERS (Al-Ansar) ARE FURIOUS AT THE MESSENGER OF ALLAH (peace be upon him) :

At first the Prophet's policy of distribution was uncomprehended by many a man. Therefore sharp-tongued people started expressing their objections. The Helpers were among those who were afflicted by this policy. They were deprived of Hunain gifts though they had been the ones who were summoned at Hunain hard times and they were the first to rush to fight with the Messenger of Allâh (peace be upon him) and standfast till the defeat turned into victory. Now here they are watching those who escaped fill their hands with booty while they are given nothing.

On the authority of Ibn Ishaq: "When the Messenger of Allâh (peace be upon him) had given Quraish and Arab tribes those gifts and allotted nothing to the Helpers, a group of the Helpers felt so uneasy about it that a lot of ill-statements against the Prophet (peace be upon him) were spread among them to an extent that one of them said: "By Allâh, the Messenger of Allâh (peace be upon him) was ill-spoken of by his folksmen!" And those ill-statements went on spreading till Sa'd bin 'Ubadah met the Messenger of Allâh (peace be upon him) , who in his turn faced his people after a while.

Sa'd bin 'Ubadah said: "O Messenger of Allâh, this group of the Helpers are furious at you about the distribution of the booty that you had won. You have allotted shares to your own kinsmen and forwarded lots of gifts to the Arab tribes. But this group has obtained nothing." The Prophet (peace be upon him) asked Sa'd exclaiming: "Sa'd, what do you think of all that?" Sa'd replied: "O Messenger of Allâh. You know that I am nothing but a member of this group." "Call out on your people and bring them forth to me into this shed." Said the Prophet (peace be upon him).

So Sa'd went out and summoned them. When some Emigrants came, he let them in but forbade others. When they were all gathered together, he informed the Prophet saying: "This group of the Helpers have just arrived to meet you in compliance with your orders." As soon as the Messenger (peace be upon him) faced them he thanked Allâh and praised Him, then said to them inquiring, "I have been told that you are angry with me. Didn't I come to you when you were astray and Allâh guided you? You were poor and Allâh gave you wealth. Weren't you foes and Allâh made you love one another." "Yes," they said, "Allâh and His Messenger are better and more gracious." Then he said: "What prevents you from replying to the Messenger of Allâh, O tribe of Helpers?" They said, "What should be the reply, O Messenger of Allâh, while to the Lord and to his Messenger belong all benevolence and grace."

The Prophet (peace be upon him) again said:

- "But by Allâh, you might have answered and answered truly, for I would have testified to its truth myself: 'You came to us belied and rejected and we accepted you; you came to us as helpless and we helped you; a fugitive, and we took you in; poor and we comforted you'.

    You Helpers, do you feel anxious for the things of this world, wherewith I have sought to incline these people unto the Faith in which you are already established?

    Are you not satisfied, O group of Helpers that the people go with ewes and camels while you go along with the Messenger of Allâh (peace be upon him) to your dwellings. By Him in Whose Hand is my life, had there been no migration, I would have been one of the Helpers. If the people would go through a valley and passage, and the Helpers go through another valley and passage, I would go through the valley and passage of the Helpers. Allâh! Have mercy on the Helpers, their children and their children's children."

The audience wept until tears rolled down their beards as they said:

- "Yes, we are satisfied, O Prophet of Allâh (peace be upon him) ! with our lot and share."

Then the Prophet (peace be upon him) left the gathering and the people also dispersed.

ARRIVAL O FTHE HAWAZIN DELEGATION:

Hawazin's delegation arrived a Muslims just after the distribution of spoils. They were fourteen men headed by Zuhair bin Sard. The Messenger's fosteruncle was one of them. They asked him to bestow upon them some of the wealth and spoils. They uttered so touching words that the Messenger of Allâh (peace be upon him) said to them: "You surely see who are with me. The most desirable speech to me is the most truthful. Which is dearer to you, your wealth or your women and children?" They replied: "Nothing whatsoever compares with kinship." Then when I perform the noon prayer, stand up and say:

"We intercede with the Messenger of Allâh (peace be upon him) to exhort the believers, and we intercede with the believers to exhort the Messenger of Allâh (peace be upon him) to forego the captives of our people fallen to their lot." So when the Messenger of Allâh (peace be upon him) performed the noon prayer, they stood up and said what they had been told to say. The Messenger (peace be upon him) , then, said: "As for what belongs to me and to the children of Abdul Muttalib, you may consider them, from now on, yours. And I will ask my folksmen to give back theirs." Upon hearing that the Emigrants and the Helpers said: "What belongs to us is, from now on, offered to the Messenger of Allâh (peace be upon him) ." But Al-Aqra' bin Habis said, "We will grant none of what belongs to me and to Bani Tamim,"; so did 'Uyaina bin Hisn, who said: "As for me and Bani Fazarah, I say 'No'." Al-'Abbas bin Mirdas also refused and said: "No" for Bani Saleem and him. His people, however, said otherwise: "Whatever spoils belong to us we offer to the Messenger of Allâh (peace be upon him) " "You have undermined my position." Said Al-'Abbas bin Mirdas spontaneously. Then the Messenger of Allâh (peace be upon him) said: "These people have come to you as Muslims. For this I have already tarried the distribution of the booty. Besides, I have granted them a fair option but they refused to have anything other than their women and children. Therefore he who has some of theirs and will prefer willingly to give them back, let them do. But those who favours to keep what he owns to himself, let them grant them back too, and he will be given as a recompense six times as much from the first booty that Allâh may provide us." People then said, "We will willingly offer them all for the sake of the Messenger of Allâh." The Messenger of Allâh (peace be upon him) said: "But in this way we are not able to find out who is content and who is not. So go back and we will be waiting for your chiefs to convey to us your decisions." All of them gave back the women and children. The only one who refused to comply with the Messenger's desire was 'Uyaina bin Hisn. He refused to let an old woman of theirs go back at first. Later on he let her go back. The Messenger of Allâh (peace be upon him) gave every captive a garment as a gift.

LSSER PILGRIMAGE (Al-'Umrah) TO MAKKAH AND LEAVING FOR MADINAH:

Having accomplished the distribution of the spoils at Al-Ji'ranah he left it while wearing Al-'Umrah clothes and proceeded to Makkah to perform Al-'Umrah. The Messenger of Allâh صلى الله عليه وسلم turned back from there to Madinah after appointing 'Itab bin Usaid on Makkah as governor. His arrival to Madinah was by the last six nights of Dhul-Qa'dah, in the year 8 A.H. On this occasion Muhammad Al-Ghazali said:

"What a great change it is between the victorious period of Muhammad at present which Allâh has towered with a manifest conquest, and that period of the past during which Muhammad first arrived at this town, eight years ago."

When he first came to Madinah, he was pursued and wanted. He was seeking a secure shelter. He was a lonely stranger who sought companionship and comfort. The people of Madinah welcomed him, gave him residence and aided him and embraced the light of Islam, which had been sent down upon him. They, for his sake, did not care about the enmity of other peoples. Here he is entering Madinah again, after the lapse of eight years of that first visit. Madinah, the town that had received him once, when he was a frightened Emigrant; it receives him once again when Makkah has become in his hands and at his disposal. It is Makkah that has got rid of its pride and *Jahiliyah* (i.e. pre-Islamic period and traditions). It is now proud again and mighty in Islam. The Messenger of Allâh forgave all the errors and wrongs of its people.

- "Verily, he who fears Allâh with obedience to Him (by abstaining from sins and evil deeds, and by performing righteous good deeds), and is patient, then surely, Allâh makes not the reward of the good-doers to be lost." [12:90]

MISSIONS AND PLATOONS AFTER THE CONQUEST:

Upon returning from this long successful travel, the Messenger of Allâh (peace be upon him) stayed in Madinah where he received delegates and dispatched agents and appointed preachers and callers to Islam everywhere. Those whose hearts were still full of prejudice against Islam and therefore were too proud to embrace Allâh's religion, were decisively muffled on their non-acquiescence in the status quo prevalent then in Arabia.

Here is a mini-image about the believed ones. We have already stated that the Messenger's arrival in Madinah was by the last days of the eighth year of Al-Hijra. No sooner the crescent of Muharram of the ninth year turned up than the Messenger of Allâh (peace be upon him) dispatched the believed ones, to the tribes as shown in the list below:

- 1. 'Uyaina bin Hisn to Bani Tamim.

  2. Yazeed bin Husain to Aslam and Ghifar.

  3. 'Abbad bin Bishr Al-Ashhali to Sulaim and Muzainah.

  4. Rafi' bin Mukaith to Juhainah.

  5. 'Amr bin Al-'As to Bani Fazarah.

  6. Ad-Dahhak bin Sufyan to Bani Kilab.

  7. Basheer bin Sufyan to Bani Ka'b.

8. Ibn Al-Lutabiyah Al-Azdi to Bani Dhubyan.

9. Al-Muhajir bin Abi Omaiyah to Sana'a' (Al-Aswad Al-'Ansi called at him when he was in it).

10. Ziyad bin Labid to Hadramout.

11. 'Adi bin Hatim to Tai' and Bani Asad.

12. Malik bin Nuwairah to Bani Hanzalah.

13. Az-Zabraqan bin Badr to Bani Sa'd (a portion of them).

14. Qais bin 'Asim to Bani Sa'd (a portion of them).

15. Al-'Alâ' bin Al-Hadrami to Al-Bahrain.

16. 'Ali bin Abi Talib to Najran (to collect *Sadaqa & Jizya*).

Some of these agents were despatched in Muharram, 7 A.H., others were sent later until the tribes they were heading for had completely converted into Islam. Such a move clearly demonstrates the great success that the Islamic *Da'wah* (Call) enjoyed after Al-Hudaibiyah Treaty. However, shortly after the conquest of Makkah, people began to embrace Islam in large hosts.

THE PLATOONS:

In the same way that the believed ones were dispatched to the tribes, we understand that dispatching some more platoons to all regions of Arabia is a necessity for the prevalence and domination of security on all lands of Arabia.

Here is a list of those platoons:

1. 'Uyaina bin Hisn Al-Fazari's platoon in Al-Muharram, the ninth year of Al-Hijra to Bani Tamim. It consisted of fifty horsemen, none of them was an Emigrant or a Helper.
2. This expedition was dispatched due to the fact that Bani Tamim had already urged other tribes not to pay tribute (*Al-Jizya*) and eventually stopped them from paying it.

   Therefore, 'Uyaina bin Hisn set out to fight them. All the way long he marched by night and lurked by day. He went on that way till he overtook them and attacked them in the desert. They fled back for their lives. Eleven men, twenty-one women and thirty boys were captured then. He drove them back to Madinah and were housed in Ramlah bint Al-Harith's residence. Ten of their leaders, who came to the Prophet's door, called out unto him saying: "O Muhammad come out and face us." When he went out they held him and started talking.

   He exchanged talk with them for a while then left them and went to perform the noon-prayer. After prayer he sat in the mosque-patio. They proclaimed a desire to show boasting and self-pride. For this purpose they introduced their orator 'Utarid bin Hajib who delivered his speech. The Messenger of Allâh (peace be upon him) asked Thabit bin Qais bin Shammas — the Muslim orator — to respond. He did that. In return, they brought forth their poet Az-Zabraqan bin Badr who recited some boastful poetry. Hassan bin Thabit, the poet of Islam, promptly replied back. When talks and poetcame to an end, Al-Aqra' bin Habis said: "Their orator is more eloquent than ours, and their poet is more poetically learned than ours. Their voices and sayings excel ours, as well." Eventually they announced their embracing Islam. Consequently, the Messenger of Allâh (peace be upon him) acknowledged their Islamization, awarded them well, and rendered them back their women and children.

3. A platoon headed by Qutbah bin 'Amir to a spot called Khath'am in Tabalah, a plot of land not far from Turbah. That was in Safar, 9 A.H. Accompanied by twenty men and only ten camels to mount alternatively on, Qutbah raided them and fought so fiercely that a great number of both parties were wounded and some others were killed. The Muslims drove back with them camels, women and sheep to Madinah.
4. The mission of Dahhak bin Sufyan Al-Kilabi to Bani Kilab in Rabi' Al-Awwal in the year 9 A.H. This mission was sent to Bani Kilab to call them to embrace Islam. Refusing to embrace Islam, they started to fight against the Muslims, but were defeated and sustained one man killed.
5. The three hundred men expedition of 'Alqamah bin Mujazziz Al-Mudlaji to Jeddah shores in Rabi' Al-Akhir. This expedition was dispatched to fight against some men from (Al-Habasha) Abyssinia (Ethiopia), who gathered together near the shores of Jeddah and exercised acts of piracy against the Makkans. Therefore he crossed the sea till he got to an island. But as soon as the pirates had learned of Muslims' arrival, they fled.
6. The task of the platoon of 'Ali bin Abi Talib was to demolish Al-Qullus, which was an idol that belonged to Tai' tribe. That was in Rabi' Al-Awwal in the year 9 A.H. 'Ali was dispatched by the Messenger of Allâh (peace be upon him) with one hundred fifty men. A hundred of them were on camels. The other fifty were on horseback. He held a black flag and a white banner.

- At dawn they raided *Mahallat* Hatim, demolished the idol and filled their hands with spoils, camels and sheep booties, whereas 'Adi fled to Ash-Sham. The sister of 'Adi bin Hatim was one of the captives. Inside Al-Qullus safe, Muslims found three swords and three armours. On the way they distributed the spoils and put aside the best things to the Messenger of Allâh (peace be upon him) . They did not share the Hatims.

Upon arrival in Madinah, the sister of 'Adi bin Hatim begged the Messenger of Allâh (peace be upon him) to have mercy on her and said: "O Messenger of Allâh, my brother is absent and father is dead, and I am too old to render any service. Be beneficent to me so that Allâh may be bountiful to you." He said: "Who is your brother?" She said: "It is 'Adi bin Hatim." "Is he not the one who fled from Allâh and his Messenger?" Said the Prophet (peace be upon him) then went away from her. Next day she reiterated the same thing as the day before and received the same answer. A day later she uttered similar words, this time he made benefaction to her. The man who was beside the Prophet, and whom she thought to be 'Ali, said to her: "Ask for an animal from him to ride on." And she was granted her request.

She returned to Ash-Sham where she met her brother and said to him: "The Messenger of Allâh (peace be upon him) has done me such noble deed that your father would never have done it. Therefore, willy-nilly, frightened or secure, you should go and see him." Unsecure neither protected by some one, not even recommended by a letter as a means of protection, 'Adi came and met the Prophet. The Messenger of Allâh (peace be upon him) took him home with him. As soon as he sat before him, the Messenger of Allâh (peace be upon him) thanked Allâh and praised him, then said: "What makes you flee? Do you flee lest you should say there is no god but Allâh? Do you know any other god but Allâh?" "No" he said, then talked for a while. The Messenger of Allâh went on saying: "Certainly you flee so that you may not hear the statement saying 'Allâh is the Greatest.' Do you know anyone who is greater than Allâh?" "No" he said. "The Jews are those whose portion is wrath, and the Christians are those who have gone astray," the Prophet retorted. "I am a Muslim and I believe in one God (Allâh)." 'Adi finally proclaimed with a joyous face. The Prophet ordered him a residence with one of the Helpers. From that time he started calling at the Prophet (peace be upon him) in the mornings and in the evenings.

On the authority of Ibn Ishaq, when the Prophet (peace be upon him) made him sit down in front of him in his house, the Prophet said, "O 'Adi, were you not cast in disbelief?" "Yes". 'Adi said. "Did you not share one quarter of your people's gains?" "Yes". Said 'Adi. The Messenger of Allâh (peace be upon him) said: "It is sinful in your religion to do such a thing, and you should not allow yourself to do it." "Yes, by Allâh, that is true", said 'Adi. "Thus I worked out that he was a Prophet inspired by Allâh, and sent to people. He knows what is unknown."

In another version, the Prophet (peace be upon him) said: "'Adi, embrace Islam and you shall be secure." "But I am a man of religion." Said 'Adi. "I know your religion better than you." Said the Prophet. "Do you know my religion better than me?" 'Adi asked. The Prophet replied, "Yes". He said: "Are you not cast in disbelief because you appropriate to yourself the fourth of your people's gains?" "Yes". Said 'Adi. "It is unlawful in your religion to do such a thing." The Prophet said, and "Adi added: "He did not need to say it again for I immediately acquiesced it."

Al-Bukhari narrates that 'Adi said: While we were with the Prophet (peace be upon him), a man came in and complained to him about poverty. Then another man came in and complained about highway robbery. The Messenger of Allâh (peace be upon him) then said: "O 'Adi, have you ever been to Al-Hirah? If you were doomed to live long life, you would be able to see a riding camel woman travel from Hirah till it circumambulates Al-Ka'bah fearing none but Allâh; and if you were to live long enough you would open the treasures of Kisra. And if you were to live long you would be able to see man offering a handful of gold or silver to others but none accepts to take it." At the end of this *Hadith* 'Adi later on says: "I have seen a riding camel woman travel from Al-Hirah till it circumambulates the Ka'bah fearing none but Allâh, I have also been one of those who opened the treasures of Kisra bin Hurmuz. If you were to live long life you would witness what the Prophet, Abul Qasim, (peace be upon him) had already said about 'offering a handful of …' i.e. the Prophet's prophecies did really come true."

THE INVASION OF TABUK IN RAJAB, IN THE YEAR 9 A.H.

The invasion and the conquest of Makkah was considered a decisive one between the truth and the error. As a result of which, the Arabs had no more doubt in Muhammad's mission. Thus we see that things went contrary to the pagans' expectations. People started to embrace Islam, the religion of Allâh, in great numbers. This is manifested clearly in the chapter — The delegations, of this book. It can also be deduced out of the enormous number of people who shared in the *Hajjatul-Wadâ*' (Farewell Pilgrimage). All domestic troubles came to an end. Muslims, eventually felt at ease and started setting up the teachings of Allâh's Laws and intensifying the Call to Islam.

THE UNDERLYING REASONS:

The Byzantine power, which was considered the greatest military force on earth at that time, showed an unjustifiable opposition towards Muslims. As we have already mentioned, their opposition started at killing the ambassador of the Messenger of Allâh (peace be upon him), Al-Harith bin 'Umair Al-Azdi, by Sharhabeel bin 'Amr Al-Ghassani. The ambassador was then carrying a message from the Prophet (peace be upon him) to the ruler of Busra. We have also stated that the Prophet consequently dispatched a brigade under the command of Zaid bin Haritha, who had a fierce fight against the Byzantines at Mu'tah. Although Muslim forces could not have revenge on those haughty overproud tyrants, the confrontation itself had a great impression on the Arabs, all over Arabia.

Caesar — who could neither ignore the great benefit thMu'tah Battle had brought to Muslims, nor could he disregard the Arab tribes' expectations of independence, and their hopes of getting free from his influence and reign, nor he could ignore their alliance to the Muslims — realizing all that, Caesar was aware of the progressive danger threatening his borders, especially Ash-Sham-fronts which were neighbouring Arab lands. So he concluded that demolition of the Muslims power had grown an urgent necessity. This decision of his should, in his opinion, be achieved before the Muslims become too powerful to conquer, and raise troubles and unrest in the adjacent Arab territories.

To meet these exigencies, Caesar mustered a huge army of the Byzantines and pro-Roman Ghassanide tribes to launch a decisive bloody battle against the Muslims.

General News about the Byzantines and Ghassanide Preparations for War.

No sooner news about the Byzantine's preparations for a decisive invasion against Muslims reached Madinah than fear spread among them. They started to envisage the Byzantine invasion in the least sound they could hear. This could be clearly worked out of what had happened to 'Umar bin Al-Khattab one day.

The Prophet (peace be upon him) had taken an oath to stay off his wives for a month in the ninth year of Al-Hijra. Therefore, he deserted them and kept off in a private place. At the beginning, the Companions of the Messenger of Allâh were puzzled and could not work out the reason for such behaviour. They thought the Prophet (peace be upon him) had divorced them and that was why he was grieved, disturbed and upset. In 'Umar's version of the very story he says: "I used to have a Helper friend who often informed me about what happened if I weren't present, and in return I always informed him of what had taken place during his absence. They both lived in the high part of Madinah. Both of them used to call at the Prophet alternatively during that time of suspense. Then one day I heard my friend, knock at the door saying: "Open up! Open up!" I asked wondering, "What's the matter? Has the Ghassanide come?" "No it is more serious than that. The Messenger of Allâh (peace be upon him) has deserted his wives."

In another version, 'Umar said, "We talked about Ghassanide preparations to invade us. When it was his turn to convey the news to me, he went down and returned in the evening. He knocked at the door violently and said 'Is he sleeping?' I was terrified but I went out to meet him. 'Something serious had taken place.' He said. 'Has the Ghassaindes arrived?' Said I. 'No,' he said, 'it is greater and more serious. The Messenger of Allâh (peace be upon him) has divorced his wives.'"

This state of too much alertness manifests clearly the seriousness of the situation that Muslims began to experience. The seriousness of the situation was confirmed to a large degree by the hypocrites behaviour, when news about the Byzantines' preparations reached Madinah. The fact that the Messenger of Allâh (peace be upon him) won all the battles he fought, and that no power on earth could make him terrified, and that he had always proved to be able to overcome all the obstacles that stood in his way - did not prevent the hypocrites, who concealed evil in their hearts, from expecting an affliction to fall upon the Muslims and Islam.

They used to harbour evil and ill-intentions against the whole process of Islam and the Muslims. On grounds of illusory hopes of destroying this great religious edifice, they erected a hotbed of conspiracy and intrigue in the form of a mosque — *Masjid-e-Darar* (the mosque of harm). They approached the Prophet (peace be upon him) with the request that he should come and consecrate the place by praying in it himself. As he was at the moment about to start for Tabuk, he deferred compliance with their request till his return. Meanwhile he came to know through Divine Revelation that it was not a Mosque for devotion and prayer but a meeting place for the anti-Islamic elements. On his return, therefore, the Prophet (peace be upon him) sent a party to demolish the new structure.

Particular News about the Byzantine and Ghassanide Preparations for War:

A magnified image of the prominent danger threatening the Muslims life was carried to them by the Nabateans who brought oil from Ash-Sham to Madinah. They carried news about Heraclius' preparations and equipment of an enormous army counting over forty thousand fighters besides Lukham, Judham and other tribes allied to the Byzantines. They said that its vanguard had already reached Al-Balqâ'. Thus was the grave situation standing in ambush for the Muslims. The general situation was aggravated seriously by other adverse factors of too much hot weather, drought and the rough and rugged distance they had to cover in case they decided to encounter the imminent danger.

The Messenger of Allâh's (peace be upon him) concept and estimation of the situation and its development was more precise and accurate than all others. He thought that if he tarried or dealt passively with the situation in such a way that might enable the Byzantines to paddle through the Islamic controlled provinces or to go as far as Madinah, this would — amid these circumstances — leave the most awful impression on Islam as well as on the Muslims' military credibility.

The pre-Islamic beliefs and traditions (*Al-Jahiliyah*) which were at that time dying because of the strong decisive blow that they had already had at Hunain, could have had a way to come back to life once again in such an environment. The hypocrites who were conspiring against the Muslims so that they might stab them in the back whereas Byzantines would attack them from the front. If such a thing came to light and they succeeded in their evil attempts, the Prophet and his Companions' efforts to spread Islam would collapse and their profits which were the consequences of successive and constant fights and invasions would be invalidated. The Messenger of Allâh (peace be upon him) realised all that very well. So — in spite of the hardships and drought that Muslims were suffering from — the Prophet (peace be upon him) was determined that the Muslims should invade the Byzantines and fight a decisive battle at their own borders. He was determined not to tarry at all in order to thwart any Roman attempt to approach the land of Islam.

When the Messenger of Allâh (peace be upon him) had made up his mind and took his final decision, he ordered his Companions to get ready for war and sent for the Makkans and the other Arab tribes asking for their assistance.

Contrary to his habit of concealing his real intention of the invasion by means of declaring a false one, he announced openly his intention of meeting the Byzantines and fighting them. He cleared the situation to his people so that they would get ready, and urged them to fight in the way of Allâh. On this occasion a part of *Surat Bara'a* (Chapter 9 — The Repentance) was sent down by Allâh, urging them to steadfastness and stamina.

On the other hand, the Messenger of Allâh (peace be upon him) cherished them to pay charities and to spend the best of their fortunes in the way of Allâh.

No sooner had the Muslims heard the voice of the Messenger of Allâh (peace be upon him) calling them to fight the Byzantines than they rushed to comply with his orders. With great speed they started getting ready for war. Tribes and phratries from here and there began pouring in Madinah. Almost all the Muslims responded positively. Only those who had weakness at their hearts favoured to stay behind. They were only three people. Even the needy and the poor who could not afford a ride came to the Messenger of Allâh (peace be upon him) asking for one so that they would be able to share in the fight against the Byzantines. But when he said:

- "...'I can find no mounts for you' they turned back while their eyes overflowing with tears of grief that they could not find anything to spend (for *Jihad*)." [9:92]

The Muslims raced to spend out money and to pay charities to provide this invasion. 'Uthman, for instance, who had already rigged two hundred, saddled camels to travel to Ash-Sham, presented them all with two hundred o(of gold) as charity. He also fetched a thousand dinars and cast them all into the lap of the Messenger of Allâh (peace be upon him), who turned them over and said: "From this day on nothing will harm 'Uthman regardless of what he does." Again and again 'Uthman gave till his charity toped to nine hundred camels and a hundred horses, besides the money he paid.

Abdur Rahman bin 'Awf, on his side, paid two hundred silver ounces, whereas Abu Bakr paid the whole money he had and left nothing but Allâh and His Messenger as a fortune for his family. 'Umar paid half his fortune. Al-'Abbas gifted a lot of money. Talhah, Sa'd bin 'Ubadah and Muhammad bin Maslamah, gave money for the welfare of the invasion. 'Asim bin 'Adi, on his turn, offered ninety camel-burdens of dates. People raced to pay little and much charities alike. One of them gave the only half bushel (or the only bushel) he owned. Women shared in this competition by giving the things they owned; such as musk, armlets, anklets, ear-rings and rings. No one abstained from spending out money, or was too mean to grant money or anything except the hypocrites:

- "Those who defame such of the believers who give charity (in Allâh's cause) voluntarily, and those who could not find to give charity (in Allâh's cause) except what is available to them, so they mock at them (believers)." [9:79]

The Muslim Army is leaving for Tabuk:

Upon accomplishing the equipment of the army, the Messenger of Allâh (peace be upon him) ordained that Muhammad bin Maslamah Al-Ansari should be appointed over Madinah — in another version Siba' bin 'Arftah. To 'Ali bin Abu Talib he entrusted his family's safety and affairs and ordered him to stay with them. This move made the hypocrites undervalue 'Ali, so he followed the Messenger of Allâh (peace be upon him) and caught up with him. But the Prophet made 'Ali turn back to Madinah after saying: "Would it not suffice you to be my successor in the way that Aaron (Harun) was to Moses'?" Then he proceeded saying: "But no Prophet succeeds me."

On Thursday, the Messenger of Allâh (peace be upon him) marched northwards to Tabuk. The army that numbered thirty thousand fighters was a great one, when compared with the previous armies of Islam. Muslims had never marched with such a great number before.

Despite all the gifts of wealth and mounts the army was not perfectly equipped. The shortage of provisions and mounts was so serious that eighteen men mounted one camel alternatively. As for provisions, members of the army at times had to eat the leaves of trees till their lips got swollen. Some others had to slaughter camels — though they were so dear — so that they could drink the water of their stomach; that is why that army was called "The army of distress".

On their way to Tabuk, the army of Islam passed by Al-Hijr — which was the native land of Thamud who cut out (huge) rocks in the valley; that is "Al-Qura Valley" of today. They watered from its well but later the Messenger of Allâh (peace be upon him) told them not to drink of that water, nor perform the ablution with it. The dough they made, he asked them to feed their camels with. He forbade them to eat anything whatsoever of it. As an alternative he told them to water from that well which Prophet Salih's she-camel used to water from.

On the authority of Ibn 'Umar: "Upon passing by Al-Hijr the Prophet (peace be upon him) said:

- "Do not enter the houses of those who erred themselves lest what had happened to them would afflict you, but if you had to do such a thing let it be associated with weeping."

Then he raised his head up and accelerated his strides till he passed the valley out."

Shortage of water and the army's need to it made them complain to the Messenger of Allâh (peace be upon him) about that. So he supplicated Allâh, who sent a rainful cloud. It rained and so all people drank and supplied themselves with their need of water.

When they drew near Tabuk, the Prophet said: "If Allâh will, tomorrow you will arrive at Tabuk spring. You will not get there before daytime. So whoever reaches it should not touch its water; but wait till I come." Mu'adh said: "When we reached the spring it used to gush forth some water. We found that two men had already preceded us to it. The Messenger of Allâh (peace be upon him) asked them: 'Have you touched its water?' They replied: 'Yes'. He said what Allâh inspired him to say, then he scooped up little water of that spring, thin stream which gathered together, he washed his face and hand with it and poured it back into it; consequently plenty of water spouted out of it so people watered. 'Mu'adh', said the Messenger of Allâh, 'if you were doomed to live long life you will see in here fields full of vegetation.'

On the way to Tabuk, or as soon as they reached Tabuk, the Messenger of Allâh (peace be upon him) said: 'Severe wind will blow tonight, so none of you should stand up. Whoever has a camel should tie it up.' Later on when the strong wind blew, one of the men stood up and the wind carried him away to Tai' Mountain.

All the way long the Messenger of Allâh (peace be upon him) was intent on the performance of the combined prayer of noon and the afternoon; and so did he with sunset and evening prayers. His prayers for both were either pre-time or post-time prayers.

<u>The Army of Islam at Tabuk:</u>

Arriving at Tabuk and camping there, the Muslim army was ready to face the enemy. There, the Messenger of Allâh (peace be upon him) delivered an eloquent speech that included the most inclusive words. In that speech he urged the Muslims to seek the welfare of this world and the world to come. He warned and cherished them and gave them good tidings. By doing that he cherished those who were broken in spirits, and blocked up the gap of shortage and mess they were suffering from due to lack of supplies, food and other substances.

Upon learning of the Muslims' march, the Byzantines and their allies were so terrified that none of them dared set out to fight. On the contrary they scattered inside their territory. It brought, in itself, a good credit to the Muslim forces. That had gained military reputation in the mid and remote lands of Arabian Peninsula. The great and serious political profits that the Muslim forces had obtained, were far better than the ones they could have acquired if the two armies had been engaged in military confrontation.

The Head of Ailah, Yahna bin Rawbah came to the Messenger of Allâh (peace be upon him), made peace with him and paid him the tribute (*Al-Jizya*). Both of Jarba' and Adhruh peoples paid him tribute, as well. So the Messenger of Allâh (peace be upon him) gave each a guarantee letter, similar to Yahna's, in which he says:

- "In the Name of Allâh, the Most Beneficent, the Most Merciful.

    This is a guarantee of protection from Allâh and Muhammad the Prophet, the Messenger of Allâh, to Yahna bin Rawbah and the people of Ailah; their ships, their caravans on land and sea shall have the custody of Allâh and the Prophet Muhammad, he and whosoever are with him of Ash-Sham people and those of the sea. Whosoever contravenes this treaty, his wealth shall not save him; it shall be the fair prize of him that takes it. Now it should not be lawful to hinder the men from any springs which they have been in the habit of frequenting, nor from any journeys they desire to make, whether by sea or by land."

The Messenger of Allâh (peace be upon him) dispatched Khalid bin Al-Waleed at the head of four hundred and fifty horsemen to 'Ukaidir Dumat Al-Jandal and said to him: "You will see him hunting oryxes." So when Khalid drew near his castle and was as far as an eye-sight range, he saw the oryxes coming out rubbing their horns against the castle gate. As it was a moony night Khalid could see Ukaidir come out to hunt them, so he captured him — though he was surrounded by his men — and brought him back to the Messenger of Allâh (peace be upon him), who spared his life and made peace with him for the payment of two thousand camels, eight hundred heads of cattle, four hundred armours and four hundred lances. He obliged him to recognize the duty of paying tribute and charged him with cit from Dumat, Tabuk, Ailah and Taima'.

The tribes, who used to ally the Byzantines, became quite certain that their dependence oinn their former masters came to an end. Therefore they turned into being pro-Muslims. The Islamic state had therefore enlarged its borders to an extent that it, touched the Byzantines' and their agents' borders. So we see that the Byzantine agents role was over.

Returning to Madinah:

The Muslim army returned from Tabuk victoriously, undeceived or wronged. That was because Allâh had sufficed them the evils of fight.

On the way back and at a mountain road, twelve hypocrites sought the Prophet's life and that was while he was passing along that mountain road with only Ammar holding the rein of his she-camel and Hudhaifa bin Al-Yaman driving it, at the time that people had already gone down into the bottom of the valley.

The hypocrites seized that opportunity to seek the Prophet's life. As the Messenger of Allâh (peace be upon him) and his two companions were moving along, they heard thrusts of people coming towards him from behind with their faces veiled. Hudhaifa, who was sent by the Prophet to see what was going on, saw them and stroke their mounts' faces with a crook in his hand and Allâh cast fear into their hearts. They fled away and overtook their people.

However, Hudhaifa named them to the Messenger of Allâh (peace be upon him) and informed him of their intentions. So that was why Hudhaifa was called the "confidant" of the Messenger of Allâh (peace be upon him). About this event Allâh, the Exalted says:

- "And they resolved that [plot to murder Prophet Muhammad (peace be upon him)] which they were unable to carry out." [9:74]

When his headquarters, Madinah, began to loom at the horizon, the Prophet (peace be upon him) said: "This is a cheerful sight. This is Uhud, which is a mountain, we like it and it likes us." When the Madinese learnt of their arrival they set out to meet the army. Women, youths, youngsters and small children went out of town to celebrate their home-return wholeheartedly singing:

- "The full moon shone down upon us, through the traits of Al-Wada' Mountain.
    Thanks is due to us, as long as a supplicator invokes to Allâh.."

The Messenger of Allâh 's march to Tabuk was in Rajab and his return in Ramadan. So we see that this *Ghazwah* took fifty days, twenty days of which were spent in Tabuk and the others on the way to and fro. Tabuk Invasion was the last one made by the Prophet (peace be upon him).

The People Who lagged Behind:

Due to its particular circumstances, this invasion was a peculiar severe trial provided by Allâh only to try the believers'Faith and sort them out of others. This is Allâh's permanent Will in such circumstances. In this respect He says:

- "Allâh will not leave the believers in the state in which you are now, until He distinguishes the wicked from the good." [3:179]

Lagging and hanging back from full participation in that invasion amounted to the degree of hypocrisy. Whenever the Messenger of Allâh (peace be upon him) was informed of a man's lingering, he would say: "Leave him alone! If Allâh knows him to be good He will enable him to follow you; but if he were not so, Allâh would relieve us of him."

Nobody stayed behind except those who were either hindered by a serious excuse or the hypocrites who told lies to Allâh and His Messenger.

Some of those hypocrites' lingering was due to an excuse based on forgery and delusion. Some others tarried but didn't ask for an instant permission. But there were three believers who unjustifiably lingered. They were the ones whom Allâh tried their Faith, but later on He turned to them in mercy and accepted their repentance.

As soon as the Messenger of Allâh (peace be upon him) had entered Madinah, he prayed two *Rak'a* then he sat to receive his people. The hypocrites who were over eighty men came and offered various kinds of excuses and started swearing. The Prophet acknowledged their excuses and invoked Allâh's forgiveness for them but he entrusted their inner thoughts and Faith to Allâh.

As for the three faithful believers — Ka'b bin Malik, Murara bin Ar-Rabi', and Hilal bin Omaiyah — who favoured telling the truth, the Messenger of Allâh صلى الله عليه وسلم bade his Companions not to talk to them.

Consequently they were subject to a severe boycott and were excluded from the life of the community. Everybody turned them their back. So they felt as if the whole land had become constrained to them in spite of its spaciousness and they felt awkward and uneasy. The hard times they lived and which lasted for over forty days were towered by an order to them to forsake their wives. After fifty days' boycott Allâh turned to them and revealed that in Qur'ân:

- "And (He did forgive also) the three [whom the Prophet (peace be upon him)] left (i.e. he did not give his judgement in their case, and their case was suspended for Allâh's Decision) till for them the earth, vast as it is, was straitened and their ownselves were straitened to them, and they perceived that there is no fleeing from Allâh, and no refuge but with Him. Then, He accepted their repentance, that they might repent (unto Him). Verily, Allâh is the One Who accepts repentance, Most Merciful." [9:118]

Allâh's turning to them was a great joy for both Muslims and the three concerned. The joy of the stayers behind was unaccountable in aim and degree. It was the happiest day in their lives. The good tiding cherished them and filled their hearts with delight. As for those who lingered due to disability or sickness or any other serious excuse, Allâh, the Exalted said about them:

- "There is no blame on those who are weak or ill or who find no resources to spend [in holy warfare (*Jihad*)], if they are sincere (in duty) to Allâh and His Messenger." [9:91]

When he approached Madinah, the Messenger of Allâh (peace be upon him) said:

- "Inside Madinah, there are certain men, who though being left back due to serious excuses, they have, all the time, been with you. Lingerers as they are, they have been while you were passing valleys or walking along roads." "Do you mean that they have done that while they are still in Madinah?" They wondered. "Yes though they are in Madinah." The Prophet said.

The Invasion of Tabuk and its Far-Reaching Ramifications:

The effect of this invasion is great as regards extending and confirming the Muslims' influence and domination on the Arabian Peninsula. It was quite obvious to everybody that no power but Islam's would live long among the Arabs. The remainders of *Jahiliyin* and hypocrites — who used to conspire steadily against the Muslims and who perpetually relied on Byzantine power when they were in need of support or help — these people lost their expectations and desires of ever reclaiming their ex-influence. Realizing that there was no way out and that they were to submit to the *fait accompli*, they gave up their attempts.

From that time on, hypocrites were no longer treated leniently or even gently by the Muslims. Allâh not only bade Muslims to treat them severely but He also forbade them to take their gift charities or perform prayer on their dead, or ask Allâh's forgiveness for them or even visit their tombs. Allâh bade the Muslims to demolish the mosque, which they verily appointed and used as a hiding place where they might practise their plots, conspiracy and deceit. Some Qur'ânic verses were sent down disclosing them publicly and utterly so that everybody in Madinah got to know their reality.

The great impact that this invasion produced could be perceived in of the great number of delegations who came successively to meet the Messenger of Allâh (peace be upon him). Naturally, deputations used to come to meet him at the end of an invasion particularly after Makkah Conquest but they were not as many as these nor were they as frequent as they were then in the wake of Tabuk event. It was certainly the greatest.

The Qur'ânic Verses Relating to this Invasion:

Many a verse of *Bara'a* (*Tauba*) Chapter handling the event of Tabuk were revealed. Some verses were revealed before the march, while others after setting out for Tabuk, i.e.in the context of the battle. Some other verses were also revealed on the Prophet's arrival in Madinah. All of which covered the incidents that featured this invasion: the immanent circumstances of the battle, exposure of the hypocrites, the prerogatives and special rank earmarked for the strivers in the cause of Allâh, acceptance of the repentance of the truthful believers who slackened and those who hung back, etc.

Some Important Events that featured that Year:

During this year many events of great significance took place. They were:

1. After the Messenger's return from Tabuk, the sworn allegation of infidelity between 'Uwaimir Al-'Ajlani and his wife took place.
2. Pelting with stones the Ghamidiyah woman who confessed committing adultery. She was pelted with stones only after weaning her child off her breast milk.
3. Negus Ashama; the king of Abyssinia (Ethiopia), died so the Prophet (peace be upon him) performed prayer in absentia for him.
4. The death of Umm Kulthum, the daughter of the Prophet (peace be upon him), the Prophet felt extremely sad at her death. "Had I got a third

daughter, I would let you marry her." He said to 'Uthman.

5. The death of 'Abdullah bin Abi Salool, the head of hypocrites, after the Prophet's return from Tabuk. The Messenger of Allâh (peace be upon him) asked Allâh's forgiveness for him. He also prayed for him in spite of 'Umar's disapproval and his attempt to prevent him from doing that.

   Later on a Qur'ânic verse was revealed attesting to 'Umar's right viewpoint.

SOME IMPORTANT EVENTS THAT FEATURED THAT YEAR

DURING THIS YEAR MANY EVENTS OF GREAT SIGNIFICANCE TOOK PLACE THEY WERE:

1. After the Messenger's return from Tabuk, the sworn allegation of infidelity between 'Uwaimir Al-'Ajlani and his wife took place.
2. Pelting with stones the Ghamidiyah woman who confessed committing adultery. She was pelted with stones only after weaning her child off her breast milk.
3. Negus Ashama; the king of Abyssinia (Ethiopia), died so the Prophet (Peace be upon him) performed prayer in absentia for him.
4. The death of Umm Kulthum, the daughter of the Prophet (Peace be upon him), the Prophet felt extremely sad at her death. "Had I got a third daughter, I would let you marry her." He said to 'Uthman.
5. The death of 'Abdullah bin Abi Salool, the head of hypocrites, after the Prophet's return from Tabuk. The Messenger of Allâh (Peace be upon him) asked Allâh's forgiveness for him. He also prayed for him in spite of 'Umar's disapproval and his attempt to prevent him from doing that. Later on a Qur'ânic verse was revealed attesting to 'Umar's right viewpoint.

ABU BAKR (May Allah be pleased with him) PERFORMS THE PILGRIMAGE:

In the month Dhul-Qa'dah or in Dhul-Hijjah of the very year (the ninth of Al-Hijra), the Messenger of Allâh (Peace be upon him) dispatched Abu Bakr (May Allah be pleased with him), the truthful, as a deputy prince of *Al-Hajj* (pilgrimage), so that he would lead the Muslims in performing of the pilgrimage rituals.

Soon after the departure of the Muslims, there came a Revelation from Allâh: the opening passages of the Chapter 9 entitled 'Repentance' (*Surah Tauba* or *Bara'a*) in which 'freedom from obligation' is proclaimed from Allâh in regard to those idolatrous tribes who had shown no respect for the treaties which they had entered into with the Prophet (Peace be upon him). Communication of this news went in line with the Arabian traditions of making public any change relating to declining conventions of blood and fortunes.

'Ali bin Abi Talib was deputed to make this declaration. He overtook Abu Bakr at Al-'Arj or Dajnan. Abu Bakr inquired whether the Prophet (Peace be upon him) had put him in command or he had just been commissioned to make the announcement. "I have been deputed to make the proclamation only" replied 'Ali. The two Companions then proceeded with the pilgrimage process. Towards the close of the rituals, on the day of the ritual sacrifice, 'Ali stood at *Al-Jamrah* (a spot at which stones are pelted) and read aloud to the multitudes that thronged around him and declared quittance from covenants with idolaters and giving them four months' respite to reconsider their position. As for the other idolaters with whom the believers had a treaty and had abated nothing of the Muslims' rights nor had supported anyone against them, then the terms of the treaty would run valid until the duration of which expired.

Abu Bakr then sent some Muslims to declare publicly that no disbeliever would after that year perform pilgrimage, nor would anyone be allowed to make the *Tawaf* (going round) of the Sacred House unclothed.

That proclamation in fact vetoed all aspects of paganism out of Arabia and stated quite unequivocally that those pre-Islam practices were no longer in operation.

A MEDITATION ON THE GHAZWAT:

Meditation on the Prophet's Ghazawat, missions, and the battalions he formed and dispatched, will certainly give us and everybody a true and clear impression that the Prophet (Peace be upon him) was the greatest military leader in the whole world as well as the most righteous, the most insightful and the most alert one. He was not a man of superior genius for this concern but he was also the Master and the greatest of all Messengers as far as Prophethood and Heavenly Message are concerned. Besides, all the battles that he had fought were standard in their application to the requirements of strictness, bravery, and good arrangements that fitted the terms and conditions of war. None of the battles he fought was lost as a consequence of shortage of wisdom or due to any other technical error in army mobilization or a location in a wrong strategical position. The loss of any of his battle was not due to misjudgement about occupying the best and the most appropriate sites of battles, nor was it due to a mischoice of leaders of the fight, for he had proved himself to be a peculiar sort of leader that differs from any of those leaders that our world had known and experienced. As regards Uhud and Hunain events, there were consequences of weakness in some military elements in Hunain; and disobedience to orders in Uhud. Their non-compliance with wisdom and the plan of the battle played a passive role in the course of those two invasions.

His genius was clearly shown in these two battles when the Muslims were defeated; for he stoodfast facing the enemy and managed, by his super wisdom, to thwart the enemy's aim as was the case in Uhud. Similarly he managed to change the Muslims' defeat in Hunain into a victory. Nothwithstanding the fact that serious grave developments in military operations usually leave the worst impression on the military leaders and entice them to flee for their lives.

We have, so far, discussed the mere aspects of military leadership of the invasions. On the other hand, through these invasions he was able to impose security, institute peace, diffuse dissension and destroy the military might of the enemies through relentless struggle between Islam and paganism.

The Prophet had also profound insight and could differentiate the faithful from the hypocrites and plotters.

Great was the group of military leaders who fought and excelled the Persians and the Byzantines in the battlefields of Ash-Sham and Iraq with respect to war strategy and leading the fight procedures. The very leaders, who succeeded Muhammad (Peace be upon him) , managed to drive off the enemies of Islam, from their lands and countries, their gardens and springs, and their farms. They drove them off their honourable residence and from the grace and provisions they owned and enjoyed. Those Muslim leaders were all Muhammad's men. They were imbued with the spirit of Islam at the hand of the Prophet (Peace be upon him).

Thanks to these battles, the Messenger of Allâh (Peace be upon him) managed accommodation, secured land and provided chances of work for all Muslims. He, even, made a lot of inquiries about the refugee problems who (then) had no houses or fortunes. He equipped the army with weapons, horses and expenditures. He had all that realized without exercising a particle weight of injustice. The Prophet (Peace be upon him) has altered the standards and aims of pre-Islamic wars. Their war was no more than robbing, killing, plundering, tyranny and aggression-oriented wars. Those wars focused on winning victory, oppressing the weakling and demolishing their houses and constructions. For them, war was a means by which they can rape or unveil women, practise cruelty against the weakling, the babies and small children, spoil tillage and race, and spread corruption on the earth. Islamic wars are different from pre-Islamic wars. A "war" in Islam is a *Jihad*. That is to say it is a noble sacred fight in the way of Allâh for the verification of a Muslim society that seeks to free man from oppression, tyranny and aggression. It is a society that everyone everywhere and at all times should be proud of.Pre-Islamic thoughts and traditions of *Al-Jahiliyah* period have been turned upside down by Islam. These were so hard upon the weakling that they had to invoke Allâh to enable them to get away from that pre-Islamic environment by saying:

- "Our Lord, rescue us from this town whose people are oppressors, and raise for us from You one who will protect, and raise for us from You one who will help."

The war of corruption, slaying and robbing that used to prevail has now turned into a sacred one, *Al-Jihad*. One of the greatest aims of *Al-Jihad* is to free man from the aggression, the oppression and the tyranny of men of power. A man of power, in Islam, is a weakling till after the right of the poor is taken from him. War, in Islam, is a *Jihad* for the purification of the land of Allâh from dece, treachery, sinful deeds and aggression. It is a sacred war that aims at spreading security, safety, mercy and compassion as well as observing the rights and magnanimity. The Messenger of Allâh (Peace be upon him) had issued honourable strict rules about war and bade his soldiers and leaders to comply with them. They were forbidden to break those rules under any circumstances. In reference to Sulaiman bin Buraidah's version, who said that his father had told him that whenever the Messenger of Allâh (Peace be upon him) appointed a leader on an army or on a battalion, he used to recommend him to fear Allâh, the Great and All-Mighty, when dealing with those who were closest to him and to be good with all Muslims. Then the Prophet (Peace be upon him) would say to him:

- "Let your invasion be in the Name of Allâh and for His sake. Fight those who disbelieve in Allâh. Invade but do not exaggerate nor commit treachery. Never deform the corpse of a dead person or kill an infant child."

The Messenger of Allâh (Peace be upon him) asked people to facilitate but he forbade them to bear down hard on others or constrain. "Pacify", he said, "and do not disincline". When it happened that he arrived at the battlefield by night, he would never invade the enemy till it was morning. He utterly forbade burning (i.e. torturing people) in fire, killing children and women or even beating them. He also forbade theft and robbery and proceeded so far as to say gains acquired through plundering are not less forbidden than the flesh of a corpse. Corruption of tillage and race and cutting down of trees were all forbidden unless they were badly needed and there was no other substitute:

- "Do not kill a wounded person nor run after a fleeing one or kill a captive."

He decreed that envoys cannot be killed. He also stressed on not killing those who made covenants. He even said:

- "He whoever kills one who is under pledge to a covenant shall not smell Paradise, though its smell could be experienced at a forty-year distance from it."

There were some other noble rules which purified wars from their *Al-Jahiliyah* (pre-Islamic) filthiness and turned them into sacred wars.

PEOPLE EMBRACE THE RELIGION OF ALLAH IN LARGE CROWDS:

The invasion and the conquest of Makkah was — as we have already stated — a decisive battle that destroyed paganism utterly. The Arabs as a result of that battle were able to differentiate the truth from the error. Delusion no longer existed in their life. So they raced to embrace Islam. 'Amr bin Salamah said: "We were at a water (spring) where the passage of people was. So when camel riders passed by us we used to ask them: 'What is the matter with people? What is this man (i.e. the Prophet) like?' They would say, 'He claims that Allâh has revealed so and so.' I used to memorize those words as if they had been recited within my chest. The Arabs used to ascribe their Islamization to the conquest. They would say: 'Leave him alone to face his people. If he were a truthful Prophet he would overcome them.' So when the conquest took place, peoples hastened to declare their Islam. My father was the quickest of all my people to embrace Islam. Arriving at his people he said: 'By Allâh I have just verily been to the Prophet (Peace be upon him) . And he said: 'Perform so a prayer at such a time, and so and so prayers at such and such time. When the prayer time is due let one of you call for the prayer and appoint the most learned of the Qur'ân among you to be an *Imam* (leader) of yours." This Prophetic tradition manifests the great effect of the conquest of Makkah on the phase of events. It certainly shows the influence of the conquest of Makkah upon the consolidation of Islam as well as on the Arabs' stand and their surrender to Islam. That influence was absolutely confirmed and deeply rooted after the invasion of Tabuk. A clear and an obvious evidence of that influence could be deduced from the great number of delegations arriving in Madinah successively in the ninth and tenth years of Al-Hijra. The immense crowds of people who raced to embrace the religion of Allâh and the great army which included ten thousand fighters in the invasion of the conquest of Makkah had grown big enough to include thirty thousand fighters sharing in Tabuk invasion. It was only in less than a year after the conquest of Makkah that this growth in Islamic army had taken place. A hundred thousand or a hundred and forty four thousand Muslim pilgrims shared in *Hajjatul -Wada*' (i.e. Farewell Pilgrimage); it was such an enormous number of Muslims surging — as an ocean of men — round the Messenger of Allâh (Peace be upon him) , that the horizon echoed their voices and the expanses of land shook whereby while saying *Labbaik* (i.e. Lord, here we are worshipping), glorifying and magnifying Allâh, and thanking Him.

THE DELEGATIONS:

The number of delegations listed in *Ahl Al-Maghazi* were over seventy. Investigating such a large number is not an accessible thing; besides stating them in detail is not of a great benefit. Therefore, I am going to reveal an expose about what is historically wonderful or highly significant. Anyway a reader should always keep in mind that whilst the majority of tribes arrived in Madinah after the conquest, there were also pre-conquest delegations.

1. The delegation of 'Abdul Qais: This tribe had two arrivals. The first was in the fifth year of Al-Hijra or before that date. Munqidh bin Haiyan, a member of that tribe, used to trade in Madinah. So, as soon as he heard of Islam when he had arrived in it for trading — that was after the migration — he embraced Islam and carried a pledge from the Prophet (Peace be upon him) to his people who eventually became Muslims too. Thirteen or fourteen of them came to the Prophet (Peace be upon him) in one of the *Hurum* Months. It was then that they asked the Prophet's advice about the Faith and drinks. Their chief was Al-Ashaj Al-Usri, to whom the Messenger of Allâh (Peace be upon him) said: "You have two qualities that Allâh likes: They are deliberatenessandclemency."

2. Their second arrival was in the Year of Delegations. They were forty men. Al-Jarud bin Al-'Alâ' Al-'Abdi, who was Christian but turned to be a good Muslim, was one of that group.

3. Daws Delegation: The arrival of this tribe was in the early times of the seventh year and that was when the Messenger of Allâh (Peace be upon him) was in Khaibar. At-Tufail bin 'Amr Ad-Dawsi, that we have already talked about and explained how he became a Muslim at the time the Messenger of Allâh (Peace be upon him) was in Makkah. He went back home to his people where he kept calling people to Islam but they tarried till he despaired of them and returned to the

Messenger of Allâh (Peace be upon him) and asked him to invoke Allâh against Daws but the Messenger of Allâh (Peace be upon him) invoked Allâh to guide Daws. Later on, Daws embraced Islam. So At-Tufail arrived in Madinah accompanied by seventy or eighty families of his people in the early times of the seventh year of Al-Hijra, at the time that the Messenger of Allâh (Peace be upon him) was at Khaibar, so he overtook him there.

4. Farwah Bani 'Amr Al-Judhami's messenger: Farwah was an Arab leader in the Byzantine army. He was a Byzantine agent ruler by proxy on the Arabs allied to the Byzantines. His home was at Mu'an and the surrounding area of Ash-Sham lands. Seeing the stamina and courage of the Muslims he became a Muslim. The battle of Mu'tah — which took place in the eighth year of Al-Hijra — compelled his admiration. He sent a white mule gift with a messenger of his to the Messenger of Allâh (Peace be upon him) to inform him of his conversion into Islam. When the Byzantines learnt of his embracing Islam, they sent him to prison. At first they gave him an opportunity to choose one of the two — "either he defects from Islam or death shall be his punishment." Refusing to defect they crucified him and cut his neck at a water (fountain) called 'Afra' in Palestine.

5. Sudâ' Delegation: The arrival of this delegation was after the departure of the Messenger of Allâh (Peace be upon him) from Al-Ji'ranah in the eighth year of Al-Hi. It was because the Messenger of Allâh (Peace be upon him) had already dispatched a mission that comprised four hundred Muslims and asked them to go to where Sudâ' was. Sudâ' was (a fresh-water fountain) in Yemen. While the mission was camping there at the starting point of a canal. Ziyad bin Al-Harith As-Sudâ'i learned of their stay, so he came to the Messenger of Allâh (Peace be upon him) and said: "I have come to you as a deputy of my people, so tell your army to go back and I guarantee of my people." The army were sent away off the canal. In his turn As-Sudâ'i went back, cherished and urged his people to come and meet the Messenger of Allâh (Peace be upon him). Eventually fifteen of them came and pledged allegiance to him as true Muslims. Returning home, they in their turn, urged the rest to be Muslims. Thus Islam spread among them. Later on, a hundred men joined the Messenger of Allâh (Peace be upon him) in *Hajjatul-Wada'* (Farewell Pilgrimage.)

6. The arrival of Ka'b bin Zuhair bin Abi Sulma: Ka'b who was a member of a family of poets, was considered one of the most poetic Arab poets. He used to satirize the Prophet (Peace be upon him) when he wasn't a Muslim. In the eighth year of Al-Hijra and at the time that the Messenger of Allâh (Peace be upon him) had already gone back from At-Ta'if invasion, Bujair bin Zuhair wrote a letter to his brother Ka'b warning and advising him: "The Messenger of Allâh (Peace be upon him) had killed some men in Makkah who used to satirize and harm him, and that the other poets who had survived fled in all directions for their lives. So if you want to save your skin, hasten to the Messenger of Allâh (Peace be upon him). He never kills those who resort to him as repentant. If you refuse to do as I tell, it is up to you to try to save your skin by any means." The two brothers corresponded with one another for a long time till Ka'b was awkward and felt as if the earth had constrained on him. Arriving in Madinah, he stayed at a man's house from Juhainah as a guest. They performed the dawn prayer together; but when he was about to leave, the man suggested that he go to the Messenger of Allâh (Peace be upon him). He went there, sat by him, put his hand in his. The Messenger of Allâh (Peace be upon him) who had never seen Ka'b before, did not recognize him. Ka'b then said: "O, Messenger of Allâh! Ka'b bin Zuhair has come to you as a repentant Muslim; will he be secure and forgiven if I fetch him?" The Messenger of Allâh (Peace be upon him) said, "Yes." "I am Ka'b bin Zuhair," said he. Upon hearing that one of the Helpers rose to his feet and asked the Messenger's allowance to cut his throat. "Leave him alone!" Said the Prophet (Peace be upon him), "He has become a repentant Muslim after his disposal of the past." Ka'b then recited his well-known poem *"Su'ad appeared..."* in which he praised the Prophet (Peace be upon him) , thanked him and apologized for the wrongs he had done. He acknowledged Muhammad's mission. Both Emigrants and Helpers were spoken of in this poem but differently. He praised the Emigrants but criticized the Helpers, for one of them demanded a Prophet's permission to kill him. Later on Ka'b tried to compensate for that by praising the Helpers too but that was in another poem.

7. 'Udharah Delegation: This delegation which consisted of twelve men, had arrived in Madinah in Safar, the ninth year of Al-Hijra. They spent three days there. One of them was Hamza bin An-

Nu'man. When they were asked who they were, they said "We are Bani 'Udharah, the foster brothers of Qusai to his mother. We are the ones who supported Qusai, and removed Khuza'a and Bani Bakr from the bosom of Makkah. We have relatives and kinspeople." So the Messenger of Allâh (Peace be upon him) welcomed them and gave good tidings to them, which was Ash-Sham Conquest; but he, on the other hand, forbade them from consulting a soothsayer and from eating the slain animals they slaughtered. Eventually they became Muslims, stayed there for several days then went back.

8. Bali Delegation: Their arrival was in Rabi' Al-Awwal, the ninth year of Al-Hijra. They embraced Islam, stayed in Madinah for three days. Their chief Abu Ad-Dabeeb wondered whether hospitality was rewarded by Allâh. The Messenger of Allâh (Peace be upon him) said:

-
  - "Yes, and so is any charity you offer to poor or rich people that is *Sadaqah*."

He also inquired about the time allotted to hospitality. "Three days," said he. "What about the stray ewe?" The Prophet said: "It is either yours or your brother's, otherwise it goes to the wolf." He inquired about the stray camel. "It is not of your business. Leave it alone! Its owner will try to find it."

8. Thaqif Delegation: Their arrival was in Ramadan, the ninth year of Al-Hijra, after the return of the Messenger of Allâh (Peace be upon him) from Tabuk. As to how they became Muslims, this could be deduced from the following:

9. Their chief 'Urwah bin Mas'ud Ath-Thaqafi came to see the Messenger of Allâh (Peace be upon him) after the latter's return from At-Ta'if in Dhul-Qa'dah in the year 8 A.H. 'Urwah became a Muslim. He thought that when he will tell his people and call them to embrace Islam, they would obey him, because he had always been an obeyed Master. He was even more beloved to them than their own firstborn. But contrary to that, when he called them to Islam they shot arrows at him from everywhere and killed him. They remained as they were for months before they started discussing the situation again among themselves. Upon realizing that they were incapable of fighting the neighbouring Arabs who had paid allegiance to the Prophet (Peace be upon him) and converted to Islam, they made up their mind to dispatch a man to the Messenger of Allâh (Peace be upon him). They concluded that 'Abd Yalail bin 'Amr would be the right messenger.

'Abd refused to do such a thing lest they should kill him as they had killed 'Urwah. "I will not do such a thing till you send some other men with me," said 'Abd. So they sent two men of their allies and three others from Bani Malik. The six of them including 'Uthman bin Abi Al-'As Ath-Thaqafi who was the youngest among them all.

When they entered into the Prophet's (Peace be upon him) audience, a tent was pitched up in a corner of the mosque so that they might listen to the Qur'ân and see people at prayer. During their stay they came again and again to the Prophet (Peace be upon him) who kept on calling them to embrace Islam, till their chief asked the Messenger of Allâh (Peace be upon him) to enter into a peace treaty between him and Thaqif by means of which he allows them to commit fornication, drink wine and deal with usury. They also asked him not to injure their tyrant idol "Al-Lat" or to oblige them to perform the prayer. Finally they insisted that they would not knock down the idols themselves. But the Messenger of Allâh (Peace be upon him) turned down all their requests. They went aside to council. Realizing that there were no other alternatives they yielded and professed Islam. The only condition that they insisted on was that the demolition of Al-Lat should be dealt with and handled by the Messenger of Allâh (Peace be upon him) whereas Thaqif should in no way knock it down themselves. The Messenger of Allâh (Peace be upon him) agreed and took a pledge with them.

Being the most attentive and the keenest to study jurisprudence and learn Qur'ân, 'Uthman bin Abi Al-'As was appointed by the Messenger of Allâh (Peace be upon him) a prince on his people.

His keenness and carefulness to learn the Qur'ân and study jurisprudence were clearly discernible through his behaviour during their stay.

Everyday morning, the group of delegates used to go and see the Messenger of Allâh (Peace be upon him). Being the youngest one, 'Uthman bin Abi Al-'As was left behind with their camels and things to keep an eye on. At noon when they came back and slept, 'Uthman used to go to the Messenger of Allâh (Peace be upon him) in order to learn the Qur'ân and inquire about religious matters. If it happened that the Messenger of Allâh (Peace be upon him) was asleep, he would then go to Abu Bakr for the same purpose. With the pof time, he turned out to be a source of blessing to his people. For at the Apostasy Times (Ar-Riddah) when Thaqif were determined to apostatize, he addressed them saying: "O, folkmen of Thaqif! You have been the latest at embracing Islam, so do not be the first to apostatize." Consequently they gave up apostasy and clung fast to Islam.

The group of delegates returned home but they were determined to conceal the truth for a while. They told their people to expect fight at any moment. They pretended to be grieved and depressed. They claimed that the Messenger of Allâh (Peace be upon him) demanded that they should embrace Islam and abandon adultery, drinking wine and dealing with usury and some other things, or else he would fight them. Seized by the arrogance and zeal of Al-Jahiliyah (pre-Islamic traditions), Thaqif remained for days intent on fighting. Then Allâh cast terror and dismay in their hearts in such a way that they gave up fighting and thought that the delegation should go back to him and announce their approval. It was until then that the group of delegates told them the truth and revealed the items of their peace-talk with the Prophet, consequently Thaqif embraced Islam.

The Messenger of Allâh (Peace be upon him) sent some men to demolish the idol called "Al-Lat" under the command of Khalid bin Al-Waleed. Al-Mugheerah bin Shu'bah, stood to his feet, held the hoe and the ax and said: "By Allâh, I will make you laugh at Thaqif." He struck with them, and pretended to fall down while running. The people of Thaqif trembled at that sight and said: "May Allâh dismay Al-Mugheerah off. The goddess has killed him." Hearing that Al-Mugheerah leapt up to his feet and said: "May Allâh bring shame on you. Al-Lat is nothing but a mass of dirt and stones." Then he struck the door and broke it. He mounted its highest wall, and so did the other men. They knocked Al-Lat down till they levelled it with the ground. Then they dug up its foundation and brought out its jewels and garments; to the great astonishment of Thaqif. Khalid bin Al-Waleed and his group came back to the Messenger of Allâh (Peace be upon him) carrying Al-Lat's jewels and garments. The Messenger of Allâh (Peace be upon him) distributed them and thanked Allâh for helping his Prophet and solidifying his religion.

10. The message of the Yemeni kings: After the return of the Messenger of Allâh (Peace be upon him) from Tabuk, a message came to him from the kings of Himyar, Al-Harith bin 'Abd Kilal, Na'eem bin 'Abd Kilal, An-Nu'man bin Qeel Dhi Ra'in, Hamdan and Mu'afir. Their messenger was Malik bin Murrah Ar-Rahawi. They sent him in order to inform the Prophet (Peace be upon him) about their embracing Islam and their parting with polytheism. In reply to their message, the Messenger of Allâh (Peace be upon him) gave them the pledge of Allâh and the pledge of His Messenger provided they paid the tribute, which was still overdue. He sent to them some of his Companions under the command of Mu'adh bin Jabal (May Allah be pleased with him).

11. Hamdan Delegation: The arrival of this delegation was in the ninth year of Al-Hijra after the Messenger's return from Tabuk. So the Messenger of Allâh (Peace be upon him) gave them a pledge to guarantee the fulfillment of their demands. He sent to them Malik bin An-Namt as their chief, and appointed him as an agent on those of his people who embraced Islam. Khalid bin Al-Waleed was appointed for them all with a purpose of calling them to Islam. He stayed with them for six months calling them to Islam but no one responded to his call. Later on 'Ali bin Abi Talib was dispatched there and Khalid was ordered to come back. Upon arriving at Hamdan, 'Ali communicated to them a message from the Messenger of Allâh (Peace be upon him) and called them to Islam. They responded to the call and became Muslims. 'Ali wrote to the Messenger of Allâh (Peace be upon him) informing him of the good tidings. The Messenger of Allâh (Peace be

upon him) was briefed on the content of that letter, so he prostrated, then raised his head up and said: "Peace be upon Hamdan. Peace be upon Hamdan."

12. **The Delegation of Bani Fazarah:** Upon the Messenger's return from Tabuk, the delegation of Bani Fazarah came to see him. That was in the ninth year of Al-Hijra. The group of delegates were over ten men. They came in order to profess Islam and complain about the drought of their region. The Messenger of Allâh (Peace be upon him) ascended the pulpit, lifted his hands up and implored Allâh to send rain forth onto them and said:

- "O Allâh let rain fall down, and water Your country and animals, and spread Your mercy and bring to life the dead lands. O Allâh send rain that would be saving, comforting, and sprouting grass, and overwhelming vast areas sooner and later. Let it be useful rain and not harmful. O Allâh let it be rain of mercy and not rain of torture and chastisement. Let that rain not be destructive or floody. O Allâh send us down water and help to fight the enemies."

12. **Najran's Delegation:** Najran is rather a big area of land. It was at a distance of seven trip stages southwards of Makkah towards Yemen. It included seventy three villages. It took a fast-rider one day ride to get there. Its military forces consisted of a hundred thousand fighters.

- Their arrival was in the year 9 A.H. The delegation comprised sixty men. Twenty-four of them were of noble families. Three out of twenty-four were at one time leaders of Najran. *Al-'Aqib*, i.e. who was in charge of princehood and government affairs. His name was 'Abdul Maseeh. The second was *As-Saiyid* (the Master) under whose supervision were the educational and political affairs; his name was Al-Aiham or Sharhabeel. Abu Haritha bin 'Alqamah was the third. He was a bishop to whom all religious presidency and spiritual leadership belonged and were his charge.

When that group of delegates arrived in Madinah, they met the Prophet (Peace be upon him), exchanged inquiries with him; but when he called them to Islam and recited the Qur'ân to them, they refused. They asked him what he thought about 'Isa (i.e. Jesus), (Peace be upon him), he (Peace be upon him) tarried a whole day till the following Qur'ânic reply was revealed to him:

   o "Verily, the likeness of Jesus before Allâh is the likeness of Adam. He created him from dust, then (He) said to him: 'Be!' — and he was. (This is) the truth from your Lord, so be not of those who doubt. Then whoever disputes with you concerning him (Jesus) after (all this) knowledge that has come to you, (i.e. Jesus being a slave of Allâh, and having no share in Divinity) say: [O Muhammad (Peace be upon him)] 'Come, let us call our sons and your sons, our women and your women, ourselves and yourselves — then we pray and invoke (sincerely) the Curse of Allâh upon those who lie." [3:59-61]

When it was morning, the Messenger of Allâh (Peace be upon him) told them what 'Iesa (Jesus) was in the light of the recently revealed verses. He left them a whole day to consult and think it over. So when it was next morning and they still showed disapproval to admit Allâh's Words about 'Isa or to embrace Islam, the Prophet suggested *Al-Mubahala* that is each party should supplicate and implore Allâh to send His Curse upon him or them if they were telling lies. After that suggestion of his, the Prophet (Peace be upon him) came forward wrapping Al-Hasan and Al-Husain under his garment whereas Fatimah was walking at his back. Seeing that the Prophet (Peace be upon him) was serious and prepared to face them firmly, they went aside and started consulting. *Al-'Aqib* and *As-Saiyid* (i.e. the Master) said to each other: "We shall not supplicate. For, I swear by Allâh, if he is really a Prophet and exchanges curses with us, we will never prosper nor will the descendants of ours. Consequently neither us nor our animals will survive it." Finally they made their mind to resort to the Messenger of Allâh's judgement about their cause. They came to him and said: "We grant you what you have demanded." The Messenger of Allâh (Peace be upon him) then admitted that agreement and ordered them to pay *Al-Jizya* (i.e. tribute) and he made peace with them for the provisioof two thousand garments, one thousand of them to be delivered in Rajab, the other thousand ones in Safar. With every garment they had to pay an ounce (of gold). In return they will have the covenant of Allâh and His Messenger. He gave them a covenant that provides for practicing their religious affairs freely. They asked the Prophet (Peace be upon him) to appoint a trustworthy man to receive the money agreed on for peace, so he sent them the trustworthy man of this nation Abu 'Ubaidah bin Al-Jarrah to receive the amounts of money agreed on in the peace treaty.

By the time Islam started to spread in Najran, naturally, they did not have to pay *Al-Jizya* that usually non-Muslims paid. Whatever the case was, it was said that *Al-Aqib* and *As-Saiyid* embraced Islam as soon as they reached Najran on their journey back home. It is also said that the Prophet (Peace be upon him) sent to them 'Ali too, for the collection of charities and tribute.

13. Bani Haneefa Delegation: They arrived in Madinah in the ninth year of Al-Hijra. They were 17 in number and included the Master of Liars, Musailima bin Thumamah bin Kabeer bin Habeeb bin Al-Harith of Bani Haneefa The group of delegates were housed in a Helper's house. They came to the Prophet (Peace be upon him) and declared their Islamization. As for Musailima the liar, versions vary concerning his embracing Islam. Contemplation of all these versions shows clearly that Musailima expressed disapproval and revealed haughtiness, boastful spirit and expectations to be a prince.

- At first the Prophet (Peace be upon him) attempted going on well with him. he dealt with him nicely and charitably but that did not do with him. The Messenger of Allâh (Peace be upon him) perceived evil in his soul and recognized that he was one of those three evils he dreamt of while asleep.

The Prophet (Peace be upon him) had already dreamt that he had been granted the treasures of earth. His hand fell upon two golden bracelets, which distressed and worried him a lot. He was taught by inspiration to blow them off, so he did that and they were gone off. They were interpreted to be two liars who would turn up after the death of Muhammad (Peace be upon him). So when Musailima acted that way and showed disapproval, he realized that he would be one of the two liars. However Musailima used to say, "If Muhammad appointed me a successor of his, I would be a Muslim. Later on the Messenger of Allâh (Peace be upon him) came to him, with a piece of palm leaf in his hand, and in the company of his orator, Thabit bin Qais bin Shammas. He was among some of his friends. The Prophet (Peace be upon him) talked to him but Musailima addressed him saying: "If you agree to transfer the whole thing to me after your death, I will not stand in your way." The Messenger of Allâh (Peace be upon him) replied: "If you asked me to give you this (i.e. a piece of a palm leaf), I would not grant it to you. You are doomed. Even if you repented and stopped what you were doing, Allâh appointed that you would be slain. By Allâh, I swear, that I see you now in the very state that has been revealed to me. Here is Thabit! You will hear my answer (from him)." Then he went away.

Finally, the Prophet's predictions of Musailima came true; for when Musailima returned to Yamama, he kept on thinking about the Prophet (Peace be upon him) and how he would be his partner. His dreams and thoughts went so far as to claim that he himself was a prophet. To confirm his prophecy he started uttering rhymed statements. He said that it was lawful to drink wine and commit adultery. He, however, bore witness that the Messenger of Allâh (Peace be upon him) was a real Prophet. His people, who were fascinated by what he allowed them to do, followed him and made bargains with him. He grew so prominent among them that they called him the beneficent of Al-Yamama. He wrote to the Messenger of Allâh (Peace be upon him) saying: "I have been appointed an associate with you, so I will have a half and Quraish will have the other half of the people's affairs." The Messenger of Allâh's reply was a letter saying that:

   o "Verily, the earth is Allâh's. He gives it as a heritage to whom He will of His slaves, and the (blessed) end is for the *Muttaqûn* (pious)." [7:128]

On the authority of Ibn Mas'ud, he says: When the two messengers of Musailima — Ibn An-Nawaha and Ibn Athal — came to the Messenger of Allâh (Peace be upon him), he asked them: "Do you bear witness that I am the Messenger of Allâh?" Their reply was "We testify that

Musailima is the Messenger of Allâh." "I believe in Allâh and in His Messenger," said the Prophet (Peace be upon him), "If I had ever thought of killing a messenger I would have killed you both."

Musailima's pretence to prophethood was in the tenth year of Al-Hijra. But he was killed in Al-Yamama war during Abu Bakr As-Siddeeq era, in Rabi' Al-Awwal, in the twelfth year of Al-Hijra. He was killed by Wahshi, the killer of Hamzah. The second person who claimed to be a prophet was Al-Aswad Al-'Ansi who was in Yemen. He was killed by Fairuz. His head was cut off a day and a night before the Prophet's death. So when the delegates came he told them the news that reached him through Divine Revelation. News about his death reached Abu Bakr (May Allah be pleased with him) from Yemen.

14. The Delegation of Bani 'Amir bin Sa'sa'a: Among the group of delegates were 'Amir bin At-Tufail — the enemy of Allâh, Arbad bin Qais — Labid's maternal brother, Khalid bin Ja'far, and Jabbar bin Aslam. All of them were the leaders and satans of their people. 'Amir was the one who double-crossed the group of Ma'una well. When this delegation made their mind to come to Madinah, 'Amir and Arbad conspired to kill the Prophet (Peace be upon him). So when the group of delegates arrived, 'Amir kept on talking to the Prophet (Peace be upon him) whereas Arbad turned aside trying to draw his sword. He managed to draw a span of hand long but Allâh stilled his hand so that he was unable to proceed with its withdrawal. Allâh protected the Prophet (Peace be upon him). The Prophet (Peace be upon him) invoked Allâh against them. So when they returned, Allâh sent down a thunderbolt unto Arbad and his camel and he was burnt. As for 'Amir he called at a house of a woman who was from Bani Salul and had a gland sore. He eventually died while he was saying: "What am I like? I have a gland similar to a camel's. And here I am dying in the house of the woman from Bani Salul."
15. In *Sahih Al-Bukhari* it is narrated that 'Amir came to the Prophet (Peace be upon him) and said: "I grant you an opportunity to choose one of two: you will have the flat land people and I will have townspeople; or I will succeed you. Otherwise, I will invade your people with a thousand he-camels and a thousand she-camels." But, later on he got plague-stricken in a woman's house. So he said: "What! I have a gland similar to a camel's, and here I am in a woman's house of Bani so and so people. Fetch me my mare!" He mounted it but died on its back.
16. Tujeeb Delegation: They came to Madinah carrying the surplus of charities (*Sadaqat*) of their people. That is to say the extra charities they had after they had distributed the poor-due. They were thirteen men. They asked about the Qur'ân and *Sunnah* (the Prophet's saying, deeds and sanctions) so that they might learn them. They demanded things from the Messenger of Allâh (Peace be upon him) to which he gave them pledges. They did not stay long; so when the Messenger of Allâh (Peace be upon him) acknowledged their demands and allowed them to depart, they sent him a boy whom they had already left at their property. The young man said to the Prophet (Peace be upon him): "By Allâh, I swear, I have left my home (for Madinah) with a purpose that you invoke Allâh, the Great and All-Mighty for me to forgive me and have mercy on me and to make my heart a source of content and sufficiency." The Messenger of Allâh (Peace be upon him) supplicated Allâh to grant him what he demanded.
17. From that time on, he was the most contented person. In *Ar-Riddah* (i.e. the Apostasy Times), he stoodfast as a Muslim and warned his people and reminded them of Aâh and went on preaching them till they stoodfast and did not apostatize. The group of delegates met the Prophet (Peace be upon him) again in the Farewell Pilgrimage in the tenth year of Al-Hijra.
18. Tai' Delegation: One of that group of delegates who came to meet the Prophet (Peace be upon him) was Zaid Al-Khail. They talked to the Prophet (Peace be upon him) who urged them to embrace Islam. They agreed and grew good Muslims. About Zaid, the Messenger of Allâh (Peace be upon him) said: "The Arabs are never exact at estimating people. They have never told me about the virtues of a man correctly; for when I see the man concerned I realize that they have overestimated him except Zaid Al-Khail, when I met him I knew that they had underestimated him." Then he named him 'Zaid Al-Khair' (i.e. Zaid, the bounteous).

The delegations arrived successively in Madinah during the ninth and tenth of Al-Hijra. Biographers and invasion-writers have written down about some of Yemen delegations. They were Al-Azd; Bani Sa'd Hadheem from Quda'ah, Bani 'Amir bin Qais; Bani Asad, Bahra', Khaulan, Muharib, Bani Al-Harith bin Ka'b, Ghamid, Bani Al-Muntafiq, Salaman, Bani 'Abs, Muzainah, Murad, Zabid, Kinda, Dhi Murrah,

Ghassan, Bani 'Aish, and Nakh' which were the last group of delegates. Nakh' Delegation comprised two hundred men and they arrived in the middle of Muharram in the eleventh year of Al-Hijra. The majority of these groups of delegates arrived during the ninth and tenth years of Al-Hijra. The arrival of some of them tarried till the eleventh year of Al-Hijra.

The succession of these delegations indicated the great degree of the entire acceptance which the Islamic Call reached. It manifested its influence and domination on vast areas of Arabia . The Arabs observed Al-Madinah with such a great respect and estimation that they could do nothing but surrender and submit to it. Al-Madinah had become the headquarters of all Arabia; so it was impossible to avoid it. We dare not say that all the Arabians were possessed and enchanted by this religion. There were lots of hard-hearted bedouins — among the Arabs — who surrendered (i.e. became Muslims) only because their master did so. Their souls were not sanctified yet. Their tendency to raids had been deeply rooted in their souls. The teachings of Islam had not crystallized their souls well yet. Accounting some of them the Qur'ân says:

- "The bedouins are the worst in disbelief and hypocrisy, and more likely to be in ignorance of the limits (Allâh's Commandments and His legal laws, etc.) which Allâh has revealed to His Messenger. And Allâh is All-Knower, All-Wise. And of the bedouins there are some who look upon what they spend (in Allâh's cause) as a fine and watch for calamities for you, on them be the calamity of evil. And Allâh is All-Hearer, All-Knower." [9:97,98]

The Qur'ân praised others saying:

- "And of the bedouins there are some who believe in Allâh and the Last Day, and look upon what they spend in Allâh's cause as approaches to Allâh, and a cause of receiving the Messenger's invocations. Indeed these are an approach for them. Allâh will admit them to His Mercy. Certainly Allâh is Oft-Forgiving, Most Merciful." [9:99]

Those of them who were present at Makkah, Madinah and Thaqif and in many other areas of Al-Yemen and Al-Bahrain were different because Islam had been firmly rooted in their souls. Some of them were great Companions and Masters of Muslims.

THE SUCCESS AND IMPACT OF THE CALL:

Before we move one more step and meditate on the last days of the Messenger of Allâh's life, we ought to cast a quick glance at the great work that was a peculiarity of his. That very peculiarity that made him excel all other Prophets and Messengers and made him so superb that Allâh made him atop the formers and the latters. It was him that was addressed by:

- "O you wrapped in garments [i.e Prophet Muhammad (Peace be upon him)]! Stand (to pray) all night, except a little." [73:1,2]

And said:

- "O you [Muhammad (Peace be upon him)] enveloped (in garments). Arise and warn!" [74:1,2]

So he arose and kept on like that for over twenty years. During those years he undertook to carry the burdens of the great expectations on his shoulders for the sake of the whole mankind and humanity, the Faith and *Jihad* in various fields.

The Messenger of Allâh (Peace be upon him) undertook the burdens of struggle and *Al-Jihad* in the conscience of mankind which was then drowning in the illusions of *Al-Jahiliyah* and its images that were loaded with the ground weights and gravitations. He took upon his shoulder to free man's conscience which was chained with desires and lusts. As soon as he had freed the conscience of his Companions from the burdens and heaps of *Al-Jahiliyah* and earthly life, he started another battle in another field or rather successive battles against the enemy of Allâh's Call, and against those who conspired against it. It was a battle against those who conspired against the believers and against those who were so careful to tend that pure plant in its implantation before it grew up and stretched its roots in soil and extended its branches up into the air and thus dawned upon other areas. No sooner had he finished the battles in the Arabian Peninsula than the Byzantines began preparations to destroy this new nation on the northern borders.

The first battle — i.e. the battle of conscience — was not over yet. It was in fact a perpetual one. Satan, who was its leader did not spare a moment without exercising his activity in the depth of human conscience. Muhammad (Peace be upon him), on the other hand was attending on calling to Allâh's religion there and he was keen on fighting that perpetual battle in all fields in spite of their hard circumstances and the world's conspiracy against him. He went on calling effectively and actively surrounded by the believers who were seeking security through ceaseless toil and great patience.

The Companions acted perpetually and patiently by day and they spent the night worshipping their Lord, reciting and memorizing the Qur'ân glorifying and magnifying Allâh and imploring Him by night; all that at the behest of their Lord, the All-Mighty.

For over twenty years the Messenger of Allâh (Peace be upon him) had been leading that progressive steady battle, disregarding any other affairs that kept him off that noble goal. He went on that way till the Islamic Call proved to be successful on a large scale that puzzled all men possessed of good reason.

The Islamic Call eventually prevailed all over Arabia. It removed all traces of *Al-Jahiliyah* from the horizon of the peninsula. The sick minds of *Al-Jahiliyah* grew healthy in Islam. They did not only get rid of idol-worship, but they also knocked them down. The general atmosphere began to echo "there is no god but Allâh." The calls to prayers were heard five times a day penetrating space and breaking the silence of the dead desert and bringing back life through the new belief. Reciters and memorizers of the Qur'ân set out northwards and southwards reciting verses of the Qur'ân and carrying out Allâh's injunctions.

Scattered people and tribes were united and man moved from man's worship of man to man's worship of Allâh. There were no more oppressors nor oppressed; no masters nor slaves, nor people bound to other people, nor aggressors that would practise aggression. All people were slaves of Allâh. They were beloved brothers obeying Allâh's rules. Thanks to Allâh they disposed of arrogance and the boastful spirit:

- "An Arab is no better than a non-Arab. In return a non-Arab is no better than an Arab. A red raced man was not better than a black one except in piety. Mankind are all Adam's children and Adam was created from dust."

Thanks to the Islamic Call, the Arab unity had become a reality, and so was the case with human unity and social justice as far as their earthly and heavenly affairs were concerned. The time course of events had changed, the features on the earth's surface and the crooked line of history had grown straight and the mentality had been rectified.

The spirit and the corrupted conscience of people, the distorted valand measures of *Al-Jahiliyah* had overwhelmed the whole world during that period of *Al-Jahiliyah.* The prevalence of slavery, injustice, extravagant luxury, adultery, depression, deprivity, disbelief, stray from the straight path and darkness; all of those were *fait accomplis* in spite of the existence of the heavenly religions. The teachings of those religions had grown weak and lost all influence on men's souls and spirits and became mere lifeless ritual traditions.

When this Call had accomplished its role in human life, it freed mankind's spirit of superstitions, illusions, white slavery, corruption and man's worship of man. Islam had freed the human society of filth, dissolution, injustice and tyranny. There were no more social distinctions, nor clergymen's or governors' dictatorship. Islam had set up a world built on solid virtuous and clean foundations, it was based on positivity, righteous construction, freedom and renewal. Truth, faith, dignity active steady deeds, the development and improvement of means of living and reclaim of rights were all bases upon which the Islamic state was built.

Thanks to these evolutions, Arabia witnessed such an unprecedented blessed resurrection, since construction and establishment found its way to it. Never had its history been so religious, pious and brilliant as it had been during those peculiar days of its life.

THE FAREWELL PILGRIMAGE:

After the accomplishment of the Call, the proclamation of the Message and the establishment of a new society on the basis of 'There is no god but Allâh,' and on Muhammad's mission, a secret call uprose in the heart of the Messenger of Allâh (Peace be upon him) telling him that his stay in the Lower World was about to terminate. That was clear in his talk to Mu'adh whom he had dispatched to Yemen in the tenth year of Al-Hijra: "O, Mu'adh! You may not see me after this current year. You may even pass by this very Mosque of mine and my tomb." Upon hearing that Mu'adh cried for fear that he would part with the Messenger of Allâh (Peace be upon him).

Allâh's care was so bounteous as to let the Prophet (Peace be upon him) see the fruits of his Call for the sake of which he suffered various sorts of trouble for over twenty years. Those twenty years had elapsed actively. He used to spend his last days meeting, at the outskirts of Makkah, members of tribes and their representatives who used to consult him and learn the laws and legislation of Islam from him, and in return he used to exact their testimony that he had delivered trust and communicated the Message and counselled the people.

The Messenger of Allâh (Peace be upon him) announced an intention to proceed with this blessed pilgrimage journey himself. Enormous crowds of people came to Madinah, all of whom seek the guidance and *Imamate* of the Messenger of Allâh (Peace be upon him) in the pilgrimage (*Al-Hajj*). On a Saturday of the last four days of Dhul-Qa'dah, the Prophet (Peace be upon him) started the departure preparations procedure. He combed his hair, applied some perfume, wore his garment, saddled his camel and set off in the afternoon. He arrived at Dhul-Hulaifa before the afternoon prayer. He performed two *Rak'a* and spent the night there. When it was morning he said to his Companions:

- "A comer, sent by my Lord, has called on me tonight and said: 'Pray in this blessed valley and say: I intend '*Umrah* combined with pilgrimage ('*Umrah* into *Al-Hajj*).

Before performing the noon prayer, he bathed for *Ihram* (ritual consecration), and 'Aishah (May Allah be pleased with her) perfumed him on both his body and head with her hand with a *Dharira* (a plant) and with a perfume containing musk. The thick sticky layer of perfume could be seen among his parts of hair and beard. He left it unwashed, wore his loincloth and garment. He performed the noon prayer shortened, two *Rak'a*. He proclaimed pilgrimage procedure associated with '*Umrah* at his prayer-place. He, then mounted his she-camel 'Al-Qaswa', and proclaimed: 'There is no god but Allâh'. When he moved into the desert, he acclaimed the Name of Allâh.

He proceeded with his journey till he approached Makkah. He spent the night at Dhi Tuwa and entered Makkah after performing the dawn prayer. He had a bath on Sunday morning, the fourth of Dhul-Hijjah the tenth year of Al-Hijra. He spent eight days on the way, which was an average period. As soon as he entered Al-Haram Mosque he circumambulated Al-Ka'bah and walked to and fro (*Sa'i*) between As-Safa and Al-Marwah. He did not finish the *Ihram* (ritual consecration) because he was *Qarin* (i.e. intending '*Umrah* and *Al-Hajj* associated). He then took *Al-Hadi* (i.e. the sacrificial animals) in order to slaughter them. He camped on a high place of Makkah — Al-Hajun. As for circumambulation, he performed only that of *Al-Hajj* (pilgrimage circumambulation).

Those of his Companions who had no *Hadi* with them to sacrifice, were ordered to observe *Ihram* (i.e. the state of ritual consecration) into '*Umrah* (i.e. lesser pilgrimage), and circumambulate Al-Ka'bah and stride ritually to and fro between As-Safa and Al-Marwah. After that they could relieve themselves from *Ihram*. They, however, showed reluctance to do what they had been told. Thereupon, the Messenger of Allâh (Peace be upon him) said: "Had I known beforehand what I knew afterward, I would not bring *Hadi*, and if I did not have *Hadi*, I would break *Ihram*. On hearing these words, his Companions obeyed the orders to the latter.

On the eighth day of Dhul-Hijjah — that is the Day of *Tarwiyah,* he left for Mina where he performed the noon, the afternoon, the sunset, the evening and the dawn prayers. — i.e. five prayers. Then he stayed for a while till the sun rose up then he passed along till he reached 'Arafah, where there was a tent built for him at Namirah. He sat inside till the sun went down. He ordered that Al-Qaswa', his she-camel, should be prepared for him. They saddled it and had it ready, so he went down the valley where a hundred thousand and twenty-four or forty-four thousand people gathered round him. There he stood up and delivered the following speech:

- " O people! Listen to what I say. I do not know whether I will ever meet you at this place once again after this current year. It is unlawful for you to shed the blood of one another or take (unlawfully) the fortunes of one another. They are as unlawful, (*Haram*) as shedding blood on such a day as today and in such a month as this *Haram* month and in such a sanctified city as this sacred city (i.e. Makkah and the surrounding areas)."

"Behold! all practices of paganism and ignorance are now under my feet. The blood-revenge of the Days of Ignorance (pre-Islamic time) are remitted. The first claim on blood I abolish is that of Ibn Rabi'a bin Harith who was nursed in the tribe of Sa'd and whom Hudhail killed. Usury is forbidden, and I make a beginning by remitting the amount of interest which 'Abbas bin 'Abdul Muttalib has to receive. Verily, it is remitted entirely."

"O people! Fear Allâh concerning women. Verily you have taken them on the security of Allâh and have made their persons lawful unto you by Words of Allâh! It is incumbent upon them to honour their conjugal rights and, not to commit acts of impropriety which, if they do, you have authority to chastise them, yet not severely. If your wives refrain from impropriety and are faithful to you, clothe and feed them suitably."

"Verily, I have left amongst you the Book of Allâh and the *Sunnah* (Traditions) of His Messenger which if you hold fast, you shall never go astray."

"O people, I am not succeeded by a Prophet and you are not succeeded by any nation. So I recommend you to worship your Lord, to pray the five prayers, to fast Ramadan and to offer the *Zakat* (poor-due) of your provision willingly. I recommend you to do the pilgrimage to the Sacred House of your Lord and to obey those who are in charge of you then you will be awarded to enter the Paradise of your Lord."

"And if you were asked about me, what wanted you to say?"

They replied:

- "We bear witness that you have conveyed the message and discharged your ministry."

He then raised his forefskywards and then moved it down towards people while saying:

- "O Allâh, Bear witness."

He said that phrase thrice.

The one who repeated the Prophet's (Peace be upon him)statements loudly at 'Arafat was Rabi'a bin Omaiyah bin Khalaf.

As soon as the Prophet (Peace be upon him) had accomplished delivering the speech, the following Qur'ânic verse was revealed to him:

- "This day I have perfected your religion for you, completed My Favour upon you, and have chosen for you Islam as your religion." [5:3]

Upon hearing this verse 'Umar cried. "What makes you cry?" He was asked. His answer was: "Nothing succeeds perfection but imperfection."

Bilal called for prayer after the speech, and then made the second call. The Prophet (Peace be upon him) performed both of the noon and the afternoon prayers separately, with no prayers in between. He then mounted his she-camel Al-Qaswa', approached the location of the vigil, directed his face towards *Al-Qiblah*, kept on standing till sunset when the sky yellow colour vanished a bit and the disc of the sun disappeared. Osamah added that the Prophet (Peace be upon him) moved onward to Muzdalifa. where he observed the sunset and the evening prayers with one 'First call' and two 'second calls'. He did not entertain the Glory of Allâh between the two prayers. Then he lay down till it was dawn prayer time. He performed it with one first call and one second call at almost daybreak time. Mounting on his Al-Qaswa', he moved towards *Al-Mash'ar Al-Haram*. He faced *Al-Qiblah* and started supplicating: "Allâh is the Greatest. There is no god but Allâh." He remained there till it was clear morning and before the sun rose high, he made his way to Mina. He walked a little and threaded the mid-road leading to the big *Jamrah* where he stopped and pelted seven pebbles at it saying "Allâh is the Greatest" each time. They were like small pebbles hurled from the bottom of the valley. Then he set off to the sacrificial place, where he sacrificed sixty-three camels with his hands, and asked 'Ali to slaughter the others, a hundred and thirty-seven altogether. He made 'Ali share him in *Al-Hadi*. A piece of meat from each slaughtered animal was ordered to be cooked in a pot and from which both men ate, and drank the soup.

Then the Messenger of Allâh (Peace be upon him) mounted his she-camel and returned to the House where he observed the noon prayer at Makkah and there he came upon the children of 'Abdul Muttalib were supplying drinking water to people at Zamzam Well. "Draw up water, children of 'Abdul Muttalib, I would draw up with you if I were not afraid that people would appropriate this honour after me." They handed him a pail of water and he drank to his fill.

At the daytime of the tenth of Dhul-Hijjah on the Slaughtering Day (*Yaum An-Nahr*) The Prophet (Peace be upon him) delivered another speech. That was at high time morning, while he was mounting a grey mule. 'Ali conveyed his statements to the people, who were standing or sitting. He repeated some of the statements that he had previously said the day before. The two Sheikh (Bukhâri and Muslim) reported a version narrated by Abi Bakrah who said:

- The Prophet (Peace be upon him) made a speech on *Yaum An-Nahr* (day of slaughtering) and said:

    o "Time has grown similar in form and state to the time when Allâh created the heavens and the earth. A year is twelve months. Four of which are Sacred Months (*Hurum*). Three of the four months are successive. They are Dhul-Qa'dah, Dhul-Hijjah, and Al-Muharram. The fourth Month is Rajab Mudar, which comes between Jumada and Sha'ban."

    "What month is this month?" He asked. We said: "Allâh and His Messenger know best of all." He kept silent for a while till we thought he would attach to it a different appellation. "Is it not Dhul-Hijjah?" He wondered. "Yes. It is." We said. Then he asked, "What is this town called?" We said: "Allâh and His Messenger know best of all." He was silent for a while till we thought he would give it a different name. "Is it not *Al-Baldah*? (i.e. the town)" asked he. "Yes. It is." We replied. Then he asked again, "What day is it today?" We replied: "Allâh and His Messenger know best of all." Then he kept silent for a while and said wondering: "Is it not '*An-Nahr*' (i.e. slaughtering) Day?" "Yes. It is." Said we. Then he said:

    "(Shedding) the blood of one another and eating or taking one another's provisions (unwillingly) and your honour are all inviolable (*Haram*). It is unlawful to violate their holiness. They must be as sacred to one another as this sacred day, in this sacred month, in this sacred town."

"You will go back to be resurrected (after death) to your Lord. There you will be accounted for your deeds. So do not turn into people who go astray and kill one another."

"Have I not delivered the Message (of my Lord)?" "Yes you have." Said they. "O Allâh! Bear witness! Let him that is present convey it unto him who is absent. For haply, many people to whom the Message is conveyed may be more mindful of it than the audience,." said he.

In another version it is said that the Prophet (Peace be upon him) had said in that very speech:

- "He whoever plunges into misfortune will certainly aggrieve himself. So let no one of you inflict an evil upon his parents. Verily Satan has utterly despaired being worshipped in this country of yours; but he will be obeyed at your committing trivial things you disdain. Satan will be contented with such things."

The Messenger of Allâh (Peace be upon him) spent *At-Tashreeq* Days (11th, 12th and 13th of Dhul-Hijjah) in Mina performing the ritual teachings of Islam, remembering Allâh (praying), following the ways of guidance of Ibrahim, wiping out all traces and features or polytheism. On some days of *At-Tashreeq* he delivered some speeches as well. In a version to Abu Da'ûd with good reference to Sira,' the daughter of Nabhan; she said: "The Messenger of Allâh (Peace be upon him) made us a speech at the *Ru'us* (Heads) Day in which he said: "Is it not this the middle day of *At-Tashreeq* Days."

His speech that day was similar to that of *An-Nahr* Day's. It was made after the revelation of *Surat An-Nasr*.

On the second day of *An-Nafr* (i.e. Departure) — on the thirteenth of Dhul-Hijjah, the Prophet (Peace be upon him) proceeded with *An-Nafr* to Mina and stayed at a high place of a mountain side at Bani Kinanah from Al-Abtah. He spent the rest of that day and night there — where he performed the noon, the afternoon, the sunset and the evening prayers.

Then he slept for a short while and mounted leaving for the Ka'bah. He performed the Farewell Circumambulation (*Tawaf Al-Wada'*), after ordering his Companions to do the same thing.

Upon the accomplishment of his religious rituals he quickened his move to the purified Madinah. He went there not to seek rest but to resume the strife and struggle in the way of Allâh.

THE LAST EXPEDITIONS:

The pride of the Byzantine State made it deny Muslims their right to live. The Byzantine arrogance made them even kill those agents of theirs, who embraced Islam. Killing Farwah bin 'Amr Al-Judhami, who was their agent on Mu'an, was an evidence of their arrogance. Due to that arrogance and presumptuousness of the Byzantines, the Messenger of Allâh (Peace be upon him) started to mobilize a great army in Safar in the eleventh year of Al-Hijra and made it under the command of Osamah bin Zaid bin Haritha with orders to have the horses of Muslims tread on the lands bordering Al-Balqa' and Ad-Darum of Palestine. His aim was to terrorize Byzantines and to implant confidence into the hearts of Arabs who were settled at the borders of the Byzantines. His other purpose was to deliver a message to everybody there, so that no one may dare say that the Church brutality can't go with impunity; and that Islamization is not synonymous with fear and vulnerability.

The leadership of Osamah was subject to criticism. Because he was still too young, people tarried at joining his expedition. The Messenger of Allâh (Peace be upon him) addressed people saying:

- "No wonder now you contest his leadership, for you have already contested the ex-leadership ofhis father. Yes, by Allâh, his father, who was one of the most beloved people to me, was quite efficient for leadership; and this son of his is one of the most beloved individuals to me after his father."

So people started tending towards Osamah and joined his army. The number of volunteers in his army was so enormous that they formed such a long queue that they had to descend the escarpment — which was a parasang off Madinah. The anxiety-provoking news about the Messenger of Allâh's sickness, however, made the expedition tarry again in order to know what Allâh had willed as regards His Messenger (Peace be upon him).

It was Allâh's Will that Osamah's expedition would be the first one dispatched during the caliphate of the veracious Abu Bakr.

THE JOURNEY TO ALLAH, THE SUBLIME

SYMTOMPS OF FAREWELL:

When the Call to Islam grew complete and the new faith dominated the whole situation. The Messenger of Allâh (Peace be upon him) started to develop certain symptoms that bespoke of leave-taking. They could be perceived through his statements and deeds:

1. In Ramadan in the tenth year of Al-Hijra he secluded himself for twenty days in contrast to ten, previously.
2. The archangel Gabriel reviewed the Qur'ân twice with him.
3. His words in the Farewell Pilgrimage (i.e. *Al-Wida'*):
4. "I do not know whether I will ever meet you at this place once again after this current year."
5. The revelation of *An-Nasr* Chapter amid *At-Tashreeq* Days. So when it was sent down on him, he realized that it was the parting time and that *Surah* was an announcement of his approaching death.
6. On the early days of Safar in the eleventh year of Al-Hijra, the Prophet (Peace be upon him) went out to Uhud and observed a farewell prayer to the martyrs. It looked like saying goodbye to both the dead and the living alike. He then ascended the pulpit and addressed the people saying:
7. "I am to precede you and I have been made witness upon you. By Allâh, you will meet me at the 'Fountain' very soon. I have been given the keys of worldly treasures. By Allâh, I do not fear for you that you will turn polytheists after me. But I do fear that acquisition of worldly riches should entice you to strike one another's neck."
8. One day, at midnight he went to Al-Baqee' cemetry, and implored Allâh to forgive the martyrs of Islam. He said: "Peace be upon you tomb-dwellers! May that morning that dawns upon you be more relieving than that which dawn upon the living. Afflictions are approaching them like cloudy lumps of a dark night — the last of which follows the first. The last one is bearing more evil than the first." He comforted them saying: "We will follow you."

THE START OF THE DISEAS:

On Monday the twenty-ninth of Safar in the eleventh year of Al-Hijra, he participated in funeral rites in Al-Baqee'. On the way back he had a headache, his temperature rose so high that the heat effect could be felt over his headband.

He led the Muslims in prayer for eleven days though he was sick. The total number of his sick days were either thirteen or fourteen.

THE LAST WEEK:

When his sickness grew severe he asked his wives: "Where shall I stay tomorrow?" "Where shall I stay?" They understood what he wanted. So they allowed him to stay wherever he wished. He moved to 'Aishah's room leaning — while he was walking — on Al-Fadl bin Al-'Abbas and 'Ali bin Abi Talib. Head banded as he was, he dragged his feet till he came into her abode. It was there that he spent the last week of his life.

During that period, 'Aishah used to recite *Al-Mu'awwidhat* (Chapters 113 and 114 of the Qur'ân) and other supplications which he had already taught her.

FIVE DAYS BEFORE DEATH:

On Wednesday, five days before he died the Prophet's temperature rose so high signalling the severeness of his disease. He fainted and suffered from pain. "Pour out on me seven *Qirab* (water skin pots) of various water wells so that I may go out to meet people and talk to them." So they seated him in a container (usually used for washing) and poured out water on him till he said: "That is enough. That is enough."

Then he felt well enough to enter the Mosque. He entered it band-headed, sat on the pulpit and made a speech to the people who were gathering together around him. He said:

- "The curse of Allâh falls upon the Jews and Christians for they have made their Prophets' tombs places of worship."

Then he said:

- "Do not make my tomb a worshipped idol."

Then he offered himself and invited the people to repay any injuries he might have inflicted on them, saying:

- "He whom I have ever lashed his back, I offer him my back so that he may avenge himself on me. He whom I have ever blasphemed his honour, here I am offering my honour so that he may avenge himself."

Then he descended, and performed the noon prayer. Again he returned to the pulpit and sat on it. He resumed his first speech about enmity and some other things.

A man then said: "You owe me three Dirhams." The Prophet (Peace be upon him) said: "Fadl, pay him the money." He went on saying:

- "I admonish you to be good to *Al-Ansar* (the Helpers). They are my family and with them I found shelter. They have acquitted themselves credibly of the responsibility that fell upon them and now there remains what you have to do. You should fully acknowledge and appreciate the favour that they have shown, and should overlook their faults."

In another version:

- "The number of believers would increase, but the number of Helpers would decrease to the extent that they would be among men as salt in the food. So he who from among you occupies a position of responsibility and is powerful enough to do harm or good to the people, he should fully acknowledge and appreciate the favour that these benefactors have shown and overlook their faults."

And said:

- "Allâh, the Great, has given a slave of His the opportunity to make a choice between whatever he desires of Allâh's provisions in this world, and what He keeps for him in the world, but he has opted for the latter."

Abu Sa'îd Al-Khudri said: "Upon hearing that, Abu Bakr cried and said: 'We sacrifice our fathers and mothers for your sake.' We wondered why Abu Bakr said such a thing. People said: 'Look at that old man! The Messenger of Allâh (Peace be upon him) says about a slave of Allâh who was granted the right between the best fortunes of this world and the bounty of Allâh in the Hereafter, but he says: We sacrifice our fathers and mothers for your sake!' It was later on that we realized what he had aimed at. The Messenger of Allâh (Peace be upon him) was the slave informed to choose. We also acknowledged that Abu Bakr was the most learned among us."

Then the Messenger of Allâh (Peace be upon him) said:

- "The fellow I feel most secure in his company is Abu Bakr. If I were to make friendship with any other one than Allâh, I would have Abu Bakr a bosom friend of mine. For him I feel affection and brotherhood of Islam. No gate shall be kept open in the Mosque except that of Abu Bakr's."

FOUR DAYS BEFORE HIS DEATH:

On Thursday, four days before the death of the Messenger of Allâh (Peace be upon him), he said to people — though he was suffering from a severe pain: "Come here. I will cause you to write something so that you will never fall into error." Upon this 'Umar bin Al-Khattab said: "The Prophet of Allâh (Peace be upon him) is suffering from acute pain and you have the Qur'ân with you; the Book of Allâh is sufficient unto you." Others however wanted the writing to be made. When Muhammad (Peace be upon him) heard them debating over it, he ordered them to go away and leave him alone.

THE DAY HE RECOMMENDED THREE THINGS:

1. Jews, Christians and polytheists should be expelled out of Arabia.
2. He recommended that delegations should be honoured and entertained, in a way similar to the one he used to do.
3. As for the third — the narrator said that he had forgotten it. It could have been adherence to the Holy Book and the *Sunnah*. It was likely to be the accomplishment and the mobilization of Osamah's army, or it could have been performance of prayers and being attentive to slaves.

In spite of the strain of disease and suffering from pain, the Prophet (Peace be upon him) used to lead all the prayers till that Thursday — four days before he died. On that day he led the sunset prayer and recited:

-
  - "By the winds (or angels or the Messengers of Allâh) sent forth one after another." [77:1]

In the evening he grew so sick that he could not overcome the strain of disease or go out to enter the Mosque. 'Aishah said: The Prophet (Peace be upon him) asked: "Have the people performed the prayer?" "No. They haven't. They are waiting for you." "Put some water in the washing pot." Said he. We did what he ordered. So he washed and wanted to stand up, but he fainted. When he came round he asked again "Have the people prayed?" Then the same sequence of events took place again and again for the second and the third tifrom the time he washed to the time he fainted after his attempts to stand up. Therefore he sent to Abu Bakr to lead the prayer himself. Abu Bakr then led the prayer during those days. They were seventeen prayers in the lifetime of Muhammad(Peace be upon him).

Three or four times 'Aishah talked to the Prophet (Peace be upon him) to exempt Abu Bakr from leadership in prayer lest people should despair of him, but he refused and said:

- "You (women) are like the women who tried to entice Joseph (Yusuf) into immorality. Convey my request to Abu Bakr to lead the prayer."

A DAY OR TWO PRIOR TO DEATH:

On Saturday or on Sunday, the Prophet (Peace be upon him) felt that he was well enough to perform the prayer; so he went out leaning on two men in order to perform the noon prayer. Abu Bakr, who was then about to lead the prayer withdrew when he saw him coming; but the Prophet (Peace be upon him) made him a gesture to stay where he was and said: "Seat me next to him." They seated him on the left hand side of Abu Bakr. The Prophet (Peace be upon him) led the prayer, and Abu Bakr followed him and raised his voice at every '*Allâhu Akbar*' (i.e. Allâh is the Greatest) the Prophet (Peace be upon him) said, so that the people may hear clearly.

A DAY BEFORE HIS DEATH:

On Sunday, a day before he died, the Prophet (Peace be upon him) set his slaves free, paid as a charity the seven Dinars he owned and gave his weapons as a present to the Muslims. So when night fell 'Aishah had to borrow some oil from her neighbour to light her oil-lantern.

Even his armour was mortgaged as a security with a Jew for thirty *Sa`* (a cubic measure) of barley.

THE LAST DAY ALIVE:

In a narration by Anas bin Malik, he said: "While the Muslims were performing the dawn prayer on Monday — led by Abu Bakr, they were surprised to see the Messenger of Allâh (Peace be upon him) raising the curtain of 'Aishah's room. He looked at them while they were praying aligned properly and smiled cheerfully. Seeing him, Abu Bakr withdrew to join the lines and give way to him to lead the prayer. For he thought that the Prophet (Peace be upon him) wanted to go out and pray." Anas said: "The Muslims, who were praying, were so delighted that they were almost too enraptured at their prayers. The Messenger of Allâh (Peace be upon him) made them a gesture to continue their prayer, went into the room and drew down the curtain."

The Messenger of Allâh (Peace be upon him) did not live for the next prayer time.

When it was daytime, the Prophet (Peace be upon him) called Fatimah and told her something in a secret voice that made her cry. Then he whispered to her something else which made her laugh. 'Aishah enquired from her after the Prophet's death, as to this weeping and laughing to which Fatimah replied: "The first time he disclosed to me that he would not recover from his illness and I wept. Then he told me that I would be the first of his family to join him, so I laughed."

He gave Fatimah glad tidings that she would become the lady of all women of the world.

Fatimah witnessed the great pain that afflicted her father. So she said: "What great pain my father is in!". To these words, the Prophet (Peace be upon him) remarked:

- "He will not suffer any more when today is over."

He asked that Al-Hasan and Al-Husain be brought to him. He kissed them and recommended that they be looked after. He asked to see his wives. They were brought to him. He preached them and told them to remember Allâh. Pain grew so much severe that the trace of poison he had at Khaibar came to light. It was so sore that he said to 'Aishah: "I still feel the painful effect of that food I tasted at Khaibar. I feel as if death is approaching." He ordered the people to perform the prayers and be attentive to slaves. He repeated it several times.

THE PROPHET BREATHES HIS LAST:

When the pangs of death started, 'Aishah leant him against her. She used to say: One of Allâh's bounties upon me is that the Messenger of Allâh (Peace be upon him) died in my house, while I am still alive. He died between my chest and neck while he was leaning against me. Allâh has mixed his saliva with mine at his death. For 'Abdur Rahman — the son of Abu Bakr — came in with a *Siwak* (i.e. the root of a desert plant used for brushing teeth) in his hand, while I was leaning the Messenger of Allâh (Peace be upon him) against me. I noticed that he was looking at the *Siwak*, so I asked him — for I knew that he wanted it — "Would you like me to take it for you?" He nodded in agreement. I took it and gave it to him. As it was too hard for him, I asked him "Shall I soften it for you?" He nodded in agreement. So I softened it with my saliva and he passed it (on his teeth).

In another version it is said: "So he brushed (*Istanna*) his teeth as nice as he could." There was a water container (*Rakwa*) available at his hand with some water in. He put his hand in it and wiped his face with it and said:

- "There is no god but Allâh. Death is full of agonies."

As soon as he had finished his *Siwak* brushing, he raised his hand or his finger up, looked upwards to the ceiling and moved his lips. So 'Aishah listened to him. She heard him say: "With those on whom You have bestowed Your Grace with the Prophets and the Truthful ones (*As-Siddeeqeen*), the martyrs and the good doers. O Allâh, forgive me and have mercy upon me and join me to the Companionship on high." Then at intervals he uttered these words: "The most exalted Companionship on high. To Allâh we turn and to Him we turn back for help and last abode." This event took place at high morning time on Monday, the twelfth of Rabi' Al-Awwal, in the eleventh year of Al-Hijrah. He was sixty-three years and four days old when he died.

THE COMPANIONS' CONCERN OVER THE PROPHET'S DEATH:

The great (loss) news was soon known by everybody in Madinah. Dark grief spread on all areas and horizons of Madinah. Anas said:

- "I have never witnessed a day better or brighter than that day on which the Messenger of Allâh (Peace be upon him) came to us; and I have never witnessed a more awful or darker day than that one on which the Messenger of Allâh (Peace be upon him) died on."

When he died, Fatimah said: "O Father, whom his Lord responded to his supplication! O Father, whose abode is Paradise. O Father, whom I announce his death to Gabriel."

'UMAR ATTITUDE:

'Umar, who was so stunned that he almost lost consciousness and stood before people addressing them: "Some of the hypocrites claim that the Messenger of Allâh (Peace be upon him) died. The Messenger of Allâh (Peace be upon him) did not die, but went to his Lord in the same way as Moses bin 'Imran did. He stayed away for forty nights, but finally came back though they said he had been dead. By Allâh, the Messenger of Allâh (Peace be upon him) will come back and he will cut off the hands and legs of those who claim his death."

ABU BAKR'S ATTITUDE:

Abu Bakr left his house at As-Sunh and came forth to the Mosque on a mare-back. At the Mosque, he dismounted and entered. He talked to nobody but went on till he entered 'Aishah's abode, and went directly to where the Messenger of Allâh (Peace be upon him) was. The Prophet (Peace be upon him) was covered with a Yemeni mantle. He uncovered his face and tended down, kissed him and cried. Then he said: "I sacrifice my father and mother for your sake. Allâh, verily, will not cause you to die twice. You have just experienced the death that Allâh had ordained."

Then he went out and found 'Umar talking to people. He said: "'Umar, be seated." 'Umar refused to do so. People parted 'Umar and came towards Abu Bakr, who started a speech saying:

- "And now, he who worships Muhammad (Peace be upon him). Muhammad is dead now. But he who worships Allâh, He is Ever Living and He never dies. Allâh says:

    'Muhammad (Peace be upon him) is no more than a Messenger, and indeed (many) Messengers have passed away before him. If he dies or is killed, will you then turn back on your heels (as disbelievers)? And he who turns back on his heels, not the least harm will he do to Allâh, and

Allâh will give reward to those who are grateful.'" [3:1]

Ibn 'Abbas said: "By Allâh, it sounded as if people had never heard such a Qur'ânic verse till Abu Bakr recited it as a reminder. So people started reciting it till there was no man who did not recite it."

Ibn Al-Musaiyab said that 'Umar had said: "By Allâh, as soon as I heard Abu Bakr say it, I fell down to the ground. I felt as if my legs had been unable to carry me so I collapsed when I heard him say it. Only then did I realize that Muhammad (Peace be upon him) had really died."

BURIAL AND FAREWELL PREPARATIONS TO HIS HONOURABLE BODY:

Dispute about who would succeed him (Peace be upon him) broke out even before having the Messenger of Allâh's body prepared for burial. Lots of arguments, discussions, dialogues took place between the Helpers and Emigrants in the roofed passage (portico) of Bani Sa'ida. Finally they acknowledged Abu Bakr (May Allah be pleased with him) as a caliph. They spent the whole Monday there till it was night. People were so busy with their arguments that it was late night — just about dawn of Tuesday — yet his blessed body was still lying on his bed covered with an inked-garment. He was locked in the room.

On Tuesday, his body was washed with his clothes on. He was washed by Al-'Abbas, 'Ali, Al-Fadl and Qathm — the two sons of Al-'Abbas, as well as Shaqran — the Messenger's freed slave, Osamah bin Zaid and Aws bin Khauli. Al-'Abbas, Al-Fadl and Qathm turned his body round, whereas Osamah and Shaqran poured out water. 'Ali washed him and Aws leant him against his chest.

They shrouded him in three white Sahooli cotton cloth which had neither a headcloth nor a casing and inserted him in.

A sort of disagreement arose with regard to a burial place. Abu Bakr said: "I heard the Messenger of Allâh (Peace be upon him) say: 'A dead Prophet is buried where he dies.' So Abu Talhah lifted the bed on which he died, dug underneath and cut the ground to make the tomb.

People entered the room ten by ten. They prayed for the Prophet (Peace be upon him). The first to pray for him were people of his clan. Then the Emigrants, then the Helpers. Women prayed for him after men. The young were the last to pray.

This process took Tuesday long and Wednesday night (i.e. the night which precedes Wednesday morning). 'Aishah said: "We did not know that the Prophet (Peace be upon him) was being buried till we heard the sound of tools digging the ground at the depth of Wednesday night."

THE PROPHETIC HOUSEHOLD

1. Khadijah Bint Khuwailid: In Makkah — prior to Hijra — the Prophet's household comprised him (Peace be upon him) and his wife Khadijah bint Khuwailid. He was twenty-five and she was forty when they got married. She was the first woman he married. She was the only wife he had till she died. He had sons and daughters with her. None of their sons lived long. They all died. Their daughters were Zainab, Ruqaiya, Umm Kulthum and Fatimah.

- Zainab was married to her maternal cousin Abu Al-'As bin Al-Rabi' and that was before Al-Hijra. Ruqaiya and Umm Kulthum were both married to 'Uthman bin 'Affan (May Allah be pleased with him) successively (i.e. he married one after the death of her sister). Fatimah was married to 'Ali bin Abi Talib; and that was in the period between Badr and Uhud battles. The sons and daughters that Fatimah and 'Ali had were Al-Hasan, Al-Husain, Zainab and Umm Kulthum.

  It is well-known that the Prophet (Peace be upon him) was exceptionally authorized to have more than four wives for various reasons. The wives he married were thirteen. Nine of them outlived him. Two died in his lifetime: Khadijah and the Mother of the poor (*Umm Al-Masakeen*) — Zainab bint Khuzaima, besides two others with whom he did not consummate his marriage.

2. Sawdah bint Zam'a: He married her in Shawwal, in the tenth year of Prophethood, a few days after the death of Khadijah. Prior to that, she was married to a paternal cousin of hers called As-Sakran bin 'Amr.
3. 'Aishah bint Abu Bakr: He married her in the eleventh year of Prophethood, a year after his marriage to Sawdah, and two years and five months before Al-Hijra. She was six years old when he married her. However, he did not consummate the marriage with her till Shawwal seven months after Al-Hijra, and that was in Madinah. She was nine then. She was the only virgin he married, and the most beloved creature to him. As a woman she was the most learnèd woman in jurisprudence.
4. Hafsah bint 'Umar bin Al-Khattab: She was *Aiyim* (i.e. husbandless). Her ex-husband was Khunais bin Hudhafa As-Sahmi in the period between Badr and Uhud battles. The Messenger of Allâh (Peace be upon him) married her in the third year of Al-Hijra.
5. Zainab bint Khuzaimah: She was from Bani Hilal bin 'Amir bin Sa'sa'a. Was nicknamed *Umm Al-Masakeen*, because of her kindness and care towards them. She used to be the wife of 'Abdullah bin Jahsh, who was martyred at Uhud, was married to the Prophet (Peace be upon him) in the fourth year of Al-Hijra, but she died two or three months after her marriage to the Messenger of Allâh (Peace be upon him).
6. Umm Salamah Hind bint Abi Omaiyah: She used to be the wife of Abu Salamah, who died in Jumada Al-Akhir, in the fourth year of Al-Hijra. The Messenger of Allâh (Peace be upon him) married her in Shawwal of the same year.
7. Zainab bint Jahsh bin Riyab: She was from Bani Asad bin Khuzaimah and was the Messenger's paternal cousin. She was married to Zaid bin Haritha — who was then considered son of the Prophet (Peace be upon him) . However, Zaid divorced her. Allâh sent down some Qur'ânic verses with this respect:

- "So when Zaid had accomplished his desire from her (i.e., divorced her), We gave her to you in marriage." [33:37]

  About her, Allâh has sent down some verses of *Al-Ahzab* Chapter that discussed the adoption of children in detail — anyway we will discuss this later. The Messenger of Allâh (Peace be upon him) married her in Dhul-Qa'dah, the fifth year of Al-Hijra.

8. Juwairiyah bint Al-Harith: Al-Harith was the head of Bani Al-Mustaliq of Khuza'ah. Juwairiyah was among the booty that fell to the Muslims from Bani Al-Mustaliq. She was a portion of Thabit bin Qais bin Shammas' share. He made her a covenant to set her free at a certain time. The Messenger of Allâh (Peace be upon him) accomplished the covenant and married her in Sha'ban

in the sixth year of Al-Hijra.
9. Umm Habibah: Ramlah, the daughter of Abu Sufyan. She was married to 'Ubaidullah bin Jahsh. She migrated with him to Abyssinia (Ethiopia). When 'Ubaidullah apostatized and became a Christian, she stoodfast to her religion and refused to convert. However 'Ubaidullah died there in Abyssinia (Ethiopia). The Messenger of Allâh (Peace be upon him) dispatched 'Amr bin Omaiyah Ad-Damri with a letter to Negus, the king, asking him for Umm Habibah's hand — that was in Muharram, in the seventh year of Al-Hijra. Negus agreed and sent her to the Prophet (Peace be upon him) in the company of Sharhabeel
10. her after that conquest in the seventh year of Al-Hijra.
11. Maimunah bint Al-Harith: The daughter of Al-Harith, and the sister of Umm Al-Fadl Lubabah bint Al-Harith. The Prophet (Peace be upon him) married her after the Compensatory *'Umrah* (Lesser Pilgrimage). That was in Dhul-Qa'dah in the seventh year of Al-Hijra.

Those were the eleven women that the Messenger of Allâh (Peace be upon him) had married and consummated marriage with them. He outlived two of them — Khadijah and Zainab, the *Umm Al-Masakeen.* Whereas the other nine wives outlived him.

The two wives that he did not consummate marriage with were, one from Bani Kilab and the other from Kindah and this was the one called Al-Jauniyah.

Besides these, he had two concubines. The first was Mariyah, the Coptic (an Egyptian Christian), a present gift from Al-Muqauqis, vicegerent of Egypt — she gave birth to his son Ibrâhim, who died in Madinah while still a little child, on the 28th or 29th of Shawwal in the year 10 A.H., i.e. 27th January, 632 A.D. The second one was Raihanah bint Zaid An-Nadriyah or Quraziyah, a captive from Bani Quraiza. Some people say she was one of his wives. However, Ibn Al-Qaiyim gives more weight to the first version. Abu 'Ubaidah spoke of two more concubines, Jameelah, a captive, and another one, a bondwoman granted to him by Zainab bint Jahsh.

Whosoever meditates on the life of the Messenger of Allâh (Peace be upon him), will conceive that his marriage to this great number of women in the late years of his lifetime, after he had almost spent thirty years of his best days of youth sufficing himself to one old wife — Khadijah and later on to Sawdah, was in no way an overwhelming lustful desire to be satisfied through such a number of wives. These marriages were in fact motivated by aims and purposes much more glorious and greater than what normal marriages usually aim at.

The tendency of the Messenger of Allâh (Peace be upon him) towards establishing a relationship by marriage with both Abu Bakr and 'Umar and his marriage to 'Aishah and Hafsah — and getting his daughter Fatimah married to 'Ali bin Abi Talib, and the marriage of his two daughters, Ruqaiyah and Umm Kulthum to 'Uthman — indicate clearly that he aimed at confirming the relationship among the four men — whose sacrifices and great achievements in the cause of Islam are well-known.

Besides this, there was that tradition of the Arabs to honour the in-law relations. For them a son or a daughter-in-law was a means by which they sought the consolidation of relationship and affection with various phratries. Hostility and fights against alliances and affinities would bring an unforgettable shame, disgrace and degradation to them.

By marrying the Mothers of believers, the Prophet (Peace be upon him) wanted to demolish or break down the Arab tribes' enmity to Islam and extinguish their intense hatred. Umm Salamah was from Bani Makhzum — the clan of Abu Jahl and Khalid bin Al-Waleed. Her marriage to the Messenger of Allâh (Peace be upon him) produced good results. Khalid's deliberately undecisive attitude at Uhud — for instance — was due to the Messenger's marriage to Umm Salamah. Khalid went even further than that, in a short time he willingly became a keen obedient Muslim.

After the Messenger of Allâh's marriage to Umm Habibah, Abu Sufyan, her father, did not encounter him with any sort of hostility. Similarly his marriage to Juwairiyah and Safiyah made the two tribes stop all sorts of provocation, aggression or hostility against Islam. Better still, Juwairiyah, herself, was one of the greatest sources of blessing to her own people. On the occasion of her marriage to the Prophet

(Peace be upon him), his Companions set a hundred families of her people free. They said: "It is for their affinity with the Messenger of Allâh (Peace be upon him)." No need to say what great good impression this gratitude had on everybody's soul. One of the greatest motives of all is Allâh's bidding his Prophet to educate and purify the souls of people who had known nothing whatsoever about courtesy, education and culture. He had to teach them to comply with the necessities of civilization and to contribute to the solidification and the establishment of a new Islamic society.

An essential fundamental rule of the Muslim society is to prohibit mixing of men and women. Providing direct education for women, though highly compelling, is impossible in the light of this Islamic norm. Therefore, the Prophet (Peace be upon him) had to select some women of different ages and talents, and indoctrinate them systematically in order to educate she-bedouins and townswomen, old and young, and thus furnish them with the instruments of propagating the true faith. The Mothers of believers [i.e. wives of the Prophet (Peace be upon him)] were in such a convenient position that they could convey the state of the Prophet (Peace be upon him) and his affairs to people (men and women). Being educated and taught the teachings and rules of Islam, his wives, especially those who outlived him, played a very important role in conveying Prophetic traditions *Ahadith* to the Muslims. 'Aishah, for instance, related a large number of the Prophet's deeds and statements.

His marriage to his paternal cousin Zainab bint Jahsh was a peculiar case which aimed at eradicating a deeply rooted pre-Islamic tradition — i.e. the adoption of children. In *Al-Jahiliyah* the Arabs used to consider an adopted person exactly like a real son or daughter as far as rights and sanctities are concerned. That *Jahiliyah* tradition had been so deeply rooted in their hearts that it was not easy to remove or uproot it. This tradition in fact affronts the basic principles of Islam; especially those concerned with marriage, divorce and inheritance and some other cases, and brought about lots of corruptions and indecencies. Naturally Islam stands against such deeds, and attempts to remove them from the Islamic society.

For the eradication of this tradition, Allâh, the Exalted, bid His Messenger (Peace be upon him) to marry his cousin Zainab bint Jahsh, who was an ex-wife to Zaid. She was at variance with Zaid to an extent that he intended to divorce her — that was at the time when the Confederates (*Al-Ahzab*) were making an evil alliance against the Messenger of Allâh (Peace be upon him) and against the Muslims. The Messenger of Allâh (Peace be upon him) feared that the hypocrites, the idolaters, and the Jews would make a propaganda out of it and try to influence some Muslims of weak hearts. That was why he urged Zaid not to divorce her, in order not to get involved into that trial.

Undoubtedly this hesitation and partiality were alien to the character of the Prophet (Peace be upon him). They did not apply to the power of determination and will with which he had been sent. Allâh, the Exalted, blamed him for that by saying:

- "And (remember) when you said to him [Zaid bin Haritha (May Allah be pleased with him) — the freed slave of the Prophet (Peace be upon him)] on whom Allâh has bestowed grace (by guiding him to Islam) and you [O Muhammad (Peace be upon him)] have done favour (by manumitting him), 'Keep your wife to yourself, and fear Allâh.' But you did hide in yourself (i.e. what Allâh has already made known to you that He will give her to you in marriage) that which Allâh will make manifest, you did fear the people [i.e. Muhammad (Peace be upon him)] married the divorced wife of his manumitted slave] whereas Allâh had a better right that you should fear him." [33:37]

Finally Zaid divorced Zainab and the Messenger of Allâh (Peace be upon him) married her at the time he laid siege to Bani Quraiza. That was after she had finished her *Iddat* (i.e. period during which a widow or a divorcee may not remarry). Allâh Himself had already ordained it, and so gave him no other alternative. Allâh had even started the marriage Himself by saying:

- "So when Zaid had accomplished his desire from her (i.e. divorced her), We gave her to you in marriage, so that (in future) there may be no difficulty to the believers in respect of (the marriage of) the wives of their adopted sons when the latter have no desire to keep them (i.e.

they have divorced them)." [33:37]

And that was in order to break down the tradition of child adoption in practice after He had done it in words:

- "Call them (adopted sons) by (the names of) their fathers, that is more just near Allâh." [33:5]

"Muhammad (Peace be upon him)] is not the father of any man among you, but he is the Messenger of Allâh, and the last (end) of the Prophets." [33:40]

Lots of deeply-rooted traditions cannot be uprooted or demolished or even adjusted by mere words. They must be matched and associated with the action of the advocate of the Message himself.

This could be perceived through the deeds practised by the Muslims at Al-Hudaibiyah *'Umrah* (Lesser Pilgrimage) during which 'Urwah bin Mas'ud Al-Thaqafi saw certain Muslims tend to pick up any expectoration that fell down from the Prophet صلى الله عليه وسلم . He also saw them race to the water of his ablution and they almost quarrelled for it. There were others who competed to pledge allegiance to death and some others pledged not to flee from (the battlefield). Among those people, were eminent Companions like 'Umar and Abu Bak, who although dedicated all their lives to the Prophet (Peace be upon him) and to the cause of Islam, but refused to carry out the Messenger's ordres with respect to slaughtering sacrificial animals after the ratification of Al-Hudaibiyah Peace Treaty, the thing that perturbed and caused the Prophet (Peace be upon him) to feel anxious. However, when Umm Salamah (May Allah be pleased with her) advised that he take the initiative and sacrifice his animals, his followers raced to follow his example; a clear evidence in support of the saying: Actions speak louder than words, in the process of exterminating a deeply-established tradition.

Hypocrites aroused a lot of suspicions and made a broad false propaganda against that marriage. Their acts and talks about that marriage had ill-effects on those Muslims whose Faith was still weak, particularly that Zainab was the fifth wife — and the Noble Qur'ân limited the number up to four only; Zaid was traditionally his son, and so a father marrying his son's divorcee was a heinous sin in the eyes of the Arabians.

Al-Ahzab Surah was revealed to shed full light on the two issues, i.e. Islam does not recognize adoption of children, and the Prophet (Peace be upon him) is given (by Allâh) more freedom as regards the number of wives he can hold than other Muslims in order to achieve noble and honourable purposes.

However, the treatment of the Messenger of Allâh (Peace be upon him) to his wives was of honourable, noble, and superb nature. His wives were on tops in respect of honour, satisfaction, patience, modesty, and service (that is to say the performance of housework and marriage duties). Although the Messenger's house-life was hard and unbearable, none of his wives complained. Anas said about the Prophet's life: "According to my knowledge, the Messenger of Allâh (Peace be upon him) has never tasted a thin flattened loaf in all his lifetime, nor has he ever seen with his own eyes roasted mutton."

'Aishah said: "Over two months have elapsed — during which we have seen three crescents — and yet no fire has been kindled in the houses of the Messenger of Allâh (Peace be upon him) (i.e. they did not cook food)." "What did you eat to sustain yourselves?" 'Urwah asked. She said "The two blacks: dates and water". Lots of information about the hard life of the Prophet (Peace be upon him) were told.

In spite of these hardships, straits and adversity of life in the house of the Prophet (Peace be upon him), none of his wives uttered a word of complaint worthy of reproach — but once. This exception was required by human instinctive inclinations. However, it was not so important and consequently it did not require the decree of a legislative rule. Allâh has given them an opportunity to choose between two things, as clearly stated in the following verses:

- "O Prophet [Muhammad (Peace be upon him)]! Say to your wives: 'If you desire the life of this world, and its glitter, — then come! I will make a provision for you and set you free in a handsome manner (divorce). But if you desire Allâh and His Messenger, and the Home of the Hereafter, then verily, Allâh has prepared for *Al-Muhsinat* (good doers) amongst you an enormous reward.'" [33:28,29]

They were so noble and honest that none of them preferred 'the life of this world and its glitter' to the abode in the Hereafter.

Although they were many in number, nothing of the dispute occurrences that normally happen among co-wives, took place in their houses. Very few cases could be the only exception; but they were quite normal. Allâh reproached them for that, so they ceased to do such a thing. This incident is mentioned in *At-Tahreem* Chapter:

- "O Prophet! Why do you ban (for yourself) that which Allâh has made lawful to you …" [66:1] (to the end of the fifth verse).

Discussing polygamy — in my opinion — is not a necessity; since a person who is familiar with the Europeans, and indecent practices, sufferings, wickedness, their sorrows and distresses, the horrible crimes they commit in this respect as well as the trials, the disasters that they are involved in, and which emanate directly from their disregard of the principle of polygamy form a good reason (to justify the soundness of polygamy). The distorted picture of life in Europe with the ill-practices featuring it, could truthfully justify the existence and practice of polygamy. In this, there are Divine signs for all people possessed of lucid mind.

THE PROPHET (Peace be upon him), ATTRIBUTES AND MANNERS

The Prophet (Peace be upon him) combined both perfection of creation and perfection of manners. This impression on people can be deduced by the bliss that overwhelmed their hearts and filled them with dignity. Men's dignity, devotion and estimation of the Messenger of Allâh (Peace be upon him) were unique and matchless. No other man in the whole world has been so honoured and beloved. Those who knew him well, were fascinated and enchanted by him. They were ready to sacrifice their lives for the sake of saving a nail of his from hurt or injury. Being privileged by lots of prerogatives of perfection that no one else had been endowed with, his Companions found that he was peerless and so they loved him.

Here we list a brief summary of the versions about his beauty and perfection. To encompass all which is, addmittedly, beyond our power.

BEAUTY OF CREATION:

Describing the Messenger of Allâh (Peace be upon him), who passed by her tent on his journey of migration, Umm Ma'bad Al-Khuza'iyah said to her husband:

- "He was innocently bright and had broad countenance. His manners were fine. Neither was his belly bulging out nor was his head deprived of hair. He had black attractive eyes finely arched by continuous eyebrows. His hair glossy and black, inclined to curl, he wore long. His voice was extremely commanding. His head was large, well formed and set on a slender neck. His expression was pensive and contemplative, serene and sublime. The stranger was fascinated from the distance, but no sooner he became intimate with him than this fascination was changed into attachment and respect. His expression was very sweet and distinct. His speech was well set and free from the use of superfluous words, as if it were a rosary of beads. His stature was neither too high nor too small to look repulsive. He was a twig amongst the two, singularly bright and fresh. He was always surrounded by his Companions. Whenever he uttered something, the listeners would hear him with rapt attention and whenever he issued any command, they vied with each other in carrying it out. He was a master and a commander. His utterances were marked by truth and sincerity, free from all kinds of falsehoods and lies."

'Ali bin Abi Talib describing him said: "The Messenger of Allâh (Peace be upon him) was neither excessively tall nor extremely short. He was medium height among his friends. His hair was neither curly nor wavy. It was in between. It was not too curly nor was it plain straight. It was both curly and wavy combined. His face was not swollen or meaty-compact. It was fairly round. His mouth was white. He had black and large eyes with long haired eyelids. His joints (limbs) and shoulder joints were rather big. He had a rod-like little hair extending from his chest down to his navel, but the rest of his body was almost hairless. He had thick hand palms and thick fingers and toes. At walking, he lifted his feet off the ground as if he had been walking in a muddy remainder of water. When he turned, he turned all. The Prophethood Seal was between his shoulders. He is the Seal of Prophets, the most generous and the bravest of all.

His speech was the most reliable. He was the keenest and the most attentive to people's trust and was very careful to pay people's due in full. The Prophet (Peace be upon him) was the most tractable and the most yielding companion, seeing him unexpectedly you fear him and venerate him. He who has acquaintance with him will like him. He who describes him says:

- 'I have never seen such a person neither before nor after seeing him.'

Jabir bin Samurah reported that Allâh's Messenger (Peace be upon him) had a broad face with reddish (wide) eyes and leanheels.

Abu At-Tufail said: "He was white, good-looking. He was neither fat nor thin; neither tall nor short."

Anas bin Malik said: "He had unfolded hands and was pink-coloured. He was neither white nor brown. He was rather whitish. In both his head and beard there were as many as twenty grey hairs, besides some grey hairs at his temples." In another version: "and some scattered white hairs in his head."

Abu Juhaifa said: "I have seen some grey colour under his lower lip." Al-Bara' said: "He was of medium height, broad-shouldered, his hair went up to his earlobes. I saw him dressed in a red garment and I (assure you) I have never seen someone more handsome. At first he used to let his hair loose so as to be in compliance with the people of the Book; but later on he used to part it."

Al-Bara' also said: "He had the most handsome face and the best character." When he was asked: "Was the Messenger's face sword-like?" "No," he said: "it was moon-like." But in another version: he said, "His face was round." Ar-Rabi' bint Muawwidh said: "Had you seen him, you would have felt that the sun was shining." Jabir bin Samurah said, "I saw him at one full-moony night. I looked at him. He was dressed in a red garment. I compared him with the moon and found that — for me — he was better than the moon."

Abu Huraira said: "I have never seen a thing nicer than the Messenger of Allâh (Peace be upon him). It seems as if the sunlight were moving within his face. I have never seen one who is faster in pace than the Messenger of Allâh (Peace be upon him). It seemed as if the earth had folded itself up to shorten the distance for him. For we used to wear ourselves out while he was at full ease."

Ka'b bin Malik said: "When he was pleased, his face would shine with so bright light that you would believe that it was a moon-piece." Once he sweated hot at 'Aishah's, and the features of his face twinkled; so I recited a poem by Abu Kabeer Al-Hudhali:

- "If you watch his face-features, you will see them twinkling like the lightning of an approaching rain."

Whenever Abu Bakr saw him he would say:

- "He is faithful, chosen (by Allâh), and calls for forgiveness. He shines like a full-moon light when it is far from dark (clouds)."

'Umar used to recite verses by Zuhair describing Haram bin Sinan:

- "Were you other than a human being, you would be a lighted moon at a full-moon night."

    Then he would add: "Thus was the Messenger of Allâh (Peace be upon him) .

When he got angry his face would go so red that you would think it were "an inflected red skin-spot with pomegranate grains on both cheeks."

Jabir bin Samurah said: "His legs were gentle, delicate and in conformity. His laughter is no more than smiling. Looking at him will make you say 'He is black-eyed though he is not so.'"

Ibn Al-'Abbas said: "His two front teeth were splitted so whenever he speaks, light goes through them. His neck was as pure and silvery as a neck of doll. His eyelids were long haired but his beard was thick. His forehead was broad; but his eyebrows were like the metal piece attached to a lance, but they were unhorned. His nose was high-tipped, middle-cambered with narrow nostrils. His cheeks were plain, but he had (little hair) running down like a rod from his throat to his navel. He had hair neither on his abdomen nor on his chest except some on his arms and shoulders. His chest was broad and flatted. He had long forearms with expansive palms of the hand. His legs were plain straight and stretching down. His other limbs were straight too. The two hollows of his soles hardly touch the ground. When he walks away he vanishes soon; but he walks at ease (when he is not in a hurry). The way he walks seems similar to one who is leaning forwards and is about to fall down."

Anas said: "I have never touched silk or a silky garment softer than the palm of the Prophet's (Peace be upon him); nor have I smelt a perfume or any scent nicer than his." In another version, "I have never smelt ambergris nor musk nor any other thing sweeter than the scent and the smell of the Messenger of Allâh (Peace be upon him)."

Abu Juhaifa said: "I took his hand and put it on my head and I found that it was colder than ice and better scented than the musk perfume."

Jabir bin Samurah — who was a little child then — said: "When he wiped my cheek, I felt it was cold and scented as if it had been taken out of a shop of a perfume workshop."

Anas said, "His sweat was pearl-like." Umm Sulaim said: "His sweat smelt nicer than the nicest perfume."

Jabir said: "Whoever pursues a road that has been trodden by the Messenger of Allâh (Peace be upon him), will certainly scent his smell and will be quite sure that the Messenger of Allâh (Peace be upon him) has already passed it." The Seal of Prophethood, which was similar in size to a pigeon's egg, was between his shoulders on the left side having spots on it like moles.

THE PERFECTION OF SOUL AND NOBILITY:

The Prophet (Peace be upon him) was noted for superb eloquence and fluency in Arabic. He was remarkable in position and rank. He was an accurate, unpretending straightforward speaker. He was well-versed in Arabic and quite familiar with the dialects and accents of every tribe. He spoke with his entertainers using their own accents and dialects. He mastered and was quite eloquent at both bedouin and town speech. So he had the strength and eloquence of bedouin language as well as the clarity and the decorated splendid speech of town. Above all, there was the assistance of Allâh embodied in the revealed verses of the Qur'ân.

His stamina, endurance and forgiveness — out of a commanding position — his patience and standing what he detested — these were all talents, attributes and qualities Allâh Himself had brought him on. Even wise men have their flaws, but the Messenger of Allâh (Peace be upon him), unlike everybody, the more he was hurt or injured, the more clement and patient he became. The more insolence an ignorant anybody exercised against him the more enduring he became.

'Aishah said:

- "The Messenger of Allâh (Peace be upon him), whenever he is given the opportunity to choose between two affairs, he always chooses the easiest and the most convenient. But if he is certain that it is sinful, he will be as far as he could from it. He has never avenged himself; but when the sanctity of Allâh is violated he would. That would be for Allâh's not for himself. He is the last one to get angry and the first to be satisfied. His hospitality and generosity were matchless. His gifts and endowments manifest a man who does not fear poverty."

Ibn'Abbas said: "The Prophet (Peace be upon him) was the most generous. He is usually most generous of all times in Ramadan, the times at which the angel Gabriel (Peace be upon him) comes to see him. Gabriel used to visit him every night of Ramadan and review the Qur'ân with him. Verily the Messenger of Allâh (Peace be upon him) is more generous at giving bounty or charity than the blowing wind."

Jabir said:

"The Prophet (Peace be upon him) would never deny anything he was asked for."

His courage, his succour and his might are distinguishable. He was the most courageous. He witnessed awkward and difficult times and stoodfast at them. More than once brave men and daring ones fled away leaving him alone; yet he stood with full composure facing the enemy without turning his back. All brave men must have experienced fleeing once or have been driven off the battlefield at a round at a time except the Prophet (Peace be upon him) 'Ali said: "Whenever the fight grew fierce and the eyes of fighters went red, we used to resort to the Prophet (Peace be upon him) for succour. He was always the closest to the enemy."

Anas said: "One night the people of Madinah felt alarmed. People went out hurriedly towards the source of sound, but the Prophet (Peace be upon him) had already gone ahead of them. He was on the horseback of Abu Talhah which had no saddle over it, and a sword was slung round his neck, and said to them: 'There was nothing to be afraid for.'"

He was the most modest and the first one to cast his eyes down. Abu Sa'îd Al-Khudri : "He was shier than a virgin in her boudoir. When he hates a thing we read it on his face. He does not stare at anybody's face. He always casts his eyes down. He looks at the ground more than he looks sky-wards. His utmost looks at people are glances. He is willingly and modestly obeyed by everybody. He would never name a person whom he had heard ill-news about — which he hated. Instead he would say: 'Why do certain people do so....'"

Al-Farazdaq verse of poem fits him very much and the best one to be said of:

- "He casts his eyes modestly but the eyes of others are cast down due to his solemnity, and words issue out of his mouth only while he is smiling."

The Prophet صلى الله عليه وسلم is the most just, the most decent, the most truthful at speech, and the honestest of all. Those who have exchanged speech with him, and even his enemies, acknowledge his noble qualities. Even before the Prophethood he was nicknamed *Al-Ameen* (i.e. the truthful, the truthworthy). Even then — in *Al-Jahiliyah* — they used to turn to him for judgement and consultation. In a version by At-Tirmidhi, he says that 'Ali had said that he had been told by Abu Jahl that he (Abu Jahl) said to the Messenger of Allâh (Peace be upon him): "We do not call you a liar; but we do not have faith in what you have brought." In His Book, Allâh, the Exalted, said about them:

- "It is not you that they deny, but it is the Verses (the Qur'ân) of Allâh that the *Zalimûn* (polytheists and wrong-doers) deny." [6:33]

Even when Heraclius asked Abu Sufyan: "Have you ever accused him of lying before the ministry of Prophethood?" Abu Sufyan said: "No."

He was most modest and far from being arrogant or proud. He forbade people to stand up at his presence as other people usually do for their kings.

Visiting the poor, the needy and entertaining them are some of his habits. If a slave invited him, he would accept the invitation. He always sat among his friends as if he were an ordinary person of them. 'Aishah said that he used to repair his shoes, sew or mend his dress and to do what ordinary men did in their houses. After all, he was a human being like others. He used to check his dress (lest it has some insects on). Milking the she-sheep and catering for himself were some of his normal jobs. The Prophet (Peace be upon him) was the most truthful to his pledges, and it is one of his qualities to establish good and steady relationship with his relatives — '*Silat-Ar-Rahim*'. He is the most merciful, gentle and amiable to all people. His way of living is the simplest one. Ill-manners and indecency are two qualities completely alien to him. He was decent, and did not call anybody names. He was not the sort of person who cursed or made noise in the streets. He did not exchange offences with others. He pushed back an offence or an error by forgiveness and overlooking. Nobody was allowed to walk behind him (i.e. as a bodyguard). He did not feel himself superior to others not even to his slaves (men or women) as far as food or clothes were concerned.

Whoever served him should be served by him too. 'Ugh' (an utterance of complaint) is a word that had never been said by him to his servant; nor was his servant blamed for doing a thing or leaving it undone. Loving the poor and the needy and entertaining them or participating in their funerals were things the Prophet (Peace be upon him) always observed. He never contempted or disgraced a poor man for his poverty. Once he was travelling with his Companions and when it was time to have food prepared, he asked them to slaughter a she-sheep. A man said: I will slaughter it, another one said: I will skin it out. A third said: I will cook it. So the Messenger of Allâh (Peace be upon him) said: I will collect wood for fire. They said: "No. We will suffice you that work." "I know that you can do it for me, but I hate to be privileged. Allâh hates to see a slave of his privileged to others." So he went and collected fire-wood.

Let us have some of the description of Hind bin Abi Halah: "The Messenger of Allâh (Peace be upon him) was continually sad, thinking perpetually. He had no rest (i.e. for long). He only spoke when it was necessary. He would remain silent for a long time and whenever he spoke, he would end his talk with his jawbone but not out of the corners of his mouth, i.e. (snobbishly). His speech was inclusive. He spoke inclusively and decisively. It was not excessive nor was it short of meaning. It was amiable. It was in no way hard discoroning. He glorified the bounty of Allâh; even if it were little. If he had no liking for someone's food, he would neither praise nor criticize.

He was always in full control of his temper and he would never get seemed angry unless it was necessary. He never got angry for himself nor did he avenge himself. It was for Allâh's sanctity and religion that he always seemed angry.

When he pointed at a thing he would do so with his full hand-palm, and he would turn it round to show surprise. If he were angry he would turn both his body and face aside. When he was pleased, he cast his eyes down. His laughter was mostly smiling. It was then that his teeth which were like hail-stones were revealed.

He never spoke unless it was something closely relevant to him. He confirmed the brotherhood relationship among his Companions; and thus he made them intimate and did not separate them or implant enmity among them. Those who were honourable with their peoples, were honoured and respected by him and were assigned rulers over their own peoples. His cheerfulness was never withdrawn at anyone's face; even at those whom he warned his people from or those whom he himself was on the alert of. He visited friends and inquired about people's affairs. He confirmed what was right and criticized the awful and tried to undermine it. He was moderate in all affairs. He was equal to others and was not privileged. He would never act heedlessly, lest the others should get heedless. Each situation was dealt with in its proper due.

Righteousness was his target; so he was never short of it nor indifferent to it. People who sat next to him were the best of their people and the best of them all were — for him — those who provided common consultations. For him, the greatest ones and the highest in ranks were the best at providing comfort and co-ordination and succour. Remembrance (of Allâh) was a thing he aimed at and established whenever he sat down or stands up. No certain position was assigned for him to sit on. He sits at the end of the group, seated next to the last sitter in the place. He ordered people to do the same. He entertained his participants in social gatherings alike so that the one addressed would think that there was no one honoured by the Prophet (Peace be upon him) but himself. He whoever sat next to him or interrupted him in order to ask for his advice about an affair of his, would be the first to start the talk and the one to end it. The Prophet (Peace be upon him) would listen to him patiently till he ended his speech. He never denied a request to anyone, if unapproachable, then few gratifying words would work, instead.

His magnanimity, broad mindedness his tolerance could embrace all people and entitled him to be regarded as father for them all. In justice, all of them were almost equal. Nobody was better than another except on the criterion of Allâh fearing. A favoured one, to him, was the most Allâh fearing. His assembly was a meeting of clemency, timidness, patience and honesty. Voices were not raised in rows or riots. Inviolable things were never violable. Fearing Allâh and worship were their means to sympathy and compassion. They used to esteem the old and have mercy on the young. They assisted the needy and entertained strangers.

The Messenger of Allâh (Peace be upon him) was always cheerful, easy, pleasant-tempered and lenient. He was never rude or rough nor clamorous or indecent. He was neither a reproacher nor a praiser. He overlooked what he did not desire, yet you would never despair of him. Three qualities he disposed of: hypocrisy, excessiveness, and what was none of his concern. People did not fear him in three area: — for they were not qualities or habits of his —: He never disparaged, or reproached nor did he seek the defects or shortages of others. He only spoke things whose reward was Divinely desirable. When he spoke, his listeners would attentively listen casting down their heads. They only spoke when he was silent. They did not have disputes or arguments about who was to talk. He who talked in his presence would be listened to by everybody till he finished his talk. Their talk would be about the topic discussed or delivered by their first speaker. The Messenger of Allâh (Peace be upon him) used to laugh at what they laughed at and admired what they used to admire. He would always show patience with a stranger's harshness at talk. He used to say:

- "When you see a person seeking an object earnestly, assist him to get his need. And never ask for a reward except from the reward-Giver, i.e. Allâh."

Kharijah bin Zaid said: "The Prophet (Peace be upon him) was the most honoured among the people with whom he sat. His limbs could hardly be seen. He was often silent and rarely talked when speech was not a necessity. He turned away from those whose speech was rude or impolite. His laughter was no more than a smile. His speech, which was decisive, it was neither excessive nor incomplete. Out of reverence and esteem and following the example of their Prophet (Peace be upon him), the Companions' laughter at his presence — was smiling, as well."

On the whole the Prophet (Peace be upon him) was ornamented with peerless attributes of perfection. No wonder to be like that for he was brought up, educated and taught (the Qur'ân) by Allâh. He was even praised by Allâh:

- "And verily, you [O Muhammad (Peace be upon him)] are on an exalted standard of character." [68:4]

Those were the attributes and qualities that the Prophet (Peace be upon him) enjoyed which made the hearts of souls of the people close to him, draw near to him and love him. Those traits made him so popular that the restraint and enmity of his people grew less and they started to embrace Islam in large crowds.

This description is in fact no more than a rapid review or rather short brief lines of Muhammad's (Peace be upon him) aspects of full perfection. Trying to encompass the whole perfect picture of the Prophet (Peace be upon him). No one can ever claim to be possessed of full knowledge or complete mastery of the great attributes of the greatest man in this universe. No one can ever give this man, the top of perfection, his due descrpition. He was a man who always sought Allâh's light, to such an extent that he was wholly imbued with the Qur'ânic approach.

- O Allâh! send your blessings (and the Holy Words of Yours) upon Muhammad and the family of Muhammad, as You have send blessings upon Ibrâhim and the family of Ibrâhim. You are worthy of all praise, All Glorious.

    O Allâh! bless Muhammad and the family of Muhammad as You have already blessed Ibrâhim and the family of Ibrâhim. You are worthy of all praise, All Glorious.

Islamic Books

www.al-Qarni.com

www.ingramcontent.com/pod-product-compliance
Lightning Source LLC
Chambersburg PA
CBHW082200070526
44585CB00020B/2216